CITY OF FORTUNE

ALSO BY MASON B. WILLIAMS

City of Ambition:
FDR, La Guardia, and the Making of Modern New York

Shaped by the State:
Toward a New Political History of the Twentieth Century
(co-editor with Brent Cebul and Lily Geismer)

CITY OF FORTUNE

INEQUALITY AND THE MAKING OF CONTEMPORARY NEW YORK

MASON B. WILLIAMS

W. W. NORTON & COMPANY
Independent Publishers Since 1923

Printed in the United States of America
First Edition

Parts of chapter 3 appeared previously in Mason B. Williams, "How the Rockefeller Laws Hit the Streets: Drug Policing and the Politics of State Competence in New York City, 1973–1989," *Modern American History* 4, no. 1 (March 2021) 67–90.

Manufacturing by Lakeside Book Company
Book design by Brooke Koven
Production manager: Louise Mattarelliano

Library of Congress Cataloging-in-Publication Data

Names: Williams, Mason B. author
Title: City of fortune : inequality and the making of contemporary New York / Mason B. Williams.
Other titles: Inequality and the making of contemporary New York
Description: First edition. | New York : W. W. Norton & Company, [2026] | Includes bibliographical references and index.
Identifiers: LCCN 2026001674 | ISBN 9780393292855 hardcover | ISBN 9780393292862 ebook
Subjects: LCSH: New York (N.Y.)—History—1951– | New York (N.Y.)—Politics and government—1951–
Classification: LCC F128.55 .W554 2026 | DDC 974.7/1—dc23/eng/20260128
LC record available at https://lccn.loc.gov/2026001674

W. W. Norton & Company, Inc., 500 Fifth Avenue, New York, NY 10110
www.wwnorton.com

W. W. Norton & Company Ltd., 15 Carlisle Street, London W1D 3BS

Authorized EU representative: EAS, Mustamäe tee 50, 10621 Tallinn, Estonia

10 9 8 7 6 5 4 3 2 1

To Mom and Dad,

and to Emerson and Johanna

CONTENTS

Preface xi

PART I: CRISIS 1970–1982

1 Power Failure 3
2 Austerity 46

PART II: QUALITY OF LIFE 1983–2001

3 From Survival to Revival 79
4 Gorgeous Mosaic 122
5 The Republican Moment 160

PART III: PROGRESS AND POVERTY 2002–2019

6 City of Choice 209

7 A Tale of Two New Yorks 247

Postscript 277

Acknowledgments 283

Notes 287

Index 353

PREFACE

Shortly after noon on December 31, 1974, New York governor-elect Hugh Carey emerged from his apartment building in Park Slope, Brooklyn, Robert Caro's recently published biography of Robert Moses, *The Power Broker*, under his arm. He and eleven of his twelve children, together with assorted spouses, friends, aides, reporters, and a pet Labrador named Jet, crowded onto a chartered Silver Eagle bus, bound for Albany, where Carey was to be inaugurated as the Empire State's fifty-first governor. Carey had lost his wife to cancer that spring, and he had kept the family together through the campaign. As the bus wound out of Brooklyn and up First Avenue, the Carey kids reminisced about other trips they had taken that year—Winnebago rides to state and county fairs, fire engines in small town parades, puddle-jumping in the tiny chartered planes they nervously dubbed "toothpaste tubes." The bus skirted the South Bronx before leaving the city behind and traveling the 150-some miles that separated New York's great metropolis from its seat of power.[1]

For Carey, the occasion marked the unexpected culmination of a distinguished career. Raised by middle-class parents in the Irish enclaves of interwar Brooklyn, he had graduated from St. John's University with tuition help from Franklin Roosevelt's National

Youth Administration and, after a spell in the army during which he helped liberate the Nordhausen concentration camp, finished first in his class at St. John's Law School. In 1960, he won election to Congress, a Kennedy Democrat who helped enact Lyndon Johnson's Great Society legislation. Honest and exceptionally smart but sometimes easy to underestimate—"an outwardly genial Irish pol who did not wear his emotions or his intelligence on his sleeve," one of his great admirers wrote—he pulled a surprise victory in the 1974 Democratic primary, then swept into office on the post-Watergate tide. Except for Averell Harriman's single term, Republicans had held the Governor's Mansion since 1943. Now the party of Al Smith, Franklin Roosevelt, and Herbert Lehman would return to power. The band at Carey's election-night victory party had struck up FDR's 1932 campaign anthem, "Happy Days Are Here Again."[2]

By the time of his inauguration, the spirit of jubilation had faded in the face of daunting challenges. Both the City of New York and the Urban Development Corporation, a state-backed public authority, were approaching bankruptcy. "I had the champagne," former governor Nelson Rockefeller told him; "you have the hang-over."[3]

A week after his swearing-in, Carey strode to the front of the Assembly Chamber to deliver his first State of the State speech, his solemn countenance foreshadowing what was to follow. "Sudden storms have swept across our economy and all of American life, shattering our hopes and our illusions of comfort; and the storms do not abate," he said. "This government, and we as a people, have been living far beyond our means. What we did was limited only by our imagination and our desire. . . . Now, the times of plenty, the days of wine and roses, are over." That spring the market for New York City's debt issuances collapsed, bringing America's largest city to the brink of insolvency.[4]

The scenes that followed are etched in the city's collective consciousness: the leaflets bidding tourists "WELCOME TO FEAR CITY"; the *Daily News*'s "FORD TO CITY: DROP DEAD" headline after President Gerald

Ford pledged to veto a package to save New York from bankruptcy; the piles of trash that collected on city streets amid draconian budget cuts and municipal strikes; the plumes of smoke and tongues of fire pouring forth from apartment buildings set ablaze by arsonists-for-hire. By the end of the 1970s, homicides in the city were up 38 percent, the number of public school teachers had fallen by a quarter due to budget cuts and attrition, and the city's older neighborhoods had lost hundreds of thousands of housing units. "There was a time when every American community contained people who wanted to get to New York," the scholar Andrew Hacker wrote in 1975. Now, for the first sustained period in the city's modern history, more people were leaving than arriving.[5]

Some forty years later, by the second decade of the twenty-first century, the crisis of the 1970s was a distant memory. New York was the safest big city in America. It had rebuilt many of the public institutions that fell into disrepair in the 1970s—the subway, the parks, the public schools. Millions of new residents had arrived in the city, from all over the world, reviving its economy and repopulating its neighborhoods. Tourists came in unprecedented numbers. The city had even recovered something of the ambitious civic spirit of mid-century, the imagination and desire that the chastened Carey had urged New Yorkers to rein in. "For the first time since La Guardia was mayor and FDR created the WPA," Mayor Michael Bloomberg proclaimed in his 2013 State of the City speech, "we're not only conceiving big plans that fundamentally change the landscape of our city, we're achieving them."[6]

But if New York was flourishing in many respects, it was also a city of staggering inequality. A single express stop on the Lexington Avenue subway line carried riders from a census tract with a median household income of $120,000 per year to one where the figure was $19,000. In the part of Carnegie Hill near the 86th Street stop, 5 percent of the population lived in poverty; near the 125th Street stop in East Harlem, 46 percent did. Less than 1 percent of residents in the

Carnegie Hill tract were incarcerated; 3.8 percent of the residents in the East Harlem tract were. Children's prospects for the future tracked these extremes of wealth and power. A child growing up poor in the Carnegie Hill tract could expect to earn $45,000 a year at age thirty-five; a child growing up in the East Harlem tract could expect to earn a little more than half that.[7]

This unequal geography of opportunity aligned closely with the geography of race, which changed abruptly at 96th Street. In Carnegie Hill, 82 percent of residents were white; in East Harlem, 2 percent were. Such racialized extremes of wealth and opportunity, though particularly stark in this corner of Manhattan, could be found across the five boroughs. And they were replicated in the public institutions that gave everyday meaning to citizenship in the city. New York's public schools were among the most segregated in the nation. Police violence and harassment of people of color sparked regular protests. And though soaring housing costs were a problem for nearly everyone, poor and working-class New Yorkers in particular found themselves squeezed by high rents and threatened by eviction and displacement. Early twenty-first-century New York had become a city of fortune in two senses of the term: a city whose vast accumulations of wealth facilitated the revival of civic ambitions, and one in which, for those on the wrong side of its sharp divisions, life's prospects could depend on factors far beyond one's control.

ACCOUNTS OF NEW YORK CITY'S history since the crisis of the 1970s tend to tell one of two stories. The first, more common in popular culture than in scholarly accounts, is a story of renaissance, revitalization, and rebirth, a phoenix rising from the ashes. Sometimes this story credits political leaders and public officials for making the tough choices necessary to put the city on a path to recovery. In these tellings, the city's post-crisis history is a tale of a city "taken back" from the ravages of disorder, crime, and political dysfunction by tough-minded public officials who "reclaimed" it and "restored" its quality of life. Sometimes it emphasizes the work of grassroots organizations, community leaders, and everyday New Yorkers who rebuilt the city's neighborhoods block by block in the wake of the urban crisis.[8]

The second story is a tale of diminished public values. In this story, the crisis of the 1970s marks a turning point in which mid-twentieth-century New York, a working-class city of democratic ambitions uncommon in modern American history, gives way to the luxury city of the twenty-first century, much of its public sphere privatized and what remains captured by the imperatives of real estate development and commercial boosterism. This story tends to strike a note of loss: a city's democratic promises betrayed, the distinctive qualities of its streetscape given over to Whole Foodses and Equinox gyms, ATM lobbies and luxury high-rises and other manifestations of the hegemonic forces of global capital.[9]

This book takes a different approach. If narratives of renaissance fail to make sense of the persistent poverty, racial marginalization, and inequality so evident in today's New York, tales of a lost democratic promise risk both exaggerating the virtues of the mid-century city and overlooking the persistence of working-class power in the post-crisis city. Mid-century New York, while in many ways more generous, inclusive, and democratic than the contemporary city, was also racially segregated and politically unequal—enough so that the Bronx, Brooklyn, and Manhattan, the three boroughs with the largest Puerto Rican and Black populations, all violated the preclearance provision of the 1965 Voting Rights Act due to their low voter turnout, three of only a handful of counties outside the South to do so. And if the public ambitions of mid-century have been diminished, in New York they have also survived, at least to some degree, the broader trends toward privatization, marketization, retrenchment, inequality, and disenfranchisement that have characterized recent American history. As the historians Joshua Freeman and Kim Phillips-Fein observe, contemporary New York continues to reserve some of the most valuable real estate on earth for public housing. This is a testament not only to the persistence of mid-century visions but also to the tenacity of contemporary advocates and their political allies.[10]

Rather than emphasize renaissance or civic diminishment, this book examines the relationship between the two, showing how the reconstruction of state authority in the wake of the crisis of the 1970s restored the city's public capacities while embedding racial and class inequalities in new institutional forms. The book begins in the late 1960s, toward the tail end of a long era of progressive reform that began in the early twentieth century and culminated during and after the New Deal. During this era, the city's labor movement empowered workers, and the city government provided new opportunities for professional accomplishment and upward mobility for previously underrepresented groups. New Deal agencies such as the Works Progress Administration helped the city government provide poor and working-class people access to goods and services—new forms of education, recreation, health care—that they could not afford to buy, and built up a sense of social citizenship and public good. In tandem with Washington, the city sought to provide affordable, decent, and stable housing through the creation of public and subsidized housing and the implementation, in 1943, of rent regulation. In the decades after World War II, New Yorkers, powered by the labor movement, the left, and community-based organizations, extended this legacy, putting the city on the vanguard of postwar liberal reform. The city's civic credo could be heard in the municipal radio station's identification tag: "This program comes from WNYC, New York City's own station, where seven-and-half-million people, who have come from all parts of the world, are now living in peace and enjoying the benefits of democracy."[11]

Like the New Deal writ large, however, New York City's tradition of postwar urban liberalism was shot through with modes of exclusion. Gains by the labor movement meant little to workers who could not join unions. Public works and urban renewal projects tore at the social networks of working-class and poor communities while offloading environmental costs onto them. Liberal mayors did relatively little to rein in police brutality and harassment, particularly of young New Yorkers of color. The prevalence of concentrated poverty and neighborhood disinvestment grew as the phenomenon of ghettoization spread from upper Manhattan into Brooklyn and the Bronx. New York, the bastion of urban liberalism, was rocked by protest movements in the 1960s precisely because discrimination and disfranchisement remained so pervasive.[12]

New York therefore entered the crisis of the 1970s in a precarious position. Because of its long tradition of progressive reform and public works, the city had an extensive, entrenched public realm, supported by many different kinds of institutions, interest groups, and constituencies—not only by everyday citizens but also by businessmen, real estate owners, and powerful public sector agencies. At the same time, the exclusions and inequalities of the mid-century city made it harder for those institutions to work. Even before New York's economy declined in the 1970s, the city's housing stock, public schools, and public spaces were under strain because of deep-rooted racism and concentrated poverty. The inequalities of the mid-century city laid the groundwork for the crisis of the 1970s while ensuring that its consequences would be felt primarily by those New Yorkers worst equipped to bear them.

For half a decade after New York's 1975 near-bankruptcy, city officials muddled through under conditions of extreme austerity, patching together partnerships with community and business groups in the hopes of arresting the deterioration of the city's quality of life—and retaining what remained of the middle-class population they believed to be essential to the city's future. Then, as the finance sector expanded in the early 1980s, the fiscal clouds began to lift. By mid-decade, a city beset by and accustomed to the constraints of austerity had an opportunity to move, as Mayor Edward Koch put it, from survival to revival. The question was: What would that revival look like? How should the city rebuild? What, and whom, should it prioritize, and who would have the power to decide?

This book examines the contending visions and clashes of interests that remade the city between the crisis of the 1970s and the eve of another epochal crisis in 2020, and the new landscape these struggles produced. In telling this story, I have focused on three aspects of city life: housing, schools, and the policing of public space. These three interconnected areas embody the tensions—in some ways, the contradictions—at the heart of political life in a democratic capitalist city. Housing is both home and investment: the foundation of private and neighborhood life as well as a source of profit. Public education embodies ideals of community and democratic citizenship even as it provides young people with the skills to navigate the contemporary economy. Public space is at once the infrastructure that facilitates the lived experience of urban democracy and a key source of value for property owners (and in turn, an important source of revenue for the city government). Cities need good housing, schools, and spaces in order to thrive. Yet because they embody such profound tensions, the very meaning of "good" housing, schools, and public space, as well as the terms on which they should be provided, are bound to be contested. And so these three realms have been the central issues in New York's democratic politics for most of the last half-century.[13]

Of course, the history of each of these aspects of city life on its own could fill more than one book. In order to bring them together, I have focused on particular developments within each area. The sections on housing focus primarily on laws regulating when and how landlords could raise rent, the chief way in which New York has tried to maintain affordable and stable housing. The sections on schools focus on the rise of public school choice—the creation of new kinds of schools such as small "alternative" schools, magnet schools, gifted-and-talented programs, and charter schools and the shift from neighborhood zoning to a system in which students apply to attend the school of their choice. The sections on policing deal specifically with what is often called "quality of life" policing, active street policing of low-level offenses. Each of these stories has its own idiosyncrasies, its own cast of characters and political dynamics. Considering them in relation to one another illuminates the broader historical processes that yielded what is sometimes known as the neoliberal state.[14]

How to make sense of a history as sweeping and tangled as that of New York City's politics in the last half century? The venues in which crucial decisions were made ranged from the backrooms of Albany to police precinct houses to the halls of the Federal Reserve, from City Hall and One Police Plaza to elementary school principals' offices. The forces that bore on the city's politics ranged from federal policy to the flows of global capital to the actions of individual New Yorkers in their homes and schools and on their streets. Moreover, this period saw vast upheavals in the city's economic and social life. Its economy shifted away from the manufacture and movement of goods and toward the provision of services and the manipulation of information, while the old working-class city of predominantly white-ethnic, African American, and Puerto Rican citizens became a global metropolis of staggering diversity.

How to lay out the contours of so complex a history? Is New York's recent political history a story of clashing ideologies—of liberalism, neoliberalism, neoconservatism, progressivism—the local equivalent of the liberalism-versus-conservatism story so familiar from national politics? Or conversely, is it a tale of consensus, a story of how the limits of the possible in American politics have shrunk into contending versions of neoliberalism? Ideology matters deeply in the following pages, but not quite in the way we are used to employing the term. This story is full of politicians and activists doing things that do not fit well with their purported politics. We will see people doing similar things for very different reasons—democratic socialists and free-market neoconservatives alike championing public school choice, for instance. And we will see very different politicians doing similar things for similar reasons and then justifying them to the public in very different terms. Democrats and Republicans both, for example, encouraged the NYPD to adopt policing strategies that targeted low-level offenses via an active street presence—Democrats explaining their approach primarily as one of responsive "community" (later "neighborhood") policing, Republicans as "zero tolerance," Broken Windows policing.

Such analytical oddities tell us something about the difficulty that ism-based political histories have in accounting for factors outside the ambit of partisan ideology: the interplay of interest groups; the structures of state institutions; ideological shifts that cut across partisan categories (such as the turn to punishment characteristic of the late twentieth century)—and not least the importance of ideas, which had a way of escaping the clutches of the political ideologies to which they purportedly belonged. Above all, they tell us something about the dilemmas of governing a volatile, unequal city: What appear to be coherent ideologies are often the readymade narratives of politicians scrambling, under intense pressure, to calculate their own political advantage while, ideally, doing their best to match problems and solutions.[15]

Given the shortcomings of the liberalism-versus-conservatism narrative, the consensus framing has some analytical advantages. Yet even if actors from across the political spectrum often alighted on similar approaches to governance, it would be a mistake to envision this era as one in which varieties of neoliberalism began to look to people of all political stripes like the only viable options. The political clashes of this era were grounded in radically different visions of the city, and they mattered because they made real differences in people's lives. Whether a family could keep its home and stay in its community, what kinds of educational possibilities existed for young people, the chances that a person would be stopped and searched by the police on the way home from work—all these intimate details of daily life could turn on the outcomes of political contests. In that light, it is perhaps not surprising that the political rhetoric of this era was so pitched: that tenants and landlords squared off in a series of "rent wars"; that education reformers accused each other of stealing young New Yorkers' futures; that advocates of different approaches to policing effectively charged each other with murder. The neoliberal state, whatever its structures and coherence, contained space for fundamental political conflict—even on issues where broad consensus sometimes prevailed at the national level.[16]

ONE WAY TO TELL A STORY that defies a straightforward thematic narrative is to follow the people. And indeed, to sketch this book's cast of characters is to suggest something essential about its argument. Many of its major figures were famous politicians, the types whose names adorned front pages before they moved onto bridges, tunnels, and municipal buildings across the city and state: Governor Nelson Rockefeller, a political titan struggling toward the one prize that had eluded him; the liberal Republican mayor John Lindsay, his mid-1960s idealism derailed by the harsh realities of the early 1970s; the boisterous, irrepressible, sometimes tetchy Ed Koch and the brilliant, enigmatic son of immigrant shopkeepers, Mario Cuomo; the thoughtful, courtly, and at times languorous David Dinkins and the operatic, self-righteous Rudy Giuliani; the business data maven and philanthropist turned mayor, Michael Bloomberg, who bestrode the city as had no mayor since La Guardia until his power splintered on the shoals of the city's inequalities; and another duo in a long line of disputatious chief executives, the high-minded (and sometimes high-flown) progressive mayor, Bill de Blasio, and the imperious prince of Albany, Andrew Cuomo, a commanding political tactician whose core principles, unlike his father's, often remained shrouded in mystery.

Other key politicians and political activists, famous in their own times, may be less familiar today. Still, the mention of their names will cast a spark in the memories of longtime New Yorkers. Because so much political power in New York City resides not in City Hall but in Albany, the leaders of the state legislature are essential to this story—people like the phlegmatic, calculating Lower East Sider, Democratic Assembly speaker Sheldon Silver, and his primary antagonist, the pugnacious upstate conservative Joe Bruno, leader of the Senate Republican majority. So, too, are a host of nonelected public officials: police commissioners Benjamin Ward, Raymond Kelly, and Bill Bratton above all, but also the people who actually ran the city agencies and gave New York a sense of continuity through time, like the omnipresent commissioner, adviser, and keeper of the city's civic flame, Bobby Wagner. And so are political strategists and advisers such as the legendary, mysterious Republican pollster Arthur Finkelstein, who, after lifting conservative Republicans Alfonse D'Amato and George Pataki to power in New York State, would help do the same with Benjamin Netanyahu in Israel and Viktor Orbán in Hungary.

But political history is incomprehensible if told only through the stories of politicians, politicos, and public officials. And so this book is also filled with people who wielded power in other ways. Some, like the outer-borough real estate scion Donald Trump—whose business interests, personal ambitions, and sense of grievance led him repeatedly into the center of the city's political life even before he made his unlikely entry into politics—sought to leverage the post-crisis city's economic anxieties to advance their own agendas. Some introduced and circulated new ideas: people like the Harlem education advocates Preston Wilcox and Babette Edwards; the progressive educator Deborah Meier and her adversary-turned-ally Diane Ravitch; the scholars James Q. Wilson and George Kelling, authors of the Broken Windows approach to policing; and the scores of intellectuals and journalists who debated housing policy. Still others brought everyday New Yorkers together to make their numbers felt in the halls of power—union leaders and charter school advocates, police reform activists like the Reverend Al Sharpton; the heads of the big state- and citywide tenant groups and their neighborhood-level counterparts—all those people whose success, to borrow from the novelist Don DeLillo, depended on expressing their dissatisfaction in interesting ways.[17]

Not least, there are those everyday New Yorkers, the kinds of political thinkers and actors whose names do not always make it onto the letterhead of the organizations in which they participate or into newspaper coverage of their actions, whose political lives, to the extent they are preserved at all, appear as flecks in archives bearing other people's names and—maybe—as registered voters in the city's records. Their politics was politics as most New Yorkers experienced it, and when circumstances permitted, their actions provided grist for the major political debates that swept the city in these years. They are the Harlem parents who pulled their students out of public schools in the mid-1970s to protest their inadequacy and the Brooklyn and Queens families that flooded public notice meetings three-plus decades later to protest school closures. They are the tenants who bused to Albany and showered their state senators with letters and phone calls when the rent laws were up for renewal. They are the teachers, principals, community leaders, and clergy who were on the front line helping young New Yorkers, particularly Black boys and young Black men, through the everyday violence and humiliation of stop-and-frisk—and the young New Yorkers themselves who had to figure out how to make their lives in the city while being treated as suspicious by their own government. They are the New Yorkers who gave the keys of City Hall to Ed Koch instead of Mario Cuomo, to David Dinkins instead of Rudy Giuliani—and then to Giuliani instead of Dinkins.

For all their differences, nearly all these people were united in their belief that the city and its key institutions were not working the way they should. They disagreed, though, in their understanding of why. For some, such as Giuliani and his admirer Trump, the city's problems were rooted primarily in the decline of social order and traditional authority, a decline they thought responsible for the "moral deregulation" they believed began in the 1960s—evident in what James Q. Wilson called the proliferation of "public obscenity, unconventional morality, and social and political heresy." They sought ways to reassert authority, restore order, and enforce what they viewed as traditional norms. For others, the city's ills resulted from the imbalances of power in New York's politics and the inequalities of resources built into its institutions. Explicitly concerned with equity and belonging, these New Yorkers—David Dinkins and Bill de Blasio were their most prominent representatives in City Hall—repeatedly took up the banner of "a tale of two cities" in advocating for what they called "the other New York"; they were critical of approaches they felt neglected (or harmed) disadvantaged New Yorkers in the name of the common good, and they looked for new ways to elevate the lives of those who could not get ahead through economic clout or social position. For still others, such as Koch and Bloomberg, the city's struggles were the product primarily of its failure to attract middle-class and affluent residents and business investment—the types of people and organizations that would bring the city stability and provide the resources with which skilled managers and data-driven experts could find innovative solutions to the city's social problems (an approach their opponents on the left felt represented a kind of trickle-down urbanism).[18]

Order and authority, equity and empowerment, growth and technocracy—these were more clusters of emphasis than firm positions, their salience rising and falling through time and according to the matter in question, and they were by no means static or exclusive. Moreover, meaningful differences in how New Yorkers viewed the city's problems should not obscure important commonalities in how they went about attempting to address them. Nearly all of New York's politicians pursued local development, if only because it provided the quickest route to the fiscal resources necessary for ambitious social programs. Nearly all believed a middle-class presence to be essential to the stability of the city and its neighborhoods. And nearly all came to rely on the NYPD as a primary instrument of governance. Still, these different ways of viewing the city's dilemmas can give us insight into how different political actors thought about problems and solutions and went about the messy work of building and maintaining coalitions, setting agendas, claiming resources, pushing through policies, making institutions function—the actual stuff of local statecraft. The history that unfolds in the following pages thus may be understood as a series of contests and accommodations between different ways of envisioning and addressing the city's problems—filtered through the ever-changing matrix of institutions, interests, and ideas that made up New York's political universe, all within the context of a shifting economy, radically changing demographics, and an evolving national political environment.

At the heart of that tangled history, in some ways the most fundamental fact running through fifty years of politics, was the existence of concentrated, racialized deprivation. Some of the best American political-historical writing of the last four decades has examined the making of mid-twentieth-century metropolitan racial segregation and the toxic ways segregation intersected with racial discrimination in employment, access to credit, housing, education, health, and policing. By creating landscapes of concentrated deprivation in the hearts of America's metropolises, segregation rendered entire swaths of great American cities fundamentally vulnerable. Although its economic diversity and its position at the hinge point of the American and world economies shielded it from the fate suffered by many other older American cities in the 1960s and '70s, New York could hardly escape the consequences of deeply entrenched inequality. As the first chapter of this book explains, the crises that began in New York in the late 1960s were crises of racialized inequality: A city built in such a fashion simply could not work—it could not maintain the housing stock, could not prevent street crime, and could not educate large numbers of its children adequately.

New York City was distinct, however, in that it did not suffer nearly the same degree of white and middle-class flight as other industrial cities in the second half of the twentieth century. As a consequence, it remained highly segregated by race and class, encompassing within its political boundaries many of the dynamics that elsewhere were structured by the city-suburb divide. On the one hand, its inequalities were thus more subject to formal democratic politics; on the other, its racial politics came to involve a kind of internal white flight, implicating institutions and governing practices in addition to space, as more advantaged New Yorkers sought to protect their interests within the city.[19]

Because inequality was racialized, and because the crises of the 1960s and '70s were in large measure crises of inequality, contests over how to rebuild the city inevitably implicated race. Those who prioritized social order and authority dealt at turns in explicit racism, in thinly veiled evocations of the white-ethnic city of the 1950s, and in ostensibly universalist (but to their opponents, obviously coded) appeals to civility and a "single standard" of behavior; theirs was a coalition rooted in the white electorate, though they also succeeded in drawing significant numbers of nonwhite voters. The efforts of those who stressed inequality sometimes took the form of movements for community self-determination, but because issues that disproportionately affected Black and Latino New Yorkers touched plenty of other New Yorkers as well, they could also be broad-based and interracial. Their ambitious efforts faced many challenges: finding allies and building coalitions that would allow them to wield power in Albany and Washington; transcending the inter- and intraracial class divisions that often ran through such coalitions; navigating the inherent stickiness of the political status quo (what social scientists call "path dependencies"); fending off efforts to co-opt particular elements of their program in ways that ignored their broader egalitarian visions.[20]

Those who emphasized an investment-driven political economy

and a technocratic, "problem-solving" approach to governance typically sought to decenter and deemphasize race. They attempted to dissolve distributional questions, inevitably racialized in a segregated city, into claims about the public good: the need for a stable tax base, better test scores, a lower crime rate, a refurbished housing stock. If it took some segregated gifted-and-talented programs to keep affluent white families in the public school system, or if many of the young people stopped in the search for illegal guns were innocent, or if people lost homes in the process of opening up and improving the city's housing stock, these were the costs of progress. Such an approach, of course, did not always square with the city's democratic institutions and culture. In practice, problem-solving often involved shifting the sites of democratic contestation—or removing policymaking from democratic contestation altogether. The regime assembled by Governor Hugh Carey to address the city's fiscal crisis in the mid-1970s literally overrode the City of New York's decisions on taxing and spending—on whether to keep neighborhood firehouses and health clinics open or to continue to offer its citizens tuition-free college, all in the name of the greater good of fiscal solvency. The city's subsequent history is full of other examples—rent increases set by appointed boards, local school boards dissolved, "community" policing controlled by the NYPD, crucial decisions on city issues made 150 miles up the Hudson River by state senators unaccountable to New Yorkers. Yet such efforts to constrain democratic contestation did not always succeed. What follows, then, is not only an account of elite efforts to reshape the city but also a history of popular revolts and crises of state legitimacy fomented and managed as New Yorkers went in search of a democratic city.

THE CONTESTS RECOUNTED HERE are important in their own right, for they shaped the everyday lives of millions of people in America's largest and most cosmopolitan city. They are of broader significance because they shaped events beyond the five boroughs. People who built their careers and reputations in New York, from the progressive schooling pioneer Deborah Meier to police commissioner William Bratton to Donald Trump, went on to become national figures. The problems New Yorkers dealt with in the late twentieth century—from its intractable housing crisis to the contentious racial politics of a society undergoing profound demographic transition—are now America's problems.

New York's recent history is significant, too, because it sheds light on a question central to political life in an ever-more unequal world in which the failures of national governments have cast ever-greater responsibility on state and city governments to realize democracy's promises.[21] In the past half-century, many New Yorkers have fought to sustain a vision of a democratic public even in the face of broader trends. What happens on the streets, in the homes, and in the schools of a great city when democratic aspirations confront powerful inegalitarian forces and constraining institutions? Is a democratic city possible in a context of structural inequality and national dysfunction? As New Yorkerers continue to battle and contend over such fundamental questions, the city's recent history has much to tell us about the possibilities of metropolitan democracy in our own time.

PART I
CRISIS

1970–1982

1

Power Failure

In December 1968, in its first year-end issue as a stand-alone publication, *New York* magazine launched what would become an annual feature: "Who Runs New York?" For the first few years, the ten-person lists offered few surprises. Mayor John Lindsay and Governor Nelson Rockefeller usually ranked high. Robert Moses had fallen from power by then, but the heads of the large public authorities—the MTA, the Port Authority, the Urban Development Corporation—typically garnered mention. Leaders of organized labor featured consistently. David Rockefeller represented the nexus of Wall Street and the city's philanthropic class. The inclusion of important figures at *The New York Times* offered a nod to the city press. Usually a leader of the state legislature made the list.[1]

Within a few years, though, the careful structure of the list began to crack. By 1974, faceless, abstract entities—"Big Oil," "Arab Money Managers," "The Stickup Man" ("undisputed boss of the nighttime streets of the city")—claimed nearly half the positions. "How few *names* there are," one of the list-makers remarked that year. "One looks around to see who wields vast power, and for the moment one sees only the struggle for it." Soon the list disappeared entirely. As another list-maker later remarked, the question of who held power had been supplanted by a different question: "Is there power?" The sense that an abundance of power had been replaced by a power vacuum was symptomatic of a general breakdown of public competence and authority, both perceived and real: the schools, the streets, the subways—none of them seemed to work the way New Yorkers thought they should. Worse, no one seemed willing or able to step in and make them work.[2]

The best-remembered phase of the crisis erupted in the spring of 1975 when the city government found itself unable to borrow the money it needed for operating expenses, pushing it to the edge of bankruptcy. In the months that followed, as the city's political leaders endured the humiliating ordeal of pleading with the federal government for loan guarantees to help the city weather the storm, the state government set up an emergency financial control board, effectively taking control of the municipal budget—and demanding deep cuts. Within a few years, New York had abandoned long-standing social commitments—imposing tuition at the city's public universities, hiking the subway fare, cutting health and daycare centers, and otherwise stepping back from the style of democratic politics wrought by the long era of social reform that had defined the city to that point in the twentieth century.[3]

Yet if the fiscal crisis that began in 1975 seemed to arrive with a brutal suddenness, the broader crisis of governance that coalesced in the 1970s had been decades in the making. It was not even a singular "crisis"; nor did it entail the kind of break from the past implied by that term. Already in the boom years of the late 1960s, key city institutions were cracking under stress—the result not primarily of political indiscipline, fiscal profligacy, cultural breakdown, or any of the other reasons New Yorkers cited at the time to explain the 1970s crisis, but rather of the strain brought by racial segregation and deprivation in the context of a shifting economy. New Yorkers had barely begun to reform these institutions when they ran headlong into the fiscal crisis and the era of austerity that followed. The fiscal crisis thus functioned less as a singular turning point than as a crucial episode in a long process of grappling with the failures of governance in a segmented city, accelerating some developments and constraining or reversing others.

The 1970s saw a certain narrowing of civic ambition among the city's political classes and the outright eclipse of the more radical egalitarian visions of the 1960s. Yet some political space remained. Amid austerity and the neoliberal turn, New Yorkers fended off efforts to end rent regulation, engaged in police reform, and launched innovative new public schools. The interlocking crises of the 1970s did not determine New York's future, but they did establish the parameters within which it would unfold.[4]

NOTHING EMBODIED NEW YORK'S travails in the 1970s quite as viscerally as the destruction of its housing stock. Beginning in the late 1960s, first individual buildings, then blocks, and in some instances entire sections of the city were lost to abandonment and arson. "At best," the historian Joshua Freeman writes, "a greater shabbiness came to characterize" the city's working-class communities. "At worst, whole neighborhoods literally dematerialized, going from bustling (if not thriving) communities to acres of rubble-strewn lots in just a few years."[5]

The housing cataclysm provided the most arresting images of the era—the shots of arson-stricken neighborhoods seen from above Yankee Stadium, President Jimmy Carter striding along the barren lots and burned-out shells of Charlotte Street in the South Bronx. For everyday New Yorkers, it provided perhaps the most tangible demonstrations of the city's failed promises: the daily strain of living without heat or hot water; the monthly crunch of rent payments rising faster than paychecks; the looming threat of being displaced from home and community. And in a city still grappling with the wreckage wrought by Robert Moses's urban renewal projects—a city that had come to understand stable, intact neighborhoods as its lifeblood—the decimation of the built environment seemed to strike at the very heart of the city's social order.[6]

New York has long had an image as a city of extremes: the city of "sunshine and shadow," of great fortunes and dangerous classes in the late nineteenth century, the capital of the New Gilded Age in the twenty-first. In the mid-twentieth century, though, New York had become a remarkably middle-income city. This had in part to do with the labor movement's successful efforts to stabilize cutthroat industries and elevate the wages of laboring New Yorkers to the point where parts of the city's working class registered middle-class incomes. It had also to do with the structure of the local manufacturing sector, which consisted primarily of small-scale, non-Fordist firms with lower barriers to entry than those in heavy industry cities like Pittsburgh and Detroit: What the sociologist Daniel Bell called the "entrepreneurial wealth of small-unit firms," most famously in the garment industry, had served as the economic platform for "an extraordinar[ily] large middle class . . . probably, though no one has ever measured it, the largest middle-class aggregate in any urban center of this country." New York's middle class was distinguished from its provincial counterparts, Bell wrote, by its "hunge[r] for culture and self-improvement," which in turn created a local market for all manner of cultural production. At the same time, the growing white- and pink-collar salariat in the office economy added another source of middle-income jobs.[7]

The unionized manufacturing sector had begun to erode by the late 1960s, undermined by mechanization and relocation, and the combination of business district redevelopment and urban renewal had scattered many of the small businesses integral to the postwar middle class. But overall, the local economy was thriving: By the end of the decade, New York boasted the greatest number of jobs in its history; among major American cities, only Dallas had a lower unemployment rate. Driven by a boom in the office economy, the local real estate tax base was growing at twice the rate of inflation. New York still had the character captured by Stephen Sondheim in the 1970 musical *Company*: a bustling city of striving and dreaming *arrivants*, profane and increasingly tattered around the edges. Many of its neighborhoods, especially outside Manhattan, still had a kind of middle-class economic stability that would soon disappear. Nearly all of Queens, much of Brooklyn south of Prospect Park, much of the Bronx north of the Cross-Bronx Expressway, and rapidly developing Staten Island were home to predominantly middle-income communities. More than at any other time in the city's modern history, they were also communities of people born in the United States: In 1920, 40.8 percent of New Yorkers had been born abroad, and many more were children of immigrants. By 1970, the figure was down to 18.2 percent. With immigration halted by the various federal exclusion and quota laws, the largest foreign-born population in the city still consisted of Italian Americans, most of whom had arrived in New York at least a half-century earlier.[8]

That was one New York. The same years that saw New York's development from an immigrant city into a working- and middle-class white-ethnic metropolis also witnessed the development and proliferation of what were then called "ghettoes." Deploying a suite of tools, the real estate industry and white property owners had constrained the hundreds of thousands of Black people from the American South and the West Indies who arrived in the city during the era of the Great Migration and the Puerto Rican migrants of the interwar and postwar years to a handful of neighborhoods, first in northern Manhattan, then in central Brooklyn, the southern stretches of the Bronx, the Lower East Side of Manhattan, and scattered parts of Queens. Racial steering by real estate agents, building-by-building discrimination, and violence seem to have been the primary mechanisms; deed restrictions and racially restrictive covenants, which became common practice in northern cities in the 1920s, were relatively uncommon in Manhattan and the older parts of Brooklyn and the Bronx, where property development predated their use, though they were common in parts of Queens and continued to privilege white access to the suburbs even after the Supreme Court rendered them unenforceable in 1948. Beginning in the 1930s, the federal government lent its support to this process of racialized city-building, making federal mortgage insurance contingent on a measure of racial and class homogeneity in neighborhoods—a process known as redlining, which locked areas populated by Black and Puerto Rican New Yorkers (and areas soon to open up to them) out of new investment. During the postwar decades, a phenomenon that had existed primarily in Harlem and East Harlem in upper Manhattan spread to neighborhoods in the Bronx and Brooklyn, sometimes with astonishing quickness through blockbusting and white flight.[9]

By 1970, these intensely disinvested neighborhoods stretched across three of the city's boroughs: a suite of adjacent neighborhoods in the South Bronx, especially east of Morris Avenue; Central Harlem, East Harlem, and parts of Washington Heights in upper Manhattan and parts of the Lower East Side downtown; and a large stretch of Brooklyn north of Prospect Park, from Fort Greene in the west to Brownsville and East New York in the east. These were, as one contemporary study put it, "area[s] of agitation and ferment"—the seedbeds of vibrant political and cultural movements driven by young people. They were also places of deprivation and desperation. The unequal housing market had downstream consequences: renting and buying in restricted markets, Black and Puerto Rican New Yorkers paid more for equivalent housing; locked out of suburbia, they had unequal access to the perks that were flowing, albeit unevenly, to the postwar middle class. Life in disinvested New York, the East Harlem–born, Bronx-raised brothers Eddie and Charlie Palmieri noted in the opening lines of their legendary jazz-funk and Latin soul album *Harlem River Drive* (released the year Sondheim's

Company was sweeping up Tonys), consisted of "several shades of living, from diamonds to mud."[10]

As social scientists have long stressed, racial and class segregation, combined with discrimination in the labor markets, left poor and working-class communities of color particularly vulnerable to economic downturns and restructurings. This is what began to occur in New York in the 1960s. In the aggregate, even as New York was losing ground in relative terms to other American metropolises, the local economy was soaring to new heights. Yet the city's economic health rested on a fragile foundation. As well-paying, unionized jobs in manufacturing left the city, they removed a crucial rung from the ladder of upward mobility. Employment in the garment industry, a vital resource to the Jewish and Italian immigrant communities of the early twentieth century, and in many ways the engine of mid-twentieth-century New York's distinctive middle class, fell by 20 percent in the two decades after 1950, resulting in some 200,000 lost jobs; likewise, the construction industry, which had only begun to open up to nonwhite workers, lost 17,000 jobs over the course of the 1960s. Young New Yorkers of color were hit particularly hard—by the end of the 1960s, youth unemployment among white teens was 9.1 percent; among Black teens, it was 16.7 percent. For those who could find work, the rising class of jobs—secretaries, typists, sales clerks, restaurant workers—typically paid less. But as researchers from the Bureau of Labor Statistics discovered, the consequences of economic restructuring for New York's communities of color ran much deeper than unemployment and sagging wages. By the late 1960s, the BLS had devised a new concept, "subemployment," which accounted for those not captured by the unemployment index—people engaged in part-time work and people who had stopped looking for formal employment altogether. Even as the citywide unemployment rate fell to a startlingly low 3.1 percent, the subemployment index rose to 28.6 percent in Central Harlem and 33.1 percent in East Harlem.[11]

While New York's economy boomed, half a million families could not afford the levels of rent needed to maintain their housing in satisfactory condition (while delivering profits to landlords). Because segregation concentrated poverty at the neighborhood level, this declining purchasing power hit a handful of neighborhoods especially hard. And so when the problem of housing abandonment captured the attention of public officials and the city press in the late 1960s, it happened first in neighborhoods with some of the city's oldest and least desirable housing stock, row houses and tenements, where the impact of deindustrialization and stagnant incomes was felt most keenly—predominantly Black Harlem and Brownsville, Brooklyn; the mostly Puerto Rican Lower East Side, East Harlem, and parts of what had recently become known as the South Bronx.[12]

In the early 1970s, this crisis of disinvestment, having begun in a handful of extraordinarily impoverished neighborhoods, spread out to engulf large parts of the city—working- and middle-class neighborhoods with solid housing stock. The precise dynamics varied from neighborhood to neighborhood, and even from building to building, but a few basic factors tended to drive the process. The costs of operating rental housing rose considerably, due to a variety of local factors as well as national inflation, which, after being low and steady throughout much of the postwar period, jumped amid the monetary uncertainty and oil shocks of the early 1970s. Costs rose in the form of escalating property, sewer, and water taxes; in labor and capital expenses as incinerators, boilers, and plumbing systems reached the end of their useful lives; in higher interest rates (which jumped by roughly a third between the mid-1960s and the mid-1970s) for renewal of ten-year mortgages; and eventually, in the soaring cost of energy. At the same time, middle-class and even working-class New Yorkers—especially though not exclusively white New Yorkers—enjoyed more housing options than they once possessed, with the continuing growth of suburbia and the opening of new middle-income complexes such as Co-op City in the Bronx and LeFrak City in Elmhurst, Queens, within the five boroughs. As these residents left and the real incomes of remaining workers and welfare recipients stagnated or fell (particularly amid the national economic recession of 1969–71, which hit New York City especially hard), rising housing costs steadily outpaced tenant incomes. In some buildings, New York's system of rent control placed an additional constraint on landlord revenues; in others, especially in neighborhoods where abandonment was most severe, tenant incomes were too low for landlords to charge even the legal rents.[13]

Finally, racial prejudice facilitated the spread of disinvestment into fundamentally sound neighborhoods: owners and banks, a 1971 study by the National Urban League found, demonstrated a consistent tendency "to withdraw residential investment capital from black and potentially black areas," which in turn "created a situation in which the viability of the cities as a whole must be questioned." "Housing economists have finally discovered what all American families have always known," the housing scholar Peter Salins wrote at the decade's end. "Although the physical characteristics of units, structures, and neighborhoods are important, nothing matters as much in a family's choice of housing as the characteristics of their prospective neighbors." Because many white New Yorkers refused to live next door to Black or Puerto Rican New Yorkers, demand was falling even in neighborhoods with good housing stock.[14]

A self-reinforcing cycle took hold: In order to maintain profits, landlords declined to make needed repairs to their buildings (encouraged by banks, which refused to lend for rehabilitation in "declining neighborhoods"); tenants withheld rents, as was their right in buildings with code violations; landlords not only found their income further reduced, but also came to see their buildings as bad investments and stopped paying property taxes. By the early 1970s, abandonment had become a feature, rather than a bug, in an important segment of the New York housing market. As costs rose and profits fell, a study by the Rand Institute found, institutional investors were withdrawing from the field of low- and middle-income housing, opening the door to unscrupulous owners whose business was to acquire properties at bargain-basement prices, collect what rents they could for a few years while declining to pay property taxes or make repairs, then walk away. Some landlords sought one final payday, engaging "large-scale arson rings involving insurance adjusters, organized crime, neighborhood youth," in order to collect on federally sponsored insurance policies. Others simply left buildings to crumble. As buildings and blocks emptied, drug workers and building strippers moved in. The latter were not entirely confined to people who needed the money: By 1977, *The New York Times* was running features on a "new urban sport" called "shopping"—"the urban homeowner's euphemism for illegal salvaging, the removal from other people's buildings of such ornamentation as wall paneling, lighting fixtures, stained glass, mantles [*sic*], . . . and other 'Victoriana.' "[15]

Thus New York confronted a kind of urban equivalent of stagflation. Rents continued to outpace incomes, yet in its most densely settled parts, the city was losing more units of housing than it was building. Landlords, bankers, tenant leaders, policy experts, politicians, and journalists struggled for superlatives with which to describe the city's housing problems. New York was facing "the greatest housing crisis in its history," the Citizens Budget Commission held—a state of "impending utter collapse." " 'Crisis' is an understatement," the city's housing administrator remarked. "Disaster may be more appropriate." Roger Starr, who would soon lay out the grisly logic of disinvestment in an approach he called "planned shrinkage," spoke of "a breakdown in the institution of private ownership."[16]

IN THEIR LOCAL AFFAIRS, New Yorkers, like all Americans, are semi-sovereign people. In the century or so leading up to the early 1970s, the city's municipal government developed the immense capacity necessary to manage most of the areas touching on day-to-day life in the city—police, fire, sanitation, public health, public transportation, public broadcasting, municipal higher education, and much more. After the Second World War and especially in the 1960s, New York State entered into what had been, traditionally, the municipal domain, especially with the development of the State University of New York system and the creation of the Metropolitan Transit Authority, which took over management of the subway from the city. But responsibility for the agencies managing the day-to-day quality of life in the city remained primarily local.

Even so, New York City is legally a creature of the State of New York, its powers granted by the state constitution, its state-conferred municipal charter, and state law. Those instruments grant the municipal government extensive authority known as "home rule": powers to make local laws, to tax and spend within limits established by the state, to exercise zoning and police powers. Still, the state government has the final word on major issues of city governance. In addition, as more and more of the New York City metropolitan area spilled out over the city's political boundaries into suburbia, the municipal government became increasingly reliant on state aid, a process that was well underway by the early 1970s. By fiscal year 1970–71, 26.6 percent of municipal revenue came in the form of state aid—the same as the property tax, the city's largest local source, and more than the 16.6 percent in aid from the federal government.[17]

Albany is central to the city's public affairs, yet the ability of New York City citizens to make their wishes felt in Albany is constrained and contingent. During the period examined in this book, with the important exception of the early 1970s, the State Assembly was dominated by Democrats, who tended to represent urban areas. The speaker of the State Assembly was often thus the primary champion of urban interests in the state government and the person most responsible for holding together a coalition whose members spanned from Brooklyn to Buffalo, from the representatives of well-off liberal districts to those of the most severely underserved communities. The State Senate, by contrast, was almost always controlled by the Republican Party, the great majority of whose members hailed either from suburbia or from outside the state's major metropolitan areas, a situation that often made the small contingent of downstate metropolitan Republicans—mostly from Queens, Staten Island, the northern Bronx, and Nassau and Westchester counties—crucial players when urban issues came before the state legislature. The state's governors tended to be as responsive to New York City's constituencies as their electoral coalitions, political agendas, and governing strategies dictated.

A certain structural tension is thus built into the relationship between the mayor of New York City and the governor of New York State. Mayors tend to see Albany as at once parochial and imperial, needlessly thwarting their efforts to govern the city that elected them. Governors tend to view mayors as local officials gumming up the political works by attempting to impose their own agendas and bringing them problems they did not ask for and do not want. With big personalities and high stakes, it can be a combustible dynamic.

In 1965, John Lindsay, a dashing, Yale-educated liberal Republican congressman based on the Upper East Side, broke the Democrats' two-decade hold on City Hall. He brought to office both a genuine interest in racial justice—he would serve as vice-chair of the famous National Advisory Commission on Civil Disorders, better known as the Kerner Commission, which issued the famous warning that the United States was moving toward two societies, one Black and one white, separate and unequal—and a modernizing, technocratic bent: He vowed to address the knotty problems of urban governance by bringing "modern men" into government, experts in management and problem-solving who would rationalize city government. Lindsay was particularly fond of think tanks and managerial consultants—during his first term, city spending on consulting fees rose from $8 million to $70 million. He was drummed out of the GOP in its 1969 mayoral primary but won reelection on the Liberal Party line and was beginning to eye the Democratic nomination for president.[18]

Lindsay's counterpart in Albany was Governor Nelson Rockefeller, standard-bearer of the moderate wing of the national Republican Party and grandson of the oil tycoon who had once been the richest man in the world. First elected governor in 1958, Rockefeller had built the New York State government into a titan, expanding its role in education, housing, transportation, urban development, environmental protection, and much else. Though his aspirations toward the Republican nomination for president had been frustrated, Rockefeller was approaching the peak of his considerable power in New York, having been elected to a fourth term in a landslide in 1970. His presidential ambitions still burned bright. He also harbored an intense dislike for Lindsay, whom he considered something of a dilettante as well as a political rival. When Rockefeller spoke Lindsay's name, one aide recalled, "his lips compressed, his brow furrowed, and his voice lowered to a contemptuous rasp."[19]

In searching for a response to the housing emergency, Lindsay and Rockefeller alighted, in different ways, on the same target for reform: the city's singular system of rent regulation. Commonly referred to then and after simply as "rent control," rent regulation in New York City actually consisted of two different programs: rent control and rent stabilization. Rent control dated to 1943. Originally a wartime anti-inflation measure undertaken by the federal government under Franklin Roosevelt, it won ardent support from tenant organizations, labor unions, and progressive politicians, who pushed successfully for New York State to take over administration when the federal program lapsed in the late 1940s. Under the law, so long as the city's vacancy rate remained under 5 percent, landlords could not raise rents except under particular circumstances:

upon making major improvements and rehabilitations, when the government sanctioned occasional across-the-board increases, and when they could show that they were not making a "fair" return of 6 percent on the building's assessed value. Tenants, in turn, enjoyed statutory rights of tenancy and relatively strong protections against evictions. Across the postwar decades, officials sanctioned decontrol for a limited number of units. But as of 1970, rent control still covered about 1.3 million apartments, all constructed before 1947. Rent stabilization was a smaller, newer program created by Lindsay and the City Council in 1968 in response to sharp rent hikes in uncontrolled units built after 1947. As of the early 1970s, the program covered some 375,000 units. Neither program applied to future construction, with the significant exception of some units built with government tax abatements, in which case those units were typically regulated for the duration of the tax benefit.[20]

Rent regulation represented only one part of the broader housing picture. From the post–World War II period onward, New York has been distinctive, though not altogether exceptional, in the share of its population that rents rather than owns: Only one-quarter of the city's housing units were owner-occupied in 1970, according to the U.S. Census. Eighty-four percent of owner-occupied units consisted of what the Census called "conventional" owner-occupied housing: single-family detached homes, row houses, brownstones, and the like; 16 percent consisted of either condominiums, in which residents owned their individual unit within a multiunit building, or, more frequently, cooperatives (often referred to as co-ops), in which residents owned shares in a corporation that owned the building. The remaining three-quarters of New Yorkers rented. Of the more than 2 million rental housing units in the city, 5.5 percent consisted of public housing, run by the New York City Housing Authority, that housed predominantly poor New Yorkers; a state program aimed at middle-class renters known as Mitchell-Lama contributed about 2.5 percent of the city's housing. More than 1 million units—58 percent of the rental stock and 44.6 percent of all the housing in New York—fell under one of the two primary rent regulation programs.[21]

Rent regulation did nothing to produce new housing, and indeed its critics charged it with constraining production by making it more difficult to clear sites for redevelopment and, less plausibly, by introducing uncertainty about future rent levels (a claim that held up better in theory than in practice, given the fact that regulations did not apply to unsubsidized new construction). Though it limited rent gouging within the market as a whole, it did not account for the conditions of particular renters and landlords. It did not seek, for instance, to ensure that renters paid only the recommended 25 to 30 percent of their income on rent. Other policy approaches were better suited to addressing key facets of the housing problem: the expansion of rental vouchers, such as the chronically underfunded federal Section 8 program, which aimed to make up the difference between low-income tenants' ability to pay and the cost of maintaining rental housing; alternative ownership models and novel approaches to the construction of new affordable housing; and the reform of inequitable taxation and easing of various impediments to new construction, such as onerous building codes, permitting fees and processes, and land-use restrictions.[22]

Still, rent regulation engendered remarkable political passion: from tenants, who saw it as protection not only against exorbitant rents but also against the potential loss of their homes and communities; and from landlords, who saw both programs as an unfair constraint on their profits and a violation of their property rights—and, increasingly, as the driving cause of housing deterioration and abandonment. Pro- and anti-regulation proponents alike accused each other of privileging their own self-interest over the well-being of the city as a whole. And yet both offered compelling arguments that transcended their own individual or group interests: Landlords claimed that rent regulation was inhibiting them from making improvements to the physical condition of the city's housing, something universally recognized as necessary; tenants argued that regulation contributed to urban vitality, stability, and community by making it possible for working- and middle-class people to stay in their neighborhoods and contribute to city life.[23]

For Lindsay, regulatory reform was one of the few levers the city could pull on its own to get badly needed capital into the housing stock—in the aggregate, housing experts estimated that the city was suffering an annual shortfall of some $260 million in rehabilitation spending, and with banks refusing to lend in redlined neighborhoods, additional rental income seemed like a potential resource. Befitting its technocratic ethos, Lindsay's administration insisted on "liberat[ing] the rent-control issue from the political arena," as his housing commissioner put it, and treating it instead as a technical problem with an optimal solution. Following a suggestion from the Rand Institute, one of the think tanks with which the Lindsay administration had formed a partnership, the city designed a computerized system that would rationalize the rent regulation regime by calculating a "Maximum Base Rent," or MBR—roughly, the cost of providing the housing plus an 8 percent profit. To the Lindsay administration, their proposal was a "sophisticated, almost scientific system." In an indication of how profoundly the abandonment crisis had shaken up the politics of rent control, Lindsay's proposal won some support from liberal Democrats: Brooklyn congresswoman Shirley Chisholm, then a year away from her landmark bid for the Democratic presidential nomination, warned that without an infusion of rental income, sound housing in stable neighborhoods such as Eastern Parkway, Crown Heights, and the Grand Concourse "would go." The City Council passed it in 1970.[24]

Lindsay's MBR program elicited howls of protest from tenant advocates, who pointed out that the permitted rent hikes could add up quickly and noted that the measure contained no enforcement mechanism to ensure that a fair share of the additional rent was going back into the housing stock. Worse, the technocratic order

Lindsay had promised conspicuously failed to materialize. The private contractors hired by the city to implement the program could not get the computerized system to function; eventually, they ditched it altogether and reverted to a "hand-tooled operation" that, because of the delays, frequently ran more than a year behind schedule in establishing Maximum Base Rents. A New York State study deemed the program a "disaster"; newspaper reports described it as "bewildering." "I've never been so confused in all my life," a top official in the Department of Rent and Housing Maintenance remarked. "After three years in this department I'm ready for the straitjacket."[25]

While Lindsay endeavored to reform rent regulation at the city level, Rockefeller sought to scale it back altogether. Unlike Lindsay, Rockefeller outright objected to rent control, though his political advisers, much to the consternation of the city's residential real estate organizations, had persuaded him not to take such a stance publicly. But the housing crisis had created an opening. In 1971, fresh off his commanding reelection and with unified Republican control of the state legislature, Rockefeller proposed to put rent control on a path to extinction by removing controls on apartments as they were voluntarily vacated by their tenants—a policy that became known as vacancy decontrol. Only the free play of "natural market forces," the governor argued, could stanch abandonment and stimulate new construction; a group of developers duly promised to "embark on a multibillion dollar housing program" in New York City if Rockefeller's bill went through. Lindsay denounced the plan as "unsound on every count," predicting that soaring rents "would drive middle-income families from our city." Other opponents of decontrol pointed to the incentives it created for tenant harassment.[26]

As the bitterly contentious legislative session of 1971 wound to a close, it appeared that the Democratic minority in the Senate could bring over enough Republicans to block decontrol. But Rockefeller would not be denied: by folding a two-year extension of upstate rent control into the vacancy decontrol bill, he was able to get the measure through the Senate with four votes to spare. Percy Sutton, the borough president of Manhattan, denounced the last-minute deal as "without a doubt the most cynical and perfidious move ever taken by the man who is the most cynical and perfidious politician in America." The real estate community was ecstatic. "It's the single greatest step forward in the history of New York City's effort to solve its housing problems," said the president of the Real Estate Board of New York. An accompanying measure, known as the Urstadt Law after state housing commissioner (and real estate executive) Charles Urstadt, prohibited cities from enacting local rent laws more restrictive than the state's, effectively taking regulation out of local democratic politics. In all, John Lindsay's chief aide in Albany described the legislative session to the mayor as "anti-city" and "the single most reactionary in modern memory."[27]

In the wake of Maximum Base Rent and vacancy decontrol, rents rose, yet little materialized in the way of new construction, and abandonment continued apace. By one account, the median rent in decontrolled apartments rose 52 percent between 1971 and 1973, while spending on renovations fell by nearly $1 million per month compared to what it had been before deregulation; new housing permits rose slightly in 1972 before falling back to pre-1968 levels in 1973. City housing officials documented a spike in rents and a major upsurge in harassment cases. "Vacancy decontrol does more than give an equitable return to the landlord," Commissioner Nathan Leventhal charged; "it gift-wraps the tenant and presents him to the landlord to do with as he pleases." Rockefeller's top aides were taken aback by the media reaction to vacancy decontrol, and by early 1972 one aide reported with alarm that Urstadt was being viewed as "a spokesman for the landlords." With living costs rising across the board, Rockefeller assembled a State Commission on Living Costs and the Economy, chaired by Democratic Assemblyman Andrew

Stein, son of the wealthy law journal publisher and Rockefeller ally Jerry Finkelstein. In 1973, concerned by the politics of rising rents in advance of the 1974 gubernatorial election, Rockefeller asked Stein's commission to suggest possible state action to hold down rents. In early February 1974, Stein released the commission's report and called for vacancy decontrol to be repealed and for large municipalities to regain the right to enact their own rent regulations.[28]

By then Rockefeller was gone, having stepped down in December 1973 to prepare for yet another presidential bid and allow his long-serving lieutenant Malcolm Wilson to stand as an incumbent in the 1974 gubernatorial election. As soon as the legislative session opened, New Yorkers flooded the hopper with rent control legislation. Personally, Wilson was no more supportive of rent control than Rockefeller, but with suburban Republicans coming under pressure from their constituents, tenant groups mobilizing effectively, and an election on the horizon, he bowed to political reality and endorsed a plan to roll back vacancy decontrol.

"Every rent-controlled building in the city will be abandoned within a year" if vacancy decontrol were ended, claimed the young developer Donald Trump, who had recently become president of his father Fred Trump's Brooklyn and Queens rental empire. Trump, whose organization had been sued by the federal Department of Justice the previous fall for violating the 1968 Fair Housing Act (a lawsuit that was ultimately settled with no admission of wrongdoing)—the 3,700-unit Trump Village complex in Brooklyn was home to only seven Black families—put together a lobbying fund that he claimed amounted to $250,000. Vacancy decontrol, he wrote in an urgent letter to the governor, "must remain in full force" or else "every middle-income apartment house unit in the city will become abandoned, within a short period of time," and "the decay and squalor which will inevitably follow will be unprecedented in our nation's history." But he failed to get a hearing from Governor

Wilson. "As I am sure you realize," an assistant to the governor replied, Wilson and his staff were thoroughly familiar with the situation, "and it would be unusual if you could convey to him or his staff any more information on the subject than he already has."[29]

Shortly before midnight on the final day of the session, the GOP legislative leaders hashed out a thirty-nine-page bill, the Emergency Tenant Protection Act of 1974, that placed vacated rent-controlled apartments under the city's rent stabilization system after allowing a one-time "negotiated first rent"—a framework that meant that rent stabilization, a looser system administered by the mayor's appointees, would gradually replace the more stringent rent control regime as the city's primary form of regulation. At the insistence of a group of Queens Republicans in the Assembly, the final terms were somewhat more favorable to landlords than what Wilson had proposed, let alone what the city Democrats and tenant organizations wanted. Most tenant groups opposed the act, with one calling it a "weak, cosmetic" bill, and the great majority of New York City Democrats voted against it. Still, Rockefeller's program of full vacancy deregulation was effectively dead.[30]

Even as the state legislature was working out the details of rent regulation, the city's housing disaster continued to compound. In 1973 and 1974, oil prices spiked. Heavily dependent on foreign oil, which was nearly twice as expensive as domestic oil, New York City saw its heating and utility costs skyrocket—amounting in some instances to an entire third of the rent roll. The Real Estate Board of New York pleaded with the federal government to equalize oil costs across the nation, warning of a "major regional depression, including severe job losses and widespread abandonment." As yet more owners defaulted on their mortgages, banks offloaded their properties at prices that practically implied abandonment as a business model. The Bronx in particular suffered. "South Bronx landlords are like California prospectors a hundred years ago," one city official lamented. "They rushed in, took out the gold, and left a ghost town."

On the eve of the fiscal crisis, the city had already experienced a housing cataclysm—and the worst was yet to come.[31]

IF HOUSING REPRESENTED the most profound—and confounding—failure of governance in the decade leading up to the fiscal crisis, the proliferation of crime and disorder in the city's streets and public spaces emerged as perhaps the primary symbol of the failure of public authority. "No aspect of the environment so concerns the people of New York City as its streets," the City Planning Commission wrote in its 1969 master plan. "They think they are not only too dirty, they think that they are much too dangerous."[32]

If the destruction of the housing stock struck at the quintessential urban social unit, the neighborhood, street crime threatened one of the city's most remarkable features: what the urbanist Marshall Berman called its "intense and vibrant street life," a constellation of public spaces "of a breadth and depth undreamt of in the rest of the US (and possibly unmatched in the entire world)"—places that not only facilitated the comings and goings of daily life but also embodied the energies of the cosmopolitan city. The 1960s was hardly the first time that crime and disorder had moved to the center of city politics—witness the panic over "juvenile delinquency" in the war and postwar years. But it was this emphasis on public space that most clearly distinguished anxieties about crime and disorder in the 1960s from earlier "crime wave" panics. New phrases like "street crime" and "crime in the streets" entered the lexicon. A new attention to surveillance and the management (and eventually, "reclaiming") of public spaces characterized the city's official response.[33]

During his first mayoral campaign in 1965, John Lindsay made street crime a central theme: "No problem facing New York City and no issue in this campaign is more important than the problem of rising crime and the safety of our cities. The fear which wracks our citizens today is the fear to walk the streets and ride the subways and . . . enjoy the parks. It is a fear that has made thousands and thousands of our citizens prisoners in their own city. It is a fear that more than any other factor has staggered the city's spirit and morale." Lindsay's focus on street crime appears to have been at least to some extent grounded in reality—crime statistics are notoriously unreliable and prone to misuse, but they did rise across every major category in the first half of the 1960s (though nowhere near as much as they would in the decade that followed). Reporters, politicians, and citizens from communities across the city blamed the New York Police Department for failing to curtail street crime. Some simply demanded more policing; others, particularly Black and Puerto Rican leaders, assailed police abuse as well as unresponsiveness and ineffectiveness, calling for measures such as an independent civilian complaint review board as well as investments in housing, education, and jobs that would address the "root causes" of crime. During the 1965 campaign, Lindsay had endorsed a civilian review board and vowed to provide a twenty-four-hour police presence on every single block of the city. After a high-profile clash with the Patrolmen's Benevolent Association, Lindsay's review board went down to defeat in a public referendum. But Lindsay did succeed at growing the force by some four thousand officers.[34]

In the second half of the 1960s, the problem of crime in the streets became closely associated in public discourse and policymaking with the use and marketing of illicit drugs, particularly heroin. The actual connection between increasing drug use and rising crime was complicated. Statistics showed that 21.8 percent of people arrested for burglary and 18.1 percent of people arrested for robbery in New York in 1971 described themselves as drug addicts; the figure for murder and homicide was 10.6. The monetary demands of addiction were clearly driving some growth in property crime. But drug use and markets also served as a kind of scapegoat for a broader social phenomenon that defied easy solutions.[35]

The purported connection between drugs and street crime became a rare point of agreement between Governor Rockefeller and Mayor Lindsay. In 1966, Rockefeller called for new civil commitment programs, arguing that "addicts" were responsible for one-half of the crimes committed in New York City, a claim that became something of a refrain. In his bid for reelection that year, he ran ads that read: "Get the addicts off the streets, put the pushers behind bars, and this crime will stop." Lindsay likewise subscribed to the connection between crime and the drug economy. Narcotics addiction, he wrote in a letter to Rockefeller, "breeds crime and terrorizes communities. . . . And it precipitates the deterioration of once stable neighborhoods. . . . An expanded fight against narcotics is absolutely essential to the stability of this City."[36]

Pressed by his rivals during the 1969 mayoral election, Lindsay and the NYPD launched a concerted crackdown on street-level drug markets, requiring every precinct captain to make narcotics traffic their top priority and to report drug arrest statistics weekly. Overall, drug arrests nearly tripled between 1967 and 1970. But intensive street-level drug policing did not produce the effects Lindsay and the NYPD hoped. The policy was extraordinarily expensive: one study found that nearly a full man-week of effort was required to obtain the evidence necessary to make a street-level sale arrest stand up in court. Drug cases seemed to soak up valuable criminal justice resources toward no discernible ends. In part because mass drug arrests overwhelmed the courts, the conviction rates for those arrested on felony drug charges had been a low three in ten. And with no meaningful decline in property crimes, the city seemed to have little to show for this massive investment of public resources. Powerful voices within the local criminal justice establishment began, with renewed force, to disparage the idea of treating narcotics addiction through the criminal justice system. "As long as drug abusers are treated as outlaws," Lindsay's Criminal Justice Coordinating Council wrote in its 1972 annual report, "any real progress in helping them or even making them harmless will be impossible."[37]

Then there were the opportunities for corruption that street-level drug policing afforded unscrupulous officers. When a series of scandals rocked the NYPD in the early 1970s (portrayed in the 1973 film *Serpico*), Lindsay assembled an investigatory body known as the Knapp Commission whose hearings uncovered a startling range of abuses: in addition to the usual shakedowns, officers had sold drugs, helped to finance drug sales, and shielded sellers from arrest in a variety of ways—by revealing the identity of government informants, tipping off dealers about wiretaps and upcoming raids, and even kidnapping key witnesses. When the NYPD took steps to guard against corruption in the wake of these disclosures, it included a "general prohibition on self-initiated enforcement actions"; patrol officers who enforced the narcotics laws found themselves reprimanded by supervisors and forced to fill out extensive reports. And so, beginning in 1972, the city and its police department largely abandoned the street-policing experiment and shifted its attention to mid- and upper-level traffickers.[38]

Rockefeller, though, like the national Republicans during Richard Nixon's presidency, was moving in precisely the opposite direction. In November 1971, he delivered a major address calling for an all-out war on drugs. Then in early 1973 he introduced the measures that would become known as the Rockefeller Drug Laws. Intended to scare drug users into treatment programs while removing ostensibly incorrigible "pushers" from the state's communities, the legislation established severe penalties for the sale and possession of narcotics and other drugs; a concurrent measure set new mandatory minimums for second felony offenders. Whatever Rockefeller's sincere hopes for the measures, his aims were also transparently political: Just as the laws were going into effect, one of his top aides arranged a publishing deal with Doubleday for a ghostwritten book on the Rockefeller laws' success, intending to distribute complimentary copies to all potential delegates to the 1976 Republican National Convention.[39]

Many New Yorkers were appalled by Rockefeller's proposals. "When are we going to open the concentration camps?" asked State Senator Manfred Ohrenstein, a Democrat from Manhattan. Long-serving Manhattan district attorney Frank Hogan described the proposed laws as "impractical, inequitable, and inexplicable" and predicted they would grind the criminal justice system to a standstill; liberal groups noted that the city was full of people in recovery leading productive lives who would have been incarcerated under the Rockefeller laws. John Lindsay excoriated the measures. "We all know how empty it is to promise victory over crime by an emotional call to lock the criminals up and throw away the key," he said. "This is not a battle plan. It is merely a deceptive gesture, offering nothing beyond momentary satisfaction and inevitable disillusionment." They watched helplessly as a modified version of Rockefeller's proposals passed through the GOP-dominated state legislature. The NYPD, which also opposed the laws, was in a position to act. "We could destroy Rocky's program in two months just by making a lot of arrests," one anonymous officer told the *Times*. "There are people who would like to do that, to give the legislators what they've asked for." Instead, the department went in the other direction, continuing its preferred policy of nonenforcement in defiance of Rockefeller and the state legislature. By 1974, the number of felony drug arrests in the city had fallen from a high of 26,378 during Lindsay's enforcement surge to a mere 7,439.[40]

The first major departure from this policy of nonenforcement came in 1975, not at the NYPD's initiative but because political leaders, businesses, and media outlets in Harlem called for it. "All of us know," argued an editorial in the Harlem newspaper *Amsterdam News*, "that a police campaign . . . is not the answer to the narcotics problem in Harlem or anywhere else. Many fundamental social and economic changes must take place before any lasting alleviation comes about. But the people of Harlem do have a right to possess their streets; they do have a right not to be subjected to the blight of 'marketplaces.'" More intensive street policing was something the government appeared relatively able and perhaps willing to provide, and something that could be put into operation quickly. In late 1975, the *Amsterdam News* declared a community-level "war on crime," calling for greater action against street-level "pushers." Press coverage, in turn, galvanized the neighborhood's political leaders, most notably Manhattan borough president Percy Sutton and Congressman Charles Rangel. They convinced Commissioner Michael Codd to sign off on an effort called Operation Drugs, which sent some 150 uniformed personnel and 75 members of the Narcotics Division into the neighborhood to make street-level arrests—nearly five thousand in the course of the next four months.[41]

Foisted on the department, Operation Drugs never really received buy-in from the NYPD. Police officials speaking anonymously described the operation as "a cynical and perhaps futile product of political pressure." Whatever skepticism Harlem residents themselves may have felt toward more intensive street policing proved well founded: the police department, unable and unwilling to devote the resources required, engaged not in street-level drug policing but in street sweeps that made Operation Drugs an exercise in harassment for many neighborhood residents. Newspaper reporters who combed the arrest records learned that many of the arrests were for disorderly conduct, not for drug sales or possession, and that they had occurred because "crowds of young men refused to move off street corners when told to do so." Prosecutors found that the "number and quality of arrests we are getting from the police is way down." The entire episode seemed only to affirm the NYPD's decision in the early 1970s to cut back on street-level enforcement.[42]

Into the mid-1970s, a decade after Lindsay had called it the city's most important issue, New York had done little to bring street crime under control. Compromised by its own institutional weaknesses and with little capacity to address the underlying economic dynamics driving street crime, the NYPD floundered. As the fiscal crisis approached, police officers and a wide range of New Yorkers were voicing skepticism about the NYPD's ability to significantly reduce crime in the streets. The police "[did] not have the cure" for rising crime, one police captain told a meeting in Brooklyn Heights. The police could only "play checkers" with muggers, another told a group on the Upper West Side. "We increase the patrols on one street and they move to the next."[43]

ON FEBRUARY 3, 1964, some 460,000 New York City students and teachers took part in what may have been the largest single-day civil rights demonstration of the 1960s, staying home from school to protest the Board of Education's failure to desegregate the public schools. "Our children must be given quality education in a de-segregated school system," the Jamaica, Queens, branch of the NAACP and the Queens chapter of the Congress on Racial Equality wrote in a joint statement. "Every child, whether he lives in South Jamaica or Kew Gardens, is entitled to the same opportunity to develop his abilities." Ten years after the U.S. Supreme Court's landmark *Brown v. Board* decision, this bastion of urban liberalism effectively had two school systems, one with adequate resources, experienced and effective teachers, and avenues for parental and community involvement, the other without.[44]

In the wake of *Brown*, many New York City activists pushed for integration as a technique for achieving their broader aims of equality and empowerment. No one disputed that New York's public schools were racially segregated: A 1955 study found that nearly three-quarters of New York's public elementary schools had student populations that were more than 90 percent white or 90 percent nonwhite. But while civil rights leaders pointed to the role of policy decisions, such as the drawing of district lines and the selection of sites for new construction in reinforcing segregation (itself the product of racist housing policy and practices), schools officials claimed that "racial imbalance"—they resisted even the term *segregation*—though perhaps undesirable, could be addressed only slowly. "We have natural segregation here," New York's superintendent of schools said in 1954—"it's accidental."[45]

Convinced that segregation, along with other forms of discrimination and prejudice, underpinned the unequal distribution of educational resources and learning opportunities in the city, civil rights leaders and families of color pushed the city to work toward integration. They were met by reluctance from the Board of Education and vocal opposition from many white parents, who stressed the importance of "neighborhood schools." A coalition led by the psychologist and educator Kenneth Clark and the legendary civil rights organizer Ella Baker had been able to leverage the public attention brought by *Brown* to win a committee on integration, but the Board of Education took little action on its recommendations. At the same time, white parents resisted even small-scale, localized plans to transfer Black and Puerto Rican students in overcrowded schools to nearby white-majority schools. Education officials sought to walk a line between these forces, expressing a desire for a better "racial balance" while accusing desegregation advocates of being "extremists" who wanted "instant racial balances." As more Black and Puerto Rican children arrived in the segregated city, the schools became still more divided. In the half-decade after *Brown*, a study by the Brooklyn chapter of the NAACP found, the number of segregated elementary schools in New York City had risen by more than 70 percent.[46]

As the campaign for integration mobilized in the mid-1960s, so too did white opponents of desegregation: The month after the 1964 student boycott, a group of more than ten thousand white parents calling themselves "Parents and Taxpayers" gathered at the Board of Education building in downtown Brooklyn and marched across the Brooklyn Bridge to City Hall in protest against the city's desegregation plans, bearing signs that read "FOR QUALITY EDUCATION," "LOVE THY NEIGHBORHOOD SCHOOL," and "SHIP CATTLE—NOT CHILDREN." They followed with their own boycott, some 275,000 children strong, in September 1964.[47]

As the political obstacles to desegregation were becoming clear, many policy experts, parents and students of color, and community leaders began to search for alternative approaches to school equity. For some Black and Puerto Rican thinkers and activists, this meant shifting the focus from integration toward community empowerment. Preston Wilcox, a former professional basketball player turned Columbia School of Social Work professor, knew the experience of quiet bigotry firsthand. At the predominantly white school he attended in Youngstown, Ohio, he recalled, his teachers were "friendly enough to me personally." But even though he was an honor roll student, not a single one had encouraged him to go to college. Integration on such terms, he later wrote, could amount only to a systemic effort "to enable Black students to perceive virtues in those who oppress them" while subjecting them to teachers and principals who acted "instinctively and negatively toward Black students."[48]

The answer, Wilcox believed, was direct community control over the public schools through elected local boards. "If it is true that the public school system can do no more than it is already doing," Wilcox wrote, "then the communities of the poor must be prepared to act for themselves. The residents of the ghetto must seize the opportunity to assume a leadership role in the education of their own children." In 1966, a group of activists calling themselves the People's Board of Education, many of whom had been prominent members of the integration movement, occupied the Board of Education building in downtown Brooklyn. The president of the newly formed organization, Brooklyn minister the Reverend Milton Galamison, one of the chief organizers of the 1964 boycott, charged the Board of Education with "abdicat[ing] its responsibility and continu[ing] to neglect the needs of our ghetto schools." The People's Board published a report that "demonstrated a 2- to 5-year achievement gap between students in predominantly black and Puerto Rican schools and students in predominantly white schools." To address these failures, they called for "community participation in support of 'creative innovation' in schools," as well as community control of schools to provide "quality control and accountability for how resources were spent to meet local needs."[49]

In 1967, in response to growing grassroots pressure from parents and community leaders (and with support from the Ford Foundation), the Board of Education authorized three "demonstration" districts—in East Harlem, the Lower East Side, and in the adjoining Brooklyn neighborhoods of Ocean Hill and Brownsville—that gave community school boards control over staffing, curriculum decisions, and uses of school buildings for community activities. When the community board in Ocean Hill–Brownsville tested its powers over staffing in the spring of 1968 by dismissing nineteen teachers and administrators on grounds that they had been ineffectual, the United Federation of Teachers responded with a series of strikes, first in the district and then citywide, that closed New York schools for six weeks. The standoff—which became ugly and racially charged, yielding ill sentiments that would linger for decades—pitted Lindsay, Black and Puerto Rican activists and teachers, and major corporations and nonprofits against the UFT and its mostly white membership. When the scene shifted to Albany, Lindsay and other community control advocates found that they had lost the support of upstate legislators, outer borough Democrats, suburban lawmakers, and Nelson Rockefeller, who was courting the support of the UFT in advance of the 1970 gubernatorial election. The state legislature resolved the crisis in 1969 by designing a new system that would remain in place for the next three decades. Rather than citywide administration or community control, the legislature opted for "decentralization": a hybrid system composed of thirty-two community school districts—significantly larger than the community control demonstration districts—whose locally elected school boards governed elementary and middle schools but with considerably less authority than community control advocates had envisioned. The central Board of Education retained control of high schools.[50]

Many advocates saw the decentralization law as a cruel hoax, a watered-down version of the community control ideal. "The local school boards are powerless, the election procedures are undemocratic, and the district lines are illegitimate," argued United Bronx Parents, a wide-ranging community advocacy group. Yet the law also created a framework within which a new generation of activists, teachers, and school leaders could apply some of the ideas of the community control movement—and it was in this context that efforts at innovative pedagogy and school choice coalesced. Inspired in part by liberal intellectuals who suggested that integration could be achieved by allowing parents to choose between distinctive, innovative public schools, experiments in progressive education popped up around the city: John Dewey High School, a prototype magnet school, was opened by the Board of Education in Brooklyn in 1969; the experimental P.S. 3 in Greenwich Village was founded by parents in 1971; and City-as-School, a teacher-driven alternative school, opened its doors in Brooklyn in 1973.[51]

But no district pushed the approach of small, theme-driven public schools and school choice as far as District 4, which covered the heavily Puerto Rican neighborhood of East Harlem. In 1973, the local school board hired a young educator, Anthony Alvarado, to serve as district superintendent. Alvarado, who had grown up in a working-class family with Puerto Rican and Cuban parents in the South Bronx, announced that he was willing to pursue any "original vital idea" that might improve the district's schools. He quickly partnered with a progressive educator named Deborah Meier.

Also a native New Yorker, Meier had grown up with the left-labor politics of the postwar city, and she remained a committed socialist, becoming a founding member of one of the forerunners to the Democratic Socialists of America (DSA) in 1973. (Over the years, the FBI amassed a 163-page surveillance file on her.)[52]

As a young teacher in underresourced schools in Chicago, Philadelphia, and Central Harlem, Meier had struggled to understand why students with obvious verbal and conceptual ability were being labeled "slow learners." The problem, she began to believe, lay not with the children but with an approach to education that viewed poor students of color as culturally and linguistically deprived, a problem to be fixed through "compensatory education." Such an approach was destined to fail, Meier thought, because it refused to work with students on their own terms: Rather than engage their curiosity, schools were fostering "an alienation so severe as to make the school and the teacher a relatively useless educational instrument." In 1974, with Alvarado's support, Meier launched Central Park East, a small, integrated school with no fixed curriculum—Meier viewed it as a "teachers' collective"—that she hoped would foster a sense of community and give students an experience of learning that was, in her words, "both conceptual and *tangible*." Central Park East started with only thirty-two students—kindergartners and first-graders—in space borrowed from a local public school. It quickly grew and provided a kind of proof of concept in District 4, which created twenty new schools over the course of the next decade.[53]

By then, the political tide had turned decisively against remaining proponents of desegregation. Kenneth Clark, now a member of the State Board of Regents, noted ruefully that the direction of policy had turned from lackluster implementation of a "very strong integration policy" to an effective state policy that "encourages and supports racial segregation." As national Republican politicians increasingly adopted antibusing rhetoric and policies to court suburban voters, he believed, the Republican leadership of the New York State legislature had become more aggressive in screening potential appointees to the Board of Regents for their attitudes toward desegregation. "The fact is," Clark charged during a Sunday-morning broadcast on WNYC-TV, that the "Board of Regents . . . has become nothing more than a subcommittee of the Legislature reflecting what the political officials, the elected political officials, [take] to be the desire of the majority of whites in New York State." "An absurd statement," Clark's fellow regent Emlyn I. Griffith responded. But when pressed, Griffith offered his opinion that "the fact that the Regents are reflecting some of the facts of life at the present time is an indication that they are responsible."[54]

If Griffith was content to refer obliquely to segregated schools as "facts of life," his fellow appointee, former New York City teacher Genevieve Klein of Bayside, Queens, happily provided more detail: Desegregation "soured race relations" and created "conflict and bitterness," she wrote. How? "If two black, two Irish or two Jewish kids get into a fight in school, it's nothing," she explained to a reporter. "But the moment you mix it, it becomes a big hoo-ha." ("I'm not a racist by a longshot," she quickly added.) By late 1976, opponents of desegregation had gained enough seats on the Board of Regents to oust the pro-integration state commissioner of education, Ewald Nyquist. The New York City Board of Education, for its part, had largely thrown up its hands in the face of white flight, arguing, in the words of Chancellor Irving Anker, that its own efforts had been "eroded or nullified by changes in the pupil population." Integration was no longer possible within the five boroughs, city officials suggested, because the number of white public school students had fallen so far.[55]

Even as the broader visions of the 1960s faded, the rise of the small-school movement suggested that progressive change might just flower from the grassroots. Still, it remained to be seen whether experiments like District 4's could be brought to scale, and whether progressive reform was really possible within a system that remained so deeply segregated—and which was soon to see its resources slashed to the bone.

ON THE FIRST DAY OF 1974, control of City Hall passed from John Lindsay to Abraham Beame, a Democrat who had served two nonconsecutive terms as city comptroller before easily winning the mayoralty in 1973. Sixty-eight years old at the time of his inauguration, Beame's political and personal journey was representative of a generation of Jewish New York. Born in London to Eastern European Jewish parents on the run from the czar's police, he arrived at Ellis Island in 1906, three months old, and grew up in a series of tenement apartments on the Lower East Side before graduating cum laude from tuition-free City College and opening an accounting firm. Once a young socialist, he became a New Dealer and a Democratic Party regular, building his political career through Brooklyn's Madison Democratic Club and remaining firmly committed to programs such as rent control, tuition-free college, and affordable transportation that defined the city's post–New Deal tradition.[56]

By the time Beame took office, the city was in deep fiscal trouble. The outflow of residents and jobs that had begun in 1970 had cut into the city's revenues just as inflation, rising health and social service costs, and the long-term expansion of the municipal workforce had driven up its expenditures. Beame quickly promised some budget cuts but not on a scale that would close what had become a structural deficit. Rather than face the political choice of raising taxes or cutting expenditures head-on, Beame and the Board of Estimate, like Lindsay before them, resorted to borrowing to cover short-term expenses. In 1969, the City of New York had issued $747 million in short-term notes; by Beame's second year in office, 1975, the figure had risen to $4.5 billion. That spring the city's major underwriters, suspicious of its accounting practices and seeing better value in investments elsewhere, pulled out of the market for municipal debt, forcing the city to seek support from the state and federal governments.[57]

New York State's response was overseen by first-year governor Hugh Carey, the Brooklyn Democrat who had warned of stormy times ahead in his 1975 State of the State address. To help the city regain access to the financial markets, Carey created a new agency, the Municipal Assistance Corporation, consisting of leading figures from the finance and business communities and informally directed by the Vienna-born investment banker Felix Rohatyn, whom Carey had been leaning on for advice. MAC, as it was known, was authorized but not required to issue $3 billion in bonds to finance the city's debts. It was able to pressure the city into budget-balancing cuts by threatening to withhold resources. MAC was indeed able to force Beame to propose drastic budget cuts—including eliminating some thirty-eight thousand jobs. But even these reductions failed to reassure the financial markets. In September 1975, Carey created another new entity, the Emergency Financial Control Board, consisting of the governor, the mayor, the comptrollers of New York State and New York City, and three private members appointed by Carey. The board effectively took control of the city's finances.[58]

Still, New York remained on the fiscal brink. President Gerald Ford and the group of conservative advisers who surrounded him were generally unsympathetic. New York's difficulties, they believed, were primarily the consequence of a profligate and undisciplined local political culture. The city's crisis, Ford suggested in an address to the National Press Club, was not simply the result of "long-range economic factors" such as suburbanization and deindustrialization. "Most other cities in America have faced these very same challenges," he argued, "and they are still financially healthy today." Instead, he believed, the city had brought itself to the brink through its generous spending, not only on its poor but also on its middle class—in the form of good wages and pensions for a unionized municipal workforce, a tuition-free college, an expansive municipal hospital system, and a low subway fare. A lack of discipline and responsibility, Ford claimed, had led to a fiscal reckoning. As the crisis unfolded, he insisted on the need to get tough. "Must do what's right. Bite bullet," he wrote in a note to himself in advance of a meeting with Mayor Beame and Governor Carey. On October 29, 1975, he memorably vowed to veto any congressional rescue measure, inspiring the *Daily News* to publish the most famous tabloid headline in the city's history: "FORD TO CITY: DROP DEAD."[59]

Ford may have intended his speech to force the city and state to make more drastic cuts; in any case, the notion that the federal government would refuse to aid New York proved untenable. The financial community remained concerned that a New York City default would ripple across the global economy. Republicans, in turn, worried that an economic downturn would hurt them in the 1976 elections. In the meantime, the Emergency Financial Control Board had produced a plan to ensure a budget surplus within three years through additional deep cuts. On December 9, Ford signed off on a program of seasonal loans, ending the acute phase of the fiscal crisis. The cost of New York's return to solvency, Felix Rohatyn remarked, was "the most brutal kind of financial and fiscal exercise any community in the country will ever have to face." In the next three years, New York lost 69,672 municipal workers. The effects were felt in nearly every aspect of city life: day care centers closed, libraries cut their hours, parks went undermaintained, the streets were swept and repaired less frequently, schools lost teachers and staffers. Police and fire services became less reliable, safety inspections occurred less frequently, and vital maintenance work was deferred as infrastructure decayed.[60]

If the fiscal crisis fundamentally changed how New Yorkers experienced government, it also reshaped how the political classes envisioned government's role in the city. The Democrats and liberal Republicans who retained most of the key political positions in New York emerged from the fiscal crisis chastened, more likely to emphasize limits and the need for discipline and tough choices, more willing to write city issues off as beyond the purview of government. They also acquired a greater interest in working with the business community to stimulate property and commercial development. In fact, liberal politicians helped organize the business community as a coherent political force in the city precisely in order to pursue their own objectives. In early 1975, New York's senior U.S. senator, the liberal Republican Jacob Javits, who at that time was pushing for a full-employment bill in Washington, brought a coalition of businessmen led by Chase Manhattan president (and younger brother of the former governor) David Rockefeller, and labor leaders led by Harry Van Arsdale, longtime head of the New York City Central Labor Council of the AFL-CIO, to form a new organization, the Business/Labor Working Group (B/LWG), to pursue shared solutions to the city's problems.[61]

While they accepted austerity as necessary and saw tax reductions as important to restoring the city's economic competitiveness, the coalition of liberals and businessmen that emerged during the crisis were by no means anti-state. What they desired above all was a return to the shared public- and private-sector focus on growth and development of the New Deal and postwar eras. The B/LWG's primary objectives were a new convention center and, especially, a controversial highway-and-park project along the Hudson River known as Westway. And even as they accepted austerity, they felt that private investment alone could not restore the city to economic health. "Direct economic actions will not work effectively unless they are accompanied by an actual and perceived improvement in the 'quality of life'—better security and schools, cleaner streets, etc.," the group's final report argued. Quality of life was paramount because it promised to secure the middle class on which the group presumed New York's future to depend. "A better 'quality of life' is key to New York's future economic and social vitality. . . . *[all] policies and actions should increasingly focus on maintaining and attracting middle-income families.*" Even in the midst of austerity, a certain vision of pro-growth investment in city services, not only for business but also for the middle classes, was starting to appear.[62]

Politicians who held firm to the New Deal tradition of activist government, too, did so by emphasizing the importance of a stable middle class. If the imposition of austerity struck older liberals like Beame as a betrayal of the social compact that had shaped their lives in New York, it seemed self-defeating to many younger, idealistic Democrats. Former mayor Robert F. Wagner's son Bobby, Harvard- and Princeton-educated, a member of the City Council, and in his thirties a rising star in the city's Democratic party, likened threats to free tuition at CUNY and the end of rent control to America's strategy in Vietnam—"in order to save the city, you must destroy it." The institutions threatened by the fiscal crisis, he believed, were the same institutions "which help hold [the city's] middle class and prevent it from going the way of Newark, Buffalo, Cleveland, Philadelphia, and Baltimore." New York's problems were real, he acknowledged, but "without federal recognition that poverty is a national problem, no real answer will be found. . . ." Meanwhile "it is madness to make the city even less attractive to its middle and lower-middle class. . . . Such policies would leave New York a shell of its former self." Liberals like Wagner and business leaders like Rockefeller disagreed fundamentally on issues like rent regulation. But they shared the assumption that the city's future depended on its appeal to the middle class.[63]

This new liberal outlook had little room for considerations of racial equity and empowerment. The conflicts of the 1960s, such as Ocean Hill–Brownsville, were still raw. More than that, though, white liberals had arrived at a sense that responsiveness to the concerns of Black and Hispanic New Yorkers had contributed to the breakdown in political discipline that had led to the fiscal crisis—that a broad coalitional politics was inconsonant with the demands facing the city and state in the 1970s. A decade earlier New York's power structure had seemed responsive, if only grudgingly, to the freedom movements that swept the city. Now it refused to engage even in the kind of small-scale representation that might a few years prior been regarded as mere tokenism—as when Carey rejected demands for a Black person to be appointed to the EFCB. As the tenor of life in the city changed, the horizons of liberatory politics unmistakably receded.[64]

WITH THE CITY EVIDENTLY AT a crossroads, the 1977 contest for mayor drew one of the most remarkable fields of candidates in the city's history. Beame chose to stand for reelection and remained formidable, though the fiscal crisis had weakened his standing to the point that many other leading politicians entered the fray. Manhattan borough president Percy Sutton, a former Tuskegee airman and onetime lawyer for Malcolm X who was among the city's most prominent Black politicians, entered the race, as did Herman Badillo of the Bronx, the first Puerto Rican member of Congress, who had run second to Beame in the 1973 mayoral primary. The strongest early challenge came from former U.S. representative Bella Abzug, a feminist icon and champion of the New Left whose indefatigable efforts on behalf of everyday New Yorkers had gained her a reputation as the people's representative—New Yorkers from outside her district and even outside the city frequently wrote to her congressional office asking her to take up their problems.[65]

The Democratic primary also boasted two lesser-known figures. Mario Cuomo was the Queens-raised son of Italian immigrants, a onetime professional baseball prospect who had gone on to law school, graduating, like Hugh Carey, first in his class at St. John's

Law. First gaining notice as the attorney for community organizations in Queens, he had risen through the ranks of the Democratic Party to become New York's secretary of state. Widely admired in political and journalistic circles for his intelligence, eloquence, and character, he seemed to his supporters like a successor to Robert F. Kennedy—liberal, humane, and idealistic, but also someone who appealed to the white-ethnic working-class voters of Brooklyn and Queens. He had the support of Jacqueline Kennedy Onassis, who said that he reminded her of her late husband, as well as Kennedy-affiliated liberals such as Arthur Schlesinger, Jr. But he was also Carey's preferred candidate, which meant that he risked being viewed by voters as the governor's puppet.[66]

The final major candidate was Congressman Edward Koch of Manhattan. Born in the Bronx to Jewish immigrant garment workers, Koch had grown up in Newark. After serving in the 104th Infantry during World War II, he attended City College and NYU Law before starting his own practice. Koch entered politics as an idealistic reformer based in Greenwich Village, part of a group of independent Democrats who sought to overthrow the last great boss of Tammany Hall, Carmine de Sapio. After a term on the City Council, Koch ran for Congress in John Lindsay's old district and won, taking his seat in 1969.[67]

Through the mid-1960s, Koch was in essence a Great Society liberal. He traveled to the South to support civil rights during Freedom Summer of 1964 and helped draft the measure that became John Lindsay's ill-fated Civilian Complaint Review Board. But his stance began to change in the late 1960s and early '70s as key political contests in the city increasingly positioned Black and Jewish New Yorkers at odds. Koch opposed busing for school integration as well as a plan to integrate public housing into the Queens neighborhood of Forest Hills—a controversy he called his "political Rubicon." By the time of the 1977 mayoral race, he had developed an instinctive suspicion of Black politicians and activists. "My experience with blacks," he said in 1975, "is that they're basically anti-Semitic." Backed by the New York political guru David Garth, who had advised Lindsay's campaigns, Koch mixed strong support for traditional liberal causes such as rent control with a tough-on-crime attitude and an embrace of the new liberalism of limits. "The City of New York," he cautioned, "cannot be a W.P.A."[68]

If the contenders for office in 1977 were among the strongest the city had to offer, the campaign itself was something of a disappointment. Badillo and Sutton, two of the harshest critics of austerity, struggled to articulate an alternative vision, and Sutton, though perhaps the candidate best prepared for the mayoralty, had difficulty getting a hearing outside the city's Black communities. Abzug, ahead in the polls, relatively new to municipal issues, and aware that her perceived radicalism could work to her disadvantage as the city struggled to regain solvency, ran a tempered race. As a consequence, the Democratic primary was less than a full-on reckoning with the vital issues facing the city. Following that July's blackout and widespread looting, the campaign came to focus primarily on issues favorable to Koch and Cuomo, the candidates most at home on the terrain of law and order. Abzug and Beame remained in front in the polls as late as a month after the blackout. But by early September, both had begun to slide, and the race turned into a contest between Koch and Cuomo, conducted in three stages: the Democratic primary, a head-to-head Democratic runoff, then a general election in which Cuomo, on the Liberal Party line, squared off with Koch yet again.[69]

Abzug and a number of her labor backers swung their support to Cuomo before the head-to-head run-off that would determine the Democratic nominee. But Koch won Beame's endorsement, which helped him consolidate the support of Jewish Democrats, and he garnered the support of Brooklyn Democratic boss Meade Esposito. He also secured the endorsement of the Harlem political establishment, despite his habit of deploying what Sutton had delicately called "code words" during the primary campaign. After the initial primary, Percy Sutton and his campaign manager, Harlem's young U.S. representative Charles Rangel, went to meet with the two remaining candidates. Sutton was looking for a reason to endorse Cuomo. But when Sutton and Rangel raised the question of whether Black New Yorkers would be represented in a Cuomo administration, Cuomo (as Rangel recalled) "took great pains to explain that he was color blind, and therefore could not promise a certain number of positions." When they went to see Koch, Rangel wrote, "all he wanted to know was, 'What do you want?' 'Sure we're going to have a black deputy mayor. . . . What do you need? How are we going to work this out?' "[70]

It was, in the end, largely a matter of ethnic and religious arithmetic. Koch won some two-thirds of votes from predominantly Jewish neighborhoods, doing well across lines of class, age, and ideology, and carried smaller but still significant majorities in predominantly Black neighborhoods. Cuomo won about two-thirds of the vote in predominantly white Catholic neighborhoods. In all, Koch prevailed with 50.4 percent to Cuomo's 41.4 percent; the Upper East Side Republican state senator Roy Goodman and the Conservative Party's candidate, talk-radio pioneer Barry Farber, ran a distant third and fourth.[71]

WITH KOCH'S ASCENT TO CITY HALL, New York was by 1978 presided over entirely by development-minded Democrats: Koch in New York, Carey in Albany, and the former Georgia governor Jimmy Carter in the White House. They confronted a dramatically changed city. The fiscal crisis was largely over, though the city still needed seasonal loans from the federal government to ensure its solvency. The crises of governance that had preceded it were ongoing, exacerbated by austerity and underpinned by persistent inequalities of race and class. The city's Democratic leaders found themselves in a bind: On the one hand, they had accepted austerity as unavoidable. On the other, disinvestment threatened the vision of a middle-class city that they intended their development schemes to realize. How could they square such a circle? How could they work toward their vision of the city without the means to do so?

2

Austerity

On the first day of 1978, a crowd of some 2,500 people braved a cold, overcast morning to witness Ed Koch's inauguration ceremony. New Yorkers, Koch told his audience, were "the trustees of a national treasure: the City of New York itself, the greatest national treasure in this country." If the city was to survive, he warned, "we must give more than we ask." The city government "cannot do what the people will not do. In calling upon the people of New York City to join me in the hard work needed to bring this city back to the top again, I call upon the only people who can do that job."[1]

Koch's paean to the do-it-yourself metropolis reflected the turn toward discipline and limits that had characterized the liberal response to the fiscal crisis. But it also reflected a blunt reality: Many New Yorkers were deeply dissatisfied with the conditions of austerity politics, yet the city government on its own did not possess the means to pursue an alternative. The challenges of governing without adequate resources risked saddling city agencies and public officials with a humiliating image of incompetence that they were eager to escape. Seeking to shore up their own legitimacy despite the post-fiscal-crisis budgetary straitjacket, city officials began to envision new methods of delivering services, new resource pools upon which to draw, and new ways of partnering with private actors and organizations in hopes of restoring their own capacities.

Evoking the city's "great living neighborhoods," from Harlem to Rego Park, Koch concluded his address with an ode to what would soon come to be called gentrification. "There are houses to be rehabilitated, schools to be reclaimed and preserved, neighborhoods to be freed from the oppression of crime and the stranglehold of unemployment. . . . And that is why I ask those of you who are not with us now, those who are seeking a challenge, come east and join us, come east and grow up with the new pioneers, grow up with the City of New York." With the power of the law and new ideas but very little in the way of budget revenues, New York's governing officials set out to build a city for Koch's urban pioneers—and to negotiate the conflicts that inevitably arose from their efforts.[2]

For poor and working-class New Yorkers, the resolution of the fiscal crisis via austerity, self-help, and a renewed growth politics oriented toward the expansion of the middle and professional classes only exacerbated the challenges of everyday life in the city. Budget cuts fell especially hard on New Yorkers of color, who were less able to access private alternatives to withering public services. The loss of public sector jobs removed a vital channel of upward mobility and economic security in communities that were still largely excluded from key sectors of the private sector workforce. Given the city's racial segregation, this loss of opportunity at the individual and family levels rippled out into neighborhood life. By the early 1980s, even as the local economy began a strong recovery, New York was experiencing a degree and kind of concentrated poverty that was largely unknown in its history—and that has shaped the city profoundly ever since.

AS THE CITY GOVERNMENT STRUGGLED in the aftermath of the fiscal crisis, opponents of rent regulation moved in for the kill. Amid the crisis, a cause once dominated by the real estate industry became a broader movement: the finance and business communities, some housing experts and advocacy groups, the construction unions, and newspaper editorial boards came to see rent regulation as a cause not only of the decline of the city's housing stock but also of its diminished tax base and sluggish local economy.

Nothing animated the city's business community quite like rent regulation. When the subject arose in the final meeting of David Rockefeller and Harry Van Arsdale's Business/Labor Working Group, there ensued "a general discussion of the basic ills of the city and the downward spirals connected with it [that] covered everything from Culture to Education to Tourism." Turning the table on proponents of regulation who argued that rent control was essential for retaining the city's middle class, the B/LWG claimed that by abolishing the existing system of rent regulation and shifting to housing subsidies (perhaps through an expansion of the federal Section 8 program), the city could not only create jobs in housing rehabilitation and new construction but also make neighborhoods more attractive to middle-class residents, which in turn would stimulate additional development. "Without a satisfactory housing inventory," the group argued, "we cannot hope to retain what remains of the middle-income wage earner, or to create the solid housing market that must be a basis for successful new construction."[3]

In this context, even some Democrats started to question rent regulation. Before taking office in 1975, Governor Hugh Carey created a blue-ribbon housing task force chaired by the economist and former HUD secretary Robert C. Weaver. (Donald Trump, whose father had long been close with the Brooklyn Democratic machine, received an appointment, a sharp break from how the Wilson administration had treated him the year prior.) The task force ended up supporting regulation, but the issue proved contentious enough that the developer Richard Ravitch, another task force member, suggested they scrap plans to do a formal presentation of their findings. In late 1975, Carey told a closed-door meeting of planning officials that the system "d[idn't] work" and that the "time [was] ripe" for reform. A little over a year later, U.S. senator Daniel Patrick Moynihan became "the first prominent New York Democrat in recent memory even to suggest that rent control might well be phased out" (though his spokesman quickly noted that Moynihan did not "really know the details on these things"). Even Abraham Beame, then in his final year as mayor, reluctantly allowed that rent control might be undermining the city's property tax base. Tenant organizations like the West Side Tenants Union fretted that Democrats were no longer willing to make rent regulation "a real priority."[4]

As the 1977 state legislative session opened, the journalist Linda Greenhouse wrote, "politicians of both parties predict that this will be the year that rent control goes the way of free tuition at CUNY," perhaps the most high-profile casualty of the fiscal crisis. Then seemingly out of nowhere, the Republican leaders of the legislature announced that they had agreed on a four-year extension, leaving Democratic lawmakers agape and tenant groups overjoyed. Regulation had survived the concerted mobilization of some of the most powerful political forces in New York, in essence because it was too popular to be gotten rid of. Republican senator Roy M. Goodman of the Upper East Side, a strong champion of rent regulation, was planning to run for mayor in 1977; Senate majority leader Warren M. Anderson of Binghamton was contemplating a run for governor in 1978. "We are practical people," said one upstate Republican senator who opposed regulation on principle but acceded to its extension. "We realize the tremendous political problems."[5]

Even as rent regulation survived the business mobilization of the 1970s, the policy itself was struggling to meet the upheavals in the city's housing market. In many parts of the city, rent regulation was practically irrelevant to the ongoing problems of falling tenant incomes, capital flight, and building abandonment. Across the city, rents were rising faster than tenant incomes: The median rent rose 57 percent between 1970 and 1975 and again by 23 percent between 1975 and 1978; the median income of the city's renters rose only 17 percent and 7 percent, respectively. Austerity measures increased the pain, particularly for low-income New Yorkers: In 1974, the state froze the value of its welfare housing allowance and did not raise it for a full decade, by which time rising rents had eaten away much of its value. For the first time in the city's history, the urban planning scholar Peter Marcuse noted, a majority of tenants were spending more than 25 percent of their income on rent, making it difficult for the New York's most recent working class to achieve the kind of upward mobility New Yorkers had long enjoyed. "What we are seeing is people knocking themselves out doing the classic American thing, but they are not getting the traditional rewards," one housing policy specialist told *The New York Times*. "Unfortunately, the situation hits many of the minority families that have been struggling to make it into the middle class."[6]

For the most vulnerable New Yorkers, the situation was even worse. The city's poor had long relied on low-rent single-room housing—boardinghouses and what were called "single-room occupancy" (SRO) hotels, often with shared kitchen and bathroom facilities. Between 1960 and 1978, the city lost more than 100,000 such units to dilapidation and, increasingly, to conversion into upmarket housing and hotels (underwritten after 1975 by a provision in the tax code known as J-51, which provided tax abatements for building upgrades in rental housing). The population in need of such housing grew due to economic dislocation and the state's ongoing efforts to deinstitutionalize patients in its Dickensian psychiatric hospitals, which discharged some 58,000 resident patients between 1965 and 1979. Yet there was less and less of it to go around. In the mid-twentieth century, homelessness in New York had existed primarily in a small number of skid row districts, most notably on the Bowery. By the late 1970s, unhoused people had become prominent in the parks, on the streets, and in transit facilities. Advocates responded by claiming that the New York State constitution included a right to shelter, and the city agreed in the *Callahan* consent decree of 1981. But the increasing need simply overwhelmed the government's pledge to provide housing of last resort. The shelter census nearly doubled between 1979 and 1982, and New Yorkers began to speak of "the new homeless"—no longer detached single men but increasingly families, many of them with working parents, who by the end of the 1980s would make up two-thirds of the people in the city's shelters.[7]

AS MORE AND MORE HOUSING passed from rent control to rent stabilization under the terms of the Emergency Tenant Protection Act of 1974, the city's Rent Guidelines Board (RGB) emerged as a critical actor in New York's housing politics. The board consisted of nine mayoral appointees—two representing tenants, two representing landlords, and five representing the public—tasked with setting guidelines for rent increases for one-, two-, and (until 1983) three-year leases. The board's mandate in setting those guidelines was ambiguous. Most explicitly, the rent stabilization law instructed it to consider "the economic condition of the residential real estate industry"—factors such as operating costs, mortgage rates, local taxes, and water and utility rates that determined the cost of providing rental housing. Landlords urged the board to establish its rent guidelines in response to these data. However, the text of the law also made clear that rent stabilization was intended to ensure fair rents for tenants. Rapidly rising rents "were uprooting long-time city residents from their communities," the act noted, and the law left room for the board to emphasize rent increases' effects on tenants. The board conducted annual public hearings before holding its final vote at a public meeting in June. Rent stabilization's structure, in short, allowed tenants to impose a measure of democratic contestation onto what might otherwise have been a technical, expert-led, ostensibly apolitical process.[8]

And contestation there was. Fuel costs spiked again during the oil shocks of the late 1970s; in the early 1980s mortgage interest rates soared in response to tight federal monetary policy. The ever-widening gap between what lower- and middle-income tenants could afford to pay in rent and the operating costs of rental housing placed increasing strain on a regulation system that was already tasked with mediating fundamental clashes of interest. The hapless Rent Guidelines Board—a part-time agency with a minimal budget and skeletal staff, created before the Emergency Tenant Protection Act of 1974 and hence not designed to regulate such a vast number of buildings—was tasked each year with reconciling the irreconcilable. Its annual meetings, appropriately held at police headquarters, turned into raucous displays of protests and arrests, yielding outcomes that outraged both tenants and landlords. In 1979 the tenant leader Jane Benedict denounced the board's rent increases as "atrocious . . . I can't describe it in decent English," even as the leading landlord organization was threatening to sue. "Being on this board is the most masochistic thing I've done in my life," the longtime public servant Sid Davidoff griped. As the board muddled through, its ad hoc adjustments to the turmoil in the housing market—fuel pass-alongs, vacancy allowances to compensate owners for unforeseen costs—produced more and more irrationalities within the system. By the early 1980s, accounts abounded of tenants with similar incomes who had moved into equivalent units in the same building at roughly the same time paying radically different rents, simply because they had renewed their leases at different times.[9]

With the system under such strain, calls for radical reform came from landlords and tenants, conservatives and liberals. "How can we attract important business to the city if we don't have housing for employees?" argued Samuel LeFrak, developer of LeFrak City, the massive apartment complex in Elmhurst, Queens. "How can we keep valuable people in the city if there are no apartments in which they can live? How about those starry-eyed youngsters who want to come to New York and want to find their fortune here but can't find a place to live?" The leading landlord organization, the Rent Stabilization Association, proposed in 1980 that apartments renting above $600 a month be deregulated (an approach known as "high-rent" deregulation). The Real Estate Board of New York followed up three years later with a call for vacancy and "luxury" deregulation. (The latter referred to the deregulation of high-earning tenants, not high-rent units; in practice, high-rent and luxury deregulation were often conflated.) To test the strategy's appeal to the public, they commissioned a survey by two young pollsters named Mark Penn and Doug Schoen, who had cut their teeth with Koch in 1977 and would go on to advise Bill Clinton and many others.[10]

When the national elections of 1980 swept a new cohort of conservative Republicans into office, it looked once again like proponents of deregulation might have gained the upper hand. Ronald Reagan's transition team recommended in late 1980 that federal grants be withheld from cities with rent regulation laws. "It's a joke," Koch responded. But New York's newly elected senator, Alfonse D'Amato, was not amused. Boisterous and at times loutish, the Nassau County Republican machine politician had unseated the liberal Republican Jacob Javits in the 1980 party primary and narrowly won a contentious general election. Now, in one of his first acts in office, he backed a congressional bill tying access to federal new-housing subsidy programs to deregulation. "This is a terrible thing that he's done," Koch lamented. When the House and Senate spending bills went to committee, Reagan's Housing and Urban Development secretary let the conference committee know that the administration viewed the policy as contrary to its efforts to devolve authority to states and localities. D'Amato, self-styled champion of "the forgotten middle class" and a political pragmatist before all else—"the only thing you understand is power and power relationships," his top strategist once chided him—came away from the experience chastened by the backlash to his proposal. "I opened my big mouth before I understood the facts," he later said. It would not be the last time New York's junior senator found himself entangled in one of the thorniest issues of state politics.[11]

Tenant groups and their political allies, too, called for far-reaching reforms of the rent regulations. The two largest groups, the Metropolitan Council on Housing and New York State Tenants and Neighbors Coalition, had split acrimoniously in 1980 over how precisely they wished to see the regulations improved; MetCo favored a statewide system akin to New York City's rent control system, whereas Tenants and Neighbors introduced a new measure in which individual buildings would be regulated on the public utility model used to regulate ConEd's provision of electricity. By 1983, they had reunited behind a bill sponsored by Bronx Democratic assemblyman John Dearie and Republican senator John E. Flynn, whose district spanned Yonkers and part of the Bronx—the "Flynn-Dearie bill," which eschewed the public utility model but incorporated some of its spirit.[12]

By the 1983 legislative session, the pressure for reform had reached a new pitch. "The housing issue right now politically is like a hot griddle—you start dropping water on it and everyone starts dancing around," said Alexander Grannis, chair of the Assembly Housing Committee. The residential real estate organizations pushed for luxury and vacancy decontrol. Tenant organizations dreamed of Flynn-Dearie and hoped to bring buildings with three to five units and absentee owners into the rent stabilization system (which required six or more units), certain that real estate corporations and individual speculators had bought out the old mom-and-pop landlords, particularly in Brooklyn, and were subjecting their tenants to monthly rent increases and evictions—though the GOP Senate negotiators quickly ruled such a measure off the table. Tenant hopes burned bright because Mario Cuomo, who had won election as governor after upsetting Koch in the Democratic primary, had announced his support for "the principles" of Flynn-Dearie during the campaign.[13]

But Cuomo had no intention of expending the political capital it might have taken to corral the last few Republican votes in the Senate, and it is uncertain at best that he would have succeeded had he tried. As spring turned to summer and the session drew to a close, the outlines of a tenuous deal came into view. The city's Rent Guidelines Board would continue to set annual increases, but the better-resourced state government would take over administration and would establish, for the first time, a central registry of rents that would allow tenants to see what previous tenants had paid so as to ensure that their own rents were legal. Tenants also gained the right to pursue triple damages if overcharged. In exchange, landlords were no longer required to offer three-year leases, the guidelines for which had consistently trailed inflation, and were entitled to seek a hardship exemption if they could prove they were making less than a 5 percent profit. "I am sorry to hear that your group is disappointed," Cuomo wrote a Queens tenant council after the dust had settled. "The new law is very much in the spirit of Flynn-Dearie." To tenant organizations, the legislation—officially the Omnibus Housing Act of 1983—was far from what they had envisioned, and they were particularly concerned that the new rent registry system would allow landlords to legitimize what had been above-ceiling rents. Still, one tenant leader wrote, the act did "represent the death of the landlord dream of phasing out controls"—a forecast that time would put to the test.[14]

New Yorkers had preserved rent regulation, a signature policy of the city's New Deal and labor tradition, even amid the conservative mobilizations of the fiscal crisis and the early Reagan years. Absent major political change, no large-scale reforms were possible—neither the vacancy and luxury deregulation pushed by the Real Estate Board of New York and others, nor the sweeping expansion and reconfiguration of regulation proposed by Dearie and Flynn. Yet as the politics of rent regulation settled into a period of stasis, the policy itself continued to come under major stress as poverty spread and housing demand continued to grow in Manhattan and the gentrifying neighborhoods of Brooklyn and Queens. Low-income New Yorkers got a reprieve in 1979, when a coalition led by Upper West Side councilmember Ruth Messinger won restrictions on the use of the J-51 tax break for upmarket development, and another in 1984, when Governor Cuomo and the state legislature hiked the welfare housing allowance for the first time in a decade. But the benefits of rent regulation, at least so far as affordability was concerned, accrued primarily outside impoverished neighborhoods.[15]

By the mid-1980s, the housing crisis of the 1970s—of abandonment, arson, and capital flight—was increasingly a thing of the past. But a new housing crisis, of overcrowding and homelessness and an inadequate supply of affordable housing—in which rents steadily outpaced incomes and regulation protected the working and middle classes while contributing little to housing affordability for low-income New Yorkers—was taking its place.

ON SEPTEMBER 13, 1976, New York's 1.1 million public schoolchildren returned from summer break to discover the consequences of austerity firsthand. Some 47,000 teachers were there to greet them—nearly 15,000 fewer than only two years earlier. "We will be able to provide little more than a teacher for every class," one Brooklyn district superintendent told the press. "We will have no science teachers, no music or art teachers, no guidance counselors, no librarians. If conditions get any worse, we won't have anything left that is worth calling a school system." "Last year our problems were staggering," Chancellor Irving Anker remarked. "This year, they seem almost insurmountable."[16]

Though the political failure of the desegregation and community control movements of the 1960s had constrained broader ambitions for reform, advocates for innovation in the public schools had made some real, if only local, progress in the wake of the decentralization law of 1969. Now the fiscal crisis threatened to undo much of that work. Within a few years, the Board of Education laid off a full quarter of the teaching force; because of seniority rules, the cuts disproportionately hit younger teachers, including many Black and Hispanic educators, who fell from 11 percent of the teaching force before the crisis to only 3 percent in its wake. The board also closed nearly all elementary school libraries, cut programs such as music and arts, and pared back a thriving paraprofessional movement that had offered valuable resources to schools as well as job training opportunities for community-based educators. With capital spending at a standstill, older school buildings fell into disrepair. The city school system would be playing catch-up into the late 1990s on maintenance and facility modernization deferred during the fiscal crisis.[17]

The cuts hit poor and working-class New Yorkers particularly hard as the city pulled resources out of "under-utilized" schools in neighborhoods in the South Bronx, upper Manhattan, and central Brooklyn, where the population count had fallen due to middle-class flight, housing abandonment, and arson. While middle-class families responded by moving to the suburbs or placing their children in private schools, some families in poorer communities began looking for a way out of the public school system, too. In early 1975, the Harlem-based Citizens Committee for Effective Education wrote to the New York State commissioner of education Ewald Nyquist to demand a voucher program—the beginning of a campaign that brought them together with such unlikely allies as the Libertarian Party and antibusing activists, just one instance of the ways in which the search for solutions amid austerity could make for unlikely alliances. When the Board of Regents proved unresponsive, a group of seven parents pulled their eleven children, grades two through eight, out of schools in Brooklyn, the Bronx, and Manhattan, with the Harlem Parents' Union arranging for volunteer public school teachers to tutor them. "We believe that the money allotted for a child's attendance in a school which is failing should be withdrawn from the school, on parental request, and given to the parent . . . to purchase alternative education," the Citizens Committee for Effective Education wrote on the parents' behalf. The following year the organization's leader, Babette Edwards, presented a voucher plan to the platform committee at the Democratic National Convention.[18]

The "bloodletting" of the mid-1970s, the progressive educator Deborah Meier later recalled, "crushed" the nascent alternative schools movement, draining resources and making it more difficult to hire teachers. Even so, and despite some skepticism from leaders and parents in East Harlem's traditional public schools, District 4 superintendent Anthony Alvarado continued to support the creation of new, teacher-driven alternative schools, which often used a theme—the arts, science and technology, maritime studies—as a way to build traditional academic skills. By 1982, half of the district's junior high students were enrolled in alternative schools. That year Alvarado lifted the district's remaining zoning rules, moving to a system of full public school choice.[19]

As the teacher-driven movement gained steam in East Harlem, the city Board of Education got in on the act of creating new, alternative schools. If the teachers in East Harlem were motivated primarily by the promise of pedagogy to equalize the educational playing field, the Board of Education's efforts responded to two other imperatives. Reflecting the new liberal outlook, the board wanted to keep middle-class students in the system. At the same time, the board was caught between the imperative of desegregation demanded by *Brown* and the political power of white parents, who continued to resist approaches such as busing and transfers between paired majority-white and majority-nonwhite schools. Out of this dilemma came a new type of public school: "magnet" schools, so called because they would attract students from outside the neighborhood or district.

In 1974, in response to a lawsuit by the NAACP, federal judge Jack B. Weinstein demanded a desegregation plan for Mark Twain Junior High School on Neptune Avenue in the Brooklyn neighborhood of Coney Island, an overwhelmingly Black and Puerto Rican school in the majority-white District 21. Weinstein appointed an expert, Columbia University law professor Curtis J. Berger, to design a desegregation approach. Meeting with the all-white district school board, Berger was duly informed that local officials had no intention of acquiescing to the NAACP's integration plans—even the district board's court-mandated proposal, which involved turning Mark Twain into a gifted-and-talented school, had drawn the wrath of parents (and some board members) who preferred a posture of open defiance. Given the political climate, Berger said, "forced busing must be a solution of last resort and not the place to begin." Instead, he called for Mark Twain to be reorganized as a selective magnet school, a model that had begun to spring up in other cities in the late 1960s and with which the New York City Board of Education had begun to experiment, though tentatively: Rather than mandate integration, the courts and the board would seek to induce it by creating a public school capable of attracting white students.[20]

Proponents of desegregation were aghast at Berger's proposal. The psychologist Kenneth B. Clark, whose research on the damage segregation inflicted on Black children had informed the *Brown* decision and who had helped lead the New York City integration movement of the 1950s and '60s, argued in a brief for the NAACP that Berger's proposal was simply "a sophisticated, elaborate pattern of equivocation" that sought to "evade the politically explosive issue of desegregation" through an approach that "subordinates the constitutional rights of minorities to the willingness of whites to comply with the legal requirements for desegregation of public schools."[21]

To Clark, the notion that the city would pursue desegregation by creating a school that was by design exclusionary represented a profound perversion of educational justice. "This report," he wrote, ". . . suggests that the more pernicious forms of American racism have become normative and have transcended region and ideology. The immorality of American racism is no longer an isolated problem but has now infected and threatens the rights of all human beings without regard to race or color." Under the court's proposal, Clark argued, "average white children have no more rights worthy of educational respect than do minority group children. Segregation of children in public schools according to intellect and talent is offered as an acceptable cure forr [*sic*]—or evasion of—racial desegregation." It was the "responsibility of a civilized and democratic society," he concluded, "to see that whatever educational advantages are possible for human intelligence to devise are made available to all children. . . . To advocate or do otherwise is obscene, immoral, illegal, unconstitutional."[22]

Berger had been cagey about the details of his proposed magnet school; it was, rather, the District 21 school board that insisted that the remade Mark Twain be a school for the gifted and talented. Judge Weinstein adopted the board's proposal, and pursuant to his orders, Mark Twain Junior High School for the Gifted and Talented opened in the fall of 1975. School officials expected the magnet school to cost about 50 percent more than a typical middle school—an expense that could be partially funded with federal and state grants intended to incentivize voluntary desegregation plans. The influx of white students came with extraordinary security measures—teachers received personal alarms, and the school adopted policies intended to prevent students from leaving the school property and going out into the surrounding neighborhood. Mark Twain was not New York's first magnet school. But it was the first to explicitly connect the magnet approach, and thereby the imperative of attracting white families, to the conceit of serving gifted and talented students—the first to institutionalize the relationship of whiteness to ability in the name of desegregation.[23]

The rise of the magnet school approach, in turn, facilitated the expansion of District 4's alternative school network. If the district could attract enough white families from outside East Harlem to transfer into the alternative schools, it would be eligible for more than $1 million in federal and state money. The district promptly took out newspaper advertisements boasting of the "rigorous academic standards" and "accessible location" of its primary and middle schools. The efforts succeeded: By 1981, Meier's Central Park East, which had started with nearly all Puerto Rican and Black students, was a quarter white. District 3 on the Upper West Side, from which the East Harlem schools were drawing many of their white students, responded by launching its own handful of magnet schools.[24]

By the early 1980s, the magnet school approach was drawing widespread acclaim in New York and across the country. Mark Twain topped the city in reading scores year after year, later joined by other selective magnet schools—Philippa Schuyler in Bushwick, Brooklyn, IS 223 in Harlem, P.S. 308 in Bedford-Stuyvesant. Though officially a desegregation measure, many white parents embraced magnets as an alternative to school pairing and busing. This new approach seemed to be a response to austerity that stakeholders with different values and priorities could agree to. Congress, which had provided funding for magnet schools between 1972 and 1981, resumed doing so in 1984 through amendments to the Education for Economic Security Act, with New York senator Daniel Patrick Moynihan a major proponent.[25]

Still, there were rumblings of discontent from advocates of the traditional public schools, who believed the magnet schools were skimming off their best students and claiming an outsize share of resources. The public school system, they felt, was dividing into a new set of haves and have-nots. For the time being, these protests remained muted. But in the mid-1980s, they would break into the open, forcing New Yorkers to confront fundamental questions about the meanings of excellence and equity and the purposes of public education in a democratic, capitalist city.

GIVEN THE SALIENCE OF CRIME in mid-1970s New York, the NYPD might have hoped to be spared the kinds of cuts made to education and housing. Yet the police, too, found their budget slashed. Over the second half of the decade, the department dismissed some four thousand police officers and instituted a five-year hiring freeze, which would cost it an additional eight thousand officers by attrition. By the end of the 1970s, according to one calculation, the NYPD had lost 34 percent of its workforce. Already plagued by accusations of ineffectiveness, corruption, bias, and brutality, the department now had to make do with far fewer officers.[26]

The NYPD's leaders responded by trying to build capacity and credibility through strategies that did not require major commitments of resources. With its own ranks so deeply diminished, the department made a virtue of necessity and began to embrace the civilian patrols that had started popping up in the late 1960s—dismissed at the time as "vigilantes" and untrained amateurs, "a misfit army of scabs" in the words of the Patrolmen's Benevolent Association. "In light of the present fiscal crisis," Police Commissioner Michael Codd argued, "it is imperative that as many civilian volunteers as possible become involved . . ."; these volunteers, he suggested, could "act as extended eyes and ears of the Police Department." (One effort to expand the department's footprint, the Auxiliary Police initiative, took a public relations hit in the summer of 1977 when a former trainee, David

Berkowitz, went on a killing spree in what were dubbed the Son of Sam murders.)[27]

How the NYPD approached its would-be partners in policing depended on how well those groups promised to help the department realize its own objectives. Volunteer patrol groups organized by neighborhood associations seemed to offer useful information at best and good public relations at worst—a visible demonstration that safety was a public priority and thus deserved more in the way of public resources. The NYPD launched a series of initiatives to train and equip civilian volunteers, and by the early 1980s, some fifteen thousand New Yorkers were involved with patrols, and tens of thousands more participated in block watches and other surveillance programs.[28]

The rise during the same years of business improvement districts (BIDs)—special assessment districts in which property owners raised funds to provide supplementary services, especially additional security and sanitation—presented both opportunities and potential challenges for the NYPD. Initially intended as a self-help mechanism for smaller merchants dealing with city service cutbacks in what were then becoming known as the outer boroughs, BIDs became big business in the 1980s and early '90s, especially in Manhattan, where the largest—the Bryant Park Restoration Corporation, the Grand Central Partnership, the Times Square Alliance, the 34th Street Partnership, the Union Square Partnership—collectively spent in the tens of millions of dollars each year. With so much command over the streetscape of the city's marquee areas, BIDs represented an institutional threat (writes the sociologist Alex Vitale) to the NYPD's "role as guardians of public order and safety." But well-resourced BIDs often hired former officers, and in 1984 began to hire off-duty officers, to provide security within their perimeters. As such, they represented a way of offloading the cost of a larger force and new equipment onto big property owners.[29]

The more independent citizens' patrols, in contrast, could

represent a source of embarrassment. In the late 1970s, subway riders began to encounter a patrol force of young volunteers, uniformed and capped with red berets—the Guardian Angels, a group of some seven hundred members, 85 percent Black or Hispanic, founded by Curtis Sliwa, a twenty-six-year-old native of Canarsie from a blue-collar, white-ethnic background. Patrolling the subway lines (and later the streets) in teams, monitoring spaces and making occasional citizens' arrests, the Angels quickly garnered widespread attention, including a 1980 cover feature in *New York* magazine. Their impact on crime was debatable, but their presence and notoriety served as an embarrassment to the NYPD and the Transit Police.[30]

Sliwa himself, brutal in his language toward those he held responsible for street and subway crime, was gleefully dismissive of the police. The Angels, he claimed, were protecting their own communities, whereas the police were simply "mercenaries"; the Angels were on the job, he boasted, while the police "were just hanging around at the doughnut stands." When Police Commissioner Benjamin Ward described the Angels as a "lynch mob," Sliwa replied that "Koch and Ward spend more time in the Hamptons than they do in Hollis, Harlem, and Hunt's Point." City officials, in turn, denounced the Angels as vigilantes and renegades, an example, *The New York Times* noted, of how the police felt "antagonistic toward groups that appear to symbolize official failure to stop crime." Mario Cuomo, who considered himself "a strong supporter" of the Angels and considered them (as he wrote to a constituent) "an example of the family spirit that is the real strength of New York," expressed the sense of humiliation the Angels caused public officials in bluntly racialized terms: It was "a dramatic embarrassment," Cuomo said, "that riders in our subways should pray for the appearance of a band of young minority people in berets and t-shirts."[31]

Chastened by their failure to address the visible deterioration that had swept the city in the 1970s, yet without the resources to launch a widespread campaign against it, the NYPD and the city's political leaders responded by targeting prominent manifestations. The city's subway system became a leading laboratory for these efforts. Unlike the sprawling city above, the subway was relatively contained and hence amenable to efforts on the scale the city could muster given the fiscal constraints. It was also an integrated and democratic space, a kind of microcosm of the city as a whole, and a place where public efforts would be visible. Not least, it was a leading symbol of the city's loss of control, of which the proliferation of graffiti and tagging was a preeminent manifestation.[32]

Many of the people involved in the campaign against subway graffiti recognized that it bore at best a distant relation to violent crime. Instead, the stakes of the contest had to do with status, control, emotion, psychology, even narrative: Graffiti represented a leading instance of "disorder," a concept that had come into vogue in the aftermath of the 1960s urban upheavals, especially among (neo) conservative thinkers, to refer to what they saw as the proliferation of nonnormative, at times illegal behavior rooted in the breakdown of traditional authority. Though the subway was relatively safe, the sociologist Nathan Glazer wrote in a 1979 essay for *The Public Interest*, it was suffused with signs that made it seem frightening on some subliminal level. "While I do not find myself consciously making the connection between the graffiti-makers and the criminals who occasionally rob, rape, assault, and murder passengers," he wrote, "the sense that all are part of one world of uncontrollable predators seems inescapable. Even if the graffitists are the least dangerous of these, their ever-present markings serve to persuade the passenger that, indeed, the subway is a dangerous place." That graffiti did not contribute to serious crime was beside the point: To straphangers, Glazer wrote, graffiti artists were "part of the story of 'crime in the subway.' "[33]

The year Glazer's essay appeared, Koch launched the first in a series of initiatives intended to improve the subway's image, assigning police officers to every train instead of every station between the hours of six p.m. and two a.m. When reporters asked why the city would undertake such an expensive effort when the subways were statistically safer than the streets, Koch replied bluntly: "Are we responding to the exaggerated fears conveyed by the media? The answer is yes." Anyway, he added, "perception is reality"—if New Yorkers felt the subway was safer, they would be more likely to ride it.[34]

The impulse to enlist civilians in the quest for police capacity and the new attention to symbols of disorder came together in the form of a novel approach to policing: Communities, neighborhoods, and public spaces, a range of theorists argued, could be naturally self-regulating if the police worked with residents and business owners to remove disorder and uphold so-called community norms. This idea had its roots, in part, in a theory of urban life that had been percolating since the late 1950s and that was most closely associated with two thinkers: William H. Whyte and Jane Jacobs. Whyte, a former Marine intelligence officer who had garnered renown as the author of the 1955 bestseller *The Organization Man* and become an editor at *Fortune*, invited Jacobs to write a piece for the magazine; that essay, "Downtown Belongs to People," previewed the ideas she would introduce three years later in her seminal book *The Death and Life of Great American Cities* (1961).[35]

To both Jacobs and Whyte, public spaces could be largely self-regulating if they were used legitimately by a critical mass of people. The flow of street life in dense, mixed-use neighborhoods, Jacobs wrote in *Death and Life*, facilitated order by ensuring "eyes on the street." "If someone flouts one of the unposted rules," Whyte added eighteen years later, "it is likely as not the regulars who will set him straight." The police, Whyte thought, could tip the balance in favor of the informal "mayors" and "regulars" who kept order in public spaces. "It is clear that there is a severe policing problem," he wrote in 1979, advising the Rockefeller Fund on how to restore Bryant Park. "But it is also clear that the police alone will not resolve it. If a strong police presence were the answer, there would be no problem in front of us. Right now the police are all over the place." Instead, he believed, "the improvement of the policing of the park—in the broad sense of the term—will most likely be achieved by an increase in the number of full time regulars in the park." But Whyte did not mean to suggest that the park could be entirely self-policing—he suggested "supplemental guards . . . : friendly types who like to keep everything normal but who are in walkie-talkie communication with a security base and thence to the police." "Choice of personnel for the various installations planned will be important. Their job is not fighting crime, but along with the guards and the maintenance men they will greatly affect peoples [*sic*] perception of crime—and that's a big part of the battle."[36]

In 1982, the criminologist George Kelling and the renowned political scientist James Q. Wilson took up the notion of regulation-through-perception, with its attendant emphasis on the role of "regulars," and developed it into a new approach to policing. Their March 1982 feature for *The Atlantic*, entitled "Broken Windows: The Police and Neighborhood Safety," put forward two somewhat contradictory claims. The first was that police foot patrols could make people feel safer even if they were not actually any safer. Describing the results of a foot-patrol experiment in Newark, New Jersey, they observed that "to the surprise of hardly anyone," increased numbers of officers walking the streets "had not reduced crime rates. But residents of the foot patrolled neighborhoods seemed to feel more secure than persons in other areas, tended to believe that crime had been reduced, and seemed to take fewer steps to protect themselves from crime (staying at home with the doors locked, for example)." To explain this apparent disconnect, Kelling and Wilson turned to the sort of psychological thinking that had underpinned Glazer's criticism of graffiti. Most city residents, they argued, feared "being bothered by disorderly people. Not violent people, nor, necessarily, criminals, but disreputable or obstreperous or unpredictable people: panhandlers, drunks, addicts, rowdy teenagers, prostitutes, loiterers, the mentally disturbed. What foot-patrol officers did was to elevate, to the extent they could, the level of public order in these neighborhoods." In this sense, the article made a political intervention. Most people in urban neighborhoods wanted the kind of order grounded in traditional authority and norm enforcement that had supposedly broken down in the 1960s and '70s, the argument went. The police could respond to legitimate public sentiment by helping to reconstitute it.[37]

Kelling and Wilson's second claim, advanced with precious little supporting evidence, was that foot patrols *could* make people safer by elevating the level of public order, regardless of what the Newark experiment had shown. "At the community level," they wrote, "disorder and crime are usually inextricably linked, in a kind of developmental sequence. Social psychologists and police officers tend to agree that if a window in a building is broken *and is left unrepaired*, all the rest of the windows will soon be broken." Such disorder, they argued, rendered an area "vulnerable to criminal invasion. Though it is not inevitable, it is more likely that here, rather than in places where people are confident they can regulate public behavior by informal controls, drugs will change hands, prostitutes will solicit, and cars will be stripped. That the drunks will be robbed by boys who do it as a lark, and the prostitutes' customers will be robbed by men who do it purposefully and perhaps violently. That muggings will occur."[38]

Like the urbanists Whyte and Jacobs, Kelling and Wilson emphasized the role of "regulars": "both 'decent folk' and some drunks and derelicts who were always there but who 'knew their place.'" More than the urbanists, Kelling and Wilson called attention to the menace of "strangers," whom they believed regulars were fair in viewing with apprehension. The job of a foot patrol officer was to "keep an eye on strangers, and make certain that the disreputable regulars observed some informal but widely understood rules"—rules "defined and enforced in collaboration with the 'regulars' on the street." This could be done by enforcing the law, but it might also mean "taking informal or extralegal steps to help protect what the neighborhood had decided was the appropriate level of public order." Communities—"neighborhoods"—had rights that transcended the rights of individuals, they argued; the members of those neighborhoods were anxious about the erosion of order and authority. The NYPD's job was not only to clean up disorder but also to set the members of those communities at ease by reaffirming authority.[39]

Kelling and Wilson were well aware that the kind of discretion they were calling for—the distinction between "regulars" and "strangers" and legitimate and disorderly uses—created a risk of discriminatory policing. "How do we ensure that age or skin color or national origin or harmless mannerisms will not also become the basis for distinguishing the undesirable from the desirable? How do we ensure, in short, that the police do not become the agents of neighborhood bigotry?" Alas, they answered, "We can offer no wholly satisfactory answer to this important question. We are not confident that there is a satisfactory answer except to hope that by their selection, training, and supervision, the police will be inculcated with a clear sense of the outer limit of their discretionary authority."[40]

Koch read "Broken Windows" shortly after its publication and passed it along to Police Commissioner Robert McGuire with a note emphasizing that the Broken Windows approach had "nothing to do with crime but rather deal[t] with the fear of unruly behavior by others." A few weeks later McGuire responded with a long memo outlining the results of two foot patrol projects the NYPD had implemented: a pilot patrol on the Lower East Side, and a set of "neighborhood stabilization units" that were deployed flexibly. Though McGuire credited the Lower East Side experiment with a modest reduction of street crime, he, like Koch, singled out the favorable public perceptions. Foot patrols were "immediately hailed by community and business leaders. . . . Such officers create a favorable public impression. . . . These officers make clear to the public the Department's commitment to restore a feeling of safety and security to all the streets of the City." Unfortunately, McGuire explained to Koch, budgetary austerity made it impossible to expand the patrols—in fact, the NYPD had already discontinued the Lower East Side experiment. All McGuire could do was to commend the street patrol approach for a time when the NYPD had the officers to implement it.[41]

THOSE DAYS WERE CLOSER than New Yorkers might have imagined. Despite the ongoing fiscal strictures, the city's economy had begun to turn the corner in the late 1970s. "Everything that makes the American hinterland uneasy about New York—its large foreign population, cultural diversity, intellectual leadership—is a source of attraction to foreigners," the economist Eli Ginzberg noted in 1978. When growing global capital markets and a weak U.S. dollar yielded a surge in foreign investment in the late 1970s, New York was able to capture a disproportionate share of the benefits—a pattern amplified by the growing financialization of the U.S. economy. As the returns to finance capital grew amid deregulation and global restructuring, New York, which possessed considerable first-mover advantages, benefited disproportionately.[42]

The city had been primed for this moment: Long a center for corporations doing international business, New York boasted an unequaled array of services—"firms specializing in legal matters, management consulting, tax counseling, computer operations, marketing, public relations, and advertising and in economic information and forecasting"—along with excellent telecommunications systems and good international air transportation, an around-the-clock ethos, and a thriving and diverse cultural life. Already by the late 1970s, the signs of New York's transformation into a "global city" were evident. The number of passengers arriving in the metropolitan area's three major airports rose by 10 percent. Restaurant sales were up about 10 percent, and theater sales about 19 percent. Hotels were close to full even as prices surged. The Midtown office vacancy rate was down sharply.[43]

New commercial establishments popped up to cater to the city's growing young professional and managerial classes in neighborhoods such as the Upper West Side and Park Slope, Brooklyn. "To the old candy stores and hardware stores" of a "formerly shabby stretch" of Columbus Avenue, a *New York* magazine profile announced, "have been added a spectacular array of emporiums dispensing exotic cheeses, outré fashions, and French-made Mickey Mouse chalkboards." Writers kicked around a variety of terms to describe such processes of neighborhood transition: *revitalization*, *renaissance*, *fancification*, and a new word recently imported from England, *gentrification*.[44]

A no-less-remarkable transformation was occurring in many of the city's less chic neighborhoods. Despite a citywide loss of some 823,159 residents in the 1970s, New York's immigrant population had actually grown by 233,141. Whereas the city's foreign-born population had long consisted predominantly of people born in Europe, the immigrants of the 1970s came from across the globe. In the aftermath of Lyndon Johnson's Immigration and Nationality Act of 1965 (which he signed in New York harbor) and the increase in immigration that followed normalized relations with China, the number of New Yorkers born in Colombia, the Dominican Republic, Ecuador, Honduras, Mexico, Haiti, Jamaica, and China roughly doubled in the 1970s; migrants from the Philippines and Trinidad and Tobago tripled; from India, quadrupled; and from Pakistan, quintupled. The largest rate of growth was among New Yorkers born in the Korean Republic, a population that grew from less than 3,000 in 1970 to more than 20,000 in 1980. The arrival of new New Yorkers would continue more or less unabated into the twenty-first century, with the countries of origins expanding over time to encompass most of the globe. By the twenty-first century, the native-born ethnic city of the mid-twentieth century had become, not just the city of immigrants it had long been prior to the restriction acts of the 1920s, but for the first time a city populated en masse by people from around the globe. (One consequence of the new migration was that the city's Spanish-speaking population was no longer dominated by New Yorkers of Puerto Rican ancestry, a development that led to a new sociocultural formation scholars have labeled *latinidad*. From this point forward, the book will use the term "Latino" to refer to New Yorkers of Latin American ancestry in the collective.)[45]

Especially as it accelerated in the 1980s, New York's transformation into a new global city of immigrants would induce consternation in some longtime residents. The talk-radio personality Bob Grant, whose afternoon program on WABC was the city's most-listened-to, would build a large audience with his diatribes against the ills associated with what he called "Third Worldism." The task of incorporating arrivals from around the world did present real challenges, particularly in the schools, which were faced with the task of accommodating a far more linguistically diverse population. On the whole, though, the effects of this new migration were precisely the opposite of what Grant and his listeners imagined. Ambitious and resilient enough to undertake the challenging task of resettling in a strange land, these new New Yorkers, many of whom performed grinding, bone-tiring jobs in the service sector, small retail, and informal manufacturing—what the novelist Chang-Rae Lee memorably described as "the dwindle of irredeemable hours beneath the cheap tube lights"—proved essential to the city's recovery. They provided the labor on which the city's economic recovery and subsequent expansion depended, contributed to the tax base, afforded new opportunities for small-scale entrepreneurship, stabilized and revitalized depopulated neighborhoods, and, over time, helped bring the crime rate down. Their arrival lent the city a new air of vitality;

without mass immigration, New York would have remained the aging, shrinking city it had been in the 1970s.[46]

IF THE CITY'S RECOVERY WAS the work of many hands, its benefits flowed almost entirely to the middle and upper classes. As New York came back from the fiscal brink, the city as a whole actually became poorer: In constant dollars, the median family income fell from $16,818 in 1979 to $14,880 in 1982. The poverty rate rose from 17.5 percent in 1976 to 24 percent in 1982. The growth of child poverty was particularly alarming—by 1984, 40 percent of the city's children were growing up in poverty. These figures reflected the ongoing loss of industrial jobs and the expansion of a low-wage service sector. They also reflected a less generous welfare policy. New York State had capped the maximum income limit for its primary relief programs in 1974 and did not raise it again until 1982, despite the era's high inflation, preventing large numbers of the working poor from receiving benefits: Though New York City had some 227,000 more poor people in 1982 than it had in 1970, nearly 54,000 fewer New Yorkers were able to access the primary welfare programs. And those who could saw their benefits erode in value as they failed to match the rate of inflation. The growth of poverty amid economic growth—rendered palpable by the explosion of homelessness—left analysts disoriented and reaching for new categories of description. "Poverty in New York City today is fundamentally different from two or three decades ago" one study concluded. Observers began to speak of a "new" poverty, concentrated by neighborhood and apparently impervious to aggregate economic expansion.[47]

The impacts of the local economic restructuring and rising poverty levels fell especially on Black and Latino New Yorkers—and, because of racial segregation, on predominantly Black and Latino neighborhoods. At the beginning of the 1970s, official unemployment rates among white and Black New Yorkers—an imperfect measure, to be sure—had been fairly similar: 6.4 percent of white New Yorkers were unemployed in 1971, compared to 7.8 percent of "Black and Other" New Yorkers. By 1981, Black New Yorkers were unemployed at more than double the rate of white New Yorkers (15 and 7 percent, respectively, with "Hispanic Origin" New Yorkers, whom officials started counting separately only in 1981, at 11.6 percent). Black and Latino New Yorkers were largely trapped in declining industries and cut out of the sectors that drove the city's growth in employment and, especially, income: One hundred and thirty of the city's 193 major industries—from professional jobs in finance, the law, higher education, medicine, advertising, and media to good-paying craft work in trades such as printing and construction—were barely open to New Yorkers of color. Exclusion of this kind fed on itself, making it even more difficult for marginalized New Yorkers (as one study noted) "to develop the informal networks and linkages that play a large role in occupational and job mobility."[48]

Because of residential segregation, poor Black and Latino New Yorkers were likely to experience poverty differently than poor white New Yorkers. Poor white New Yorkers, by and large, lived in mixed-income neighborhoods: about 70 percent of poor white New Yorkers lived in neighborhoods where the poverty rate was below 30 percent. Precisely the opposite was true for poor Black and Latino New Yorkers, about 70 percent of whom lived in neighborhoods with poverty rates above 30 percent. These New Yorkers were thus much more likely to live not just with poverty but with the structural effects of concentrated poverty—the systematic deprivation of resources to the neighborhood as a whole.[49]

Federal policy had played an important, if somewhat obscure, role in these transformations. On the one hand, Washington had contributed significantly to the city's economic difficulties. In the aggregate, as Senator Moynihan noted, the federal government returned in services about three-quarters of every tax dollar it raised in New

York State—whereas a state like California regularly received something like $8 billion to $12 billion more in federal spending than it paid in taxes. New Yorkers called repeatedly, to little avail, for the federal government to assume the full burden for expenses that were contributing to the city and state's fiscal stress, especially Aid to Families with Dependent Children and other conditional relief programs (a major cause of Senator Javits's) and Medicaid. More broadly, Washington's turn away from the War on Poverty and its decision not to make a robust commitment to full employment undercut poor- and working-class incomes in the city.[50]

At the same time, the federal government's choices on regulatory and monetary policy, which contributed to the immense growth of the financial and legal industries headquartered in the city, sent the upper reaches of its economy soaring to extraordinary heights. Even as Washington contributed less to the city, the new political economy made it possible for the city government to claim more revenue in the form of property, income, and business-derived taxes. Receipts from the city's income tax grew from 3.8 percent of total municipal revenue on the eve of the fiscal crisis to 9.3 percent in 1985; taxes gleaned from a variety of business activities—sales, stock transfers, hotel occupancies—rose concomitantly. The growth of the city's finance sector—and a bit later, the corporate law, consulting, and related industries—shaped much of New York's subsequent development, putting new pressure on the city's housing stock (through both demand and speculation), providing the local revenue to rebuild the NYPD, and creating pools of philanthropic money that would indelibly shape school reform. The shifting basis of the city's revenues also implied a new set of incentives: To the extent that it received less money from Washington earmarked for public purposes, the city now had to raise it locally by stimulating real estate development, luring high-income residents, and encouraging business and tourism.[51]

In all, the resolution of the fiscal crisis had done precious little to address the problems of New Yorkers who were cut out of the local recovery by historical and ongoing discrimination. To the contrary, cuts to social spending and public services exacerbated the deepening crisis of concentrated poverty. And yet even as these problems worsened, public officials were turning away from them, rejecting an emphasis on poverty and the "root causes" of urban problems and envisioning instead ways to manage the consequences of poverty and deprivation for a middle-class "public" in whose name they acted.

IN THE EARLY 1980S, as Wall Street began its prolonged expansion, returns from the city's income tax grew by double digits every year, far outpacing inflation. Koch was able to produce his first balanced budget in 1981; he even found he had the money to hire thousands of police officers, rehire teachers and firefighters, and put some $35 million into upgrading the subway. "This does not mean that the days of wine and roses have returned," Koch told the Board of Estimate in the letter accompanying his budget proposal. ". . . It does mean, though, that the worst pain is behind us, and that cutting can be balanced with some new initiatives."[52]

By the summer of 1981, Federal Reserve chair Paul Volcker's decision to raise interest rates in an effort to curb the runaway inflation of the 1970s had plunged the U.S. economy into its deepest slump since the Great Depression. Working-class New Yorkers, like Americans across the country, were hit hard; yet the booming sectors of the local economy felt little impact (indeed, the Volcker shock served as a stimulant to the city's financial sector), and the city was spared the pain of renewed budget cuts. Between 1983, when the Volcker recession fully lifted, and the end of his mayoralty in 1989, Koch would be able to expand the city budget in real terms by more than a quarter. The city now had the resources to begin rebuilding. How would it use them?[53]

PART II
QUALITY OF LIFE

1983–2001

3

From Survival to Revival

By early 1984, Mayor Koch was ready to declare New York City's long crisis over. The local economy, he claimed, had improved to the point that the city could now move from "questions of survival to questions of revival." That February he appointed a group of eminent New Yorkers to study the city's future and offer a coherent set of recommendations for how it should move toward the twenty-first century. Koch's Commission on the Year 2000 was an impressive and diverse group: in addition to leading figures from government, business, and the public sector unions, it included Donna Shalala, then the president of Hunter College; Vartan Gregorian, the widely admired president of the New York Public Library (and soon to become an important figure in the public school choice movement); Manuel Bustelo, publisher of *El Diario–La Prensa*, the city's leading Spanish-language newspaper; and Charles V. Hamilton, the Columbia political scientist who, together with Stokely Carmichael, had developed the concept of "structural racism" in the 1967 book *Black Power: The Politics of Liberation*.[1]

To chair the committee, Koch chose one of the most respected and pedigreed figures in city government: Robert F. ("Bobby") Wagner, Jr. Wagner's grandfather, Robert F. Wagner, had immigrated with his parents from Germany in the late nineteenth century and grew up in Yorkville before making his way in Democratic politics: first in the state legislature, where he advocated for new labor protections in the wake of the Triangle Shirtwaist Factory fire of 1911, then in the U.S. Senate, where he sponsored such signature New Deal legislation as the National Labor Relations Act, the Social Security Act, and the Housing Act of 1937. Senator Wagner's son, the first Robert F. Wagner, Jr., extended New York's local New Deal during three terms as the city's mayor from 1954 to 1965.[2] (Mayor Wagner dropped the "Jr." after his father's death; Bobby, the third Robert F. Wagner, thereafter became "Robert F. Wagner, Jr.")

If a new generation of political leaders were to pull New York's New Deal tradition through the upheavals of the 1970s, Bobby Wagner might have seemed at first glance a natural candidate. Franklin Roosevelt himself had welcomed Wagner into the world, taking time amid the demands of the Second World War to send him a "personal and confidential" letter offering a "word of greeting." By the time he was forty, Wagner had graduated magna cum laude from Harvard, earned a Ph.D. on a Marshall Scholarship, collected a master's in public affairs from Princeton, and knocked off an incumbent to get elected as Manhattan's at-large member of the City Council, from which post he assailed the strictures of the fiscal crisis regime as wrongheaded and self-defeating. He was a rising star, "the class of the under-40 Democratic field in New York," as one journalist wrote.[3]

Then suddenly his trajectory shifted. Unassuming and gentle of manner, instinctively intellectual, Wagner had never been a natural fit for the rough-and-tumble of New York politics. After losing a bid for borough president of Manhattan in 1977 to the flashier Andrew Stein—a blow that continued to hurt years later—he recognized that he was more at home with urban policy, both the world of ideas and the day-to-day operation of government, than with the family business of electoral politics. By the mid-1980s, though still only in his mid-forties, he had amassed a remarkable résumé: deputy mayor for policy, chair of the City Planning Commission, head of the Health and Hospitals Corporation, and president of the New York City Board of Education. He had advised both Hugh Carey and Ed Koch in an informal capacity and, observers noted, was one of the few people who seemed able to tell them that they were wrong. People who worked with him frequently came to revere him. But those who knew him also sensed an undertow of restlessness. "He has a sense of history," his friend Donna Shalala remarked, "and he's trying to find his place in history."[4]

The commission's report, entitled *New York Ascendant* and delivered in mid-1987, began with a striking renunciation of the era of limited horizons that had marked the response to the fiscal crisis. "The fiscal crisis taught New York many lessons," the commissioners wrote. ". . . All of these are lessons to keep in mind. At the same time the discipline needed to overcome the fiscal crisis diminished our sense of daring, made us too accepting of inadequate services, narrowed our vision of what New York can and should be." Yet even as it sought to break from the constraints of the crisis era, the commission's report showed how deeply a certain interpretation of the fiscal crisis had reshaped liberal thought. Poverty, the commission asserted, was the number-one problem facing the city. But the 1970s had shown that the city "cannot be a vehicle for a major redistribution of income." Instead, the commission called on the city to make major investments in public education and low- and moderate-income housing.[5]

As Koch himself had done throughout his mayoralty, the commission placed heavy emphasis on the importance of the middle class as an economic base and as a social and cultural force. "Despite its glamour, New York has always been at its base a middle-class city of middle-class neighborhoods and mores. The challenge of the future is to build on this middle-class strength." A city grounded in the middle class would be not just a city of opportunity but also a city of civility—and civility, the commission held, "should be a goal for the twenty-first century." The report went on to propose scores of policies meant to facilitate social mobility and middle-class mores.[6]

Not everyone found the optimistic view of *New York Ascendant* convincing. Though the commission's report cited poverty as the single most important problem facing the city, Manhattan borough president David Dinkins, the leading Black elected official in city government, believed that the report could have focused more closely on those left behind by the economic expansion of the 1980s. Manhattan, he wrote in response, "is midtown businesses and the Wall Street financial district, but it is also the Lower East Side, Harlem, Chelsea and El Barrio." The commission, he charged, had obscured this " 'other' Manhattan," the problems of which, he thought, closely resembled those of the "outer borough[s]," a term that had recently come into widespread use to refer to the parts of the city bypassed by the Manhattan boom. Dinkins lauded the commission for its emphasis on low-income housing and improved social services but took it to task for failing to recognize how deeply entrenched inequalities of race and class were in the city. "We New Yorkers should be genuinely proud of much of our past; however, we must also be aware of historical inequities which have formed the root of many of today's social problems. Trends toward greater income and racial polarization and segregation with worsening conditions for the poor are not new; rather they reflect deepening fissures in what was already in some ways an unequal system." To Dinkins, 1980s New York was not a city ascendant. It was, in the Charles Dickens line he would later borrow from Mario Cuomo, a tale of two cities.[7]

Another study arrived the following year to less fanfare. *New York Unbound* was sponsored by a relatively new conservative think tank called the Manhattan Institute, founded in 1978, in the wake of the fiscal crisis, by the British businessman Antony Fisher and by the future Ronald Reagan campaign director (and later Director of Central Intelligence) William J. Casey. Prior to the late 1980s, the Manhattan Institute had devoted most of its efforts to national affairs, sponsoring books such as George Gilder's *Wealth and Poverty* (1981) and Charles Murray's *Losing Ground* (1984), both of which became closely associated with the Reagan White House and the New Right. *New York Unbound*, edited by Manhattan Institute fellow Peter Salins, applied some of the same ideas—about the power of markets and the failures of regulation and the welfare state—to city issues. The volume presented, Salins wrote, "an entire point of view regarding New York's problems and prospects that has not found expression in the New York literature to date." In the contributors' view, New York was a city of "enormous natural vitality," but it had become a "paradigm of urban failure" because misguided public policies had stifled that vitality and left it with an inadequate housing stock, a "shambles of an education system," and unsafe spaces. "Let us consider solving the city's problems by harnessing rather than repressing its dynamism and energy," the volume proposed, calling for pro-market policies like school vouchers and rent deregulation.[8]

As New York moved from survival to revival, questions of distribution that had been bracketed by the imposition of austerity returned to the forefront of city politics. Who should have access to public space? Who should get to live in New York's housing? Who should get to attend its best schools? "I speak out for the middle class," Koch declared. His plans for the city turned on providing "quality of life"—a term that was coming to mean not the presence of things that made urban life enjoyable and meaningful but rather the absence of those that made it unpleasant and perhaps dangerous. While Koch would stake out middle-of-the-road positions on school reform and rent regulation, he would use the fiscal windfall to target forms of disorder that threatened his administration's ideal of a middle-class city, launching a campaign against street-level drug markets that would send incarceration rates soaring and fundamentally change how police operated in the city. In the end, Koch's inability to resolve the distributional conflicts of the mid-1980s would lead to growing dissatisfaction across the political spectrum with his brand of post-fiscal-crisis liberalism. The issues of justice and equity raised by David Dinkins in his response to *New York Ascendant* could not be kept at bay indefinitely. And neoconservatives such as the contributors to *New York Unbound* demanded more fundamental reforms to achieve the quality of life Koch had promised. By the decade's end, Koch's center could no longer hold.[9]

AS THE TOP END OF THE New York economy took off and working-class wages stagnated in the 1980s, street commerce bloomed across the city like spring shoots—or like ragweed, depending on one's perspective. Astor Place, the writer Lucy Sante recalled, "became a vast flea market, with vendors ranging from collectors of old comic books to optimists attempting to unload whatever they had skimmed from the garbage cans the night before. . . . The daily spectacle was delirious, uncanny, the range of goods boundless and utterly random." Though most pronounced in dense areas with high foot traffic, informal street markets spread throughout the city, wherever New Yorkers could find space to assert their entrepreneurial ambitions or earn what they needed for daily survival: musicians performed; breakdancers toted their boom boxes; small businesspeople sold food, clothing, and printed matter of all sorts; jobless people asked for money from passersby; independent operators stopped automobiles at tunnel exits and intersections, seeking payment in exchange for windshield squeegee jobs; and drug workers peddled their wares in open-air markets that observers likened to bazaars and outdoor supermarkets.[10]

For most of Koch's first term, the NYPD had maintained the policy of street-level nonenforcement that it had adopted in 1971 and affirmed after the passage of the Rockefeller drug laws in 1973. Koch himself, despite his tough-on-crime posture and notwithstanding a few target campaigns such as the war on graffiti, had declined during his first term to prioritize policing over public education, saying he would not allocate money to hire more police officers until the city could stop laying off teachers. But when the fiscal situation began to improve in 1981, he launched a hiring spree that eventually included thousands of new officers and began a sustained crackdown on unsanctioned use of public space—particularly open-air drug markets. "In New York City—in every city in the country—personal safety and anger at the escalation of crime is the No. 1 issue," Koch declared. "The people of this city want something done about it [and] I want something done about it."[11]

That summer Koch and the NYPD began to break from the policing strategies of the 1970s. In July, Police Commissioner McGuire announced the formation of a new unit of one hundred plainclothes officers to "battle drugs in public places." Officially a response to a surge of complaints from "members of community boards and private citizens at meetings attended by precinct commanders," the unit targeted primarily highly trafficked public spaces and parks in workplace and tourist neighborhoods: Times Square, the Financial District, Bryant and Washington Square parks. This, Koch explained, was the first step in a "broader [campaign] against 'quality-of-life' offenses."[12]

In part, Koch and the NYPD's turn toward street-level enforcement reflected new thinking about policing: In addition to Kelling and Wilson's Broken Windows theory and the broader calls for proactive, order-maintenance policing, some scholars had begun to recast street-level policing as a way of regulating the narcotics market—a public scourge dating back to John Lindsay's first term. The police could not eliminate drug sales, Mark H. Moore of the Harvard Kennedy School argued, but they could reduce the number of new users by raising the potential cost of drug transactions. With this goal in mind, Moore urged police departments to engage in buy-and-bust operations to make dealers suspicious of unknown buyers and to eliminate copping areas through active policing—there should be "no area," he wrote, "to which an inexperienced user could come and expect to find heroin."[13]

But the turn toward street-level drug enforcement also had a political logic: Neighborhood organizations demanded it. Perhaps the most sustained campaign came from the Lower East Side, a neighborhood that was undergoing both disinvestment and gentrification. The Lower East Side market illustrated particularly clearly how informal economies developed as features of disinvestment and austerity. As *El Diario* observed, the drug industry represented one of the neighborhood's largest employers, particularly for young people (on the Lower East Side, predominantly Puerto Rican) who were hit hard by the disappearance of manufacturing and government jobs; and the neighborhood's emptied tenements provided staging grounds for street-level commerce. With decent transit connections and proximity to wealthier neighborhoods, the Lower East Side drug market served a predominantly middle-class clientele with heroin and, increasingly, cocaine.[14]

By the early 1980s, the Lower East Side drug market was growing quickly. In response, Manhattan borough president Andrew Stein issued a report on the situation, which in turn spurred Koch to create a Lower East Side Narcotics Task Force. When stepped-up enforcement efforts failed to curtail the market's growth, residents took to the streets in a series of marches and candlelight vigils. In March 1983, some three hundred protesters—a coalition of block organizations, religious congregations, and other community groups—paraded from First Avenue and East Ninth Street to Mayor Koch's apartment building in Greenwich Village.[15]

Neighborhood-level discontent and loosening fiscal constraints opened the door for the city's first sustained campaigns against open-air drug markets since the early 1970s. In January 1984, McGuire's successor, Benjamin Ward, launched a new campaign to "retake" selected public spaces through a highly visible and publicized policing initiative. The program, Operation Pressure Point (OPP), launched with more than two hundred uniformed and plainclothes police officers descending on the Lower East Side "to clean up" New York's " 'supermarket' of illegal drugs," primarily through the use of undercover buy-and-bust arrests. Several months later the NYPD launched a second OPP campaign in central Harlem. With these campaigns, New York made a highly visible, sustained commitment to quality-of-life policing.[16]

Operation Pressure Point was primarily the idea of Commissioner Ward, the city's first Black police commissioner, whom Koch had appointed at the beginning of 1984 following a congressional investigation into police brutality in New York. Ward, the son of an Irish father and a Yiddish-speaking African American mother, had grown up in Weeksville, Brooklyn, and joined the NYPD as a patrolman in 1951. By his own recollection, Ward was embarrassed by the presence of the huge open-air drug market he saw on his daily commute from Queens to One Police Plaza—and was particularly distressed that European news film crews were shooting it as evidence of "the typical American scene." "I saw it as a problem that needed to be solved in some way," he recalled. Ward faced some initial resistance from within the NYPD. Some upper-level officials harbored lingering fears of corruption; some officers viewed the open-air markets as places to boost their arrest numbers—an opportunity rather than a problem. Mayor Koch, whose support Ward felt he needed to ensure himself the resources OPP required, told Ward to go ahead with the program even though he thought it unlikely to work—"the courts are going to let them go," Ward remembered Koch saying.[17]

Despite the neighborhood calls for NYPD action, Operation Pressure Point quickly stirred up opposition from churches and community groups. Still fearing corruption, the NYPD deployed patrolmen with little experience in the neighborhood; many of the officers were recent graduates of the police academy, part of the hiring spree of the early 1980s. Unsurprisingly, community leaders found that officers "[couldn't] tell the good guys from the bad guys" and were "grabbing our children . . . because they think everyone black and Hispanic is a drug dealer." "Some residents admitted," an internal NYPD study found, "that they are frequently more fearful of the officers than the addicts and dealers." Both Koch and the NYPD believed most of the drug dealers chased off the streets by OPP simply moved—to nearby streets, into the subways, into public housing projects, from one park to another.[18]

Even so, OPP became a political success for Koch. One of the city's leading tabloids, the *New York Daily News*, ran a two-page photo spread lauding Koch and the NYPD for "giving the ABCs back to the neighborhood," complete with action shots of surveillance of the lettered thoroughfares, showing searches and arrests, and a shot of Koch and Ward inspecting a collection of seized drugs and weapons. *The New York Times* ran a similarly illustrated feature. A year into the first OPP campaign, armed robberies had decreased by 47 percent and homicides by 60 percent on the Lower East Side; in Harlem, the second staging area, robberies fell by some 39 percent in the first eleven months of OPP 2. Statistics like these eluded the questions of whether crime simply moved, whether falling rates of violent crime in the staging areas were due to the OPP campaigns or caused by other factors, and whether they were permanent or merely temporary. But decontextualized, such numbers provided a language with which Koch and the NYPD could assert the city government's competency at a moment when they had relatively little success decreasing crime citywide.[19]

In 1986 Koch and Harlem congressman Charles Rangel mobilized America's big-city mayors to pressure the Reagan administration to devote more resources to the war on drugs, which the U.S. Conference of Mayors assailed as "grossly underfunded." They pointed to OPP as a local success story—a model that could be scaled up if the federal government supplied the fiscal resources. "Is it not . . . correct to say that Americans could stop the drug epidemic in America if we really wanted to?" Koch wrote in an op-ed. "I believe that Operation Pressure Point has demonstrated what can be done . . . in American cities."[20]

Koch and Ward's local war on crime won support across much of the political spectrum. When, in 1985, City Council president Carol Bellamy challenged Koch in the Democratic primary (she also ran in the general election on the Liberal Party line), she called for more police officers and a citywide extension of OPP. Community-level political leaders and organizations in neighborhoods outside the two OPP sites had yet to see firsthand the civil liberties abuses wrought by OPP. But they well understood the threat that street-level drug markets (and drug markets operating in abandoned housing) posed to their own neighborhood-based community-building projects, especially their efforts to rebuild their housing stock. For these reasons, the NYPD's expansion of OPP and similar initiatives often garnered the support of neighborhood leaders, at least at first—indeed, it sometimes came at their insistence. In the spring of 1985, Councilman Fernando Ferrer of the Bronx wrote to Deputy Mayor for Operations Stan Brezenoff to propose a Pressure Point area in his district. In 1985, a coalition of "homeowners, tenant groups, block associations, and churches" in the West Bronx staged a series of marches and demonstrations that led to meetings between the NYPD and community leaders, then to "additional foot patrol on streets with the heaviest activity and with selective attention to several specific vending locations." In Brownsville and East New York, Reverend Johnny Ray Youngblood of the East Brooklyn Churches coalition pressured the NYPD (through Koch) to take stronger action against the "plague of drug locations in our area"; the NYPD in response promised to make "a strong, good faith effort . . . to close 40 drug locations by the end of 1985." Everywhere, Ward found, favorable media coverage raised public expectations. "Everyone wants their own Pressure Point," he said.[21]

Like the campaign against graffiti, the turn toward street-level drug policing represented a response to yet another embarrassing example of the city's and the NYPD's inability to assert authority. For Koch, the "plague of street dealers" targeted by OPP represented "the transcendent urban problem of our time" because it had become "a dreary symbo[l] of human failure," evoking in people "a sense of despair and contempt for the ability of law and government to deliver them from crime and addiction." Ward's seemingly bland statement to newspaper reporters on the morning of OPP's launch suggested that the NYPD, too, felt the need to make a public demonstration of capability and competence. "I can't not do anything," he remarked. "I must do something."[22]

The campaigns also reflected Koch's desire to restore (or "stabilize") public spaces by removing the kinds of incivility and disorder that made them unappealing to many everyday New Yorkers. Drawing on Jacobs's, Whyte's, and Kelling and Wilson's notion of community self-regulation, Koch and Ward believed that the key to restoring public spaces lay in encouraging a visible presence of orderly people within them: Once such people became predominant in a particular public space, the theory went, they could enforce social norms—citizen surveillance would effectively extend the NYPD's order-maintenance capacity. The task of the police within this framework was to re-regulate public space such that small-time sellers became seen as neighborhood "outsiders." Ward, especially, envisioned street-level drug enforcement as the first phase of a police-"community" partnership that would reconstruct "community-based" social control and behavioral standards: "We try to mobilize the community to take charge of their neighborhood, once we get the outsider/drug dealers out of there." Where OPP was most successful, an early study noted, buyers and sellers did indeed become " 'outsiders,' their presence readily apparent to OPP personnel and to residents, many of whom were eager to report them to the police." The NYPD set up special drug complaint hotlines to facilitate precisely that.[23]

Particularly in neighborhoods with hot real estate markets, street-level drug policing quickly became bound up with contests over gentrification. Initially, neighborhood activists and block associations had viewed street-level drug enforcement as a tool in the fight against gentrification. Some participants in the 1983 East Side antidrug marches held signs that said "STOP GENTRIFICATION"; one woman explained to the Greenwich Village community paper *The Villager* that residents felt their neighborhood had been "zoned for drugs" so as to break down community resistance to redevelopment. By 1985, this language had largely vanished, and many Lower East Siders came to view OPP as part of a broader effort to make their neighborhood safe for the forces of gentrification. The Lower East Side Joint Planning Council professed that, while they were "grateful when drug traffic is under control," they were "convinced safe streets for Lower East Side residents was not the objective of this police crackdown." Rather: "As rising rents and the new boutiques attest, the area is being made safe for well-heeled outsiders, not the working-class people who have traditionally lived here." As the campaign unfolded, voices could be heard applauding what the city was doing as a way of improving real estate markets. "Not only are young couples coming in because of it," noted one real estate agent, "but parents are buying apartments for their sons or daughters attending N.Y.U." A feature in the Sunday *New York Times* made it practically official: "THE FORTUNES OF THE LOWER EAST SIDE ARE RISING," the headline read: "Thanks to Operation Pressure Point, Art Galleries Are Replacing Shooting Galleries."[24]

In the mid-1980s, Ward returned from a trip to Los Angeles and pulled some of his top aides aside. The LAPD was struggling with a new crystallized form of cocaine people were calling "rock," he explained, and if it ever hit New York, all the progress the NYPD had achieved with Operation Pressure Point would be reversed. Sure enough, crack cocaine, a cheap, easy-to-manufacture derivative of powder cocaine, spread across the city in 1985 and 1986, ushering in a crisis of health and safety that devastated disinvested neighborhoods. The NYPD responded with a new round of street policing—organizing Tactical Narcotics Teams (TNTs) that filled the streets of selected neighborhoods with undercover officers who conducted buy-and-bust operations. The operation differed from OPP in that it focused specifically on crack and did not entail a visible uniformed presence. But as the closest study of the program notes, Koch and Ward launched it despite "persistent skepticism within the NYPD and among government officials that [street-level drug policing] was anything more than a 'numbers game,'" in large measure because "the results of Operation Pressure Point suggested that TNT had a good chance of being seen by the public as successful." Ward also created a special new Anti-Crack Unit, and acting on the assumption that crack represented a more dangerous commodity than previous drugs, city officials also launched "a campaign to make more arrests that would hold up in court as serious felonies."[25]

In the first years of OPP, the odds were relatively slight that a person arrested for buying, selling, or possessing drugs in an NYPD street sweep would go to prison. Only 37 percent of drug arrests resulted in felony charges, and only a third of those arrests led to indictments. Yet the sheer number of arrests produced by street-level drug policing quickly added up, and over time repeat arrests left sellers and buyers exposed to more severe penalties. After 1985, the incarcerated population swelled as the city sought to make crack arrests stand up in court; the city, state, and federal governments invested in prosecutorial, court, and carceral capacities, and attitudes toward drug offenses on the part of judges hardened. New York governor Mario Cuomo and the state legislature accommodated the rising number of felony convictions by financing new prison construction through the state's Urban Development Corporation, which could issue bonds without voter approval. Cuomo also supported a series of strict anticrack laws law, intended specifically to subject more small-time sellers (many of whom were arrested for misdemeanor possession) to Class D felony charges.[26]

One consequence of Koch's turn toward quality-of-life policing, then, was a sharp rise in drug-related incarceration. On the eve of OPP, drug offenders had represented some 10 percent of New York State inmates. By the end of the 1980s, that figure neared 35 percent. These arrests helped triple the state prison population compared to what it had been in Koch's first year in office. Despite the similar rates at which Black, white, and Latino New Yorkers used and sold drugs, the burden of the city's war on drugs fell overwhelmingly on communities of color. As of 1990, Black men between the ages of twenty and twenty-nine were twenty-three times more likely to be incarcerated in New York State than white men of the same age. Young Latino men were eleven times more likely. In all, Black and/or Latino New Yorkers accounted for about 82 percent of the prison population and 95 percent of the jail population.[27]

Such statistics scarcely begin to capture the myriad ways mass incarceration shaped, not only the lives of tens of thousands of New Yorkers and their families, but also the city's communities and neighborhoods. Incarceration contributed to neighborhood depopulation, heightened social stresses, put people at increased risk of homelessness, deprived many New Yorkers of voting rights and political representation, diminished job opportunities and access to public services, and channeled public resources that might have been directed toward disinvested communities into the prison system. It meant, in short, a wholesale diminishment of democratic citizenship in New York.

BY THE MID-1980S, New York had largely managed to quell the crisis of disinvestment that had destroyed so much of its housing stock in the 1970s—only for a new crisis, of affordability, overcrowding, and homelessness, to emerge. The roots of that crisis lie in part in the secular decline in profitability of mass-market housing in the five boroughs. New housing development had been economically viable in the mid-twentieth century because working-class incomes were high by historical standards and undeveloped lots were still available, which held down construction costs. But with a built-up city and declining working-class incomes, the old model no longer worked.

Compounding the situation, parts of the housing market faced new pressures amid the city's economic recovery. With the deregulation of the finance sector and the mergers-and-acquisitions mania of the 1980s, New York become a magnet for talented and well-credentialed young people eager to reap the rewards of the rapidly financializing economy. The banking and corporate law sectors added tens of thousands of jobs in the span of a few years, and Manhattan began hoovering up graduates from elite colleges and universities who a decade or two earlier might have headed to cities closer to home. Reporters dubbed the new class of young urban professionals "Yuppies," and their tastes and mores became one of the major fascinations of the 1980s. At the same time, as dual-career marriages grew and family sizes shrank, mid-career professionals and managers who might have moved to the suburbs increasingly chose to remain in the city.[28]

New York's real estate industry might conceivably have responded to rising purchasing power at the top of the city's housing market by adding new units. By and large, it did not—only once during the boom years of the 1980s did the city issue permits for more new units than it had granted in 1974, on the eve of the fiscal crisis. The reasons are many, and they are difficult to weigh. The locational preferences of the growing professional and managerial classes, in light of the historically high levels of crime and the still-ailing condition of the transit system, meant that construction would have to occur in neighborhoods where land costs were among the world's highest. The city zoning code enacted in 1961 (which became wildly complex in the decades after its adoption), the Koch administration's downzoning of residential neighborhoods, the proliferation of historic districts, and other land-use restrictions limited where developers could build and constrained how many units they could add. City building codes were particularly onerous, which meant that construction was unusually expensive in New York. And even if developers secured suitable parcels sufficiently unconstrained by land-use regulations and developed a business model consistent with the extraordinarily high cost of building in the city, they still needed to raise the money with which to build—which meant they had to compete for capital with other forms of investment, no easy task amid the 1980s bull market and the bevy of investment banking activity.[29]

But to speak only of constraints on new development for that part of the market which remained economically viable is to consider only half of the picture. If New York's real estate industry did not build to accommodate the burgeoning population of affluent professionals, this was not only because it could not do so profitably but also because it did not need to, for there existed a ready alternative. New York accommodated population growth, not primarily by adding new units but by recycling existing ones for a more affluent, more profitable market. It was a dynamic that had begun with the conversion of the old single-room occupancy hotels and boardinghouses in the 1970s, and it would continue through the second decade of the twenty-first century. There is no way to make sense of New York's modern housing crisis without accounting for it.

In the 1980s, recycling the housing stock meant, above all, converting existing rental housing into co-ops and, less frequently, condominiums. The city government had been encouraging conversions since the Lindsay years, but tenants who wished to remain as regulated renters had significant power to resist—state law required

35 percent of tenants to agree before a conversion could proceed. In the early 1980s, though, soaring demand allowed co-op conversion sponsors to buy the support of regulated tenants by offering steeply discounted purchase prices on their apartments or generous buyouts; through the early to mid-1980s, tens of thousands of rental units were converted to co-op ownership each year, rippling out from "the choicest rental apartment buildings" on the Upper East and Upper West sides to what had been predominantly middle-class developments such as Tudor City, the 1920s Tudor Revival–style complex across FDR Drive from UN Headquarters, which converted in the mid-1980s. Housing experts noted that Black New Yorkers were less able to take advantage of these discounted offerings, as intergenerational inequalities in wealth accumulation made it more difficult for them to find money for the down payment. The "new G.I. [Bill] financing," one quipped, "is good in-laws." A parallel process played out in low-rise neighborhoods, where affluent professionals provided a market for the conversion of multifamily brownstones and other row houses into single- and two-family homes. In all, the scholar Adam Brodheim estimates, the city lost some 100,000 housing units to such conversions between 1950 and 2022.[30]

In areas where the housing stock was unsuited to co-oping—in neighborhoods where old tenements rather than large apartment buildings predominated—the process of "unlocking value" required more extensive conversion or even demolition, which in turn meant emptying buildings of tenants who had a right to stay. Landlords on the Upper West Side, where gentrification was especially feverish, sometimes paid tenants five figures in cash to vacate regulated apartments, good money but often not enough for them to find someplace else in the neighborhood; tenants who remained found that the community they had known was vanishing before their eyes. "In our neighborhoods there are always bunches of people on the corners," one West Sider of Puerto Rican heritage remarked, "but you don't see many of these people now."[31]

When envelopes of cash did not work, more assertive methods were required. In 1982, in response to tenant complaints, Manhattan district attorney Robert Morgenthau formed a special task force to investigate tenant harassment. Eighteen months later his office indicted twenty-two individuals for engaging in a "routine of terror" to empty twenty-one apartment buildings of their low- and lower-middle income tenants in gentrifying neighborhoods such as the Upper West Side and Chelsea. Two landlords, Morgenthau found, had paid a criminal ring as much as $100,000 a building to "instal[l] drug addicts, prostitutes, thieves and other criminals in vacant apartments to commit burglaries and assaults against tenants, [to] caus[e] flooding, set fires, dum[p] garbage and creat[e] bedlam." Residents reported receiving death threats, and in one instance, the conspirators pushed a seventy-two-year old man down a flight of stairs.[32]

With well-located regulated apartments in ever-shorter supply, some tenants sought to game the system, keeping regulated apartments even as they spent most of the year elsewhere, handing over regulated apartments to family members who had not previously lived there, or subletting at hiked-up rates. The city responded by threatening to evict regulated tenants who did not pay full-year city income taxes; landlords, eager to take advantage of vacancy bonuses (and sometimes to warehouse apartments for co-op conversion or redevelopment), hired private investigators to alert them when a tenant was not using their regulated apartment as a primary residence. A certain degree of irrationality had long existed within the regulatory system—one reason why tenant advocates had wanted the quasi-public utility approach embodied in the proposed Flynn-Dearie legislation—but the rise of what amounted to a black market for rent-regulated units added a whole new dimension to the politics of regulation. Conservative commentators likened the system to "Moscow on the Hudson." Fascination with rent regulation's intrigues crossed into popular culture: The plot of Tom Wolfe's best-selling 1987 novel

Bonfire of the Vanities turned on evidence produced by a recording device installed by a landlord trying to oust regulated tenants.[33]

In the early 1980s, Donald Trump acquired a rent-regulated residential building on Central Park South with the intention of demolishing it and erecting luxury condominiums. To his dismay, the tenants of 100 Central Park South resisted, and Trump soon found himself battling accusations of tenant harassment. The tenants eventually won, and Trump was forced to rework his renovations to keep their homes intact. The experience inspired Trump to denounce the rent laws at length in his 1987 bestseller *The Art of the Deal.* Rent regulation, he claimed, was "a disaster for all but the privileged few who are protected by it." "As much as any other single factor," the rent laws were responsible for the housing crises of the 1970s and '80s, and even worse, they had "stopped protecting the people who needed it most." Trump offered a litany of celebrities enjoying prime apartments at cut-rate prices: Mia Farrow and Carly Simon lived on Central Park West in ten-room apartments renting for $2,000 and $2,200 a month, respectively; *New Yorker* editor William Shawn paid $1,000 a month for eight rooms on Fifth Avenue; and none other than Mayor Ed Koch, Trump's bitter enemy, had three rooms in "a beautiful part of Greenwich Village" for $350 a month. "Unlike most developers," Trump concluded, "I don't advocate eliminating rent control. I just think there ought to be a means test. . . . People with incomes above a certain sum would be given a choice between paying a proportionately higher rent for their apartments or moving somewhere else." The journalist William C. Tucker, from whom Trump and his co-writer had gotten his list of glitzy rent-controlled New Yorkers, added a Trumpian flourish: "What would happen if we scrapped rent control[?] First, there'd be so much housing in New York that you wouldn't know what to do with it. Texas millionaires would build housing. The Arabs would build housing. The Japanese probably would propose a whole new residential island off Sheepshead Bay."[34]

This was a crude caricature; the "privileged few" protected by rent regulation consisted of some 2.5 million mostly middle- and working-class New Yorkers. The reality of the New York City housing market was at once less spectacular and more profound. There were essentially three levels of renters in mid-1980s New York, the Columbia University planning expert Peter Marcuse explained. There were tenants at the top of the market, who could pay the $2,500-a-month rent that developers thought would cover construction costs on a new one-bedroom apartment. At the bottom, tenants could not afford the legally permitted rents and thus were not getting much in terms of affordability from their regulated status, though they did enjoy a measure of stability and protection against landlord abuse. "And at the middle level," Marcuse suggested, where "people cannot pay enough [for landlords to want to build new housing] but *can* pay more than operating costs, *how much more* they pay depends on the restriction of rents." From that simple question—whether New Yorkers would spend their money on rent or in some other way—flowed the larger ones about the future of the city's neighborhoods, social fabric, and housing quality.[35]

Still, the fact that a few celebrities were living on the cheap at prime addresses gave the push for deregulation a kind of populist appeal. Trump and other long-standing opponents of rent regulation clearly felt the situation afforded them a chance to go on the offensive. With New York State now administering rent regulation, the Rent Stabilization Association, the trade group of landlords that had been formed to administer the system under the original 1969 law, became an increasingly assertive lobby for regulatory reform. The RSA hired Assembly speaker Stanley Fink's top housing aide as its president and pushed the argument that regulation was primarily helping those who did not need it: Regulation had created a "Tale of Two Cities," the RSA argued in a 1986 report, a city of fortunate subsidized tenants who benefited from regulation and a city of newcomers and lower-income renters who didn't. The Real Estate Board of New York, traditionally concerned mainly with commercial real estate, lent its weight to the landlords' lobbying efforts. As the state legislature debated extending the rent laws in the spring of 1985, Larry Silverstein of REBNY issued a proposal to allow landlords to buy vacant units out of regulation for the price of a $1,000 contribution to a state housing fund. Silverstein's proposal failed, as the state extended the laws for two years in 1985 and again in 1987. But the political calculus was obvious: Armed with a new, populist rationale, the real estate lobby had an opportunity to push for deregulation if it could convince the Republicans in the State Senate to make it a priority.[36]

Democrats, too, were beginning to contemplate limited deregulation. Much as the abandonment crisis of the 1970s had prompted some Democrats to rethink their commitment to rent regulation, so now did the crisis of affordability. "We have a system that gives more protection to the people who don't need it and less protection to the people who do," Governor Cuomo's top housing aide William Eimicke suggested, floating the idea of vacancy deregulation. Cuomo tasked Eimicke with developing a "comprehensive plan to reform the system" in advance of the 1987 legislative session. During the heat of his 1986 campaign for reelection, Cuomo ruled out support for vacancy deregulation. Instead, it was Bobby Wagner's Commission on the Year 2000 that first threw liberal support behind high-rent vacancy decontrol. "Those who are wealthy enough to pay market rents should do so," *New York Ascendant* tersely suggested, calling for the beneficiaries of deregulation to pay into a housing trust fund to assist lower-income tenants. (When the Real Estate Board of New York sent Wagner its response, calling for a vacancy decontrol program for all apartments, Wagner penned in the margin: "What happens to the poor?")[37]

As affluent New Yorkers fought for—and over—the choice neighborhoods of Manhattan, low-income New Yorkers faced an ever-worsening housing disaster. The New York City Housing Authority's sprawling system of public housing, though straining under the

Reagan administration's sharp cuts to federal funding, remained the city's one reliable source of what housing policy experts called "deeply affordable" housing. In the private market, though, affordable housing was nearly impossible to find. Recognizing that the housing crisis represented a threat to neighborhood stability, Koch and Cuomo launched ambitious housing initiatives: Koch vowed to spend $4.4 billion to help private developers and nonprofits build or rehabilitate 100,000 units over five years; Cuomo promised $3.5 billion for 80,000 units.[38]

But the Koch administration, in particular, was keen to commit resources specifically to housing for the middle class. "We cannot preserve the City's long-term health if we do not address the needs of the middle class by putting public resources into creating housing for this group," his aide Stanley Brezenoff said. "If we don't, who will be here to fill the jobs and pay the taxes that support services and housing creation for the poor?" Koch's ambitious plan aided the rebuilding of neighborhoods that had been ravaged by arson and abandonment in the 1970s. But it fell far short of meeting the need for affordable housing for low-income New Yorkers, and the crises of affordability only worsened: At the start of the 1980s, about one in five tenant households spent more than half their income on rent; by the early 1990s, it was one in four.[39]

With the formal housing market incapable of meeting the need for affordable housing, many New Yorkers sought refuge through informal arrangements. Illegal subdivisions became more common. Squatters took up residence in abandoned buildings on the Lower East Side, in Harlem, and in the South Bronx. The numbers of street homeless continued to swell. Most commonly, families simply doubled up. "The data show a ballistic increase in the number of New York households crammed into overcrowded apartments," one contemporary analyst wrote. "The number of 'severely crowded' households shot up 69 percent in four years and 144 percent since 1978. The figures represent the years when foreign immigration to

New York soared and the human density of compact neighborhoods like Washington Heights, Chinatown, Crown Heights, and Flushing became more steadily apparent." With half of sheltered families coming from doubling-up units, overcrowding threatened to tip into yet more homelessness.[40]

The experiences of the mid-1980s made two things clear. First, the city had no adequate way of supplying new low-rent housing at the levels required to stabilize the new housing crisis. Second, the real estate industry would serve the profitable segments of the market primarily by recycling the existing housing stock, which meant encroaching still further on those affordable units that did exist. Rent regulation was doing relatively little to keep rents affordable for working-class New Yorkers, but it did represent protection against the continuing threat of redevelopment. Only a few years after the apparent settlement represented by the Omnibus Housing Act of 1983, political cracks had begun to appear in the regulation system. The real estate industry's efforts to profit from the new professional and managerial classes depended on breaking those cracks wide open—and the fate of working-class neighborhoods throughout the city hung in the balance.

AT NOON ON MAY 21, 1988, a crowd gathered in Sheridan Square near the corner of West Fourth Street and Seventh Avenue in Greenwich Village, not far from the Stonewall Inn, site of the pivotal 1969 riot that helped catalyze the gay rights movement. It was a warm spring day amid what had been a season of hell for the adjoining communities. Adjacent to the square sat the Ridiculous Theatrical Company, a downtown arts institution founded in 1967 by the prolific, versatile, and renowned actor and playwright Charles Ludlam. Some five blocks north stood St. Vincent's Hospital, where Ludlam had died of AIDS the previous year at the age of forty-four. The lunchtime crowd had gathered to save Ludlam's partner in life and theater, Everett Quinton, from being evicted from the apartment the two had shared for eleven years. "It's kind of gruesome," Quinton remarked. "It's awful to have your life unsettled, then the idea of having to move to a new home, having to give up all the things you've accumulated all those years, like neighbors, people you can walk down the street and wave to, where you buy your bread—the things that make life 'life.'"[41]

The question of succession rights for rent-regulated apartments became an especially urgent one amid the AIDS epidemic, which devastated New York beginning in the early 1980s. One of the briefs against regulation, from landlords and market populists alike, was that apartments were being handed down like family heirlooms. To a degree, this was true of the dwindling number of rent-controlled apartments. But in 1985, New York State's highest court found that rent-stabilized family members had no such rights, since the law did not stipulate precisely what constituted a family and what rights family members enjoyed under the law. The state Department of Housing and Community Renewal set about updating its rent stabilization regulations, and in February 1988, Governor Cuomo introduced a bill stipulating that relatives by blood and marriage were eligible to inherit the apartments in which they had been living if the leaseholder were to die. Tenant organizations and gay and lesbian rights groups alike protested the proposal, noting that it made no provision for (as one organization wrote) "gay and lesbian couples, unmarried heterosexual couples, elderly people who live together to share expenses, and many other non-traditional family units." Democratic assemblyman Richard Gottfried and Senate minority leader Manfred Ohrenstein introduced a broader measure—the policy objective of those who had gathered on Everett Quinton's behalf.[42]

Relief, it turned out, would come not through legislation but from the courts. With support from the national American Civil Liberties Union's Lesbian and Gay Rights and AIDS Projects, another man who had lost his life partner to the AIDS epidemic, Miguel Braschi, brought suit against his landlord to prevent his eviction from the apartment on East 54th Street that he had shared with his partner, Leslie Blanchard. On July 6, 1989, in a historic 4–2 decision, the New York State Court of Appeals held that Braschi and Blanchard's partnership met the definition of a family under the terms of the rent control laws. Protection against eviction, Judge Vito J. Titone wrote for the majority, "should not rest on fictitious legal distinctions or genetic history, but instead should find its foundation in the reality of family life." The majority decision went on to lay out criteria by which the definition of *family* could be met: "exclusivity and longevity of the relationship, the level of emotional and financial commitment, the manner in which the parties have conducted their everyday lives and held themselves out to society, and the reliance placed upon one another for daily family services." Though the decision was confined to the specific case of a rent-controlled apartment, the ACLU lawyer who argued the case, William B. Rubenstein, declared that *Braschi v. Stahl Associates* "marks the most important single step forward in American law toward legal recognition of lesbian and gay relationships." By the end of the year, pushed hard by the ACLU and other LGBTQ+ advocates, the Department of Housing and Community Renewal had revised its regulations to afford the same protections to unmarried families in rent-stabilized apartments. Decades later Everett Quinton was still living in the Morton Street apartment he had shared with Charles Ludlam.[43]

IN THE SPRING OF 1984, Diane Ravitch, a well-known historian of education then based at Teachers College, Columbia University, found herself chatting in a conference room in Minneapolis with a fellow New Yorker. Mary Butz was the chair of social studies at Edward R.

Murrow High School in Midwood, Brooklyn, one of the new high schools of choice that the Board of Education had opened in the early 1970s. After a quick introduction, Butz surprised Ravitch by telling her that she taught at the best school in New York City. "I was startled," Ravitch later wrote, "because over the years, I have met so many embittered teachers in the New York City school system, people who recall an era . . . when New York City public schools were widely recognized as pioneers and when their students were pressing hard for future greatness as literati or scientists." She resolved to visit the school upon her return to New York.[44]

It was an opportune moment to visit a "good school." The previous year had marked the culmination of a long-simmering national panic about education standards, most famously with the publication of *A Nation at Risk: The Imperative for Educational Reform* by a group called the United States National Commission on Excellence in Education assembled by Ronald Reagan's secretary of education, Terrel Bell. The commission's report had pinned growing challenges to the nation's "preeminence in commerce, industry, science, and technological innovation" on a "rising tide of [educational] mediocrity," urging a "standards-based" approach to improving American public education. Progressive educators were highly critical. In the name of national economic competitiveness, Deborah Meier charged in the journal *Dissent*, conservative reformers were proposing "more tests, more homework, longer school hours, mandated state requirements, stiffer standards for promotion, stricter discipline codes." "Throwing clichés at old problems is even more popular these days than throwing money was once supposed to be," she lamented. ". . . The new litany of 'toughness' will produce neither excellence nor equality—and surely not both. It won't alter the connection between social class and school achievement, beat the Russians and Japanese, nor eliminate unemployment. And it certainly won't help beleaguered children or their teachers in their daily struggle with classroom realities."[45]

To Meier, Diane Ravitch represented the respectable intellectual face of the "get tough" turn. Several months after *A Nation at Risk* was released, Ravitch published an account of postwar education reform, *The Troubled Crusade: American Education, 1945–1980*. Though Ravitch resisted any connection between her historical analysis and contemporary policy debates—and though she took issue with efforts to characterize her own politics—influential educators and scholars on the left saw her work as providing a usable past for the standards-based movement. "She is a very dangerous person," the University of Pennsylvania historian Michael B. Katz wrote to Meier. And worth watching: "I don't think her career has peaked."[46]

Edward R. Murrow, opened in 1974, was what was known as an educational-option school, or "ed-op," a variety of public choice school meant to serve students with a range of academic abilities. Ed-ops were required to fill their classes with no more than 25 percent students who read above grade level and no less than 25 percent who read below, with the remaining half consisting of students who read at grade level. Murrow was extraordinarily sought after. In 1983, it received 9,500 applications for 800 seats, which allowed it to be highly selective about its admissions within the reading-level bands established by the Board of Education. Making up about half the student body, white students were significantly overrepresented at Murrow in proportion to their share in the public high school system citywide.

When Ravitch made the trip out to Midwood, she found a highly engaged group of students learning from enthusiastic and talented teachers. She was particularly struck by the active-learning model of education that Principal Saul Bruckner, a history teacher and twenty-seven-year veteran of the public school system, had installed throughout the school. "In no instance did I see a teacher droning on to a class of bored students," she noted. The environment of the school seemed a throwback to what some New Yorkers still remembered as the good old days. "The climate of the school," Mary Butz told Ravitch, "is middle-class Jewish. These kids all believe that education will help them get ahead, move up into college and good jobs."

Ravitch wrote about her experience in an essay for *The American Scholar* entitled "A Good School." In it, she noted the frequent critique that schools like Murrow "cream[ed] away" the best students from other public schools. She defended Murrow by noting that a quarter of its students came from private or parochial middle schools: Good public schools, she argued, could increase the number of strong students in the public school system. But in other ways, she made it clear that Murrow's excellence depended on its ability to attract resources within the school system and leverage its exclusiveness to evade the most difficult challenges in public education. Bruckner, she noted, "play[ed] the teacher-selection game like a Stradivarius," drawing an outsize share of the city's teaching talent. The school's vibrant culture stemmed in part from the fact that "its students have been persuaded that Murrow is a very special school and that they are very special students." And though it served students with a range of academic performance, it was not required to enroll "those who have a well-established record of truancy, destructive behavior, or criminal activity," who remained in the purview of the traditional public schools.[47]

The exclusive nature of public schools of choice had attracted intermittent protest in the 1970s. But as inequality deepened in the mid-1980s, growing tensions between selective schools like Murrow and traditional public schools reached a flashpoint. The policy issue in question was the process by which selective schools chose their students. But the stakes were far broader, forcing New Yorkers to face fundamental questions about the purposes of public education and the meanings of excellence, equity, and fairness.

Already by the mid-1980s, the landscape of choice public schools in New York was byzantine in its complexity. At the primary and intermediate school levels, there were school-based gifted-and-talented programs, officially overseen by the community boards and their superintendents but typically run at the school level—so local in character that the Board of Education had no idea how many such programs existed. In addition, there was an eclectic array of magnet schools and other schools of choice, such as Meier's Central Park East and the court-mandated Mark Twain Intermediate School in Coney Island.

High schools, run by the central Board of Education, essentially broke down into three categories. Traditional public schools were required to offer seats to all students within their catchment areas. "Screened" schools, and screened programs within traditional public high schools, used a variety of selection mechanisms to choose their students—from a single standardized test, as at Stuyvesant, Bronx Science, and Brooklyn Tech (whose admissions practices had been fixed by a 1971 state law) to schools that required a combination of transcripts, attendance records, portfolios of work, admissions interviews, and the likelihood of parental involvement. The third type were ed-op schools like Murrow that could use a variety of selection mechanisms to choose students from each of the 25-50-25 bands of reading scores—a provision intended to make them open to a wider range of students than the screened schools. Critics of the ed-ops accused them of acting much like screened schools anyway, taking the highest-achieving students within each of the achievement bands, weeding out applicants with spotty attendance and discipline records, using interviews to learn the race of the applicants, and taking attendance at open houses to favor applicants with highly involved parents; with far more applicants than seats—Murry Bergtraum High School in Manhattan received 23,341 applications for 850 spots in 1985; Norman Thomas High School received 23,595 for 900—the most desirable ed-ops could afford to be selective. To public school principals and advocates for traditional public schools, the screened schools and ed-ops were skimming their strongest students and most involved parents, creating what amounted to a two-tiered system: schools that were permitted "to select a privileged population," according to the principal of Seward Park High School, a large traditional public school on the Lower East Side, "and others . . . given the mission of educating those more poorly prepared and at higher risk."[48]

Because ed-ops were intended to be open to a wider range of students, they became a focal point for broader dissatisfaction about inequality in admissions procedures. Ed-op leaders and their supporters responded that their admissions practices were necessary to produce excellent public schools capable of attracting students who would otherwise enroll in private or parochial schools. "If you are going to set up a particular kind of school, you have to look for students who want to go there, who show that they will go to school every day and who show that they can do the work," said the principal of Murry Bergtraum High School for Business Careers, an ed-op in lower Manhattan. "Otherwise, you are setting yourself up for failure." "I have no quarrel with taking a broad cross-section of students," echoed the principal of John Dewey High School in Bensonhurst, Brooklyn, "but I do want students who have made Dewey their first choice, and who have gone to the time and trouble of investigating our program, not just some kid chosen randomly who made a check mark on an application and might have applied to 10 other schools." Principal Saul Bruckner of Murrow suggested that the procedures were necessary to keep white students in the system. Both Murrow and Dewey were about half white, he noted; "We work to keep that 50-50 balance within the guidelines set by the Board of Education."[49]

The success of the ed-ops, proponents of admissions reform argued, came at the expense of many of the city's children. "New York is a 'tale of two cities,'" Manhattan borough president David Dinkins wrote in a 1986 *New York Times* op-ed,

> and it should come as no surprise that each of these cities has its own school system. . . . One system receives more money per pupil, has more experienced staff, better equipped

> facilities, a more creative and challenging curriculum. . . . The other system is overcrowded, receives sometimes as much as 40 percent less money per pupil, and must take the majority of the city's students with special needs—the handicapped, academically low-achieving and those with limited English proficiency. . . . One system is touted for its achievement; the other meets all the criteria for failure.

Opponents of reform, Dinkins continued, "say, 'Don't change our schools; make the others better.' They fail to see the two systems are inextricably linked; each exists, in part, because of the other. The theme schools, educational options and other special programs flourish as oases for high achievers only because we have created neighborhood dumping grounds for students who are not."[50]

In 1986, spurred by a critical report issued by the nonprofit Advocates for Children and activism from a number of civil rights groups, schools chancellor Nathan Quiñones tasked a collection of education scholars with reviewing high school admissions processes with the objective of "increas[ing] access to programs and schools for all populations without reducing school effectiveness." The committee, chaired by Frank Smith of Columbia's Teachers College, suggested that the Board of Education adopt a general stance against screened programs and the consideration of place of residence in high school admissions, and prohibit the use of locally administered tests, interviews, and references to parental interest in admissions. Ed-op admissions came in for particular scrutiny, with the committee suggesting a moratorium on new ed-op schools so as to encourage "programs of choice within all schools" as well as the use of random selection in the admissions process in order to provide "bias free access." Quiñones and Bobby Wagner, now president of the Board of Education, shepherded the recommended policy changes through. Under these reforms, ed-op high schools and the one hundred or so specialized programs within traditional schools were required to admit half of their students on a random basis and were prohibited from employing "unfair screening devices" such as interviews and assessments of parental involvement. The board concurrently affirmed its concern for the city's most elite students, guaranteeing middle schoolers who scored in the top 2 percent on the reading tests a spot in their first-choice ed-op.[51]

Diane Ravitch was dismayed by the changes. To her, the ed-ops, magnets, and other selective schools represented bulwarks of excellence that affirmed the value of public education. By reforming admissions procedures, she argued, the Board of Education was "undermining quality education throughout the system and proclaiming its commitment to mediocrity." The new measures amounted to "20th century leveling, in a system that has already been leveled. . . . There are so few schools that have high standards. Now these schools will have huge numbers of unmotivated kids and the standards will drop." The Board of Education, she said, "should be multiplying good schools, not reducing them."[52]

As New Yorkers argued over the relationship between excellence and equity, the school choice movement gathered momentum nationally. Deborah Meier's work building small schools was recognized with a MacArthur "genius" award in 1988 (the cash award generated in part from the foundation's sale of a half-billion dollars' worth of New York real estate, slated by its purchaser for co-op conversion). And in 1989, Diane Ravitch—a lifelong Democrat—took a position as assistant secretary of education in the George H. W. Bush administration. Bush, more than Reagan, made school choice a centerpiece of his education program. "Further expansion of public school choice is a national imperative," he told a White House gathering, citing the East Harlem public schools as a case in point. By 1992, Bush was calling for a voucher program that would allow students to leave the public school system altogether. His assistant secretary of education took the lesson onboard. "The issue of choice had never been important to me," Ravitch later wrote, "but I found myself trying to incorporate the arguments for choice into my own worldview." She was hardly the only one: As the 1990s dawned, school choice, previously a patchwork approach, was becoming a national program for reform.[53]

EVER SINCE HIS SERIES of triumphs over Mario Cuomo in 1977, Ed Koch had been untouchable in city elections. In 1981, after easily defeating the labor-aligned Brooklyn assemblyman Frank Barbaro in the Democratic primary, he glided to victory with a staggering 74.6 percent of the vote. Four years later, having again defeated more progressive challengers in the primary, he carried 78 percent of the citywide vote, running above 80 percent in Brooklyn and the Bronx. Given the historically low turnout of the era, though, Koch's mandate was less secure than such numbers suggested. As 1989 began, he was suffering the traditional fate of third-term mayors in New York. Public opinion polls showed his approval ratings underwater, and his own private polls indicated that only about 17 percent wanted him to serve a fourth term. Koch's problems stemmed in part from an economic downturn: A Wall Street crash in the fall of 1987 had led to layoffs in the finance sector, which in turn constrained the city's finances. Koch was also plagued by a series of scandals that enveloped his close political allies and members of his administration and by the ongoing horror of the AIDS epidemic, which had claimed more than nineteen thousand lives in New York by 1989.[54]

Koch was vulnerable to a broad political mobilization against the growing inequalities of 1980s New York. Harold Washington's successful 1983 bid to unseat the Daley machine in Chicago had inspired New York's leading politicians of color to attempt their own unity ticket against Koch in 1985; that effort had failed spectacularly due to tensions between Black and Puerto Rican politicians as to who had a claim on leadership of a coalition of color. The Reverend

Jesse Jackson's 1988 bid for the Democratic presidential nomination revived the idea. Galvanizing support in both Black and Latino neighborhoods, Jackson managed to win a plurality of the New York primary vote in the five boroughs (though he lost statewide to Massachusetts governor Michael Dukakis). If the Jackson coalition could hold together in a Democratic mayoral primary, it stood a chance of ousting Koch. On primary night, Jackson's address to his supporters was peppered with cries from the audience of "Down with Koch!"[55]

The Jackson forces chose as their candidate to contest the Democratic mayoral primary Manhattan borough president David Dinkins, sixty-one years old and a longtime veteran of city government and Democratic politics. Raised primarily in Trenton, Dinkins had briefly served in the U.S. Marine Corps before graduating from Howard University and earning his law degree from Brooklyn Law. Seeking to build his law practice, he became active in Harlem's Raymond Carver Democratic Club, where his wife, Joyce, was the daughter of a prominent member (and former state assemblyman). Dinkins joined a remarkable cohort of Black politicians in the city—Basil Paterson, Charles Rangel, and the slightly older Percy Sutton, who became an important mentor—and under the watchful eye of Harlem Democratic leader J. Raymond Jones began to rise through the political ranks. He served in the State Assembly, then as city clerk before winning, on his third try, election as borough president of Manhattan, a position that then held considerable power in city politics.[56]

Dinkins was in many respect the junior member of Harlem's "Gang of Four"; he told a journalist during the 1989 campaign that he was surprised it was he, not the pioneering Sutton, the formidable Rangel, or the brilliant Paterson, who was poised to become the city's first Black mayor. Nor did he cut a figure in the La Guardia–Koch tradition of New York City mayors who seemed to be everywhere and unavoidable. "There are undeniable stimuli to ennui in

[Dinkins's] presence," one of his most steadfast admirers, the venerable columnist Murray Kempton, wrote. Courtly and dignified if sometimes cold, Dinkins could strike observers as too measured, too deliberate, too slow to act decisively, particularly in comparison to Koch.[57]

In 1989, though, what critics called deliberation struck some knowledgeable observers as a preference for building consensus, and no one doubted his ability to put smart people to work on the major problems facing the city—the Manhattan borough president's office had been a hotbed of policy thinking in the second half of the 1980s. Dinkins, United Federation of Teachers president Sandra Feldman wrote, was a "decent, fair-minded, liberal democrat [*sic*] with an ability to get people working together." He was "not charismatic—but his office [is] efficient" and his "staff [is] extremely competent (more so than at City Hall)." His campaign released a number of detailed policy proposals aimed at the major issues of the day: city rental subsidies, expanded efforts to provide housing for the homeless, and a "New York City Housing Foundation" to tackle the housing crisis; a school-based planning model, expanded "choice" schools, and additional resources for traditional public schools; and an expansion of the city's community policing pilot programs (discussed in the following chapter) in order to double the NYPD's patrol strength and address the crime and quality-of-life problems facing the city's neighborhoods.[58]

Dinkins stood astride two political eras. He was in some respects a throwback. At a time when the party organizations had withered and well-funded, candidate-centered media campaigns had become the norm, Dinkins remained a product of the Harlem Democratic establishment. In an era in which the mayoralty had become associated with bold personalities, Dinkins's soft-spoken and deliberate style recalled Robert F. Wagner's mid-century mayoralty. At the same time, Dinkins owed his political strength to emerging forces in city politics, particularly the rising Black and Latino electorates and labor unions representing municipal and care-industry workers, which had in some ways taken over from the old industrial unions at the heart of the city's labor movement. Though Dinkins was temperamentally liberal, not radical, his politics were far enough to the left that he had been a member of the Democratic Socialists of America, and his candidacy marked the potential coalescence of a new groundswell of grassroots progressivism. Dinkins's campaign mastermind, Bill Lynch, built a labor-based operation, winning the endorsements of DC 37, the union representing municipal workers, the service workers' union SEIU, the Teamsters, and the United Federation of Teachers (the latter despite significant pushback from members who viewed Dinkins as too close to Jackson). He ran the campaign out of the offices of 1199, the health care workers union, whose members, mostly Black and Latina women, helped power the campaign's ground game. With the backing of a broad coalition, Dinkins won a comfortable primary victory—51 percent to Koch's 42 percent, with Richard Ravitch and City Comptroller Harrison Goldin a distant third and fourth.[59]

Dinkins's adversary in the general election was the former U.S. attorney for the Southern District of New York, Rudolph Giuliani. The grandson of Italian immigrants, Giuliani was born in Brooklyn, where his father tended bar in East Flatbush and served as a collector for the owner's mob-connected loan-sharking business. The family soon moved to Long Island, but Giuliani returned to the city for his education, attending Bishop Laughlin Memorial High School in Brooklyn, then Manhattan College in the Bronx, and finally NYU Law. Serious and hardworking, the young Giuliani was an ardent and idealistic Democrat—he revered Bobby Kennedy, supported George McGovern in 1972, and his friend Peter King remembered, sympathized "openly and passionately" with Black nationalists. In the mid-1970s, though, he began a political metamorphosis; a month after Ronald Reagan's 1980 election, he registered as a Republican, just in time to win an appointment as associate deputy attorney general. Taking over as U.S. attorney for the Southern District of New York in 1983, he had become a media sensation through his highly publicized campaigns against insider trading, mafia racketeering, and drug trafficking. His admirers saw him as daring, righteous, hardworking, and as policymakers got to know him, capable, not unlike Koch, of taking onboard loads of information.[60]

Though his prosecutions made him a familiar figure in city life, Giuliani's politics remained somewhat opaque. His service in the Reagan administration seemed possibly to have been a marriage of convenience rather than a matter of philosophical conviction. "He only became a Republican after he began to get all those jobs from them," his mother Helen remarked in an unpublished interview. "He's definitely not a conservative Republican. He thinks he is, but he isn't." To many of those who came to know him through city politics, this kind of political opportunism was, as the journalist Jack Newfield later wrote, "the most consistent thread running through Giuliani's career." Giuliani, said Senator Alfonse D'Amato, an on-again-off-again rival within the New York GOP, "will move to whatever drummer gives him the best beat. . . . There is no core philosophical underpinning to him."

Yet for all his flexibility, Giuliani emerged from a particular milieu, an outer-borough, white-ethnic world that emphasized respect for authority and an ethic of personal responsibility, one that lamented the permissiveness and lawlessness that many outer-borough white New Yorkers associated with the neighborhood transitions of the 1960s and '70s—a kind of popular, experiential counterpart to the ideas circulating among neoconservative intellectuals. This outlook fit naturally with Giuliani's belief in his own personal rectitude, on the one hand, and his sense of grievance, on the other. ("He's got to get back at the world," the pioneering police strategist Jack Maple remarked to colleagues in the NYPD.) Giuliani's "world view," the journalist Elizabeth Kolbert would later write, "allows for just two types of people: those who are for him and those who are either misguided, blind, or simply corrupt." To his critics, Giuliani's toughness was (Kolbert again) "an elaborate rationalization for a reflexive bellicosity," a fetishization of what amounted at the end of the day to simple meanness. As time went on, it would become clear that what his admirers saw as toughness and righteousness could also manifest as a self-destructive streak.[61]

In general, Giuliani did not take well to those who questioned what he saw as legitimate authority—especially his own. It would take some time to become unmistakably clear, but there were hints from his time as U.S. attorney onward that he reacted particularly strongly when those doing the questioning were Black. By the 1990s, Giuliani would refuse to meet with Black activists and even moderate Black elected officials. One of those officials, Manhattan borough president Virginia Fields, who had gone out of her way not to accuse Giuliani of personal racism while he was in office, later stated plainly what she had observed over years of working in city government. "I don't like to define people this way, typically," she told a reporter for *Vanity Fair*. "But [Giuliani] was just an absolute, out-of-control racist."[62]

In the mid-1980s, much of this was still in the future. Beginning in November 1986, when he won a conviction of the Bronx Democratic boss Stanley Friedman, Giuliani was openly flirting with a campaign for elected office. "He's articulate, good-looking, probably he's got a good mind," Nelson Rockefeller's former press secretary remarked. "There's no doubt—Republicans are talking about him." The office of Daniel Patrick Moynihan, who was up for reelection to the U.S. Senate in 1988, opened an opposition file on him. Cindy Adams speculated on his future in her *New York Post* gossip column. Giuliani reportedly reached out to Donald Trump to chair his finance committee in a potential campaign against Moynihan. "I hold Rudy in very high esteem and I would be very helpful to Rudy," Trump told reporters. When polls pointed to an easy Moynihan win, and with

Mario Cuomo presumed a strong incumbent in the 1990 gubernatorial election, Giuliani turned his eye to the mayoralty instead. Trump served as co-chair of his first fundraiser.[63]

Expecting to run against Koch, Giuliani positioned himself as a liberal Republican in the John Lindsay mode. He issued a notably progressive plan to address homelessness, and he sounded out Bill Lynch, perhaps the city's preeminent Black political strategist, about joining his team—an offer Lynch might well have accepted had Dinkins declined to run. But Dinkins's triumph in the Democratic primary changed the calculus. Giuliani's path to victory now went through the predominantly white neighborhoods of Queens, Brooklyn, and Staten Island. As the campaign wound on, he found himself happy to remind white voters of Dinkins's race, referring to him as a "Jesse Jackson Democrat" and predicting that he would be "the trusted servant of Jesse in City Hall."[64]

In the end, Dinkins won by the slimmest margin since 1905, carrying 50.4 percent of the vote to Giuliani's 47.8 percent. Giuliani ran even with Dinkins in affluent white neighborhoods and ran up large margins in the typically Democratic, predominantly Catholic and Jewish neighborhoods of Astoria, Whitestone, Bayside, and Forest Hills in Queens, and of Bensonhurst, Brighton Beach, and Canarsie in Brooklyn. As the political scientist John Mollenkopf would later note, the realignment of New York's mayoral politics that began in 1989 contained echoes of the movement of white southerners out of the Democratic Party and into the GOP in the wake of the civil rights revolution. Though Dinkins had narrowly triumphed with a multiracial, cross-class coalition, the racial divisions that had shaped the city during the Koch years had become the primary fault line in electoral politics.[65]

AS THE DECADE DREW TO A CLOSE, New York's egalitarian tradition appeared resurgent. Governor Mario Cuomo had established himself as the national torchbearer of New Deal liberalism in Reagan's America. A coalition of organized labor and Black, Latino, and progressive white New Yorkers had elected the city's first Black mayor. New York's liberals appeared to have come in from the wilderness, ready to challenge head on the inequalities of the post-fiscal-crisis city.

The future of the Democratic Party post-Koch, it was true, remained uncertain. The 1989 primary marked a clear repudiation of Koch, whose political career was effectively over, though he remained a civic presence until his death in 2013, a ready source of opinion on everything from politics and policy to movies. But the fragile, newly forged alliance between Black and Latino New Yorkers remained untested beyond the Jackson and anti-Koch campaigns. More broadly, electoral politics in the city was caught up in a major demographic transition. White New Yorkers had become a minority of the population sometime in the 1980s. But the electorate was still majority white. "You can see the anxiety among the new minority in New York City about this," Angelo Falcón, the president of the Institute for Puerto Rican Policy, said at a postelection roundtable. In that context, would Dinkins have the authority—and the ability—to lead the Democratic Party in New York? Or would he run into the established wing of the party represented by Cuomo, Koch, and Moynihan?[66]

The challenges facing the Dinkins administration would be staggering. The city had barely recovered its fiscal footing after a stock market crash in October 1987 cut into its tax revenues when, several months into Dinkins's mayoralty, the national economy slipped into recession as a consequence of tightening monetary policy. The recession of the early 1990s would cause New York extraordinary pain, equal in scale, if not in duration, to the long recession of the 1970s. The city's unemployment rate, down to 4.5 percent on the eve of the 1987 crash, soared to above 10 percent, spiking to 13.4 percent in January 1993—the worst since the Great Depression. In all, the city would lose some 400,000 jobs over the course of Dinkins's mayoralty. Amid acute fiscal pressures, Dinkins would struggle to make good on his campaign promises while assuaging those who saw New York's first Black mayor as a threat to the city's finances. Meanwhile his pleas for federal assistance—for a new New Deal—fell on deaf ears in the Bush administration. Even more so than in the 1970s, New York City was on its own.[67]

To make matters worse, the city was suffering a torrent of violence and property crime that surpassed the worst years of the 1970s. After declining through most of the early 1980s, crime rates rose across the major categories in the latter part of the decade, driven in large measure by the exploding crack epidemic and the drug trade that catered to it—a nationwide urban phenomenon. Robberies and burglaries had started to come down toward the end of Koch's third term, but they remained frequent—the "no radio" signs New Yorkers left in their automobiles became emblematic of the age. Homicides soared. Dinkins's first year in office would be the bloodiest in the city's modern history: 2,245 people would be murdered. The violence struck many New Yorkers as unprecedentedly random, feeding into a sense of fear over and above the actual risks of daily life in the city, with horrific instances of senseless violence making news across the nation.[68]

Though harder to quantify, the civic temper was unmistakably one of anger, frustration, cruelty—crosscut by a raw ethnic and racial animus. White rage was evident in the high-profile killings of Black New Yorkers by white New Yorkers in Bensonhurst, Brooklyn, and Howard Beach, Queens, and in the furious response to the heinous 1989 assault on a jogger in Central Park. "I want to hate," Donald Trump proclaimed in a full-page ad in the city's leading newspapers calling for New York State to restore the death penalty in the wake of the Central Park case. (The five Black and Latino teenagers imprisoned for the crime later had their convictions overturned.) For their part, predominantly Black neighborhoods were rubbed raw by the combination of poverty, discrimination, police abuse, abandonment, and the effects of the crack epidemic. A new generation of young people emerged into a world with money everywhere but few legitimate opportunities—a world of dreams and plans which failed, in which the moral philosophy of the dollar shrank and constrained the possibilities of human dignity. This context would contribute to high-profile conflicts that marked Dinkins's mayoralty, between Black communities and Korean greengrocers, on the one hand, and between the Black and the Haredi Jewish residents of Crown Heights, Brooklyn, on the other.[69]

FOR PROGRESSIVES, the timing was cruel: Just as a coalition that was focused on the needs of poor and working-class New Yorkers came to power, questions of survival returned to the center of New York politics. And as Dinkins moved into City Hall, his political opponents gathered their forces. The neoconservatives who had authored *New York Unbound* gained little traction in the 1989 campaign. But the Manhattan Institute continued its pivot to city issues, launching a new quarterly, *NY: The City Journal* (later *City Journal*) in the fall of 1990. The inaugural issue's leadoff editorial returned to Koch's emphasis on quality of life, vowing to "mak[e] the city livable once again" by offering "fundamental reforms, not simply ways of coping." And in the background stood Giuliani, fuming, with little solid evidence, that the election had been stolen from him by illegal votes in Brooklyn and Washington Heights, plotting his political revenge.[70]

4

Gorgeous Mosaic

David Dinkins took office in January 1990 amid a bewildering climate of hope and fear. "Ours will be a . . . democracy that appeals to what is best in us and strives to bring us together," he pledged in his inaugural address. "I see New York as a gorgeous mosaic of race and religious faith, of national origin and sexual orientation, of individuals whose families arrived yesterday and generations ago, coming through Ellis Island or Kennedy Airport or on busses bound for the Port Authority."

Dinkins's "gorgeous mosaic" was to be a world city that was also a people's city. He listed his policy objectives: job training, affordable housing, better access to health care, equality for women, and a more humane approach to the AIDS epidemic. Then came a line that generated as much applause as his soaring invocations of democratic revitalization: "Most of all, we must reaffirm the rule of law and fight back against the pushers and muggers and take back our streets and subways and our parks."[1]

This tension between the progressive aspiration to mend the city's inequalities and the immediate imperative of reclaiming the streets from crime and disorder was to characterize New York's liberal moment. Out of both conviction and perceived necessity, Mario Cuomo and David Dinkins would preside over key moments of reform: Cuomo would sign off on high-rent deregulation; the New York City Board of Education would make school choice its official policy; and Dinkins would expand the NYPD and formalize the problem-oriented policing approach that had developed under Koch. They did so for many different reasons. If initiatives like public school choice had genuine progressive roots, high-rent deregulation, though it had liberal antecedents, was primarily a response to actions taken by conservatives. Some initiatives, including high-rent deregulation as well as the Board of Education's partnership with private philanthropy to open new small schools, reflected the need to draw in additional resources in light of recession-driven budget constraints. The expansion of the NYPD and the rise of community policing reflected the pressures of a soaring crime rate and long-standing concerns about neighborhood stability.

As Dinkins and Cuomo, uneasy allies at best, labored to govern a city on the edge, their Republican rivals gathered forces. Giuliani would soon return to the political scene, this time in partnership with the neoconservative reformers at the Manhattan Institute and in tandem with the state's strongest Republican organizations. Senator Alfonse D'Amato, the leading power in the New York GOP, would not only mend fences with Giuliani but also train his sights on Albany. Even as neoconservatives and liberals were finding common ground in new approaches to governing, New York State's politics was cleaving along lines of class, race, geography, and ideology as at no time since the 1920s—setting the stage for a fundamental battle for power in the city.

SINCE THE TITANIC STRUGGLES of the 1970s, opponents of rent regulation had made little concrete progress. Tenant groups had come up short in their efforts to strengthen rent regulations in the early 1980s, and they had not exactly been thrilled with the year-on-year hikes sanctioned by the Rent Guidelines Board. Still, opponents of regulation had made no progress in rolling the programs back. In the 1990s, though, several factors aligned to allow proponents of deregulation their first substantial victories in more than two decades.

One crucial factor was changing conditions in the New York housing market. In the wake of the 1987 Wall Street crash, the rental market had entered a prolonged slump: For the first time since the 1930s, rents had fallen across the city. As a consequence, only in Manhattan south of 110th Street were regulated rents substantially lower than market rents. This development threatened to undermine political support for the pro-regulation coalition in several ways. Politicians from outside Manhattan might not be as adamant in defense of a program that was not immediately relevant to their constituents. And younger, affluent Manhattanites might reasonably perceive themselves as victims of a framework that favored long-standing tenants: The *New York Times* editorial board now spoke of an "unregulated silent majority" suffering at the hands of a regulated elite.[2]

These shifting market conditions allowed opponents of regulation to depict the rent laws, not as means of ensuring fair rents across the city but as subsidies for people who did not need the help. "Widows and welfare moms will be trotted out for the television cameras," the young journalist Malcolm Gladwell wrote in a *New York* magazine cover story. ". . . Don't be fooled. . . . Rent regulation is not about fairness or protecting the poor. It is a system where people with really great deals on their apartments protect the interests of other people with really great deals on their apartments." Regulation, Gladwell argued, was at the root of New York's perennial shortage of apartments: Too many New Yorkers were "hang[ing] on to their cheap apartments in the city and spend[ing] their extra money on summer houses in the Hamptons." Deregulation would create a more fluid and equitable market, bringing overall rent levels down and creating a more even playing field among renters. Gladwell recognized the hardships that would come from deregulation, particularly the displacement of older tenants from their homes, communities, and social networks. But "there is nothing intolerably mean about asking a 70-year-old widow to move into something smaller and cheaper. That's what old folks do everywhere else in the country."[3]

Analyses like Gladwell's, focused on the dwindling number of rent-controlled tenants in a handful of Manhattan neighborhoods, bore little resemblance to the rent-regulated population across the city. As a consequence, they distorted both the class and racial politics of deregulation. The argument that deregulation would affect primarily wealthy, white people overlooked the vast majority of rent-regulated tenants, who remained working class or poor. Ninety percent of rent-regulated households earned less than $60,000 a year, with 77 percent making less than $40,000 and 49 percent making less than $20,000. More than half of regulated tenants were people of color. And though critics of rent regulation argued that the programs operated on the principle of "first come, best served" at the expense of newly arrived tenants, the age distribution of regulated renters was not much different from the unregulated market—rent-controlled tenants were older by definition, but the median rent-stabilized tenant was five years younger than the market as a whole—and 60 percent had been in their apartments for less than ten years. Amid the recession of the early 1990s, these tenants were not seeing huge benefits in their rents from regulation. But the system did afford them the security of knowing that they were protected if market conditions suddenly changed—as the gentrification of the 1980s had shown was entirely possible.[4]

Even so, the fact that most of the immediate windfall of rent regulation was going to the affluent afforded deregulation proponents a means of wedging the door open in a way that the long-standing arguments for deregulation—particularly the claim that it would encourage new construction—had failed to do. By pushing for "luxury decontrol"—deregulation of apartments renting above a certain threshold or whose tenants earned above a certain income—they could get around the fact that the program enjoyed a broad, numerous constituency. The approach also offered a way of splitting the pro-regulation coalition: Politicians from outside Manhattan who would fight to the end to protect regulation as a general proposition might be willing to countenance luxury deregulation as a matter of equity.[5]

These kinds of arguments gained particular force as the city struggled through the worst fiscal straits since the 1970s. In that context, bringing valuable real estate to market rate offered a potential source of badly needed property tax revenue—and hence a way of sustaining public services. The Citizens Budget Commission and the *Times* editorial board made this argument, claiming that the city could produce $100 million in additional tax revenue each year by "tap[ping] the treasure in rent control." The president of the Rent Stabilization Association, the leading organization of residential landlords, noted almost gleefully that outer borough representatives would be "faced with the choice between closing a library or closing a pool and deregulating luxury apartments."[6]

Sensing opportunity, the landlord organizations stepped up their lobbying efforts. In 1992, the RSA created its own political action committee in order to extend its lobbying capacity. And in advance of the 1993 legislative session in Albany, campaign donors from the landlord organizations made it clear to leading Republican legislators that they expected significant reform. The Republican majority in the Senate, led by Ralph Marino, a soft-spoken Rockefeller Republican from Oyster Bay, pushed for a bill that would deregulate the apartments of people who made more than $100,000 a year and paid more than $2,000 per month in rent. Governor Cuomo pushed back. "The judgment of 50 years of Democrats and Republicans is that this system is better than the alternative," he said in a public statement. "When you try to get the occasional movie actress who has a rent-controlled apartment, you endanger two million middle-class people." Behind the scenes, though, the governor seemed willing to find an accommodation. Unable to reach a deal, the legislature extended the clock, passing an eight-day extension of the current laws—then another, followed by a one-day extension, then a three-day extension. Finally, Cuomo agreed to a four-year extension that upon vacancy would deregulate apartments renting above $2,000 as of October 1, 1993, and upon expiration of the current lease apartments renting for the same amount whose occupants earned more than $250,000 a year. The thresholds were high enough that only a tiny sliver of renters, nearly all of them in Manhattan, were affected. Still, after two decades in the wilderness, rent deregulation had returned to New York City.[7]

GIVEN DEBORAH MEIER'S DIM VIEW of the Reagan administration's approach to education reform, it may have seemed unlikely that, in the spring of 1987, District 4 superintendent Carlos Medina and deputy superintendent Seymour Fliegel—key figures in the rise of East Harlem's system of public school choice—should find themselves guests of honor at the White House. The administration was releasing a new handbook, *Schools That Work: Educating Disadvantaged Children*, that pushed the idea of school choice as a way of affording equal opportunity to low-income families; the publication singled out District 4 as an example of how the approach could work. The White House ceremony was but one event in a sequence by which District 4's program of alternative schools and public school choice rose to national prominence, in large measure because conservatives and centrist Democrats embraced it. Secretary of Education William Bennett repeatedly praised the program. British prime minister Margaret Thatcher sent both her minister of education and her chief domestic policy adviser to study it. David Osborne and Ted

Gaebler featured it in their 1992 book *Reinventing Government: How the Entrepreneurial Spirit Is Transforming the Public Sector*, which Bill Clinton described as a "blueprint" for a new liberalism.[8]

Beneath the surface, there were real differences in how leftists, liberals, and conservatives understood the purpose of education and the meaning of choice. Meier and those who shared her perspective believed the purpose of choice was to give disadvantaged students access to schools that would nurture their intellectual curiosity in an enriching, student-centered environment—the kinds of schools children from well-to-do families could already attend. It was the creation of new, progressive, small schools that really promised to improve American public education; choice was primarily a mechanism to allow all students to attend good schools. Conservatives and center-left liberals tended to place more emphasis on preparing young people for the modern labor market, equipping disadvantaged children with the skills it would take to attain upward mobility in an increasingly unequal economy, and ensuring that the nation had the human resources to avoid falling behind in an ever more competitive world. They viewed choice as an instrument for meeting these goals by subjecting public schools to the disciplining effects of market competition: Schools that did not produce good test scores, strong graduation rates, and other markers of success would lose out to those that did.[9]

Even so, in the early 1990s, the small-schools-and-choice approach appeared capable of transcending traditional partisan and ideological differences, scrambling the usual lines of confrontation and bringing progressives, liberals, and conservatives together behind a shared program. Meier, a democratic socialist, found herself lauded by the Manhattan Institute and applauded as a champion of a new liberalism by the writer Jim Sleeper, who praised her in a personal note for striking the right balance, "*idiomatically and intellectually*, between 'left' and 'right,' those outmoded terms," and for "making a little liberal self-criticism palatable." Yet the new politics of school reform did not so much transcend political contestation as shift its axis. As the mix of small schools and public school choice became a major cause of big philanthropy in the 1990s, an old question—who should govern the city's schools?—returned to the foreground.[10]

For her part, Deborah Meier still saw choice as an essential part of her project to unlock the democratic potential of neighborhood public schools. "The higher the student body's socioeconomic status, the meatier the curriculum, the more open-ended the discussion, the less rote and rigid the pedagogy, the more respectful the tone, the more rigorous the expectations, the greater the staff autonomy," she wrote in a 1991 cover story for *The Nation*. "Changing this is what education reform is about." She acknowledged the libertarian and segregationist lineages of school choice and the risk that choice might offer an opening wedge for privatization. Still, she urged progressives to view the argument over choice as an opportunity to define "a different image of what 'public' could mean."[11]

Meier's educational philosophy remained much what it had been when she launched Central Park East in the mid-1970s. To be successful, schools had to be teacher- and student-centered. The more burdens that directed time, energy, and resources away from the classroom, the less opportunity teachers had to get to know how their students' minds worked and what they needed to master the classroom material. Small schools were best. "Teachers, kids and families who do not share a common geographic, ideological, or historical community, need optimum face-to-face contact over many years to build a strong school-based community with a coherent common set of understandings," she wrote. Small schools also "made democratic governance systems feasible" and provided an "assault on the culture of anonymity that permeates our youngsters' lives. Our children need stable personal relationships more than ever." The fundamental goal remained, as Meier wrote, "that all our children . . . be educated to become the kind of thoughtful citizens a strong democracy needs"; schools, she felt, should be "communit[ies] where kids could see the complexity of democracy, and fall in love with it." Using her MacArthur grant, Meier established the Center for Collaborative Education, which would be instrumental in helping the small-school and school choice movement scale up in New York.[12]

As the historian Daniel Rodgers has noted, national-level conservatives tended to come to the concept of school choice later than Great Society liberals and community control advocates—oddly, given the right's growing affinity for free market economics in the 1970s and early '80s. But as Medina and Fliegel's visit to the White House testified, by the second half of the 1980s, conservatives, too, had embraced choice. At the national level, the George H. W. Bush administration made school vouchers one of its central domestic policy objectives. In New York, neoconservative reformers set about building right-leaning equivalents of Meier's CCE. The Manhattan Institute established a Center for Educational Innovation, staffing it with District Four veterans—Fliegel, Carlos Medina, and Colman Genn, among others. The CEI, which took up a full quarter of the Manhattan Institute's budget, produced a stream of reports touting the promise of school choice. It also helped forge the partnerships with corporations and nonprofit organizations that would allow alternative schools to proliferate in the early 1990s. CEI, for instance, brought together the leadership of District 3, which covered the Upper West Side and parts of Harlem, with the CEO of Colgate-Palmolive and the chairman of the Partnership for New York's education committee. With Colgate's support, District 3 was able to convert the old Wadleigh High School complex on West 114th Street into three specialized schools: the School of Writing and Publishing, the School of Science and Technology, and the Wadleigh Alternative Arts Middle School. At the same time, CEI worked closely with the Industrial Areas Foundation, the community organizing network founded by Saul Alinsky, to fight for better schools in East Brooklyn using the models of choice and community control pioneered in upper Manhattan in the 1960s and '70s.[13]

Although there remained real divisions between leftists, liberals, and conservatives—above all on the issue of vouchers, which liberals rejected as a threat to privatize public education and blur the line between church and state—liberals and conservatives came together on a number of major initiatives in the area of school choice in the late 1980s. The publication of John Chubb and Terry Moe's book, *Politics, Markets, and America's Schools*, which was supported by the liberal-leaning Brookings Institute and adapted for broader consumption in *City Journal*, the Manhattan Institute's quarterly, was an especially prominent intellectual event. For Chubb and Moe, both political scientists, what made the difference between effective and ineffective schools lay not in commonly cited indices of inequality— differences in "expenditures, teacher salaries, class size, graduation and promotion requirements, [and] teacher credentials"—but rather in "intangible and organizational factors" such as strong school-level leadership, clear goals, and above all autonomy. Organizational reforms, they suggested, could obviate the need to equalize resources; the task of education reform was to encourage strong leadership and autonomy. The only way to ensure autonomy was to make schools "accountable from the bottom up, to parents, rather than from the top down, to bureaucrats." The only alternative to bureaucracy, they wrote, was choice.[14]

In the mid-1990s, two leading scholars, Diane Ravitch, who had become a fellow at the Hoover Institution after leaving George H. W. Bush's Department of Education, and Joseph Viteritti, a progressive urban policy expert and John Lindsay administration alum, convened the Working Group on School Organization and Educational Quality at New York University. Their goal, they said, was to introduce "an influential audience of New Yorkers to exciting ideas" percolating within the world of education reform;

the meetings enjoyed financial support from both the free market Olin Foundation and the Democratic Leadership Council of New York, the local chapter of the organization that had helped craft Bill Clinton's policy agenda. To Ravitch and Viteritti, the traditional public school system was akin to a Taylorist production line. But a "factory-style model of schooling" characterized by large bureaucratic institutions could no longer meet the increasingly complex needs of America's children. They called instead for a "public school system that values performance, flexibility, innovation, and responsiveness." Small schools appeared to be a particularly promising vehicle for this kind of reform: In the early to-mid-1990s, research emerged showing that they offered some distinct advantages over traditional public schools. They were more personalized, they had a more defined sense of purpose, and they were more likely to produce high student achievement. Ravitch and Viteritti called for the city to create new small schools and to give families the chance to choose between them.[15]

Into this intellectual ferment strode a new schools chancellor, Joseph Fernández, a Harlem native and Columbia graduate whom Bobby Wagner had plucked from the Miami school system in 1990. Wagner himself, though not heavily involved in the small-schools-and-choice movement, had taken some steps toward school choice, issuing a plan in 1988 that envisioned permitting students to attend any neighborhood high school within their home borough. Now Fernández made a version of public school choice the city's official policy. Students had long transferred across primary school zoning boundaries and even district lines in New York. But before the early 1990s, they could do so only if there was space available at the school they wished to attend, and if administrators in both their own district and the district in which they planned to attend school were willing to sign a waiver. Public school choice thus operated in a gray zone, unregulated by the central Board of Education. The system worked best for those who could convince a school to take them and whose home districts had in-demand schools—officials in districts with declining enrollments were less likely to permit their students to leave. Which is to say, the system worked best for affluent families and for schools that had their choice of the strongest students in the city. A majority of students at P.S. 6 on the Upper East Side, long considered one of the city's best schools, came from outside the catchment area. In 1993, Fernández lifted the requirement that students receive permission from their home district, allowing students to transfer freely to any school that would take them.[16]

Aware of the new research, Fernández also planned to open a number of new small high schools—and as he was planning to do so, the philanthropist Walter Annenberg announced a national grant competition to support the creation of innovative new small schools. A coalition of the city's school reform organizations—Meier's Center for Collaborative Education, the Manhattan Institute's Center for Educational Innovation, and the Fund for New York City Public Education—came together with the community-organization group ACORN to create a new organization, New York Networks for School Renewal, which vetted proposals for new schools and provided fundraising and logistical support. The coalition secured $50 million from the Annenberg challenge, and the city provided some $150 million in additional funding for the development of new schools; by 1998, it had opened more than one hundred. Some small schools succeeded in their first years but did not reach escape velocity and gradually lost the advantages they had enjoyed when they launched: Founders left to start new projects; nonprofits and philanthropists shifted their money elsewhere. Others, like the Neighborhood School, the Earth School, the Children's Workshop School in the East Village, and Beacon High School on Manhattan's West Side, quickly became popular, in some instances attracting far more applicants than they could accommodate.[17]

If the Annenberg challenge marked a breakthrough for the

coalition of reformers that ran the spectrum from Meier to the Manhattan Institute, other longtime champions of reform felt themselves marginalized by the entry of big philanthropy. The New York City Coalition for Excellence in Black Education, a pioneering organization that dated back to the heyday of the Black Power movement, found itself calling for a picket of Meier's Central Park East Secondary School in an effort to get the leading reformers to listen to its demands for more meaningful involvement by people of color and community organizations in the Annenberg grant. "Can it be possible that a group of people who profess to be democratic, transformative educators [are] preventing a legitimate space in a public process to parents and people of color?" wrote Diana Caballero, director of the Puerto Rican/Latino Educational Roundtable and a member of the CCE's advisory board. "The Network cannot talk about democratic education for others if it does not practice inclusion as a policy and a living principle for itself," she wrote in a letter to the CCE's director, accusing the reform movement of adopting a "missionary mentality toward communities of color."[18]

While new alternative schools were opening, the public school choice approach made inroads in other ways. At the district level, principals and superintendents continued to expand gifted-and-talented programs. While alternative schools made efforts—often inadequate—to serve diverse student populations, G-&-T programs catered with little pretense to white, affluent families. White parents in diverse neighborhoods were not enrolling their children in neighborhood schools with predominantly Black and Latino populations, but perhaps they could be convinced to enroll their children in specialized programs located within those larger schools. G-&-T programs were especially important to parents in neighborhoods in transition, where affluent brownstoners lived side by side with the residents of public housing complexes and rent-regulated tenements. They were particularly prominent on the Upper West Side, where they formed one of the primary fault lines in district politics: Seven new programs sprang up in the course of the 1980s, ferociously defended by the populations they served.[19]

The challenge of reforming the public schools had brought together some unlikely collaborators in the early to mid-1990s. For a moment, these reformers worked together despite major differences in how they viewed the purposes of education and of choice, and the question of who should have control over the schools. Their efforts created new educational models and led to important policy shifts in New York; they also introduced an important new actor, private philanthropy. But the reform consensus was not a stable one. As the Center for Collaborative Education's clash with the Coalition for Excellence in Black Education illustrated, it rested on certain assumptions about who would control public education, assumptions that implicated a much bigger set of issues about race and power in the city. And even among leading reformers, those major differences over values, choice, and control remained—and could not be papered over for long.

AS THE RESPONSE TO HIS inaugural address had foretold, policing and public safety came to dominate Dinkins's mayoralty. By the summer of 1990, New Yorkers from every corner of the city were disgusted with the violence wrought by disinvestment, the proliferation of handguns, and the drug wars. "A great wave of fear and anger has swept over the city," Mario Cuomo remarked. "Either we respond to it—adequately—or we admit to the most fundamental failure—as a government and as a city."[20]

Though Dinkins's policing reforms played out in an emergency context, here, too, the transpartisan spirit of reinvention evident in the school reform movement underpinned reform efforts. A new breed of police leaders had begun to emerge in America's big cities: Highly educated, professionally trained, media savvy, and connected to the latest in academic research through workshops and forums. In New York, they used new organizational and managerial techniques to formalize Koch-era efforts to "reclaim" public spaces. But they found it was not so easy to align their grand strategies with the way the city's police departments actually worked—nor with the whims and desires of the city's largest population of street-level bureaucrats, its police officers. And for his part, Dinkins, too, encountered rank-and-file resistance to his efforts to bolster police accountability.

Dinkins's choice of police commissioner, Lee P. Brown, embodied the new style of police chief. The son of Oklahoma sharecroppers, he earned a master's degree in sociology and a doctorate in criminology before joining the faculty of Howard University. After two years, he moved into police administration, serving as public safety commissioner in Atlanta and then Houston. Particularly during his Houston years, he became part of a national network of law enforcement officials and academics who met to share new approaches to policing and new theories of organizational management in groups such as the Police Executive Research Forum and the Harvard Kennedy School's Executive Session on Policing. The latter included George Kelling and Mark H. Moore, whose theories had informed the NYPD's Operation Pressure Point.[21]

With the help of former commissioner Benjamin Ward, Brown identified a consummate insider to help him navigate the complexities of the nation's largest police department. The fifth child of working-class Irish Catholic parents, Raymond Kelly spent the first part of his childhood in a polyglot white-ethnic stretch of the Upper West Side; as he was preparing to enter eighth grade, his parents, one eye on the rising Puerto Rican presence in the neighborhood, decamped for Long Island City, Queens. As a student at Manhattan College, he stumbled across a newly established Police Cadets program that aimed to bring college students into the NYPD. He joined the department and almost immediately took a leave to join the

Marines, where, by his own account, his ideas about leadership were forged. After returning from a tour in Vietnam, he worked for the NYPD during the day while attending St. John's Law School at night, taking classes in legal research and writing with a young Queens attorney, Mario Cuomo. He later collected master's degrees in law from NYU and public administration from the Harvard Kennedy School. It was Commissioner Ward—"a terrific role model [and] an excellent police official—period," Kelly later wrote—who recognized his talent and brought him into the upper echelons of the department before recommending him to Brown. "If you needed to talk about NYPD nuts and bolts—trends, manpower, deployment—Kelly was the man," one journalist wrote. And though a department insider, he was highly attuned to the NYPD's position within the wider field of city politics. "I was surprised by his ability to step back and assess purely civilian points of view—all with an unexpected political sense," a Dinkins aide observed.[22]

Dinkins had run in 1989 on putting more police officers on the streets. And as part of his "gorgeous mosaic" philosophy, he believed that officers should reflect, and should get to know, the city's neighborhoods. He hired Brown in large measure because Brown was a leading proponent of a new policing strategy that promised to do both: "community policing." Under this approach, community patrol officers would become the focal points of the NYPD's operations. Every neighborhood in the city, Brown wrote, would "have one or more police officers who know about that neighborhood, its people, their concerns, the crime problem, the make-up of the blocks, the crises of daily living and the support systems available to help people live better." "The mission of all other department personnel, units, and programs," Ray Kelly elaborated, "is to assist those officers in solving local problems and eliminating the conditions that produce them." By "working the same neighborhoods for extended periods of time," Kelly wrote, officers would "become familiar with residents and merchants and their respective problems. As information starts to flow, the problems are accurately described and appropriate remedies are designed."[23]

Community policing incorporated Jacobs and Whyte's "eyes on the street" approach and Kelling and Wilson's Broken Windows philosophy—indeed, George Kelling described the community policing approach as in line with his ideas. As these theorists did, Brown and Kelly emphasized the role of informal social control by "regulars" and "community members." Like Kelling and Wilson, Brown and Kelly believed that a visible police presence on streets and in neighborhoods could reduce fear of crime and reconstitute order. "New York's lifeblood is its neighborhoods," Kelly wrote. "These neighborhoods have nurtured generations of great men and women. Traditionally, order was maintained in great part by informal social controls. Neighbors acted as surrogate parents. They took responsibility for their streets, parks, roadways, and the person next door." Under community policing, "people will be encouraged to use their streets and parks and provide the support for each other that will ward off criminal activity today as it did in years gone by."[24]

Brown and Kelly's vision of community policing, though, differed from Kelling and Wilson's Broken Windows theory in one important respect: It emphasized the influence of "deep-rooted social conditions" in fostering crime and disorder, and it envisioned a role for the police in addressing these conditions. Although "the cop on the beat is hard pressed to solve problems of poverty, illiteracy, underemployment, teenage pregnancy, destabilized families, homelessness, drug abuse, child abuse and disease," Kelly wrote, "by being on the street in continuous contact with residents, the officer can identify neighbors suffering from the effects of these social ills and work with community organizations to deliver services to them. A community patrol officer's armament includes referrals, interventions, and access to social service agencies and private institutions." This approach, Kelly argued, would put "officers in roles as neighborhood ombudsmen," as advocates for neighborhoods and points of access to the sprawling city bureaucracy.[25]

To Brown, community policing represented the cutting edge of expert thought on policing strategy. But as NYPD commissioner Robert McGuire had noted in the early 1980s when discussing Kelling and Wilson's "Broken Windows" article with Koch, the cop-on-the-beat approach had an additional appeal: It tended to make neighborhood-level elites look at the NYPD more favorably. The notion that community policing could help re-legitimize the department appeared to be born out in a series of precinct-level experiments that the department had mounted starting in 1984 in the diverse working-class neighborhood of Sunset Park, Brooklyn, and that, by the end of Benjamin Ward's time as commissioner, had spread to every precinct in the city. Under the program, called the Community Patrol Officer Program (or CPOP), foot patrol officers covered regular beats of some 16 to 60 blocks, seeking out partnerships with what the department called "community leaders": "merchants and business people, members of the Community Planning Boards, members of the Precinct Community Councils, officials in local tenant or block associations, civilian patrol organizations, and local clergy"—an important population though in no way representative of the neighborhood as a whole. The program got strong reviews from this population. "People are less antagonistic toward the police than they were in the past," the leader of one large community organization told scholars at the Vera Institute. "There is still a general feeling that the police goof-off and take bribes, but there is less of a feeling that the police are the enemy." If community policing represented the cutting edge intellectually, it was also good police politics, a way to justify the expansion of the force, which NYPD officials regarded as necessary to bring down the high crime numbers of the crack years.[26]

In August 1990, Dinkins asked Brown to conduct an extensive study of the NYPD's resources and needs, a task Brown handed off to Kelly, who came back with a proposal for the largest expansion of the force in the department's history: some 3,400 new officers in addition to 3,000 previously budgeted hires, to be onboarded deliberately so they could be trained properly to combat the crack epidemic and learn the techniques of community policing. Dinkins's criminal justice team designed a program called Safe Streets, Safe City that accompanied this large expansion of the uniformed forces with a host of after-school programs for at-risk youth, financed primarily through dedicated property and income taxes. Governor Cuomo backed the proposal and, after some negotiations with the New York City Republicans in the State Senate, signed it into law in February 1991. It would be Dinkins's foremost legislative achievement and the beginning of an era of police expansion that surpassed even Koch's second term.[27]

Dinkins and Brown's NYPD continued the crackdown on disorderly behavior that had begun under Koch, enacting a new city ordinance restricting sidewalk vendors; closing Tompkins Square, the site of a controversial homeless encampment, for renovations; and launching an enforcement campaign against the "squeegee men" who worked the city's high-traffic intersections. But they found it more difficult to implement an approach that would meaningfully address the kinds of social ills of which Kelly had written. Brown and Kelly's approach placed extraordinary demands on patrol officers; any chance of success would depend on the department's ability to recruit and train effective officers, and Brown and Kelly's ability to convince precinct commanders to buy in to the new paradigm.[28]

They met with mixed success. Dinkins and Brown had agreed that community policing depended on diversifying the police force. Only "officers who understand the various and diverse groups which make up our City's citizenry will be responsive and sensitive to our communities' needs and problems," Dinkins wrote to Brown in 1991. When Kelly became commissioner after Brown resigned in the fall of 1992 due to his wife's poor health, he made it a top priority to recruit more officers of color. "We need the kind of talent that is right here in this community, the kind of talent that is too often overlooked," he told one church audience during what became a regular Sunday tour. His outreach efforts, accompanied by a recruiting initiative, yielded an immediate jump in the numbers of Black and Latino New Yorkers taking the police qualifying exam. But the numbers still lagged. In a city that in 1990 was 29 percent Black, 11.6 percent of police officers were. Practically everyone in the middle and upper command—93 percent—were white men of European ancestry.[29]

Worse, the NYPD struggled to implement the new policing paradigm, which was simply too much at odds with the department's ethos for its middle managers and rank-and-file officers to take it seriously. Training sessions, a series of internal memos found, amounted to a "a superficial potpourri of makeshift time fillers"; "cursory" supervision from precinct commanders led to "slipshod attention by the beat officers," who frequently ignored community requests. Patrol officers typically worked regular hours and not nights and weekends, when crime tended to be worst. Officers began to denigrate community policing as glorified "social work," and some 40 percent of community policing officers transferred out of the program. When someone handed the memos to the press, the *Daily News* ran a blaring headline: "Community Cops Program a Bust." In all, Brown ruefully observed, the task of reorienting the NYPD's strategy and operations was like trying to "turn an aircraft carrier around in a bathtub."[30]

A SIMILAR EFFORT TO REMAKE policing was underway in the New York subway system, which prior to a merger with the NYPD in 1995 was policed separately by the New York City Transit Police. In April 1989, just as the last graffitied cars were being removed from the system after a long and expensive campaign, New York City Transit Authority president David Gunn formed a study group to design a campaign against minor infractions, bringing in George Kelling as an adviser. The subway was in many respects a perfect theater for Kelling's emphasis on psychological interventions: Serious crime was relatively uncommon, but fear of crime was acute, and unlike aboveground, subway rules and regulations had the force of law, so officers had an extra tool with which to impose Kelling's conception of order. The campaign the study group designed met with stiff opposition from civil liberties advocates—the Straphangers Campaign, a leading transit group, described it as "dangerous [and] mean-spirited," "unattainable and self-defeating"—and disinterest from subway police, who viewed the work as a distraction from real crime fighting; it lasted a scant six months. But by then Kelling had helped bring in a new commissioner of the New York City Transit Police who would go on to shape policing in the city for decades to come: William J. Bratton.[31]

As a precinct commander in Boston's District 4 (which covered roughly the neighborhoods of Back Bay, South End, and Fenway), Bratton had noticed that community groups, while concerned about major crimes, more frequently brought up "day-to-day annoyances"—the kinds of small-scale infractions that Broken Windows policing proposed to target. Addressing such quality-of-life concerns, Bratton came to realize, "opened up a tremendous amount of communication" that could help the police solve more serious crimes, such as burglaries. As he worked his way up the ladder in Boston, Bratton connected with the centers of police research that Lee Brown was frequenting. In 1988, he heard Kelling deliver a paper on "community problem solving" policing at the Kennedy School's Executive Session, and the two stayed in touch. Once Kelling started recruiting him for the transit post, Bratton—who was at least as media-savvy as Brown and Kelly—started studying the New York press with, he later wrote, an eye toward making a name for himself quickly. "If

I took the job and successfully turned that department around," he wrote, "I could legitimately begin positioning myself for the number one job in American policing, New York City police commissioner. . . . It was the ideal situation."[32]

Bratton's first priorities were visibility and morale—the presence of "uniformed police" aggressively patrolling, was "cardinal," he said. He kept Kelling on as an adviser and integrated his quality-of-life approach into the everyday operations of the transit police, focusing particularly on panhandling and fare evasion, which were costing the MTA some $80 million in lost revenue a year. Bratton soon became convinced that the problems of crime, disorder, and fare evasion were "deeply interrelated," though not exactly in the way the Broken Windows theory predicted. About one in seven people arrested for fare-beating in the early days of Bratton's initiative, the agency discovered, possessed outstanding warrants for more serious offenses; about one in twenty-one were carrying weapons. Crackdowns on small-scale offenses, it followed, could serve as a mechanism for removing weapons and ostensibly dangerous people from the subway system and, perhaps, from the city streets. On Bratton's watch, the transit police began conducting sweeps, apprehending a number of people at a time and marching them to a "bust bus" for processing and to check for outstanding warrants. People with weapons or outstanding warrants were arrested; others were typically given desk-appearance tickets, which required them to appear in court and pay a fine.[33]

The emphasis on highly visible arrests, Bratton found, helped to secure buy-in from the rank and file who, like the patrol officers above ground, sometimes chafed at quality-of-life enforcement, which they did not consider "real" policing. "The cops were motivated and getting noticed," Bratton recalled. Riders "saw cops hauling long lines of folks out of the subways and said, 'Go get 'em,' 'Great job!' 'Way to go!' 'It's about time!' . . . It was exhilarating for the cops." The comparison to Brown and Kelly's struggle to secure buy-in for community policing was telling: Police reform would succeed, apparently, to the extent that it accommodated department culture and the interests of middle managers and the rank and file.[34]

Whether or not it was due to the new enforcement approach, subway crime fell considerably on Bratton's watch. By the time he returned to Boston in 1992, he had garnered acclaim from advocates of Broken Windows policing: The "little known but profoundly important Cinderella story" over which Bratton had presided, wrote the editors of *City Journal*, offered a kind of model for policing in the city as a whole.[35]

IF COMMUNITY POLICING REPRESENTED, in part, an effort to salvage the NYPD's image, the department badly needed it. The hiring spree of the early to mid-1980s, the colonial dynamic of officers who lived in the suburbs and came into the city to police neighborhoods they did not understand and sometimes viewed with attitudes ranging from suspicion to disdain, the demands and enticements of the drug war, and the charge to manage disorder in an ever more disorderly city—it all added up to a recipe for misconduct and violence. High-profile instances of police brutality punctuated the grinding, everyday harassment that people of color experienced. The most infamous of these involved Pratt Institute student Michael Stewart, who died in police custody in 1983 after being picked up for subway graffiti (the inspiration for the culminating act of violence in Spike Lee's 1989 film, *Do the Right Thing*), and Eleanor Bumpurs, who was murdered by police with a 12-gauge shotgun the following year while resisting eviction in her Morris Heights apartment.

As the decade turned, two more episodes led New Yorkers to call for greater police accountability. The first came on August 8, 1988, toward the end of Koch's third term, when some 440 NYPD officers moved, with nightsticks flying, into Tompkins Square Park in the East Village, site of a prominent and controversial homeless encampment, to enforce a one a.m. curfew. What became known as the Tompkins Square Riot resulted in 121 complaints against NYPD officers but little follow-up action. Some four years later news broke that six NYPD officers (one retired) had been arrested as part of a drug-trafficking operation in Suffolk County, on the eastern end of Long Island. Dinkins responded by forming a commission chaired by the widely respected Judge Milton Mollen to investigate corruption in the NYPD and issue follow-up recommendations. In something of a reprise of the Knapp Commission of the early 1970s, the Mollen Commission found that officers not only stole drugs and cash from dealers but also aided drug dealers in myriad ways—allowing them to function undisturbed, providing intel on upcoming raids, and providing police escort when traffickers were moving large amounts of drugs or cash. One of the Suffolk County arrestees, Matthew Dowd, was effectively on retainer for $4,000 a week—ten times his NYPD salary (which he sometimes forgot to collect). To rein it all in, Mollen recommended the creation of an independent police monitor with subpoena power.[36]

Mollen's report, which became a kind of benchmark for police accountability advocates in New York City, would not come down until mid-1994. In the meantime, Dinkins had begun to push for a new mechanism of police accountability: an independent, civilian-run review board to investigate allegations of police abuse. Dinkins, who himself had experienced verbal abuse from the police—"you'd probably have trouble finding somebody who hasn't," he noted—had given his support to an independent board during the 1989 primary; but fearing the kind of bitter struggle that had sunk John Lindsay's proposal in the mid-1960s, he had not "aggressively pursued" it. When the City Council, led by Ronnie Eldridge and C. Virginia Fields of Manhattan and Victor Robles of Brooklyn, pushed on by the New York Civil Liberties Union, introduced a bill and prepared to hold hearings on it, Dinkins decided it was time to announce his own proposal. He envisioned a board of thirteen mayoral appointees, all of whom would be unaffiliated with the NYPD.[37]

By this time, Dinkins had drawn considerable ire from the department's rank and file—for his creation of the Mollen Commission; his offer to pay for the funeral of yet another victim of police violence, José "Kiko" Garcia, a twenty-two-year-old Dominican immigrant whose killing by a police officer had ignited an uprising in Washington Heights; and his opposition (with Brown and Kelly's support) to a state legislature initiative backed by the Patrolmen's Benevolent Association, the largest police union, to equip officers with semiautomatic nine-millimeter handguns. As Dinkins expected, the proposal for a civilian review board encountered near-hysterical opposition from the PBA and its members. In mid-September 1992, PBA president Phil Caruso held a rally in City Hall Park to demonstrate members' opposition to Dinkins's plan. Some ten thousand off-duty officers showed up, carrying racist signs and chanting racist slogans denouncing Dinkins: "THE MAYOR'S ON CRACK"; "DEAR MAYOR, HAVE YOU HUGGED A DRUG DEALER TODAY?" "DINKINS, WE KNOW YOUR TRUE COLOR—YELLOW BELLIED." Rudy Giuliani, whose narrow defeat in 1989 had made him the presumptive Republican nominee for mayor in 1993, addressed the crowd, many of whom were by this point drinking openly, calling Dinkins's proposal "bullshit" and accusing the mayor of destroying the NYPD's morale. In the course of the protest, some four thousand people "swarmed over the barricades, blocked the entry to City Hall and later marched onto the Brooklyn Bridge, where they tied up traffic for nearly an hour," kicking and punching journalists with little response from the on-duty officers. The scene was "right out of the 1950s: a drunk, racist lynch mob storming City Hall to get themselves a [racial slur]," a young Black officer named Eric Adams said. To Dinkins, the event only underlined the need for an independent review board. "If some officers in full view of camera and public and their superior officers would use racial slurs . . . then I fear how they would behave while out in the streets."[38]

Before the riot, the prospects for Dinkins's proposal seemed middling at best. City Council speaker Peter Vallone, a Queens Democrat, opposed a fully independent board. But the riot, Vallone said, had "changed the political landscape." By the end of October, he and Dinkins had worked out an agreement—the mayor would still appoint a thirteen-member Civilian Complaint Review Board, none of whom would be employed by the NYPD, but the council would be allowed to nominate five members, and the police commissioner would nominate three—and the commissioner would retain authority over disciplinary decisions. Giuliani denounced the measure as "the most irrelevant kind of symbolism" and accused its proponents of "destroy[ing]" the NYPD's morale. But a quarter-century after Lindsay's failure, the city now had an independent police review board.[39]

Among longtime New Yorkers, Dinkins's mayoralty remains a kind of Rorschach test. The same is true among scholars, though in a different way: Some have seen his mayoralty as a genuine, if short-lived, challenge to the post-fiscal-crisis order; others have argued that, with his austerity budgets and developer-friendly land use policies, Dinkins represented more continuity with Koch than his progressive rhetoric might have suggested. As his term drew to a close, his record on policing had a similar quality. Like Koch, Dinkins had poured resources into the NYPD and had cracked down on quality-of-life offenses—it was under Dinkins, not Giuliani, that the NYPD chased the much-maligned squeegee men from the city's streets. In these ways, he seemed to have legitimized and advanced an approach to policing that Koch had initiated and that Giuliani would later make the centerpiece of his mayoralty. On the other hand, community policing seemed to hold the possibility of a more responsive kind of policing. And the CCRB, for all its limitations, represented a breakthrough in the decades-long struggle for police accountability. Would the community policing approach endure and ultimately gain traction with rank-and-file officers, offering all

New Yorkers meaningful input into how their neighborhoods were policed? Or would a particular—and exclusive—construction of the concept of "community" simply afford the NYPD an additional tool with which to legitimize its exercises of power? Would the CCRB command the resources and authority to address New York's long-standing problems with brutality and harassment? Or would it be as powerless as its NYPD-dominated predecessors?[40]

One development is a simple matter of record: Crime rates declined under Dinkins. Homicides fell by 13.7 percent; robberies by 14.6 percent; burglaries by 17.6 percent. For all the dire warnings from the PBA and its supporters, Dinkins's record seemed to suggest that meaningful reform could coexist with reductions in crime. A second term, should he secure it, would test whether Dinkins could implement these reforms in a way that fit his progressive commitments rather than simply shoring up the NYPD's battered legitimacy and delivering to it an ever-greater share of city resources.[41]

WHILE DINKINS STRUGGLED to govern the city through some of the most difficult years in its history, Giuliani prepared for a rematch. In 1989, he had suffered from divisions within the Republican Party, a consequence of an ongoing feud with his onetime sponsor, Senator D'Amato, who had established himself as the most powerful force in the New York State GOP. Feisty and belligerent—he kept a pair of boxing gloves on the wall of his Senate office—D'Amato could be ruthless, but he was also capable of exercising a rough charm. ("D'Amato's kissed me," Congressman Charles Rangel once remarked; "Pat Moynihan ain't never kissed me.") His maniacal fundraising—some of his Senate colleagues dubbed him "Vacuum Cleaner"—allowed him to spend heavily on television ads and direct mail campaigns, overseen by his innovative political adviser, Arthur J. Finkelstein. Elected as a Reagan conservative, he had established himself as a master of bringing money home to his state, which won him support in Democratic cities and even among Democratic politicians and community activists. Koch consistently praised him (he would later write the introduction to D'Amato's book *Power, Pasta, and Politics*); the Reverend Al Sharpton had endorsed his 1986 bid for reelection; and Cuomo had done so little to aid his Democratic opponent in the 1986 campaign that Senator Daniel Patrick Moynihan accused the two of having a "non-aggression pact." "That's not a theory; it's a fact," Moynihan emphasized.[42]

D'Amato had also engulfed himself in an extraordinary amount of scandal, which initiated a clash with Giuliani, the crusading U.S. attorney—Giuliani, he charged, was a "publicity hound" who would "go to any length to aggrandize himself, regardless of the guilt or innocence of a person." With Giuliani the obvious front-runner in the 1989 Republican mayoral primary, D'Amato had backed a primary challenger, the cosmetics heir Ronald Lauder, whose negative campaign was transparently intended to damage Giuliani (and possibly to aid D'Amato's ally, Koch, who was still at that point the presumed favorite in the Democratic primary).[43]

In 1992, under heavy pressure from the city's GOP county leaders and presumably with an eye on the following year's mayoral campaign, Giuliani gritted his teeth and endorsed D'Amato's bid for a third Senate term. D'Amato and his party allies, in turn, backed Giuliani in 1993, which not only spared Giuliani another damaging primary fight but also allowed him to choose his own running mates for comptroller and City Council president, to take advantage of the strength of the county party organizations, and to tap into D'Amato's fundraising machine.[44]

The Giuliani of 1989 had been notably inexperienced with city issues. As the 1993 election approached, though, he connected with a group of policy intellectuals centered on the Manhattan Institute. If the Manhattan Institute had struggled to make its presence felt during the 1989 mayoral campaign, the recession and its accompanying difficulties afforded it a platform. "We were almost the only people who took the decline of the city seriously," one of its leading figures remarked. "That gave added force to our argument that there was something profoundly dysfunctional about the political culture of New York."[45]

The Manhattan Institute's quarterly, *City Journal*, gathered in former leftists turned skeptics of urban liberalism such as Nathan Glazer and education writer Sol Stern; younger Reaganites like David Brooks; a host of academics and policy experts; current and former public officials. From its inception, the journal operated in two distinct but connected registers. On one hand, it was unabashedly wonkish, which gained it notice among some of the city's liberal policy experts. It put forward "creative ideas to make government work better" on the assumption that the city could achieve desired outcomes such as lower crime and better schools through clear and disciplined policy thinking, obviating the need to examine distributional issues or structures of inequality. At the same time, it advanced a sweeping cultural narrative that aligned well with the grievance politics that had nearly fueled Giuliani to victory in 1989: It hearkened back to a halcyon mid-century city and wondered why the city's neighborhoods were reproducing poverty rather than serving as a launchpad into the professional and managerial classes—precisely the journey some of the journal's leading contributors had taken. The answer, they believed, had to do with the decline of the city's civic culture and the rise of an attitude of permissiveness and diminished standards; and so the language of restoration and reclamation ran through the journal.[46]

On a snowy morning in mid-March 1992, the Manhattan Institute sponsored a conference at the Roosevelt Hotel entitled "Rethinking New York: Policies for Renewal." Toward the front of the audience, "scribbling on a yellow legal pad," sat Rudy Giuliani. A month later *City Journal* ran an issue entitled "The Quality of Urban Life," based in part on the symposium. "Cities should be comfortable places," wrote editor Roger Starr. Instead, they were marked by "signs of deterioration." The issue of "quality of life" had risen to the center of city politics, he argued, because it represented "the common good—the interests all New Yorkers share as citizens." The journal's essays laid out a case for reform across multiple policy areas. George Kelling called on the NYPD to pay greater attention to disorder in public spaces. The historian Fred Siegel wrote frankly about the "clash of values created around contested spaces"—particularly the contests between homeless New Yorkers who used the parks to live in and neighborhood residents who saw restored parks as "a way for middle-class families to stay in the city." Colman Genn and Ray Domanico, both of whom had been active in the East Harlem school reform movement, criticized the school system for pursuing "system goals"—the priorities of the bureaucracy itself—rather than "the goals that parents, children, and most citizens value." School choice, they argued was a "fundamental precondition for reform," a way of making schools "directly accountable to the public they serve." Housing expert Peter Salins assailed rent regulation, and public ownership and management, as impediments to the provision of quality housing.[47]

Giuliani's team had already begun to make common cause with the core group at *City Journal*. Following the March symposium, Siegel helped organize a seminar series for Giuliani on issues ranging from policing to garbage collection, beginning with an extended discussion of New York City government by Bobby Wagner. Soon Giuliani could be seen waving a copy of the journal during a campaign speech, saying, "I don't know if you can plagiarize policies, but if you can, here is where I plagiarize mine." If the magazine's wonky side afforded Giuliani a more fully developed policy program, helping to establish his bona fides with the city's governing class, its account of the origins of what was broadly perceived as a crisis in the city's quality of life provided Giuliani with a coherent campaign narrative. Dinkins's permissive brand of liberalism, his unwillingness to assert authority and impose discipline, had caused a crisis of the city's quality of life, Giuliani claimed. What New York needed, he asserted, was "One City, One Standard." To Dinkins's supporters, the racial overtones of such a message were barely concealed: What Giuliani's campaign slogan really meant, the writer Kevin Baker argued, was that "black New Yorkers were getting away with something under a black mayor." (The authors of a study the Giuliani campaign commissioned in advance of the 1993 election to assess their candidate's points of vulnerability acknowledged the racial dynamics of the contest. "Simply put," they wrote, "Dinkins won't have to work hard while painting Giuliani as a racist.")[48]

In spite of all the obstacles stacked against him—the recession and its attendant fiscal pressures, the national crime wave, the inescapably racist depictions he had suffered in the local press—Dinkins came into the 1993 campaign a formidable candidate. The recession dragged on, but crime rates had begun a steady decline. Despite the economic conditions, Dinkins's approval rating remained above 50 percent, and polls showed that even New Yorkers who had voted for him in 1989 and planned to switch to Giuliani in 1993 regarded him as trustworthy. He retained the support of much of the city's business establishment, and the electoral coalition that had carried him to victory in 1989 remained largely intact.[49]

But Dinkins had won in 1989 by a hairbreadth, and operating at such slim margins, any defections threatened to prove decisive. If polls showed that New Yorkers tended to hold Dinkins in reasonably high regard personally, they also showed that most voters struggled to name a major Dinkins achievement—a product partly of the city press's tendency to report on the administration's failures and to overlook its successes, but also a statement on Dinkins's struggles to translate an ambitious policy agenda into tangible, visible results consonant with his public philosophy. His signal policy achievement, Safe Streets, Safe City, was a particularly tough hook on which to hang his political hat. Proposed in the wake of the subway murder of

Utah tourist Brian Watkins in the summer of 1990 (and the *New York Post*'s famous front-page headline "DAVE, DO SOMETHING!"), it looked like something Dinkins had been pushed into pursuing (though in fact he had tasked Brown with assessing the NYPD's staffing needs a month earlier), on an issue voters tended to associate with more conservative politicians. It had been intentionally designed, on solid policy grounds, to be rolled out slowly.

Moreover, as the campaign progressed, it became clear that Dinkins had not successfully consolidated the movement that elected him in 1989 into a coalition with the organizational and political strength to impose discipline on those who might think of breaking ranks. The United Federation of Teachers, important to Dinkins's victory in 1989 but unhappy with the administration's tight-fisted budgets, withheld its endorsement. Even staunch progressive intellectuals assailed Dinkins's leadership style and the new political syntax that accompanied the diversity of the Dinkins coalition. "The problem is that Dinkins, and progressive New York in general, speak only in the coded language of identity politics," Michael Tomasky wrote in *The Nation*. What the city needed was "a single standard for civil behavior, a standard based on decency and respect." (Despite the echo of Giuliani's campaign slogan, Tomasky doubted the GOP challenger would be much better—of Giuliani's speech at the 1992 police riot, he wrote, "Let's just say that Leni Riefenstahl should've been there to film it.")[50]

If D'Amato and his allies were pulling the GOP together behind Giuliani, the state's leading Democrats offered Dinkins considerably less help. In April, Senator Moynihan delivered a speech before the Association for a Better New York lamenting the city's moral and social decay, nostalgically invoking his own childhood in 1940s New York. "In the good old days," Dinkins told a group of Black mayors later that day, "I wore the uniform of a U.S. Marine and I had to sit in the back." Moynihan's eventual endorsement of Dinkins was so oblique that reporters asked him if it was, indeed, an endorsement—only for the senator to reply, "Ask the mayor." His subsequent endorsement statement contained barbed references to New York's quality-of-life crisis and had more to say about recent historiography on the New Deal than it did Dinkins's accomplishments.[51]

Mario Cuomo, intentionally or not, made two moves that could only have hurt Dinkins's chances. In 1990, the Democratic State Assembly had passed a measure putting a ballot question on Staten Island secession from New York City on the 1993 general election ballot as a favor to two Staten Island caucus members, assuming Cuomo would veto it. The governor, who was pushing at the time for a measure to permit state ballot referenda on major policy issues and may therefore have worried about looking hypocritical, proceeded to sign it into law despite knowing it would drive up turnout in the city's most pro-Republican borough at the next mayoral election. As the election approached, Cuomo also appeared to blame Dinkins for the NYPD's handling of the 1991 riot in Crown Heights, Brooklyn, a major flashpoint in the city's tortured racial politics.[52]

Dinkins suffered yet another blow in mid-October when two of the city's leading Democrats announced their support for Giuliani. One was Koch, who had backed Dinkins after the 1989 primary before becoming a sharp critic. He issued a scorching denunciation of Dinkins in his column for the *Daily News*. Dinkins's "gorgeous mosaic has been relegated to the dustbin of political rhetoric," he charged. "Mayor Dinkins presides over an administration in utter disarray." Perhaps anticipating that New Yorkers would find it quizzical that he would endorse a man he had once referred to as "a dog," Koch asked: "What is the alternative? Rudy Giuliani . . . is not a perfect vessel, but I have concluded he is able and intelligent and he has energy." Giuliani, he predicted, would "preside over an efficient, technocratic government dedicated to delivering service and above all setting a single standard for all citizens."[53]

The other defector was Bobby Wagner. "I'm a Democrat and very proud of that," he said, "but more than that I'm a New Yorker and

I believe the stakes of this election are incredibly important. Over the last year I've gotten to know Rudy Giuliani and realize he's a very different person than the one who comes across in the news columns and sometimes on television. He's not cold or mean." Wagner acknowledged that he found Giuliani's "extrem[ism]" off-putting. "But I think the last three and a half years have been characterized by a lack of leadership and a lack of hope for the future of the city. Certainly David conveys a picture of decency and concern, but not of leadership." The Giuliani campaign was elated. Wagner, Giuliani's deputy campaign manager noted, represented "the soul of liberal Democratic thinking in this city." As the campaign hit the home stretch, Wagner cut a television commercial for the Giuliani campaign; Giuliani's media strategist, the vastly experienced David Garth, would later speculate that Koch and Wagner's endorsements may have tipped the election.[54]

On election day, Giuliani succeeded in reversing the narrow margin by which he had lost four years earlier. He was aided primarily by a large turnout and strong performance in predominantly Catholic and Jewish neighborhoods in Queens, Brooklyn, and especially Staten Island, where Cuomo's ballot question on secession from New York City, and D'Amato ally Guy Molinari's organization, helped drive turnout. (Giuliani's campaign was accused at the time of voter intimidation tactics in predominantly Latino neighborhoods, and Giuliani himself would claim in a 2023 web stream that pro-Giuliani forces had deployed "dirty tricks" aimed at "the Hispanic illegal vote, which takes away the Hispanic legal vote." Whatever precisely occurred, the number of votes involved was not large enough to have tipped the outcome of the election.)[55]

If the thin margin was hardly the thorough repudiation of Dinkins and the Democratic Party that some New Yorkers later remembered it to be—until 2025, no winning candidate for mayor earned more votes than Dinkins did in his 1993 loss—the results nonetheless marked the end of a brief period of progressive mobilization that had begun with Jackson's 1988 primary bid. More broadly, it marked the last gasp of mass-participation electoral democracy in New York, a principal feature of the city's politics from 1933 through 1969, diminished but still alive in the 1970s, and revived in the momentous elections of 1989 and 1993. Only twice more prior to 2025, in the immediate aftermath of September 11 and again four years after that, would the number of voters in mayoral elections exceed even half of what it had been in 1969, the last election before the onset of the crises of the 1970s.

In the days after the election, some political observers anticipated that Bobby Wagner, already fielding policy suggestions and inquiries about jobs, would play a major role in the Giuliani administration's efforts to reinvent New York's government. It was not to be: During a trip to study a community development program in San Antonio, he suddenly took ill with severe flu-like symptoms and died at the age of forty-nine, apparently of heart disease. Wagner's loss hit the city's political establishment with extraordinary force. New York, the columnist Robert W. Laird wrote, had "lost one of its most decent, savvy, humane public figures at a critical juncture in its history." The editors of the *Daily News* noted that his loss deprived the mayor-elect of "the qualities Giuliani needs most—tolerance, perspective and, most of all, simple, humble kindness."[56]

Having helped elevate a potential political rival to City Hall, D'Amato turned his attention to placing an ally in the State House. To help in doing so, he sought out his longtime political consultant, Arthur J. Finkelstein. The son of a Brooklyn cab driver and part-time garment industry worker, Finkelstein had come of age as a libertarian inspired by Barry Goldwater and Ayn Rand (for whom he briefly worked)—he later described himself as a "Milton Friedman Republican." Behind his modest visage—heavy eyebrows, thinning hair, his youngish face a bit pudgy, part small-time lawyer, part character actor, part Philip Roth—lay a character of great complexity. His appearance perpetually rumpled, his tie pulled comically low, he had a habit of taking his shoes off during meetings, during which he was known for generating strings of ideas, some of them wild, a few brilliant. He was a recluse—for years, the last known photo of him had been taken in 1976—but he was also comfortable around people, modest and quick with a broad smile. Once his consulting business made him rich, he, his partner Donald, and their two daughters posted up in an Italianate Revival mansion in Ipswich, Massachusetts, north of Boston, on a forty-acre estate replete with terraced gardens and a ten-stall horse barn.

A math prodigy, Finkelstein originally entered politics through polling. "Everything that Arthur does is based on numbers," one of his many protégés later remarked, "but nobody could read the numbers like Arthur." The numbers told him two things above all. First, most Americans knew what bothered them but did not know much about the details of the issues of the day. Second, though more Americans identified as Democrats than Republicans, more identified as conservatives than as liberals. The trick to a successful Republican campaign, then, was to turn the election into a contest over ideology rather than party, and to do so by identifying a small handful of what Finkelstein called "polarizing" issues capable of breaking through with a largely ignorant public in ways that reinforced the conservative-versus-liberal division—something Finkelstein was particularly good at given his skill as a pollster. In practice, this meant engaging in what Finkelstein called "rejectionist voting" and everyone else called negative campaigning. "I plead guilty," he told an audience at CPAC. "I will continue to run ideologically arched campaigns as long as there are more conservatives than there are liberals, rather than more Democrats than there are Republicans."

Because his stock-in-trade was to focus relentlessly on his opponents' weaknesses, Finkelstein tended to do his best work with relatively unknown candidates. He had first risen to prominence in 1980, when he had helped D'Amato—an utterly unknown Nassau

County machine pol—take on Jacob Javits in the Republican Senate primary. It was a perfect match for Finkelstein's "rejectionist voting," an undefined candidate against an incumbent who could be easily pigeonholed—in Javits's case, as tired, old, and too liberal for the times. It was a formula he would repeat in 1994.[57]

Finkelstein and his colleagues had known since the mid-1980s that migration from the New York City metropolitan area had turned the mid–Hudson Valley—"from Peekskill to Hudson," one GOP strategist wrote—into the decisive battleground of New York State politics. As the 1994 gubernatorial election approached, he conducted focus groups to identify the characteristics that would give a Republican candidate a fighting shot against Mario Cuomo, and found that voters would respond best to a white-ethnic Catholic candidate with moderate credentials, especially on the question of reproductive rights. D'Amato settled on a relatively unknown state senator from Westchester County, George Pataki. The son of a postal worker and a waitress, Pataki had grown up on a farm outside Peekskill before attending Yale and Columbia Law School; after a career in law, he had gone into politics, serving two terms as mayor of his hometown, five in the State Assembly, and one in the State Senate. Tall, rhetorically bland, politically conservative, but instinctively cautious, Pataki struck his admirers as possessing the homespun earnestness of the titular character from Frank Capra's *Mr. Smith Goes to Washington*. D'Amato pushed Pataki's name through the state convention, helped staff his campaign, and supplied him with campaign contributions. Finkelstein helped craft the campaign message: Cuomo had been "too liberal for too long."[58]

Giuliani had built a strong working relationship with Cuomo in the first year of his mayoralty; he may also have been eyeing a run for governor in 1998 and certainly worried that he would be overshadowed by a pro-D'Amato Republican governor. A month before the election, he issued a stunning endorsement of the Democratic governor, accusing Pataki of being "guided, scripted, and directed by others," an obvious reference to D'Amato. But Pataki pulled through, driven by huge upstate turnout and diminished enthusiasm for Cuomo downstate, particularly on Long Island. The Democrats' two-decade turn in the governor's mansion was over.[59]

Pataki's victory marked a fundamental diminishment of New York City's power in state politics: for the first time since the 1920s, New York would be governed by an upstate conservative who owed very little of his support to the five boroughs—Pataki had carried barely over a quarter of the city's vote. It also marked the triumph of upstate conservatives over downstate moderates in a struggle for power within the state GOP. Pataki's election placed Senate majority leader Ralph Marino, who had refused to back D'Amato's efforts to make Pataki the Republican nominee, in an untenable position. Marino duly found himself ousted in favor of the far more conservative Joseph Bruno, whose upstate district encompassed primarily the suburbs of the Capital Region city of Troy.[60]

At the same time, Pataki's victory, together with Newt Gingrich's sweeping victory in the national midterm elections, forced Giuliani to recalibrate, to pivot to the right if he wanted to remain relevant in Republican politics. "Had Cuomo won," the journalist Wayne Barrett later wrote, Giuliani "would have been a starkly different mayor. . . . From 1995 on, his mayoralty pivoted around a carefully crafted national portrait: Rudy was the take-charge, no-nuance, antithesis of New York's lofty liberals." A few short years after Dinkins's victory inaugurated New York's liberal moment, the city and state had taken a sharp turn to the right—the consequences of which would soon become clear.[61]

5

The Republican Moment

The upheavals of the early 1990s shook up New York politics in ways not seen since the 1970s. Then the fiscal crisis opened the door for a new breed of Democrats; now another crisis restored the Republican Party to primacy for the first time in decades. Not since Lindsay and Rockefeller in the late 1960s had both City Hall and the Governor's Mansion been held by politicians elected on the Republican ticket. More than just a partisan or ideological takeover, the GOP ascendancy rearranged the broader constellation of power in New York. Interest groups allied with the Democratic Party lost political strength, particularly in Albany; so, too, did downstate voters in reliably Democratic neighborhoods, whose votes the governor no longer needed. Conversely, groups that had struggled to make headway under the old configuration of power, such as landlord organizations and conservative policy thinkers, found new opportunities, especially if they could shift the theater of conflict from the city to Albany.

The political reshuffling was far from absolute. Democrats and their allied interest groups would muster enough strength on some issues—such as rent regulation—to force the Republicans to compromise. In other instances, such as their push for a state charter school law, conservative Republicans would be able to win only by forging alliances with traditionally Democratic constituencies. Thus the Republican renaissance would fail to signal the full triumph of neoconservatism. Still, the Republicans' ascent to power in Albany would produce major ruptures in both housing and education policy, allowing conservatives to put their imprint on initiatives that had previously been crafted largely by Democrats.

As crucial contests over housing and schools unfolded in Albany, the political drama in the five boroughs would revolve primarily around policing, an issue that came to dominate Giuliani's mayoralty. Though Giuliani and his police commissioner, Bill Bratton, would depict their crime-fighting efforts as a sharp break from the past, in many respects they represented an extension of the initiatives of the Koch and Dinkins years: Giuliani and Bratton's emphasis on quality-of-life enforcement would echo Koch's and Dinkins's; crackdowns on street-level drug markets would hearken back to Operation Pressure Point and the Tactical Narcotics Teams; Bratton's "problem-oriented" policing style would grow out of the same nexus of academic and professional thinking that had produced Lee Brown and Raymond Kelly's community policing strategy. And in showering resources on the NYPD, Giuliani would simply be following in the footsteps of his two Democratic predecessors. The new era of policing heralded in newspapers and magazines around the world in the mid- to late 1990s was in many respects an evolutionary change, in which police leadership applied new managerial techniques and strategic approaches to long-standing priorities. Still, those innovations would matter. Bratton and his successor Howard Safir would expand the department's use of misdemeanor arrests and street-level stop-and-frisk searches—decisions with immense consequences.

If the NYPD's street-policing strategies represented a formalization of earlier practices, the way many New Yorkers viewed the NYPD underwent a remarkable transformation in the mid- to late 1990s. The crime drop that had begun under Dinkins accelerated rapidly throughout Giuliani's mayoralty. Many factors contributed, and scholars are still sorting out their relative significance. But politicians, journalists, pundits, and everyday New Yorkers assigned credit to the NYPD and particularly to Bratton's Broken Windows policing strategy—which in practice bore only a limited resemblance to Kelling and Wilson's original theory. To many New Yorkers, the NYPD had become the city's "indispensable institution," the linchpin of local prosperity and well-being.

Yet if the NYPD reasserted an image of competence after three long decades of consistently high crime rates, its crisis of legitimacy in low-income communities of color only worsened under Giuliani. The expansion of street-level activity embodied in stop-and-frisk amplified inequalities of race and class, subjecting countless New Yorkers of color to harassment, humiliation, and at times violence. Anger with Giuliani's NYPD reached a boiling point in the late 1990s amid a spate of high-profile instances of police violence, heralding the coalescence of a new, powerful movement against police brutality.

COMING OFF THEIR PARTIAL SUCCESS during the 1993 state legislative session, advocates of rent deregulation turned their attention to an unlikely venue—the City Council, traditionally a fierce defender of regulation. With the city still cash-strapped and suffering from cutbacks to public services, the arguments for high-rent vacancy deregulation advanced in the early 1990s gained greater force: Why should Manhattan apartment buildings go undertaxed when library hours were being pared back, parks undermaintained, and sanitation services stretched? Sensing opportunity, the Rent Stabilization Association launched a lobbying offensive, hiring the chief of staff of City Council speaker Peter Vallone, a Democrat of Astoria, Queens, as its new president.

The move quickly paid off. In 1994, Vallone, who had been waffling on high-rent vacancy deregulation since 1991, pushed for the city to remove the October 1, 1993, cutoff date for the measure: Under the 1993 state law, apartments renting for more than $2,000 a month as of that date were to be deregulated upon vacancy, a provision that meant that in practice, only a small share of apartments would actually be deregulated. Under Vallone's plan, apartments would be vacancy-deregulated upon renting for more than $2,000 whenever that occurred—meaning that deregulation would proceed with rising rents until the entire city was deregulated, so long as the provision remained unchanged. The measure's chief advocates made it clear that their target was rent regulation writ large, referring in council hearings on Vallone's bill to issues that had nothing to do with the deregulation of existing high-rent units. "What we have to do is encourage investment in property," Queens councilman Archie Spigner remarked during the council hearings on the measure. "We have to encourage the new construction of rental properties." Another champion of deregulation spoke during the same hearings about the importance of "send[ing] a signal" to the real estate industry.

Most Manhattan councilmembers opposed the measure vigorously. "These are not necessarily wealthy people," Upper West Side councilmember Ronnie Eldridge remarked. "They are very needed middle class people in the city. They provide the energy, they provide the workforce. They provide the backbone of this city." Critics of the bill noted that many $2,000-per-month apartments, especially in Manhattan, were occupied by young people or family members pooling their rent. But many outer-borough members believed the provision would never affect their constituents. Some, like Martin Malavé Dilan of Bushwick, argued that luxury deregulation was actually a progressive measure, a way to "end subsidies for those people who need it the least." Cuomo opposed the law but, as was typical of him on rent regulation, declined to expend much political capital on the issue. In the end, the majority of council members from the Bronx, Brooklyn, and Queens voted in favor of Vallone's measure; only one Manhattan member did.[1]

Giuliani, who despite his Manhattan Institute links considered rent regulation an untouchable third rail of city politics, opposed high-rent vacancy deregulation during the 1993 mayoral campaign and sponsored an alternative to Vallone's bill that would have extended the existing rent laws in 1994. But as Vallone's measure wound its way through the council, Giuliani, like Cuomo, largely kept his distance, declining even to meet with the tenant organizations leading the charge against it. He signed the bill, declaring that he was "not necessarily in favor of all [its] facets" but saw it as a "fair compromise." Vallone and the council Democrats had not only opened the door to deregulation in the city but had also sent a clear signal to state Republicans that they might not be willing or able to resist more immediate moves toward deregulation. Caught off guard in 1994, New York's tenant organizations gathered their forces in preparation for a conclusive showdown when the rent laws came up for reauthorization in Albany in 1997.[2]

By the time the 1997 legislative session opened, political circumstances had shifted considerably from four years earlier, when Mario Cuomo and Senate majority leader Ralph Marino had agreed to limited luxury deregulation. Governor George Pataki was on record as an opponent of rent regulation; he had voted against renewing the rent laws in 1989 and 1991 and had supported the 1993 extension only because it included high-rent vacancy deregulation. His transition team had caused a stir in the wake of the 1994 election by floating a deregulation plan. Senate majority leader Joseph Bruno, the Capitol Region conservative who had ousted Marino in the caucus room coup that followed Pataki's victory, had led the push for high-rent deregulation; tenant activists had taken to calling him "'Attila the Hun' on tenant issues." His district, he later noted almost gleefully in his memoirs, contained not a single rent-regulated unit. His

Above: Housing abandonment and arson (depicted here in the Bronx) swept across a number of New York neighborhoods in the 1970s and became a central feature of the city's crisis. (MEL ROSENTHAL / MUSEUM OF THE CITY OF NEW YORK) *Below:* Soon-to-be-mayor John Lindsay (speaking) and Governor Nelson Rockefeller in 1965. The two clashed sharply on Rockefeller's drug laws and rent-decontrol measures. (BETTMANN / CONTRIBUTOR VIA GETTY IMAGES)

Above: **Students protest segregation in New York's public schools, February 3, 1964.** (AP PHOTO / JOHN LINDSAY) ***Below:*** **A month later, white parents march across the Brooklyn Bridge to City Hall to protest the city's desegregation plans. In the wake of the political failure of the integration and community control movements, many reformers would shift their focus to creating new schools and providing greater choice.** (AP PHOTO / ANONYMOUS)

Above: Ed Koch (left) and Mario Cuomo (right) square off during the 1977 mayoral campaign. (GENE KAPPOCK / NY DAILY NEWS ARCHIVE VIA GETTY IMAGES) *Below:* U.S. Attorney Rudolph Giuliani (left) and Senator Alfonse D'Amato (right), with Parole Commission Chair Benjamin Baer, during an undercover drug raid in Washington Heights, 1986. (MISHA ERWITT / NY DAILY NEWS ARCHIVE VIA GETTY IMAGES)

Graffiti and open-air drug markets became leading symbols of the city's loss of control in the 1970s and '80s—and targets of city efforts to reassert authority. *Above:* A Guardian Angel on a graffiti-strewn subway train, 1987. (RITA BARROS / GETTY IMAGES) *Below:* Police Commissioner Benjamin Ward and Mayor Koch examine narcotics and weapons seized during Operation Pressure Point, 1984. (MEL FINKELSTEIN / NY DAILY NEWS ARCHIVE VIA GETTY IMAGES)

The late 1990s saw perhaps the largest upswell of protest politics in New York since the 1960s. *Above:* Tenants rally in Albany to preserve rent regulations during the "Rent Wars" of 1997. (THE LAGUARDIA AND WAGNER ARCHIVES, LAGUARDIA COMMUNITY COLLEGE / THE CITY UNIVERSITY OF NEW YORK) *Below:* Assembly Speaker Sheldon Silver, a Lower East Side Democrat, addresses the crowd. (AP PHOTO / TIM ROSKE)

The largest protest campaigns in the city focused on police harassment and violence. *Above:* Protesters in Foley Square shortly after the police murder of immigrant street vendor Amadou Diallo in early 1999. (JONATHAN ELDERFIELD / GETTY IMAGES) *Below:* A month later, the demonstrations had grown markedly; here the Rev. Al Sharpton addresses a rally of more than a thousand on Wall Street before his arrest for blocking traffic. (ANDREW LICHTENSTEIN / GETTY IMAGES)

Above: Street frisks (here in Harlem, 2008) proliferated in the late 1990s and 2000s, a source of anxiety and humiliation for many Black and Latino New Yorkers. (MICHAEL MATTHEWS—POLICE IMAGES / ALAMY STOCK PHOTO) *Below:* Bill Clinton swears in Bill de Blasio as the city's mayor in 2014. Standing in the front row (left to right) are David Dinkins, Charles Schumer, Michael Bloomberg, Andrew Cuomo, and Hillary Clinton. (UPI / JOHN ANGELILLO VIA ALAMY STOCK PHOTO)

School politics in the 2010s. *Above:* A pro–charter school rally in Prospect Park, 2016. (DREW ANGERER / GETTY IMAGES) *Below:* A street march protesting school segregation and inequality, 2015. (SPENCER PLATT / GETTY IMAGES) Proponents of charters felt they offered disadvantaged students opportunities for advancement; opponents thought they introduced a new mode of inequality into the city's schools.

Senate Republican Campaign Committee had been the single largest beneficiary of the nearly $700,000 that the three major landlord groups had given in the most recent election.[3]

Leadership in the Assembly had passed to Sheldon Silver, a longtime veteran of the state legislature whose downtown Manhattan district centered on the Lower East Side. Silver, an Orthodox Jew, had spent the early years of his life in a tenement on Henry Street, downstairs from his grandparents; when he was five, his family moved to the Sidney Hillman Houses, a working-class co-op sponsored by the Amalgamated Clothing Workers. On the strength of the Grand Street Jewish vote, he won election to the State Assembly in 1976 and began a steady ascent through the Democratic ranks. Phlegmatic and poker-faced, his speech filled with noncommittal "I hear ya"s and "What can I tell you?"s, Silver was renowned, one journalist wrote, for his "willingness to use time as his friend, stalling in the face of great pressure" while waiting for the opportune moment to strike a deal. His political rival Eliot Spitzer described him as "an enigma, the grandmaster of the chess game of Albany maneuvers." One of the most powerful figures in New York, Silver still lived in the Hillman Houses, "two floors below the apartment he grew up in," and got fourteen-dollar haircuts from the Astor Place barbershop.[4]

Silver represented a district full of renters. He possessed a deep desire to preserve the demographic makeup of his historically Jewish district, both out of personal preference and in order to maintain his political base (a consideration that had led him to oppose the construction of new affordable housing on the Lower East Side, which would have changed the ethnic composition of his district). He had become New York City's primary defender in a state government now dominated, for the first time since the early 1920s, by politicians who had little connection to it and who did not depend on its votes in the way Republicans like Nelson Rockefeller had. But he also faced the challenging task of holding together his caucus, which was deeply divided between liberals and moderates and torn on how much to trade off on other issues in order to preserve rent regulation.[5]

In December 1996, Bruno was scheduled to give what was supposed to be a below-the-radar address before a meeting of the Rent Stabilization Association. Sensing that something newsworthy might happen, the New York State Tenants and Neighbors Coalition, a leading tenant group, convinced two reporters to attend. Bruno duly provided them with sensational material, saying that he wanted to phase out "almost all rent regulation" within two years. If he encountered opposition, he said, he was willing simply to let the existing law lapse when it expired in mid-1997. What might otherwise have been a methodical, behind-the-scenes effort at housing deregulation was now destined to play out on the front pages of the city press and on evening news broadcasts for the next six months.[6]

Democrats immediately suspected that Bruno was staking out a far-right position in the hopes of ending up with vacancy deregulation as a compromise measure. Pataki, caught off guard by Bruno's speech, quickly came out against rapid deregulation, calling for an "intelligent transition" to a market-driven system, though he left little doubt that his ultimate goal was the same as Bruno's: full deregulation.[7]

As winter turned to spring, the outlines of the contest sharpened. Pataki and D'Amato would leverage Bruno's position to try to arrive at full vacancy deregulation and expanded luxury deregulation. As the landlord organizations lobbied behind closed doors, Democrats and tenant activists cranked up the pressure on Pataki, D'Amato, and the downstate Republicans whose support Bruno would need to push through significant deregulation. In April, tenant organizations, who had been building membership and staff and developing strategy since the fall of 1993 in preparation for this battle, launched into action, handing out flyers, staging phonebanks, and holding community meetings; as the deadline drew closer, they bused up to Albany, first by the hundreds and then by the thousands. At the same time, the Democrats ran television and radio ads urging voters to hold Pataki and D'Amato personally responsible for deregulation. Even the archbishop of the Catholic church, John Cardinal O'Connor, weighed in, suggesting in a Sunday sermon that hasty deregulation posed a threat to the church's belief in dignified housing as a human right.[8]

Pataki, wary of taking a position on such a controversial issue a year out from his reelection campaign, initially preferred to remain above the fray and to serve as a mediator between the warring camps. But as the rent regulation question began to dominate the local news, his advisers urged him to demonstrate strong leadership—and so he waded into the fight by offering his own plan. The details were unsurprising—vacancy deregulation, with an allowance for family members to take over stabilized leases and a lowering of the luxury deregulation threshold. But it quickly became clear that he had miscalculated. Pataki, the journalist Elizabeth Kolbert wrote, had made himself the "chief target of tenant ire"; at tenant rallies, he was now "portrayed as a menace not just to the tenants themselves, but to all that makes life in New York City worth living, if not to the very survival of the metropolis." Not only had he thrown away the chance to present vacancy deregulation as a compromise measure during the hectic final hours of the legislative session, with the threat of immediate deregulation hanging over the proceedings; he had also ensured that he would bear responsibility for the final deal.[9]

The pro-regulation coalition still faced significant disadvantages. They could put direct electoral pressure on only a handful of state officials; only Pataki and six downstate Republican state senators had significant numbers of regulated renters among their constituents, and most of those GOP senators were so deeply entrenched that they were more or less immune to electoral threats (though this also gave them the freedom to defy the GOP leadership). The real estate industry, always powerful, had built key fundraising and lobbying connections to the state GOP. The press generally opposed extending the existing rent laws, favoring various forms of deregulation. And after the 1994 City Council vote, it was unclear that even New York City Democrats would support the existing laws.[10]

But the coalition also had important strengths—above all, its scope and diversity. Tenant groups dotted the metropolitan area, representing people from many different backgrounds and social classes: from the Westchester Tenants Coalition north of the city to the Hempstead Tenants Council on Long Island; from the Coalición de Inquilinos del Norte de Manhattan and the Association for Neighborhood and Housing Development in upper Manhattan to the Queens League of United Tenants and the Bensonhurst Tenants Council in Brooklyn—all brought together by the citywide Metropolitan Council on Housing and the statewide New York State Tenants and Neighbors. The pro-regulation coalition also included key labor unions, particularly 1199 heath care workers, DC 37 public sector workers, the United Auto Workers, and Local 1180 of the Communications Workers of America, whose leaders viewed regulation as a bulwark against the emergence of a luxury city in which their members could no longer afford to live; 1199's phone bank, in particular, was key to the tenants' efforts to pressure downstate senators. And it included senior citizens' organizations, which were especially important in relatively pro-GOP neighborhoods such as Bay Ridge, where Pataki and D'Amato needed votes.

The coalition's breadth and diversity allowed it to engage in the range of political tasks necessary to blunt the push for deregulation. Tenant and labor groups from solidly Democratic districts could push their representatives to hold the line on regulation—not a given after the 1994 council vote. Other groups could work on the key Senate Republicans, particularly Roy Goodman of the Upper East Side and Frank Padavan of Queens, whose political stature gave them the power to undermine Pataki and Bruno's efforts. Collectively, the coalition had the numbers to keep their cause front and center—through rallies, leafleting and canvassing sessions, media outreach, phone banking, letter-writing campaigns, and more.[11]

The pro-regulation forces had gone into action when the legislative session opened in January, but they really picked up their efforts once Pataki put his proposal on the table. They kept up a campaign of unrelenting public pressure: On May 20, the Showdown '97 coalition, an alliance of tenant groups, ferried more than 160 buses to Albany, where tenants set up lobbying appointments with legislators and held a large outdoor rally on the east steps of the Capitol. Downstate, tenants picketed Pataki's Manhattan office, held candlelight vigils, and marched from REBNY's headquarters to Pataki's office led by an actor dressed as a stylized fat cat.[12]

Through May and June, Pataki's position gradually crumbled. Vallone, whose district was beginning to see the effects of the extension of high-rent vacancy deregulation he had pushed through the City Council in 1994, joined his Queens constituents as they bused up to Albany for the pro-regulation rallies. "What vacancy decontrol will do," he said, "is not only affect the people that are living in the apartments today, but will forever bar these apartments to the young working couples—the middle class that this city thrives on. That's what's at stake here." Tenants from neighborhoods across the city—mostly women, many of them elderly—traveled to Albany continuously, staging rallies and meeting with legislators. The district attorneys of Manhattan, Brooklyn, and Queens predicted that vacancy deregulation would lead to an upsurge of tenant harassment. "We are concerned that if you give corrupt landlords an incentive to get people out because of decontrol, they will go back to the professional goon squads," warned Robert Morgenthau, who had prosecuted the harrowing cases of the 1980s. Pataki's approval rating dropped precipitously—polls showed he lost a quarter of his support in New York City between March and June—and downstate senate Republicans that Bruno needed to ensure his measure's passage began to waver.[13]

By early June, Pataki had decided to limit the political damage, and he opened discussions with Silver's aides. On Father's Day, Pataki, Bruno, and Silver sat down to hash out an agreement. Bruno left for a family luncheon. When he returned, he discovered that Pataki, after consulting with D'Amato, had agreed with Silver on a framework that excluded full vacancy deregulation: a six-year extension that would drop the luxury deregulation threshold from $250,000 to $175,000 and limit vacancy deregulation to apartments renting for more than $2,000. The framework contained two additional provisions—concessions from Silver—that would prove hugely significant in the coming years. First, it afforded building owners a 20 percent bump in rent each time an apartment turned over—a new statutory entitlement that took control of vacancy bonuses away from the Rent Guidelines Board, which had typically set them around 5 percent. (The increase in the vacancy bonus had the additional effect of disincentivizing tenants from moving from one regulated unit to another.) Second, building on prior practice, landlords were permitted permanent rent increases of up to 6 percent to amortize the expense of "major capital improvements," referring to building-wide upgrades such as new roofs and boilers, an allowance meant to improve the quality of the housing stock that in practice helped landlords inch closer to the deregulation threshold. Tenant leaders accused Silver of negotiating away more than he had to, considering the leverage the movement had built up against Pataki and D'Amato. But Bruno was livid. Angrily kicking the furniture, Bruno, having failed to sweep aside a system that had stood for half a century, launched into a lecture about "the failures of social engineering."[14]

Thus Pataki and the Senate Republicans enacted the most extensive loosening of rent regulation since Nelson Rockefeller's ill-fated vacancy decontrol law of 1971. Although the immediate effects of high-rent deregulation were limited, tenants were right to worry that inflation, coupled with vacancy and capital-improvement allowances, would eat away at the real value of the $2,000 deregulation threshold. With each passing year, thousands of apartments would leave the system, bringing deregulation to bear not just on the wealthy but also on the middle and working classes. The combination of the vacancy bonus and the deregulation threshold would give landlords real incentives to harass rent-stabilized tenants. And for all that the press had focused on wealthy Manhattanites, the outcome had placed working-class and poor New Yorkers at considerable risk of displacement should gentrification and real estate speculation take off in their neighborhoods. In these ways, the law had planted the seeds of a new housing crisis.

Still, by outmaneuvering Bruno and Pataki and preventing full vacancy deregulation, the tenant movement and its Democratic allies had bought time: By keeping more than a million units—enough to house nearly the entire population of Chicago—within the system, at least for the near future, they had preserved the possibility that a future progressive movement could strengthen rent regulation. Which of these possibilities would prevail remained to be fought out as the new century dawned.

By the end of the 1990s, New York's housing stock was in markedly better condition. Under Giuliani's commissioner of housing and development, Deborah Wright, the city nearly finished the process of unloading the units it had acquired through tax default in the 1970s and early '80s, and swelling immigrant populations continued to revitalize neighborhoods that had fallen into disrepair during the urban crisis. Under the surface, though, the new housing crisis only deepened. Amid the budgetary stress of his first years in office, Giuliani had cut back sharply on spending on housing construction, ending the period of municipal investment that had begun with Koch's housing plan and continued under Dinkins. Pataki and the state legislature, following the Reagan administration's example of a decade earlier, had cut funding for NYCHA public housing, setting in motion a chain of disinvestment that would erupt in the twenty-first century. In the absence of affordable housing in the formal market, the new immigrant working class had come to rely increasingly on often dangerous informal housing, basement apartments, and illegally subdivided units prone to flooding and fire: Between 1990 and 2000, researchers estimated, the city gained 114,000 informal apartments, a testament to the city's failure to produce new, legitimate affordable units. In total, by the end of the decade, more than a quarter of New York renters were spending half or more of their household income on rent. Beneath it all, the new rent laws had just made tenant dislocation one of the more potentially profitable industries in the city.[15]

IF THE 1997 RENT WAR had been fought along relatively clear-cut partisan lines, positions in the school choice battle were far more tangled. Reformers with fundamentally different visions saw in the combination of small, innovative schools and school choice a means of achieving what they valued. As the decade unfolded, it was sometimes unclear who owned school choice. Was it a way of scaling up the teacher-driven, community-based experiments of the 1970s? An opening wedge for the creative destruction of the public school system? Or a Clintonian middle path? For a while, as people from all points on the political spectrum came together behind small-schools-and-choice, these questions seemed secondary to the question of whether the reform movement would make progress or not. As time passed, though, it would become clear just how profound these differences in vision were.

By the end of the 1990s, the reform movement had created enough successful new schools to change the city's educational landscape. In 2001, the education expert and public school parent Clara Hemphill published the first edition of a widely read book, *New York City's Best Public High Schools: A Parents' Guide*. The handbook featured several older selective schools: the long-standing four "specialized" high schools—Stuyvesant, Bronx Science, Brooklyn Tech, and LaGuardia—as well as Hunter College High School; large traditional high schools that boasted special selective programs such as Dewitt Clinton High School in the Bronx, Midwood High School in Brooklyn, and Benjamin Cardozo High School in Queens; and 1970s and '80s–era magnet, selective, and ed-op schools such as A. Philip Randolph Campus High School in upper Manhattan, Edward R. Murrow High School in Brooklyn, and Middle College High School and Townsend Harris High School in Queens.

But the bulk of the guide amounted to a compendium of the city's new public schools. In Manhattan, where the movement had spread fastest, there was an archipelago of institutions founded by Central Park East alums or affiliated with Deborah Meier's Center for Collaborative Education: East Side Community High School (1992), the Institute for Collaborative Education (1993), and the Landmark School (1993). Other recently launched high schools included the Lab School for Collaborative Studies (1987), the School of the Future (1990), the Frederick Douglass Academy (1991), the High School for Environmental Studies (1992), the Beacon School (1993), the New York City Museum School (1994), and the Young Women's Leadership School (1996).

In Brooklyn and Queens, the offerings were fewer but still ample. Among others, Brooklyn boasted Brooklyn College Academy, founded in 1986 as a collaboration between the Board of Education and Brooklyn College; Middle College High School at Medgar Evers College, established in 1993 with a grant from New Visions; and the Leon Goldstein High School for the Sciences, opened in 1993. Queens had the Robert F. Wagner, Jr. Institute for the Arts and Technology, founded in 1993 with grants from New Visions and the Annenberg Foundation, and the Academy of American Studies, established in 1996 in Long Island City with support from the Gilder Lehrman Institute of American History and the Manhattan

Institute's Center for Educational Innovation. Staten Island had Staten Island Tech, launched in 1988 as a selective high school on the model of Stuyvesant, Bronx Science, and Brooklyn Tech; and Michael J. Petrides School, an ed-op school founded in 1995 on the former campus of the College of Staten Island. Only in the Bronx, notably, had the small-school movement yet to really take root.[16]

The proliferation of new schools and the rise of public school choice spawned a new journalistic genre: tales from the "school choice wars." In feature after feature, reporters chronicled the "Darwinian struggle" over scarce seats in the most selective public schools, a competition that tested the capacities of even the savviest parents. Clara Hemphill, despite her literally encyclopedic knowledge of the city's public schools, professed that she found the rounds of tours, interviews, and tests "bewildering." "Basically, somebody has to give up their job for three months to find a school." The radio host Brian Lehrer was living on the Upper West Side when it came time to enroll his son in kindergarten. Reluctant to send him to the neighborhood school, P.S. 163, because less than a quarter of the students read at grade level, Lehrer and his partner began visiting schools both inside and outside their home district—starting two full years ahead of time. "We are working harder to get him into kindergarten than I worked to get into graduate school," Lehrer told a reporter. They applied to five schools, three of which required competitive exams; in each application, they made it known "that they would be enthusiastic volunteers and fundraisers." Even though many new selective public schools aimed for diversity, the admissions process rewarded families with the resources and social networks to navigate it.[17]

The clustering of affluent families in public schools of choice compounded the advantages those schools enjoyed. Major disparities developed between the city's parent-teacher associations (PTAs), which raised money for supplemental programs and services—additional equipment, after-school programs, more guidance counselors. By the time the city started collecting data in 2019, some PTAs were raising millions of dollars per year; fundraising per student ranged from practically nothing in the city's poorest neighborhoods to more than $2,000 per student in schools with more affluent PTAs. Better-off parents could also pool resources to surmount barriers to access, such as bad transportation connections. Parents in the Queens neighborhood of Belle Harbor hired two private buses to transport their children to the Mark Twain School for the Gifted and Talented in Coney Island. By 1996, Mark Twain—created by a desegregation court order—was seeing protests from Coney Island parents who viewed it as "an enclave for white students, largely closed to" Black and Latino children "who have to go to schools outside their neighborhood."[18]

In some instances, federal magnet school grant programs conferred additional advantages on white applicants. Because these programs required magnet schools to achieve and maintain a balance between "minority" and "nonminority" (i.e., nonwhite and white) students, some schools needed to court white students in order to retain their funding. Schools that failed to do so could pay the penalty: In 1995, the integrated P.S. 154 in Flushing, Queens, lost $70,000 in federal magnet funding because its demographics—35 percent Asian, 35 percent Black, 20 percent Latino, and 10 percent white—reflected the makeup of the surrounding community.[19]

Having gained access to outstanding new public schools, affluent parents were determined to keep it. In 1995, the superintendent of District 3 announced a plan to move one of two gifted-and-talented programs housed in P.S. 9 on West 84th Street to P.S. 166, a predominantly Black and Latino school on West 89th Street, which could be more easily renovated to make the program handicap-accessible. Hundreds of P.S. 9 parents held a candlelight vigil to protest the plan, accusing the district of seeking to sacrifice their high-performing school in order to aid P.S. 166. "In a city where so many things don't work, why tear up a school that is working?" asked one parent, an assistant managing editor at *Fortune* magazine. Even after the District 3 school board affirmed the plan, the parents continued to hold out: "I don't know if it will be a quiet behind-the-scenes fight or a loud, legal fight," one parent mused. "But we will fight." In January 1998, the district found that there were now enough gifted students to justify retaining the existing program at P.S. 9 while opening a new one at P.S. 166.[20]

For one group of parents on the Upper East Side, even the expanding menu of magnet, gifted-and-talented, and other screened programs was insufficient. The group, many of whose children attended the predominantly white neighborhood elementary school P.S. 6, worried that the traditional high schools in District 2 were inadequate in quality and that the various screened programs did not offer an appropriate alternative, since the admissions formula adopted in the late 1980s sought to balance high-, average-, and low-performing students. They therefore began to lobby for a new neighborhood high school. "Despite paying the highest tax rates in New York City," the Partnership for an Upper East Side High School argued, "we don't have a school that will prepare our children to go to the superior colleges they are qualified to attend."[21]

In June 2001, the Board of Education, together with Manhattan borough president C. Virginia Fields and Representative Carolyn Maloney, announced its intention to establish a new seven-hundred-student district high school on East 76th Street, pairing the announcement with a pledge of enhanced funding for the predominantly Black and Latino Life Sciences Secondary School. The Partnership for an Upper East Side High School reacted with skepticism—the District 2 school board, keenly aware that the school would be seen as reinforcing segregation, wanted the new high school to be open to students throughout the district and planned to adhere to the ed-op admissions formula—and denounced the plan as a sham. Their fears proved unfounded; as of 2020, two-thirds of Eleanor Roosevelt High School's students were white, and only about one-fifth qualified for a free or reduced-price lunch.[22]

The concentration of affluent parents and high-achieving students within new schools and programs exacerbated the inequalities within the system. New York State's funding formula only made matters worse: the rapid immigration of the 1980s and '90s swelled the school-age populations in a number of neighborhoods, particularly in Queens, yet the state formula placed a cap on how much additional revenue could be delivered to the schools each year. A coalition of advocates and parents called the Campaign for Fiscal Equity brought suit, accusing Albany of violating the state constitution's guarantee of a "sound basic education"; they would ultimately emerge victorious in 2004.

In the meantime, the Community Service Society, a leading local nonprofit, estimated that the Board of Education spent some $2 billion less per year than what was necessary to provide every high school student an adequate education. Inequities in teaching staff were especially stark. Schools that were disadvantaged in other dimensions badly needed effective, experienced teachers. Yet the opposite was transpiring: Elementary and intermediate schools with low reading scores were less likely to have permanently assigned, licensed, and experienced teachers; their teachers also received lower salaries, came and went more frequently, and were more often absent from class. "We have savage inequalities," said a principal whose traditional intermediate school in Queens was losing students to a neighboring magnet school. "Some kids are treated like cattle while, 13 blocks away, kids are treated like individuals. It's just not fair."[23]

Like Americans writ large, New Yorkers had come to invest their schools with an unreasonable degree of responsibility for addressing major problems—providing upward mobility, reducing intergenerational poverty, ensuring economic competitiveness—while depriving them of the resources that might have helped them contribute to such tasks. Having burdened them with such expectations, policymakers turned an increasingly critical eye toward schools that struggled to produce acceptable test scores, attendance records, and graduation rates—institutions that were increasingly labeled "failing" schools, a framing applied most often to high schools, where the cumulative costs of inequality were most evident. By the late 1990s, Governor Pataki's commissioner of education was threatening state takeovers of underperforming schools, and the city Board of Education had initiated a number of school closures.[24]

In effect, the proliferation of desirable options within the public school system, and de facto preferred access to them, allowed New York's growing population of relatively well-off families to access public institutions in a diverse city without the redistributive implications of desegregation. This state of affairs did not go unopposed. The Brooklyn chapter of the Alliance of Community Organizations for Reform Now (ACORN) conducted a series of studies of the city's gifted-and-talented programs and specialized high schools, the findings of which led to a federal Office of Civil Rights investigation of New York's gifted-and-talented programs, and which ACORN members publicized with a demonstration at Stuyvesant High School. District 26 in Queens, where Black and Latino students made up 22 percent of the district total but only 7 percent of the students in the gifted-and-talented programs, announced the relatively modest intention of delaying the intelligence test that governed admission to the programs by a year, in order to expand access for English-language learners and other underrepresented groups; the co-president of a group called Concerned Citizens for the Education of Gifted and Talented Children duly accused the district of taking "the first step toward dismantling the gifted program."[25]

Schools Chancellor Rudy Crew, appointed in late 1995 after Mayor Giuliani hounded the popular Dinkins appointee Ramón Cortines from office, also took aim at inequality within the city's selective schools. In 1997, he announced a plan to bar testing and application fees for the gifted-and-talented programs and to encourage districts to incorporate a broader range of admissions criteria; in response to ACORN's civil rights complaint, the Board of Education also agreed to take additional steps to disseminate information about special programs and their admissions procedures. The same year the Board of Education launched an eighteen-month preparatory program called the Math and Science Institute to help prepare underrepresented students for the demanding entrance exam that governed admissions to the city's three specialized high schools. The early returns were promising: Nearly 60 percent of the students in the program scored high enough to gain admission to one of the three schools; the share of Stuyvesant's incoming class who were Black rose from 4.3 percent to 5.5 percent. Still, in a city where nearly 40 percent of public school students were Black, these figures showed just how far there remained to go.[26]

WHILE PARENTS, COMMUNITY ORGANIZATIONS, and city leaders were contending over access to the city's most desired schools, Governor Pataki and his allies were working to create an entirely new set of institutions. As originally envisioned by teachers' union leaders in the late 1980s, charter schools—publicly funded schools operating independent of the traditional public school system—would have looked much like the alternative schools that had popped up in East Harlem and across the city: "collaborative R&D labs" that would afford teachers a chance to "try experimental methods, pedagogy, and curricula" in collaboration with traditional schools, teachers' unions, and local school boards. As the charter school movement took off in the early 1990s, however, it quickly became evident that some reformers saw charters not as partners working collaboratively with the traditional system but as a way of challenging the existing system. When the State of Minnesota enacted the first charter law in the country in 1991, it vested the power to create new schools in state agencies unencumbered by local school boards and teachers' unions. "That opened charter doors not only to teachers but also to outside entrepreneurs," the political scientist Paul Peterson noted. Charter laws written in such a fashion offered would-be educational disruptors an opportunity to work free from the constraints that governed the rest of the system.[27]

As the charter movement gained ground in New York in the mid-1990s, it still remained unclear which of these alternatives would prevail—which meant that some version of a charter law won support across much of the political spectrum and from very different constituencies within the city. Progressives could run hot and cold on the charter concept but were by no means outright opposed: Deborah Meier and her reform colleagues viewed charters largely as a sideshow, albeit one with the potential to distract from the real work of public education—"Charters are political, not educational," the Center for Collaborative Education claimed; in their follow-up application to the Annenberg Foundation, the CCE noted that it was seeking "to prove that innovation can flourish within a public system," noting that "no charter school, or group of charter schools, under any present charter legislation, is obligated to accept all types of children." Some progressive education scholars, such as Joseph Viteritti (who had co-convened the NYU working group with Diane Ravitch), heartily embraced charters in the name of equity. For their part, the leading figures in the city's education establishment, Chancellor Crew and United Federation of Teachers president Sandra Feldman, vowed to support the establishment of charters. "I really deeply believe in charter schools," Crew said at a 1986 meeting at the Harvard Club. The Board of Education included a law providing for district-approved charter schools along with additional start-up money for "theme based magnet schools" in its wish list for the 1998 legislative session.[28]

For reformers on the right, charters represented an opportunity, not to innovate within the traditional public school system, but rather to subject what they saw as sclerotic bureaucracies and self-dealing teachers' unions to real competition. Right-of-center education reformers in New York especially admired the results produced by the city's Catholic schools, and they might have preferred a voucher system to allow poor families the chance to attend them or other successful private schools: Vouchers, Sol Stern wrote in *City Journal*, were "the only reform that fundamentally challenges the monopoly system of public education from the outside." But vouchers were a political nonstarter in New York. Charter schools, on the other hand, had crossover support; they provided a politically feasible opportunity to subject the traditional public school system to the discipline of outside competition, especially if the charter law enabled them to operate outside the rules and strictures of the existing system.[29]

To some parents and communities underserved by the traditional public school system, the charter school movement seemed to offer something of the promise of the community control movement of the 1960s: a chance to reclaim authority from the public school system and take command of education at the neighborhood level. The appeal of the charter idea, explained Queens assemblyman Jeffrion Aubry, head of the Black and Hispanic Caucus, was "the concept that as a community, you can take control of your own destiny." Black political leaders were divided on charter schools; Latino legislators and community leaders were more uniformly in support, though they tended to view charters not as a salvation but as a response to an untenable status quo. Long underserved by magnet and educational option programs and hugely underrepresented in gifted-and-talented programs, predominantly Latino neighborhoods had now largely been passed over by the small-school movement of the 1990s. "As long as there are no viable alternatives for many of our children," said the pastor of a bilingual church in the South Bronx, "we endorse the concept of charter schools." *El Diario–La Prensa* endorsed charters as a way of facilitating parental involvement, though it was quick to warn that the approach was not a panacea. Ultimately, every Latino member of the New York City assembly delegation would vote in favor of the state charter law.[30]

Finally, the charter concept drew considerable interest from Wall Street. Some investors saw charters as a business opportunity, a chance to "mak[e] a profit while making a difference," as one private equity journal put it. Others viewed charters as an opportunity to give back to the city while demonstrating the supposed superiority of markets, private management, and nonunionized workplaces—and perhaps to state the case that upward mobility remained possible within a desperately unequal economy. Whereas the push for small alternative public schools had received support primarily from large, established philanthropies, charters operated on a scale that welcomed the involvement of individual philanthropists, their giving capacity having grown considerably thanks to the Wall Street boom and regressive changes to the federal tax code. Wall Street businessmen eager to support charter schools backed the campaign for a state charter law to the tune of $100,000 through a political action committee called School Choice Now.[31]

These contending visions would play out in Albany as lawmakers answered a handful of crucial questions. Would charter schools be required to hire state-certified teachers? Would their teachers be members of the UFT? Would they be required to win approval and funding from local school boards, as the existing alternative schools did? Or would they be free to operate more independently of existing rules and institutions? Governor Pataki first proposed a charter law at the start of the tumultuous 1997 session, only to find the issue consigned to the back burner as the rent wars raged. In 1998, he made a more concerted push for a measure, drafted in consultation with the Manhattan Institute's Center for Educational Innovation, that would minimize the role of the teachers' unions and the local school districts. As the regular session closed in June, though, Assembly speaker Sheldon Silver was still blocking the bill on account of the unions' objections.[32]

But Pataki—who had just won reelection by 20 points in a year that had seen his ally D'Amato knocked off by Democratic congressman Charles Schumer of Brooklyn—still had a card to play. Shortly after the 1998 elections, the state legislature convened for a special session to take up an issue of great importance to many of its members. Lawmakers had not seen a pay raise in ten years, during which time inflation had eaten away about a quarter of their salaries' real value. Pataki let it be known that he would go along with a pay hike—so long as he got a charter bill. Chancellor Crew and the new head of the UFT, Randi Weingarten, scrambled behind the scenes to win some concessions, but the final version of the bill closely reflected Pataki's conservative vision. The law permitted one hundred new charter schools across the state and the conversion (with approval of parents and local school districts) of an unlimited number of existing public schools, which would be exempt from a range of state and local laws, rules, regulations, and policies—opening the door, crucially, to nonunion teachers. Authority for these schools would rest not in local school boards but in the State Board of Regents, chosen by the state legislature, and the Board of Trustees of the State University of New York, controlled by the governor. The law also permitted applications from for-profit corporations so long as they partnered with nonprofit organizations. Pataki celebrated what he called "the single greatest improvement in education in state history"; Chancellor Crew described the measure as "fraught with peril." Asked about the unseemly charters-for-pay raise deal, Pataki replied tersely: "You know how the system works."[33]

The SUNY Board of Trustees chartered the first eight schools, four of them run by for-profit entities, in June 1999. New York's first charter school, the Sisulu Children's Academy, a collaboration between Harlem community activists and a partner at a leveraged buyout firm, opened that September. Within a couple of years, it was evident that the charter process as administered by the SUNY Board of Trustees and the state Board of Regents was better suited to wealthy, large-scale organizations and to those community groups that partnered with them than it was to independent grassroots operators, who struggled to provide the technical information demanded by the Board of Regents and to secure the financing necessary to meet the charter law's requirement that the school demonstrate it could be operated "in a fiscally sound manner." "The way this law is being administered, only wealthy people can create charter schools," griped District 4 alum and CEI president Seymour Fliegel. Among those who tried and failed to navigate the application process was Babette Edwards, the Harlem advocate who had pushed for vouchers in the 1970s as a way of empowering Black parents. After jumping through a number of hoops, she had her application rejected, she believed, because she had placed too much emphasis on parental involvement.[34]

By the dawn of the twenty-first century, a growing collection of alternative and charter schools had taken their place alongside the city's traditional public schools. In some respects, the unlikely consensus that had assembled behind school reform in the first half of the 1990s had hung together through the second half. Still, significant and hotly contested questions about the implantation of these new school models remained to be answered. What would be the relationship between the small-schools-and-choice movement and the regime of testing and standards that had so troubled Meier? How many charters would there be, and what would be their effect on the traditional public schools? What kinds of power would school administrators, principals, teachers, parents, students, and community members possess over education? How would New York's profound racial segregation and inequality shape its system of school choice? As city, state, and national officials took the next steps in reform in the early twenty-first century, answers to these questions would gradually come into focus.

MAYOR GIULIANI HAD PLAYED an important but ultimately secondary role in the politics of rent regulation and school reform. He declined to block City Council Speaker Peter Vallone's extension of high-rent deregulation, but it was Vallone, not Giuliani, who was the driving force behind the measure. And although tenant leaders appreciated his efforts to preserve rent regulation during the 1997 rent wars, which gave the pro-regulation movement valuable bipartisan credence, his was a minor part in a drama that starred Pataki, Bruno, Silver, D'Amato, and the tenant activists. His imprint on the schools was somewhat more substantial; in the wake of Pataki's charter law, he personally proposed a $10 million fund to help charter schools with start-up costs. (He also issued a hugely controversial proposal for a school voucher program, indelicately calling for the public school system to be "blown up" two days after the Columbine High shootings.) Still, education reform was driven primarily by chancellors, educators, philanthropists, policy intellectuals, and Albany politicians.[35]

Policing was a different matter. Giuliani, the journalist Jack Newfield wrote, "came into City Hall knowing what he wanted to do about crime. Law enforcement was his priesthood." Having grown up with four uncles who were police officers, he "knew policing in his bones. He liked cops. . . . He understood cop culture. He loathed criminals. He had been elected because the fear of crime was the biggest issue, and voters saw him as a tough, strong remedy." Though crime had been falling under Dinkins, it remained high by historical standards, giving Giuliani the latitude to make crime fighting the centerpiece of his mayoralty. Policing and crime would come to define his time in office—its legacy, its achievements, and its greatest failures.[36]

To run the NYPD, Giuliani turned to a figure closely associated with the emphasis on quality of life and public civility he had made central to his 1993 campaign: Bill Bratton, the onetime Transit Police chief whose focus on fare evasion, homelessness, and panhandling in the subways had won the admiration of *City Journal*. "Can you do in the street what you did in the subway?" Giuliani asked him. Thanks to Dinkins, Cuomo, and the state legislature, Bratton immediately inherited a windfall of some 4,200 officers funded through Safe Streets, Safe City. Giuliani, in turn, exempted the NYPD from the budget strictures that marked his first two years, a decision that split local economic elites—the Real Estate Board of New York lining up in support, the Citizens Budget Commission in opposition. The federal government delivered additional funding through the Violent Crime Control and Law Enforcement Act, signed into law by President Bill Clinton—in all, the number of uniformed NYPD officers grew by 47.4 percent between 1990 and 1997. More broadly, Giuliani's rise to power brought a cultural shift within the NYPD. Nearly everyone—from the department's ardent supporters to critics of police misconduct to the officers themselves—agreed that the department felt less constrained in its actions than it had with Dinkins in charge.[37]

Bratton's tenure as police commissioner is often regarded as revolutionary. In fact, Bratton shared key points of emphasis with his predecessors: Like Benjamin Ward, he targeted open-air drug markets. (Bratton mentioned Operation Pressure Point as a precedent in two of the policing strategy documents the NYPD produced early in his tenure.) Like Lee Brown, he emphasized proactive, problem-oriented policing. And like Ray Kelly, who had initiated the crackdowns on squeegee men late in the Dinkins years, he took aim at minor quality-of-life offenses. Where he departed from his predecessors most significantly was not in focus but in methods. Though he believed in some of the precepts of community policing, Bratton felt the approach placed an unrealistic amount of responsibility on beat cops, who were often young and inexperienced. Better, he felt, to locate problem-solving responsibility with more experienced precinct commanders, who could in turn marshal resources to address issues at the neighborhood level.[38]

But how to hold precinct commanders accountable? And how to impose his own priorities and strategies on the vast bureaucracy of the NYPD—something with which reforming commissioners had struggled for decades? Bratton and his deputy commissioner, the bow-tied, irrepressible former transit police officer Jack Maple, devised a solution: twice-weekly meetings in which precinct commanders were held to strict account for patterns of crime and disorder in their districts, displayed in near-real time through a computer system called CompStat—a digital version of the color-coded crime dot maps Bratton had put up in his precinct house back in Boston. This approach was hardly without problems: Accounts soon emerged of a precinct commander who discouraged his officers from filing assault charges unless the victim had suffered broken bones or needed stitches in the name of keeping his numbers low, and critics of the system came to feel that high-stakes CompStat meetings encouraged such manipulation. But by devolving authority to precinct commanders in exchange for this form of accountability, Bratton and Maple not only pushed their own priorities down to the precinct level but also broke through some of the NYPD's traditional stovepiping, as department brass and precinct commanders shared ideas and information in what one observer described as "high-pressure problem-solving sessions."[39]

If Lee Brown had been the paragon of community policing, Bratton was known as a leading champion of George Kelling and James Q. Wilson's Broken Windows theory, and indeed Giuliani said he had appointed him because he believed in the Broken Windows approach. Bratton consistently asserted his conviction that urban disorder was criminogenic in the ways Broken Windows suggested. In contrast, Jack Maple, a key architect of Bratton's anticrime strategy, was openly dismissive of the Broken Windows theory, which he felt rested on a "mystical link" between disorder and crime that did not hold up to the evidence. "Rapists and murderers don't head for another town when they see that graffiti is disappearing from the subway," he wrote. The real link between quality-of-life policing and crime reduction, he argued, was much more instrumental: "Quality-of-life enforcement works to reduce crime because it allows the cops to catch crooks when the crooks are off-duty," leveraging low-level arrests to apprehend people with outstanding warrants for more serious offenses. Some of the NYPD's quality-of-life initiatives under Bratton, then, simply responded to an essentially political demand for more civility in public spaces. Others served as a pretext for strategies targeting more serious crimes.[40]

One campaign, following Koch's and Dinkins's quality-of-life initiatives, took aim at the kinds of "disorderly" activities Kelling and Wilson's theory had targeted for police action. The city's "parks, playgrounds, streets, avenues, stoops, and plazas," Bratton wrote in an early strategy statement, "are the forums that make possible the sense of vitality, excitement, and community that are the pulse of urban life"—but they had been stolen, he claimed, by "aggressive panhandling, squeegee cleaners, street prostitutes, 'boombox' cars, public drunkenness, reckless bicycling, and graffiti." Bratton's NYPD departed from his predecessors' less in its emphasis on quality of life policing than in its tactics: Whereas the community policing approach had called for officers to address instances of disorder through police management, Bratton's department made greater use of criminal sanctions—summonses and misdemeanor arrests. One police captain explained the difference using the example of an open-container violation: "We have to give summonses for things that in the past we could basically *solve* on the spot. If a person was carrying an open container, we could just tell him to put it away and move along. Today, if you have a beer, you're going in. In the past, there would have had to be some kind of trigger for us to lock a guy up."[41]

Another initiative, which also built on Koch- and Dinkins-era predecessors, aimed to wipe out open-air drug markets—a major campaign pledge of Giuliani's and one of Bratton's first priorities upon taking office. Following his general managerial approach, Bratton at first shifted focus away from specialized drug enforcement and toward precinct-level problem-solving, authorizing (and tasking) precinct commanders with conducting place-appropriate antidrug initiatives in their territories and creating new Strategic Narcotics and Drug (SNAG) teams to provide them with assistance. In order to facilitate this decentralized approach—and in spite of the "Cocaine Cowboys" scandals of the late 1980s—he reversed a quarter-century of department policy by encouraging uniformed precinct cops to make drug arrests, which he described as the "most salient" feature of his drug policing program. In line with the Broken Windows approach, Bratton especially encouraged marijuana arrests, which the NYPD had previously considered too trivial to justify the police manpower required to process them.

Drug arrests were already up when, at the end of his first year, Bratton announced the largest antidrug operation in the city's history: Operation Juggernaut. The brainchild of Jack Maple, the program envisioned expanding the narcotics squad from 1,500 to 5,000 officers and launching sustained borough-by-borough campaigns beginning in Queens and moving across Brooklyn and Staten Island before continuing into the Bronx and Manhattan. Giuliani delayed the campaign, ostensibly because of the cost. But even a scaled-down version launched in central and northern Brooklyn and adjacent parts of Queens in early 1996 was the largest such initiative in the city's history. Felony drug arrests, which had soared starting in the mid-1980s, remained roughly stable. But as with the quality-of-life campaign, misdemeanor arrests jumped sharply, bringing thousands more New Yorkers who had not committed the kinds of crimes that led to long-term imprisonment into contact with the criminal justice system, including time in jail.[42]

A third street-level initiative, and the most innovative, sought to reduce violent crime by removing unlicensed guns—a huge factor in the upsurge of homicides—from city streets. Shortly after Bratton took office, James Q. Wilson published a short essay in *The New York Times Sunday Magazine* proposing a new approach to unlicensed guns. Stricter gun control laws, he argued, were not going to prevent non-law-abiding citizens from obtaining guns. The focus, then, should be on street-level police action. The 1968 Supreme Court case *Terry v. Ohio*, he noted, had created a way in which officers could search suspects without meeting the probable cause standard for an arrest: Police officers who observed "unusual conduct" that led them to conclude that criminal activity "may be afoot," the decision held, had the right to stop and question a person without violating the Fourth Amendment's prohibition on unreasonable search and seizure. (Such stops, *Terry* held, had to be based on "specific reasonable inferences," not "inarticulate hunches.") Officers who had reason to believe that the person stopped might be armed then had the right to frisk that person for weapons. The police, Wilson argued, should be encouraged to make street frisks as a way of discovering unlicensed weapons. "There will still be complaints," Wilson recognized. "Innocent people will be stopped. Young [B]lack and Hispanic men will probably be stopped more than older white Anglo males or women of any race. But . . . we must get illegal guns off the street." Bratton adopted the approach, expanding the NYPD's Street Crime Unit by 25 percent and encouraging it to be more aggressive in their pursuit of unlicensed guns. The NYPD's patrol guide gave officers wide latitude to determine who could justifiably be stopped; factors could include "the demeanor of the suspect," "time of day or night," and "the particular streets and areas involved."[43]

As Wilson had frankly acknowledged, for all Giuliani's insistence on "One City, One Standard" and an across-the-board standard of "zero tolerance," Bratton's policing approach had inequality built into it. For Broken Windows to work, Jack Maple wrote, "we needed to be more selective about who we were arresting on quality-of-life infractions. . . . The units enforcing quality-of-life laws must be sent where the maps show concentrations of crime or criminals, and the rules governing the stops have to be designed to catch the sharks, not the dolphins." Under CompStat, officers could be quickly assigned to high-crime areas; once there, they could arrest New Yorkers for low-level offenses such as marijuana possession, check them for outstanding warrants, and fingerprint them. By sending officers into predominantly poor communities of color and encouraging individual officers to concentrate on people who they thought might be serious criminals, Bratton's version of Broken Windows made racialized patterns of enforcement programmatic.[44]

In the mid-1990s, the crime drop that had begun under Dinkins accelerated, with profound and enduring consequences for city life. Homicides dropped from more than two thousand per year at the start of the decade to 673 at its end. Other violent crimes fell sharply as well. Because the crime drop happened simultaneously in many cities, it was likely driven primarily by factors outside Giuliani and the NYPD's control—a hot labor market, the changing age structure of the population, the end of the crack epidemic, and the maturation of the cocaine economy, among others. Still, violent crime fell earlier and more steeply in New York than in other cities, putting Gotham on course to becoming the safest big city in America. Controlling for other variables, criminologists have concluded that the NYPD's crime-fighting strategies, together with antiviolence work by community organizations, likely played a role in reducing violent crime in the city, though it remains unclear precisely how much.[45]

In any case, Giuliani, Bratton, the NYPD, and their allies were prepared to claim credit, and many in the local and national media were eager to deliver it. In the space of a few months, *Time* ran a cover story on Bill Bratton; *New York* announced "The End of Crime As We Knew It"; and *The New York Times* described New York's crime drop as "simply breathtaking," a "marvel," and "a miracle." Bratton's face appeared not only in city and national magazines and newspapers but also in publications around the world; much as foreign documentary crews had once filmed the Lower East Side's open-air drug markets, television programs in Brazil, Italy, and Japan now produced segments on New York's remarkable crime drop. Bratton's NYPD, the message went, was an agency capable of remarkable feats if given the kind of political support Giuliani had supplied.[46]

In these stories, Broken Windows, born as a theory and transformed under Bratton into a set of policing practices in some ways distinct from the theory, became a narrative, an explanation for why the crime drop had occurred. The journalist Malcolm Gladwell, in a widely read essay for *The New Yorker* that he later expanded into a best-selling book, credited Broken Windows policing with pushing the city past a "tipping point" where crime could drop exponentially. Crime, he argued, was akin to an epidemic, and the "sense of anarchy" in New York had facilitated its contagious spread; by tamping down on disorder, he argued, the NYPD had countered the epidemic.[47]

Giuliani and his close aides, loath to share credit for the crime drop, watched with anger as the media flocked to Bratton. By the end of their first year in office, City Hall and NYPD headquarters were openly sniping at each other, and Bratton was convinced that Giuliani's decision to delay Operation Juggernaut was due not to the cost but to the publicity its announcement had garnered for Bratton. The relationship reached a breaking point after Bratton's *Time* magazine cover story, and in April 1996, Bratton announced that he intended to leave the commissioner's post. Passing over Bratton's top deputies, Giuliani chose as his successor Fire Commissioner Howard Safir, a longtime acquaintance whose appointment seemed to promise Giuliani greater control over the department.[48]

ONE OF BRATTON'S MANY POINTS of friction with Giuliani was what he considered the mayor's benighted emphasis on arrest numbers. Bratton's street-level enforcement actions had produced many more arrests, particularly for low-level offenses. But his problem-oriented policing philosophy anticipated that this growth would be temporary—once crime had subsided, the NYPD would take fewer enforcement actions. Giuliani, Bratton believed, "was adamant that arrests were going to have to go up to keep crime going down. We tried to explain to him, 'No, it's the opposite. As crime goes down there are fewer arrests—because there are fewer criminal events occurring. . . .' Giuliani had a hard time taking this in. He was of the mindset that more is better, when actually more was not better."[49]

Though Bratton's account contains an element of self-exculpation, Giuliani's more-is-more approach was indeed to characterize street-level policing in late-1990s New York. Believing that sterner sanctions were necessary to change disorderly behavior, the department began, in 1996, to reduce the use of so-called desk appearance tickets—criminal summonses that required people to appear before a judge—in favor of misdemeanor arrests, a seemingly slight change with crucial implications. As misdemeanor arrests soared—rising 66 percent between 1993 and 1999, a time when serious crime was falling sharply in the city—more and more New Yorkers accused of minor offenses spent time in police holding cells while awaiting arraignment, a process that might last twenty-four hours. If their case went to trial and they could not afford bail, they risked spending time in the city jails, including the brutal facility on Rikers Island, typically for two weeks or more. In all, tens of thousands of New Yorkers who previously would have been released and ordered to appear in court, overwhelmingly poor and Black and Latino, now spent time in custody, oftentimes just to see their cases dismissed. A parallel process played out with more serious offenses, as an increase in felony arrests contributed to a sharp decline in the share resulting in indictment—by 1999, only 25 percent of arrests led to a felony indictment.[50]

The following year, 1997, over the protests of its former head, Commissioner Safir expanded the Street Crime Unit from 138 to

380 officers, shortening the interview process in order to get the new officers on the job. "You can't interview people that fast, to be sure they're mature enough, and not crazy," a retired police commander noted. Safir's department began to utilize gun seizures as an informal productivity measure, incentivizing officers to increase the number of stop-and-frisks. "We frisk 20, maybe 30 people a day," one officer said. "Are they all by the book? Of course not; it's safer and easier to just toss people. And if it's the 25th of the month and you haven't got your gun yet? Things can get a little desperate." Yet another antidrug operation added to the number of street stops.[51]

According to department protocol, officers were supposed to complete a one-page form, called a UF-250, following each stop-and-frisk. In practice, officers often did not bother filing one when they found nothing, unless the person they had stopped seemed so upset that they worried about a complaint or a lawsuit. For their part, citizens had the option of filing a complaint, but because the NYPD concentrated stop-and-frisks in poor neighborhoods, people who were improperly searched often lacked the resources to do so. David Dinkins's Civilian Complaint Review Board, which Giuliani had notoriously opposed, found its budget slashed and fell hopelessly behind in its own investigations.[52]

There is, therefore, no way to know precisely how many people the NYPD stopped-and-frisked in the late 1990s, and to what degree the phenomenon was accelerating. What is unambiguously clear is that, by the late 1990s, the practice of stop-and-frisk was both widespread and a source of outrage in many predominantly Black and Latino neighborhoods. Teachers and clergy could offer endless instances of innocent young people being stopped. "Every man of color in my congregation has had some sort of encounter with the police," the pastor at one Bronx church attested. She described an incident in which one of her parishioners had been wrongfully accused of armed robbery after a street stop; his family had succeeded at getting the charges dropped, but only after taking on $8,000 in legal fees, which caused them to fall behind on the ConEd bill and lose electricity. Community leaders in the Bronx received "numerous complaints each month"; even some of the community board members fielding the complaints had been stopped and searched. "It happens on a daily basis," twenty-one-year old Brooklynite Rafael Diaz told the journalist Bob Herbert. "One time there was an officer who wouldn't let me go into the building where my friend lives. I said, 'Do you have any reason to stop me?' He said, 'Shut the [expletive] up.' He said if I tried to go inside none of my family would ever see me again."[53]

The experience could be not only humiliating but also terrifying. "The modus operandi of the unit," a journalist for *The New York Beacon* noted, "was to quickly swarm on a person, with pistols drawn, all while barking commands laced with vulgarities . . . a harrowing experience for an innocent person. . . . After all, who wants to have pistols pointed at him? Who wants to have his clothes pressed against a dirty sidewalk while a stranger rifles through his pants?" The confusion innocent people could feel upon being suddenly swarmed by aggressive, plainclothes people with guns also, of course, meant a risk that situations could escalate before New Yorkers realized that they had been engaged by the police.[54]

At about ten p.m. on February 3, 1999, a team of four SCU officers, all of them added to the unit during the Safir-era expansion, departed the unit's headquarters on Randall's Island en route to the Soundview section of the Bronx. Their first two stops of the evening—one of a man "lurking" near a lobby of the Bronx River Houses project, one of a man who appeared to fit the description of a homicide suspect—found nothing. Then, at about 12:40 a.m., they stopped a third man: a twenty-two-year-old named Amadou Diallo, who had come to New York from Guinea two years earlier in the hope of getting a college education. A devout Muslim, Diallo worked long hours selling socks and videocassettes from a table outside a convenience store on Manhattan's 14th Street, near Second

Avenue; at nights he returned to a small redbrick apartment building on Wheeler Avenue, where he kept a small collection of books on Islam, Christianity, and computer science. Despite a penchant for sharing his small earnings with beggars and lending money to students at the high school across the street from his stand, Diallo had managed to amass $9,000 for tuition.[55]

That night Diallo returned home from work around midnight, talked with one of his roommates about paying the ConEd bill, turned on the television for a bit, then went back out—the roommate later told reporters that Diallo often went in search of food after getting home. The officers later offered ambiguous accounts of why they noticed Diallo, who had no criminal record. The officer who suggested the stop testified that he believed Diallo fit the description of a rape suspect, a claim that fell apart under cross-examination. The officer also offered another explanation: "He was standing on the stoop. It appeared he was looking up and down the block. . . . He steps back into the vestibule, like he doesn't want to be seen." The undercover car pulled up, Diallo stepped back into the vestibule and reached toward his pockets, and an officer shouted "Gun!" The officers drew their weapons and fired forty-one shots, nineteen of which struck Diallo, who had been carrying only his wallet, his keys, and a pager.[56]

Amadou Diallo's murder, only the latest in a series of high-profile instances of police violence during Giuliani's mayoralty, quickly became international news and a flashpoint for discussions of racial profiling and police brutality both in New York and in the nation. To many Black New Yorkers, the lesson of the Diallo murder was obvious. "Amadou Diallo was profiled to death," said former police commissioner Benjamin Ward." "Everybody out here is Amadou Diallo," said a woman in Bedford-Stuyvesant. "It's just waiting to happen. Who will it be? When will it happen?"[57]

Anti-police-violence activism had been building at the grassroots level from the mid-1990s onward, especially in upper Manhattan and the Bronx, organized through groups such as the Malcolm X Grassroots Movement, the National Congress for Puerto Rican Rights, and Mothers Against Police Brutality, with roots in Black and Latino communities. Within a few days of Diallo's murder, a wave of street protests broke out, starting with a gathering of some one thousand people outside the apartment building where the shooting took place. Demonstrations continued nearly daily, growing more diverse as they migrated south toward City Hall and One Police Plaza. A month after the shooting, the New York activist Al Sharpton began to orchestrate more organized and choreographed rallies. First, Sharpton held a thousand-person protest at the New York Stock Exchange, from which he and eleven others walked to the intersection of Wall Street and Broadway and blocked traffic until the NYPD arrested the group. More arrests followed in a series of rallies at Police Headquarters. Practically every major Black politician in the city—former mayor David Dinkins; U.S. representatives Charles Rangel, Gregory Meeks, and Major Owens; State Comptroller H. Carl McCall; and the venerable Harlem leaders Percy Sutton and Basil Paterson, among many others—was arrested. So were national civil rights leaders such as Jesse Jackson and NAACP president Kweise Mfume, and media figures such as the publishers of *Black Enterprise* and *Essence*. Giuliani told reporters that he thought the protests were "getting silly." But more and more New Yorkers were showing up to submit to arrest—ministers, rabbis, labor leaders, Latino politicians and community leaders, and everyday New Yorkers, including the eighty-three-year-old mother of the civil rights volunteer Andrew Goodman, who had been murdered in Mississippi during the Freedom Summer of 1964.[58]

The City Hall protests were but the highest profile. Smaller-scale protests were taking place across the city: students at City College tried to stop the NYPD from recruiting on campus; teachers took their students on anti-police-brutality marches; block associations and tenant groups set up pickets in front of police stations. The protests seemed to be reshaping public opinion—three-quarters of New Yorkers responded, in a survey, that they believed the NYPD treated white and Black New Yorkers differently. The movement, the veteran civil rights leader and Georgia congressman John Lewis wrote hopefully, "may mark the emergence of a broad new coalition of conscience." At the same time, Giuliani's approval rating dropped some 20 points.[59]

As protesters took to the streets, public officials and civil rights organizations responded to Diallo's murder with a wave of investigations and lawsuits. The newly elected attorney general of New York, Eliot Spitzer, announced a state inquiry into the NYPD's stop-and-frisk practices. "There is a tidal wave of concern about this issue," he said, noting that he had heard countless complaints during campaign stops the previous year. "It is impossible to be out there and not get a sense that this is perceived as the overwhelming civil rights issue facing the city." Spitzer quickly realized that the number of searches had been vastly underreported, and hence the share of innocent people stopped dramatically higher than official statistics suggested. "I've spoken to many officers who say that they do not fill out the forms, the 250, for every stop-and-frisk, and they may fill out, at most, 1 in 5, or 1 in 10," he told Brian Lehrer on WNYC. "In which case, we may have had several hundred thousand stop-and-frisks, with only the five to ten thousand arrests." A statistical analysis by the Columbia political scientist Andrew Gelman commissioned for Spitzer's report found that the Street Crime Unit stopped "16.3 blacks, 14.5 Hispanics and 9.6 whites" for every stop resulting in a corresponding arrest; the figures for the NYPD as a whole were 9.5, 8.8, and 7.9, respectively. Stunningly, less than a third of stops of Black people "took place because the officer believed the person fit [a criminal] description." Reports by the New York City public advocate's office and the U.S. attorney for the Southern District of New York produced similar findings.[60]

In March 1999, about the time when the Police Headquarters

protests were taking off, the Center for Constitutional Rights and the National Congress for Puerto Rican Rights filed a federal class action suit challenging the NYPD's stop-and-frisk practices. The suit dragged out for several years; ultimately, the city agreed to establish written stop-and-frisk guidelines, institute new training, and change the UF-250 forms that NYPD officers had been occasionally filling out. Rather than state in their own words their rationale for making a stop, officers now had to check a box indicating one of the department's acceptable reasons—though the revised form continued to offer such vague grounds as "furtive movements."[61]

Giuliani and Safir responded to the waves of protest, the inquiries, and the lawsuits with defiance. In January 2000, "as if to signal that aggressive policing is back," the journalist Dan Barry noted, the NYPD launched Operation Condor, yet another crackdown on street-level drug markets. Two months later, in March 2000, an undercover narcotics officer approached an unarmed twenty-six-year old Haitian American man, Patrick Dorismond, who was standing outside a Midtown bar looking for a cab. When the officer asked Dorismond if he had any crack, Dorismond, offended and unaware that the man was a police officer, replied "What are you doing asking me for that shit?" A scuffle ensued, in the course of which a backup officer fatally shot Dorismond in the chest. Rather than seek to defuse the situation, Giuliani responded by attempting to drag Dorismond's name through the mud, citing a number of prior charges—for robbery, assault, gun possession, and domestic violence—all of which turned out to be significantly overstated. In fact, Dorismond had never been convicted of any crime; the only mark on his record was a disorderly conduct violation.[62]

In the wake of the uproar over Dorismond's killing, Giuliani defended the NYPD by noting that police shootings were down considerably from previous decades. But for many New Yorkers of color, the most serious instances of excessive police force represented only the tip of the iceberg. High-profile cases like the killings of Diallo and Dorismond catalyzed mass protests. But the antipathy and fear expressed in those protests were grounded in much more common occurrences: stop-and-frisks that did not result in charges; a day spent in a holding cell for a small offense that led to nothing; a couple of weeks in jail awaiting trial on a minor charge; arrest on a felony charge—and with it the threat of prison time, loss of employment, loss of housing—that, considerably more often than not, did not hold up in court.

By the end of the decade, Giuliani divided the city sharply. To his supporters, he had rescued the city. "You are a very special person and I will always be with you no matter what course you follow!" Donald Trump wrote to Giuliani in August 2000. To his critics, he represented an incipient authoritarianism. "It is Giuliani time in New York whether we like it or not," the editor of Harlem's *Amsterdam News* wrote. "If we are not careful it could become . . . Giuliani time [in America] if Giuliani becomes a U.S. senator in the capital of this great nation. . . . We have in Giuliani the reality of McCarthy and the seeds of Mussolini and Hitler straining to spring forth and take over this nation. We cannot allow these seeds to develop and grow full bloom." Other New Yorkers looked on with an air of mournfulness. "I want our dear Mayor to know . . . that if he doesn't put an end to Police brutality like he's made a drop in crime, that no one will respect him or the police," a man from the Vladeck Houses on the Lower East Side wrote to Deputy Mayor Randy Mastro. "If you truly care about the plight of the people, my people especially, then help us!"[63]

For the NYPD, the Giuliani years left a paradoxical, dual legacy. On the one hand, the NYPD appeared to have resolved the long-running crisis of competence that had racked it since at least the early 1970s. For thirty years, whatever the NYPD had done—wage a war on drugs, seek to purge corruption, expand and re-expand the force, police quality-of-life offenses, implement problem-solving and community policing paradigms—it had done without cutting deeply into crime in the city. Debates about strategy, resource allocation, and accountability had proceeded with crime itself an independent variable. Now for the first time in its modern history, the NYPD could claim convincingly that it possessed the ability to reduce and control crime. And because the crime drop had coincided with—and likely contributed to—the expansion of the local economy and the growth of property values (and hence the tax base), the NYPD could claim, as the journalist Heather MacDonald wrote in *City Journal*, to be the city's "indispensable institution." If the city was to work, the argument went, the NYPD needed to be treated with deference, showered with resources, and granted autonomy.[64]

Yet if the NYPD reasserted an image of competence after three long decades of consistently high crime rates, its legitimacy in neighborhoods of color, always in question, had been deeply damaged by the rash of abuse and violence in Giuliani's second term. Large sections of the city saw the police as racist, authoritarian, and predatory. "After so much relentless criticism," MacDonald wrote in another *City Journal* essay, "the NYPD is in crisis." Indispensable, yet in crisis—in some ways, the NYPD's status in the city would never be the same; in some ways, it remained what it had long been. Meanwhile, for those New Yorkers of color who had actually lived the everyday struggles of Giuliani's New York and to the parents, teachers, religious leaders, and other community figures who had seen the daily impact of stop-and-frisk, the grinding experience of being policed in New York dragged on.[65]

"OURS IS A HOPEFUL LOOK at the city's future," Bobby Wagner and the Commission on the Year 2000 had written in 1987. "In our view New York in the next century can be not only ascendant but also triumphant." In many ways, events had exceeded even Wagner's optimistic expectations. New York, the commission had noted, was not only the headquarters of the thriving finance sector but also "the gateway to the American economy" and "the country's center of creativity in just about every field—music, theater, publishing, advertising, communications, painting, dance," industries that proved even more vital than the commission's members had foreseen, and that in turn attracted residents who were not in those fields but wished to live in proximity to such cultural ferment. With rising incomes abroad, cheaper flights, and falling crime rates, the tourism sector continued to grow. For the first time since World War II, New York City's economy, both in terms of job growth and income, was outpacing that of the nation as a whole. Wagner and the commission had confidently forecast that the city's population would continue to grow, from 7.1 million to 7.5 million by the turn of the century; in fact, the Census of 2000 revealed that New York had passed 8 million residents, with the city's population growth outpacing that of the suburbs for the first time in decades.[66]

Still, other aspects of Wagner's forecast proved prescient. "Today's poverty," the commission had written, "is different and probably more enduring than that of the past." Many of the discreet problems the city faced—in housing, education, public safety—were in essence problems of poverty, the report noted. In 1999, following the most remarkable period of economic expansion since at least the 1960s and in some respects well before that, 21.2 percent of New Yorkers lived in poverty, a higher share than in 1979—and a figure that did not account for the massive surge in incarceration of the 1980s and early '90s. And because racial segregation remained high—still higher than it had been in 1960—poverty remained spatially concentrated.[67]

The new economy was etched into the city's neighborhoods. In 1970, New York's wealthy were clustered primarily on the East Side of Manhattan, from 90th Street south to 14th Street, with a few outlying choice neighborhoods in Queens, Brooklyn, and the northwest Bronx. By the end of the twentieth century, the affluent had fanned out—across Central Park to the Upper West Side, down through much of Midtown and lower Manhattan, into the cloistered neighborhoods of Brownstone Brooklyn that had seen only the beginning stages of gentrification before the urban crisis. The disinvested neighborhoods that had been hollowed out in the 1970s and '80s remained deeply impoverished despite the affluence that had swept over the city—though some of these neighborhoods, too, particularly Harlem and parts of Brooklyn, had experienced some gentrification.

The vast middle-class stretches of Queens, Brooklyn south of Prospect Park, and the north Bronx, meanwhile, had been thoroughly remade by the waves of immigration that had swept the city in the decades after 1965. What one writer called the "checkerboard of provinces" characteristic of the white-ethnic, Black, and Puerto Rican city of mid-century gave way to a tapestry of new working-class immigrant communities: Caribbeans in Flatbush, Chinese and Koreans in Flushing, Ecuadorians, Colombians, and South Asians in Jackson Heights. For the first time in its history, New York had neighborhoods where people from around the world lived together: "Dominicans, Puerto Ricans, West Africans, Bangladeshis, Koreans, Jamaicans, Cambodians, Vietnamese, Albanians," and various Latin Americans in Bedford Park in the Bronx, people from North Africa and the Middle East alongside Bangladeshis, Brazilians, and the lingering Greek population in Astoria, Queens. The city's African-born population had more than doubled, adding considerable new diversity to New York's predominantly Black neighborhoods.[68]

In some respects, the city seemed settled, the long, interlocking crises that had begun in the 1970s ended by economic recovery, repopulation, and the crime drop. But the developments of the 1990s had sown the seeds of yet more upheavals: the school system was in the midst of profound change, the future of policing in the aftermath of the Diallo and Dorismond murders remained hotly contested, and the 1997 rent law had opened up huge swaths of the city's housing stock for redevelopment—at precisely the moment when the crime drop had made working-class neighborhoods more appealing to affluent renters. But first would come a shattering moment no one could foresee.

IF DAVID DINKINS'S VICTORY over Ed Koch in the 1989 Democratic primary had restored major-party competition to New York's mayoral elections, Giuliani's eight years in power had solidified the GOP's standing in the city. Still, the GOP was in some ways more a container for what had been a tendency within the Democratic Party—the white-ethnic component so central to Cuomo's and Koch's coalitions—than a robust organization of its own. In 2001, while Public Advocate Mark Green and Bronx borough president Fernando Ferrer fought a close, nasty, divisive contest for the Democratic nomination for mayor, with Green narrowly prevailing and City Council speaker Peter Vallone running a distant third, the Republican contest pitted two former Democrats against each other—former congressman and Bronx borough president Herman Badillo, who had sought the Democratic nomination for mayor five times before changing his registration, and a political neophyte, businessman Michael R. Bloomberg.[69]

Much like Manhattan itself, Bloomberg, a onetime Solomon Brothers bond trader, had caught the wave of financialization, becoming wealthy by selling financial markets data to traders. By the end of the 1990s, he was extraordinarily rich, an experienced manager, and a member in excellent standing of Manhattan's civic-philanthropic elite, having served on the boards of the New York Public Library, Lincoln Center, the Metropolitan Museum of Art, and the Central Park Conservancy, among others. As he began to explore a run for the mayoralty, he encountered only one problem:

The pollsters he sought out saw no way for him to get through a Democratic primary.[70]

And so in 2000, Bloomberg changed his party registration. Though he brought some Giuliani people in, his political operation was primarily built out of the old Koch-Cuomo-Moynihan wing of the New York State Democratic Party, with the influence of the recently retired Moynihan particularly pronounced. Despite running as a Republican, he still described himself as a liberal—even while campaigning next to Governor Pataki. But he also professed to be a manager, not a politician. He prioritized certain issues—especially education—and he had clear goals, but he was not closely identified with particular policies. "We ask [candidates] about policy," he mused. "But you have other people that do policy."

The mayoral contest itself was surreal, taking place in the state of almost suspended animation that characterized the immediate aftermath of the September 11 attacks. With issues of economic viability and public safety on New Yorkers' minds, Giuliani's endorsement and Bloomberg's self-funded millions—his campaign spent the unheard-of sum of ninety-eight dollars per vote—garnered him a more serious look. In the end, he won by a little over 2 percent of the vote, his coalition essentially a replica of Giuliani's. The political neophyte was to carry New York into a deeply uncertain future.[71]

PART III
PROGRESS AND POVERTY

2002–2019

6

City of Choice

The streets and stores of Midtown Manhattan were quieter than usual as 2001 wound to a close, traffic thinner at the airport terminals and train halls usually bustling at holiday time. A cloud still hung over Lower Manhattan; when the wind picked up, smoke drifted out over the river to Brooklyn. New York had seen disaster before, and it had always bounced back. Still, in the wake of the September 11 attacks, many New Yorkers found themselves asking whether the city would ever be the same. "So much of what the city was about had just been levelled," the novelist Colum McCann wrote—"not just the towers but a sense of the city itself, the desire, the greed, the appetite, the unrelenting pursuit of the present."[1]

As Bloomberg prepared to take office, the dark days of the 1970s were on New Yorkers' minds. The national recession that had begun in the spring of 2001 with the collapse of the dot-com bubble hit Wall Street particularly hard, and the consequences were felt throughout the local economy. Then the attacks of September 11 dealt a sharp blow to the many businesses—transportation, hotels, venues, restaurants—that depended on tourism. Giuliani, riding high during his second term, had taken to covering structural deficits with the temporary windfalls of the Wall Street boom, leaving the city on the hook for expenses it could not cover during normal times—and now the attacks caused municipal tax revenues to fall by some $2 billion, on top of a loss of $519 million from the recession. In that light, no less an authority than Felix Rohatyn, one of the chief architects of the fiscal crisis regime, told reporters that he thought the city's financial problems were "going to be much greater than in the 1970's."[2]

Although Bloomberg admired the fiscal responsibility that business leaders like Rohatyn had imposed on the city, he saw the experience of the 1970s as something to avoid, not emulate. "Even though we must sacrifice now," he proclaimed in his inaugural address, "let us not forget we are still a city of big dreams, of big ideas, big projects and a big heart. . . . We can never abandon our future." The crippling cuts of the 1970s, he made clear, had set the city back, rendering it undesirable to those who would come to pursue their big ideas and big dreams. Like Koch before him, Bloomberg was highly attentive to the fact that New York was competing for residents and investment. It was contending in "a worldwide market for the best and brightest," he explained in his 2003 State of the City address. "They'll build the prosperity of the next New York; our job is to make a city worthy of their ambitions."[3]

In the short term, fiscal reality won out. Bloomberg was forced to make deep cuts, including, for the first time since Koch's first term, to the NYPD—though the city avoided prolonged 1970s-style public disinvestment when Bloomberg bravely chose to raise property taxes sharply in order to sustain city services. But whereas the city in the 1970s and early '90s had been undergoing fundamental restructurings, the recession of 2001–2 and the September 11 attacks, it turned out, dealt temporary blows to a fundamentally strong local economy. Once Wall Street and the tourism sectors began to recover, Bloomberg had the resources he needed to build his city of choice.[4]

For a quarter century, the remaking of New York had proceeded piece by piece, the consequence of contending visions filtered through a tangle of political calculations, playing out in different venues amid ever-shifting contexts. With Bloomberg's ascent these processes cohered, for the first time, into something like a program. Bloomberg's vision ultimately marked the maturity of the public-investment-driven developmentalism visible in David Rockefeller and Harry Van Arsdale's Business-Labor Working Group and, a decade on, Bobby Wagner's Commission on the Year 2000, allied to a data-driven, problem-solving, managerial ethos that recalled nothing so much as the expert-led municipal reform efforts of the Progressive Era.

School reform, housing deregulation, and the extension of street-level policing all fit this program. Bloomberg would make the small-schools-and-choice approach that had developed piecemeal since the 1970s into the city's core strategy, aiming to make the school system appealing to affluent families while providing a path forward for talented, disadvantaged children. Deregulation promised to create a more flexible housing supply that would aid in the rebuilding of neighborhoods by developers seeking to profit from the influx of managerial, professional, and creative industry workers. And the remarkable fall in the city's crime rates would become one of its strongest selling point to potential residents—and to the city's voters. Crediting the NYPD for this unexpected political windfall, Bloomberg would turn a blind eye to the expansion of the aggressive street-level policing that had come into disrepute during Giuliani's second term.

Bloomberg positioned himself as an apolitical problem-solver who brought a businessman's managerial approach to major urban issues. He fondly quoted Fiorello La Guardia's maxim: "There is no Democratic or Republican way to sweep the streets." In truth, his ambitions implicated profound questions of power and values, and his efforts to change how the city's government worked thus required the reconfiguration of its politics—the shifting of loci of authority, the building up of new constituencies, the development of new ways of talking about the public good. To Bloomberg's supporters, this new mode of politics showed that government could work; to his detractors, it amounted to unaccountable management from above. Could such a politics succeed in the long run in a city where traditional democratic passions still stirred?

PRIOR TO SEPTEMBER 11, Bloomberg had made public schools the centerpiece of his campaign. "As mayor," he told an audience, "I would do for public education what Rudy Giuliani did for public safety." It was a natural fit. Bloomberg had risen to civic prominence through his philanthropic efforts just as philanthropy was becoming central to public school reform. The brand of school reform that had begun to coalesce in New York and nationally aligned closely with his style of data-driven managerialism. Not least, the promise of quality public schools fit Bloomberg's vision of building a public sector that could contribute to the economic well-being of the city—a school system that would draw professional and managerial workers with families into the city while training the workers of the future and providing avenues of upward mobility in a fundamentally unequal city.[5]

The building blocks of school reform New York–style—the small schools movement, the choice paradigm, the 1998 charter law—were mostly in place by the time Bloomberg took office. For Bloomberg and his schools chancellor, the lawyer Joel Klein, these earlier reforms became a jumping-off point for a broader vision of overhauling the entire school system. Bloomberg's first step was to win direct authority over the city schools, which meant dissolving the district-based structure of decentralization created in the wake of the school wars of the late 1960s and vesting authority instead in the mayor and the appointed schools chancellor. By 2002, proponents of mayoral control already had real momentum, part of the broader push toward accountability: Boston and Chicago had adopted it, New York's business community was staunchly behind it, and the state legislature had taken steps toward recentralization in the 1990s, though it had balked at delivering full control to the Giuliani administration. A generous donor to the New York State Republican Party, Bloomberg could count on support from the Senate. His primary obstacle was the Democratic Assembly, where Sheldon Silver was unlikely to defy the preferences of the United Federation of Teachers. Bloomberg pulled the obvious lever. The UFT's contract had expired eighteen months earlier. Bloomberg wanted teacher salaries to be competitive with neighboring suburban districts so the city could attract the best talent. The same day Bloomberg agreed to a contract that hiked teachers' salaries some 16 to 22 percent, the UFT announced its support for mayoral control.[6]

Klein's Department of Education set out to convert the byzantine, organic system that had developed at the district and schoolhouse levels under decentralization into a centralized operation with rationalized mechanisms of administration. In 2003, Klein announced a matching system for rising high school students designed by Alvin Roth, the future Nobel economist who had created an equivalent matching system for medical school residency admissions programs. Eighth graders would now list twelve choices of high school in order of preference, drawn from a 626-page directory; by 2008 the system worked well enough that students got one of their top three choices "more than 80 percent of the time." In order to help parents and students weigh the profusion of options, the Department of Education created a bevy of new resources: the Learning Environment Survey, a parent-student-and-teacher satisfaction survey; school quality reviews; annual progress reports. Well-off parents could supplement these resources with a range of private services—Bright Kids NYC, School Select NYC, NYC School Help, whose consultants charged $200 an hour or more—and, if their children were young, seek out private pre-Ks with good reputations for getting their students into desirable public kindergarten programs.[7]

Bloomberg and Klein's efforts to create a portfolio of schools were guided by a few core assumptions. Small was good; bureaucracy and the constraints imposed by collective bargaining with the UFT were bad, obstacles that needed to be removed if city government was going to work the way it needed to in order to meet the demands of the twenty-first century. Schools with low graduation rates, poor attendance records, and weak test scores should be targeted for restructuring or closure, an approach consistent with federal policy under the No Child Left Behind Act of 2001. The vast inequalities in the city, Bloomberg and Klein believed, mattered less at the end of the day than how the system was run. "From the day I became chancellor," Klein later wrote, "many people told me, 'You'll never fix education in America until you fix poverty.' I've always believed that the reverse is true: We'll never fix poverty until we fix education."[8]

Building on the Annenberg Foundation's efforts, the Gates Foundation and other philanthropies channeled tens of millions of dollars into local educational nonprofits. Whereas Chancellor Rudy Crew had viewed small schools as a complement to the larger institutions most students attended, Klein saw them as a potential replacement: one by one Klein's Department of Education phased out "failing schools," especially high schools, and replaced them with a handful of smaller ones. In all, Bloomberg and Klein began phasing out 154 schools, including 35 large high schools that were diced up into multischool "educational campuses."[9]

New York State's charter school law was scarcely three years old when Bloomberg took office; the city had only nineteen charter schools in operation. Bloomberg and Klein would become among the nation's most prominent charter supporters, building the fledgling sector into an integral part of their portfolio. Charters would be a relatively small part of the system, Klein recognized, but they would perform a vital role. Above all, charters would serve as a kind of proof of concept that the city's schools could be improved without tackling underlying structural factors such as poverty—they would force the traditional public schools, he wrote, "to stop making excuses about why they weren't successfully educating kids from poor communities." Pledging to turn New York into a "Silicon Valley for charter schools," Klein raised more than $40 million from large donors to support the sector's growth.[10]

If the charter movement had appealed to some Black and Latino community leaders and politicians because it promised a kind of community control, it soon became clear that large-scale charter management organizations would drive the sector's growth. Klein was especially drawn to an organization called Knowledge Is Power Program, or KIPP, which operated a school in the South Bronx. Klein described the model as "hiring excellent principals and teachers, training them constantly, lengthening the school day [three extra hours] and year, imposing strict discipline, and granting rewards for success that included class trips and even merchandise for individual kids." Malcolm Gladwell spelled out KIPP's philosophy in a best-selling book, *Outliers*, by tracing the experience of a Bronx middle-schooler named Marita. "Her community does not give her what she needs," he wrote. "So what does she have to do? Give up her evenings and weekends with friends—all the elements of her old world—and replace them with KIPP." KIPP was soon joined by other ambitious, well-resourced charter management organizations. The most notable of these was the Success Academy network, launched by the historian and former City Council member Eva Moskowitz in 2006, which expanded aggressively starting in upper Manhattan and the Bronx before spreading across every borough save Staten Island, utilizing a similar model and ample donations from the city's hedge-funders. In all, the city added 173 charter schools during Bloomberg's mayoralty.[11]

The rise of charter schools in New York created a kind of parallel structure to the new small schools, magnets, and gifted-and-talented programs that had grown up within the public school system starting in the 1970s. In the older structure, white students were overrepresented in proportion to their presence in the system as a whole: Some desirable new public schools, places like Beacon High, were quite diverse, though white students made up a plurality; some gifted-and-talented programs, on the other hand, were majority white even when located in mostly nonwhite districts. New York's charter schools, in contrast, served practically no white students. Many of the newer, alternative public schools bore the imprint of the progressive pedagogy and aversion to rote learning and standardized testing that had grown out of the District 4 movement and its counterparts around the city. Charters were a different story.[12]

There was real diversity in how charter schools operated. But Moskowitz's Success Academy schools became emblematic of the sector's distinctive approach. The schools were amply resourced: In 2013, the Success Academy network could count $22 million in philanthropic donations above the $72 million it received in public funds. They also ran on the labor of idealistic (and sometimes underprepared) young people capable of sustaining the long hours and intense focus that the Success Academy model required. Some school principals were still in their mid-twenties; teacher turnover was significantly higher than in traditional public schools. The schools insisted on proper behavior, down to requiring that students sit upright with hands folded, and issued far more suspensions than the traditional public schools, an approach Moskowitz said was necessary to ensure "order and civility in the classroom"—a kind of schoolhouse equivalent of Broken Windows.[13]

Success Academy's model was premised on the need to perform well on standardized tests—for the schools, in order to prove the charter model's superiority to traditional public education; for students, in order to gain a pathway out of poverty. Teaching was therefore geared toward math, science, and English, the subjects assessed in state tests: Success Academy did not offer classes in foreign languages until the eighth grade. Schools devoted extraordinary amounts of time to test prep. Stories abounded of students wetting themselves during practice tests; those who came up short on practice exams were sometimes shamed in front of peers and sent to what the schools called "effort academy." The model worked—94 percent of Success Academy students passed the state math tests compared to 35 percent of all New York City public school students. To supporters, this was what it took to provide marginalized children a chance to succeed. To skeptics, the approach subjected disadvantaged young people to a regimented, paternalistic, punitive form of education that drained away curiosity, creativity, and an intrinsic desire to learn.[14]

Gifted-and-talented programs, which had sprung up in a number of districts in the 1980s and '90s, presented Bloomberg and Klein with a different dilemma. These programs, which catered largely to elementary school students and which some 44,000 of New York's 775,000 K-8 public school students attended, were run at the school level; when Bloomberg took control of the schools, the new Department of Education had no idea how many of them existed and did not even possess a definition of what constituted a gifted-and-talented program. Klein recognized that the shadowy way the programs were administered created all kinds of opportunities for favoritism and inequity. The numbers bore him out: Surveys conducted in the late 1990s found that white students accounted for more than half of those in gifted-and-talented programs while making up less than 30 percent of the student population.[15]

Some civil rights advocates looked at the numbers and decided the entire concept was flawed. "We're against them, period," an organizer for an Upper West Side immigrant rights group said. "We think they are a kind of loophole to keep dividing up the kids and continuing to put white, middle-class kids in a different track from poor kids of color." But politically, ending or even curtailing gifted-and-talented programs was out of the question. They had strong support not only from affluent parents but also from the UFT. "The gifted-and-talented programs have been a glue that have cemented a lot of the good parts of the school system together," UFT president Randi Weingarten said. "The[y] are also magnets that have maintained the middle class in schools, whether that is a Hispanic middle class, [B]lack middle class or a white middle class." And so during his bid for reelection in 2005, Bloomberg promised not only to keep the gifted-and-talented programs so beloved by affluent parents but also to expand them into underserved parts of the city. The first seven new programs went to Staten Island, which was both underserved—the borough had no gifted-and-talented programs—and vital to Bloomberg's reelection prospects.[16]

But there remained the question of who would have access to gifted-and-talented programs. Shortly after the 2005 election, Klein announced that the city would develop a "single standardized application process" to replace the existing school-by-school hodgepodge. Two years later he announced a uniform standard for admission: Only students scoring in the top 5 percent of a citywide application test would be admitted. The aim was equity: geographic, racial, and socioeconomic. "I'm convinced that there are gifted and talented children in all communities," Klein said in announcing the new policy. In the meantime, test-prep services adjusted their offerings to prepare the city's well-off three- and four-year-olds for the new tests. "You can build a better mousetrap, it doesn't matter," said one test-prep company's founder. "There's no way you can stop it because now the idea of preparing for the kindergarten test is totally the norm. The stakes are so high."[17]

If the aim was finding academically gifted students in all communities, the initiative backfired spectacularly. The number of students admitted to gifted-and-talented programs dropped precipitously and racial and socioeconomic disparities grew wider, to the point where some of the new programs Bloomberg and Klein had opened in underserved areas were threatened with closure. District 3 on the

Upper West Side saw the number of students admitted jump from 192 to 310; District 6 in predominantly Latino Washington Heights saw it drop from 80 to 50. Education experts were left shaking their heads. "The idea that somehow making this totally reliant on tests . . . it's mindboggling," one scholar remarked. Critics dubbed the new approach the "Upper West Side Relief Act of 2008." Klein dropped the cutoff for admission from the ninety-fifth percentile to the ninetieth, and the department began a search for a less easily gamed admissions test.[18]

The end result of this onrush of school-building efforts and policy reform was a hugely complex and fractured system in which the most desirable schools picked their students rather than vice versa. Affluent families had attractive new options thanks to the proliferation of highly selective public schools of choice and gifted-and-talented programs. Charter schools posted more impressive results in New York than they did in the nation as a whole, but they also introduced a new division within communities of color, with homeless, low-achieving, special needs, and English-learning students less likely to be represented in the most successful charters than in surrounding schools. Scholarly studies found that on average, small schools tended to produce gains in graduation rates among students who had been at risk of lagging behind in older institutions. At the same time, a careful study by the education policy expert Clara Hemphill at the New School's Center for New York City Affairs found that the gains produced by new small schools had been offset by declines at older schools—exactly as skeptics from Kenneth Clark in the 1970s to David Dinkins in the 1980s might have predicted. For all the headlines about the system's aggregate performance—in test scores, attendance figures, graduation rates—the story beneath the surface remained its ever-growing inequality.[19]

IN AUGUST 2006, the MetLife corporation announced that it was seeking bids for what would become the largest real estate deal in U.S. history. The vast Stuyvesant Town and Peter Cooper Village complex—encompassing some 11,000 apartments in 110 buildings, spanning eighty acres on the east side of Manhattan, from 14th Street to 23rd—had been built in the 1940s for working-class white veterans and their families. For decades it represented New York's commitment to its middle classes, home to teachers, nurses, and civil servants. It also symbolized the long battle for inclusion in the segregated city: The struggle to do away with MetLife's whites-only policy was one of the signature civil rights campaigns of the postwar years. A who's who of developers, from New York and from as far away as Qatar, lined up to make their offers.[20]

The asking price, nearly $5 billion, was stunning on its face. But to those who looked closely at the numbers, it was also chilling. The complex's largely stabilized rent rolls could not come close to covering the cost of acquiring and running it, let alone generating the kinds of profits capable of attracting the biggest players in the real estate game. The buildings would have to be deregulated before they could provide that kind of windfall. Hidden in the eye-popping asking price, then, were some fundamental questions: Who had the right to live in the city? Who had the right to take someone's home away? What kind of city did New York want to be?

Within six months of the September 11 attacks, New York's housing market was once again booming, and the potential for profit set into motion the deregulatory machinery Pataki had signed into law in 1997. The results were predictable: Tens of thousands of units passed out of the rent-regulation system every year, and tenants faced another wave of harassment. But this time the scale was entirely different. Whereas the real estate boom of the 1980s had been limited largely to Manhattan south of 96th Street, it now swept across the city as neighborhoods from Staten Island and East Brooklyn to the Bronx gentrified. A policy approach that was supposed to generate tax revenue by opening up the high-end rental market in Manhattan now threatened tenants from Crown Heights to the Grand Concourse. And as a wider and deeper-pocketed range of investors entered the rental market, displacement and harassment became part of the business model for some of the most powerful economic actors in the city.

Housing was important to Bloomberg for much the same reason good public schools were. "Affordable housing is crucial to the future economic development of this city," his commissioner of housing preservation and development Shaun Donovan remarked. "In this new economy, the cities that will compete and win are cities that can build successful, mixed-income neighborhoods rather than the historic economic divide between city and suburb we've seen." During Bloomberg's administration, the historically low levels of new construction finally came to an end—in the four-year stretch between 2005 and 2008, the city approved more new units than it had at any time since the early 1960s. But much of this new construction catered to the still-swelling professional and managerial classes, who queued up for spots in the burnished apartment complexes that stretched along the rezoned waterfront of Williamsburg and Greenpoint, or else to the hyperrich, who parked their wealth in the glassy skyscrapers in Midtown (where 57th Street was newly christened "Billionaires' Row") whose architecture the critic Martin Filler memorably likened to three-dimensional balance sheets. Bloomberg and Donovan did launch the most ambitious affordable housing initiative since Koch, the New Housing Marketplace Plan, which sought to build or preserve 160,000 units of affordable housing. Critics noted that much of the new housing was unaffordable to surrounding residents, and in any case, the initiative was simply overwhelmed as the city lost far more affordable units than it was capable of building. In the absence of federal support for new public housing, the only alternative for many New Yorkers was informality—the number of doubled-up and illegally converted units continued to grow, as did the unsheltered population.[21]

The first indications of what was coming at Stuyvesant Town appeared in 2001, as regulated tenants noticed that MetLife was spending in the range of $30,000 to $40,000 per vacant apartment on "things like new kitchens and bathrooms," using the rent laws' major-capital improvement allowances to get the rent to the $2,000-per-month deregulation threshold. By the fall of 2002, the situation was sufficiently acute that State Comptroller H. Carl McCall, running for governor against George Pataki, held a pro-tenant rally across the street from the complex. By the time MetLife put the complex on the market, it had managed to deregulate about 27 percent of the units. Still not enough to cover the purchase price, of course, but not to worry, MetLife announced in its marketing materials—by 2018, less than 30 percent of units would still be regulated. In fact, the process of conversion was already "well underway," MetLife wrote. The offering materials practically amounted to a roadmap for displacement, noted a young housing activist named Brad Lander. "MetLife's strategy for making several billion dollars on this site is to speculate on the aggressive displacement of middle-income New Yorkers and their replacement with wealthy New Yorkers."[22]

The winning bid was proffered by one of the grand names in New York real estate, Tishman Speyer, with backing from the investment firm BlackRock. It was a sign of how hot residential real estate had become in New York: A firm that owned Rockefeller Center and the Chrysler Building, whose chairman had helmed the Federal Reserve Bank of New York, owned a piece of the New York Yankees, and served as vice-chairman of the Museum of Modern Art, was interested in owning a sea of middle-class apartment buildings. The new managers took MetLife's advice and sought to crack down hard on tenants who were not using their apartments as a primary residence. More than four out of ten cases were eventually dropped, and tenant advocates argued that, in other instances, lawful tenants were moving out because they were intimidated or wanted to avoid legal fees.[23]

Tishman Speyer's tactics could be tough, but they were legal (and they did, in fact, net a number of people who had been taking advantage of the system). Indeed, one of the reasons big money flooded into residential real estate after 1997 was because the law afforded so many legitimate ways of reaching the deregulation threshold; in turn, large investors were able to be more systematic in unlocking profit potential in residential housing, since they had the capital reserves necessary to operate over longer time horizons. The major capital improvement allowances MetLife had utilized at Stuyvesant Town were a go-to tactic. In gentrifying neighborhoods, especially, owners took advantage of a new tool. Until 2001, landlords who had offered tenants rents below the level allowed under stabilization—a so-called "preferential rent"—had only been allowed to raise rents within the bounds established by that preferential rent: If a tenant rented an apartment for $1,000 a month even though the legal limit was $1,500, and if the Rent Guidelines Board allowed a rent hike of 5 percent, the landlord could offer a maximum of $1,050 per month the next time the lease was renewed. A 2001 court decision, codified by the state legislature in 2003, removed that constraint: A landlord could now hike the rent beyond the annual limit so long as it stayed below what the limit would have been without the preferential rent. Tenants from Flatbush to Inwood suddenly found themselves asked to pay huge monthly increases simply because the market had changed.[24]

For some tenants, these hikes amounted practically to an eviction notice. Others were forced to use money that they otherwise would have spent on food, recreation, travel, education, or life's essentials: Surveys showed that 50 percent of low-income New Yorkers who fell behind on rent struggled to fill needed prescriptions, and 51 percent cut back on school supplies or clothes. All faced the risk of losing their community and all the social ties and collective efficacy that New York's neighborhoods sustained—at just the moment when increased investment promised to improve the quality of life there.[25]

Still, if the law afforded ample resources, some owners and property managers stepped closer to the line of illegality and in some cases well across it. By the mid-2000s, there existed a practical repertoire of techniques for pushing tenants out and claiming the 20 percent vacancy bonus—which, especially if paired with capital improvements, could raise the rent above the deregulation threshold: Refuse to accept rent checks, then sue the tenant for nonpayment. Send bogus notices demanding back rent or declaring a lease nonrenewal and see who had the gumption and resources to challenge them. Drag tenants into housing court by accusing them of illegal sublets. Take your time repairing the stairs, or the entryway, or the boiler, or in dealing with whatever form of infestation had visited upon a unit or building. Break the locks on the front door. Kick up clouds of dust with renovations, or make sure the construction noises continued into the deep hours of the night. Do it to enough people in the right neighborhoods, and the profits could run to hundreds of thousands of dollars a month. And if all that failed, there remained the old-school methods: In 2003, a landlord in Elmhurst, Queens, was sentenced for offering two men $700 up front and $1,800 upon completion to attack two rent-stabilized tenants; he only wanted to scare them enough to give up their apartment, he said, but the assailants got carried away and sent the two men to the hospital with stab wounds.[26]

Events in Albany offered no respite. By the time the Emergency Tenant Protection Act came up for renewal during the 2003 session, George Pataki was coming off reelection and Alfonse D'Amato, who had served as a moderating influence on the State Senate Republican caucus during the 1997 rent wars, was out of the picture, defeated in 1998 by the Brooklyn Democrat Charles Schumer. State Senate majority leader Joseph Bruno, perhaps still smarting from the denouement of his 1997 clash with Sheldon Silver, was free to play hardball. At the end of the session, after four emergency extensions of the act, he passed an eight-year extension with the same $2,000 deregulation threshold and the new preferential rent allowance, then promptly adjourned, forcing Silver and the Assembly Democrats to accept it or risk losing protections altogether.[27]

At the city level, too, tenant groups found themselves largely frustrated. They won a significant victory in 2008 when Bloomberg signed a City Council bill allowing tenants to sue over harassment. But in general, city policy under Bloomberg did little to arrest rising rents—which, to the mayor, reflected increasing demand and underwrote the continuing refurbishment of the city's housing stock. Unlike Giuliani, who occasionally pressured the Rent Guidelines Board to keep rent increases relatively low (which did not stop tenants from accusing his RGB chair of carrying out "'Giuliani's racist plot' to drive blacks and Latinos from the city"), Bloomberg tended to make landlord-friendly appointments and then keep his hands off. Yearly rent allowances were generally higher than usual, with those passed in 2003 and 2008 the largest (with one exception) since 1989.[28]

The Rent Guidelines Board's annual public meetings, never exactly tranquil, became utterly raucous as tenants, feeling disempowered at both the state and city level, opted for a strategy of disruption. In 2006, the din of chants, drums, whistles, and rattles so enveloped the venerable meeting hall at Cooper Union that the board chair had to suspend the meeting for two and a half hours. "This is fantastic," said Jumaane Williams, executive director of the group Tenants and Neighbors. "We want to stop this meeting from happening. This meeting is a sham of the democratic process." The tenant movement's turn toward disruption suggested just how powerless it had become in Bloomberg's New York. Rents kept rising, and the city kept getting less affordable, and there wasn't much Sheldon Silver or Brad Lander or Jumaane Williams or anyone else could do about it.[29]

In their darkest moment, tenants were still able to score some real victories. The well-organized, relatively well-resourced tenants in Stuyvesant Town and Peter Cooper Village discovered that MetLife and Tishman Speyer had taken J-51 tax breaks from the city while making their renovations, which should have prevented them from deregulating units; the state courts subsequently made Tishman Speyer refund rent hikes and return units to stabilization. "It's terrible for the industry," one midsize landlord said. "A lot of people bought property with the thought that they would get the rents up. People made decisions based on that. Banks made loans. This decision is another nail in the coffin." The decision, and the softening rental market amid the global economic meltdown that began in 2008, afforded renters some breathing room—though the growing ranks of jobless and underemployed were scarcely able to take advantage of it.[30]

The loss of tens of thousands of regulated units and the steeper-than-usual rent increases, together with constraints on new construction and a diminished state and federal commitment to affordable housing, contributed to the greatest jump in real rents in the city since the 1970s. By 2011, for the first time in the city's modern history, the median New York rental household was officially rent-burdened, paying more than 30 percent of its income in rent—and a third of households paid more than half. The rent-regulation system—still by far the most common kind of housing for New Yorkers in the bottom third of the income scale—was increasingly failing to ensure affordability.[31]

Yet the rent-regulation system, though patchier, remained as a bulwark for working-class neighborhoods amid gentrification. Contrary to the media image of opulent rent-controlled apartments overlooking Central Park, the most highly regulated neighborhoods were working-class neighborhoods of color: Kingsbridge Heights, Moshulu, Highbridge, South Concourse, University Heights, and Fordham in the Bronx; South Crown Heights and Flatbush in

Brooklyn; Washington Heights and Inwood in upper Manhattan. "New York is a more diverse place because of rent stabilization," the preeminent urban economist Edward Glaeser remarked in a 2012 interview, "and I say that as a staunch and steadfast enemy of rent stabilization." It would remain to be seen how much longer the vestiges of working-class New York could hold on.[32]

THOUGH HE NEVER QUITE came out and said so openly, no one who had been around the NYPD long enough could have failed to note Ray Kelly's lingering resentment at Rudy Giuliani and his first police commissioner, Bill Bratton. Kelly was widely seen to have performed well as commissioner in the last months of Dinkins's mayoralty. He approached Giuliani about keeping the job, but Giuliani wanted to signal a clean break from the Dinkins years and gave Kelly only a cursory—and by some accounts, dismissive—hearing. In the following years, Giuliani and Bratton depicted their Broken Windows style of policing as diametrically opposed to Kelly's community policing initiative, an approach they associated with the supposed permissiveness of the Dinkins years. Crime had started to fall under Dinkins and Brown and Kelly, but it was Giuliani and Bratton who got the credit for "cleaning up" New York. The politically savvy Kelly, colleagues felt, had backed the long-shot Bloomberg at least in part because he desperately wanted a chance to set the record straight.[33]

For Bloomberg, Kelly was an obvious choice for police commissioner. He had excellent anti-terrorism bona fides, essential in the aftermath of September 11. And he seemed especially well suited to the task of turning the page on the divisiveness of the Giuliani years. His outreach efforts in Black and Latino communities had earned him a reputation that stood in contrast to the NYPD under Giuliani. Even a figure as critical of the NYPD as Richie Pérez, the former Young Lord who was now directing the National Congress for Puerto Rican Rights (which had helped launch the most important post-Diallo lawsuit), thought community activists could engage with Kelly. "Don't automatically paint him as a villain," he wrote in a memo. "'He inherited a rough situation from Lee Brown and had limited time to make changes. What is he going to do now on the issues of community concern, on issues he didn't have time to address?'" For their part, right-wingers were concerned about Kelly's appointment—which, one writer for the *New York Post* worried, might represent "a throwback to the bad old days of the Dinkins' [*sic*] years."[34]

Unlike Giuliani, Bloomberg had no grand vision for the NYPD and no interest in micromanaging the department. He wanted someone he could trust to maintain or extend the gains of the 1990s, rebuild police-community relations, and develop the city's anti-terrorism capacities while he pursued other objectives. Kelly was back, eager to redeem himself, with wide autonomy; he took over a department for which post–September 11 goodwill had swept away some of the resentment of the late 1990s and which gained prestige with every month that went by without another terrorist attack. It was to be a fateful arrangement.

Kelly, like Bloomberg, was keen to move on from the divisiveness of the Giuliani years. In March, Kelly issued a department-wide memo officially forbidding the use of race and other categories (such as gender and sexual orientation) as "the determinative factor for taking police action"—a move that was reported in the press as a "ban on racial profiling" and which the executive director of the New York Civil Liberties Union described as an "important and long overdue step forward." The following month Kelly announced the dissolution of the highly controversial Street Crime Unit. A few days after that, he invited the Reverend Al Sharpton to a meeting at 1 Police Plaza. "It is not too early to say he has set a better tone," a circumspect Sharpton told reporters. "But so far, we cannot say if it is better music." Still, Kelly had been remarkably adept at changing the narrative. That month, when a police lieutenant in Brooklyn's 88th precinct named Eric Adams accused Kelly at a news conference of having "neither . . . the know-how nor the desire" to address issues affecting communities of color, the columnist Bob Herbert, a major critic of police abuse in the late 1990s, rushed to Kelly's defense: Adams, he wrote, had issued a "cheap shot," directing a "false and disgusting and dangerous charge" at "a very decent man."[35]

Though eager to change the department's tone, Kelly had no interest in scaling back the proactive street policing of the 1990s. If anything, he thought the Giuliani-era NYPD was not proactive enough. "We have to put our hands on more people," his chief of department remarked, to the commissioner's approval. Kelly sometimes referred to his approach as "Broken Windows Plus," meaning a reworked version of existing practices with a more sensitive public posture. The end of the Street Crime Unit offered one example of how what looked like significant reform could in fact amount to something quite different in practice. While headlines emphasized the demise of the unit that had killed Diallo, Kelly stated forthrightly that the move was primarily a way of redeploying officers in light of the budget cuts: By shifting the SCU's officers to precincts and other plainclothes units, he explained, he was trying to maintain the capacity to generate the kind of intelligence that CompStat ran on. As for the department's widely lauded ban on racial profiling, only time would tell what a ban on the use of race as "a determinative factor" would mean for the stop-and-frisk practices that had caused so much anguish in the Giuliani years.[36]

In January 2003, Kelly launched his signature street-policing initiative, Operation Impact. The NYPD would send recent academy graduates to sixty-one high-crime areas, chosen on the basis of statistics and "consultations with community leaders," in an approach one precinct commander likened, perhaps unfortunately, to "pinpoint precision bombing." Operation Impact was meant to be a temporary program, but the first couple of months coincided with sharp crime drops in those areas; Bloomberg extended it—"It's just too important to keeping crime down in the city to let it lapse"—and then expanded it to include fifty-two additional zones. Kelly described the program as "the prime reason" the crime rate continued to fall in New York.[37]

For a while, Kelly's balancing act seemed to work. With occasional hiccups, crime rates kept falling, and Bloomberg's city of choice gained an additional selling point: "the undisputed safest large city in the nation." "Our success in fighting crime," the mayor proclaimed at the end of 2003, ". . . is the biggest reason why the Big Apple is coming back." Curiously, by mid-decade, civilian complaints were up, with complaints about stops and searches having risen particularly sharply—a phenomenon that proved difficult to parse given the NYPD's unwillingness to provide data to the City Council (despite being required to do so under the court settlement that followed Diallo's murder). Still, the department garnered high marks in public opinion polls. Bloomberg had expected to run for reelection on the basis of his economic record and his governance of the city schools. As it happened, public safety emerged as his "not so secret weapon" during the campaign of 2005.[38]

Then on February 2, 2007, two plainclothes police officers delivered to the City Council four bound volumes of some 250 pages apiece. After years of dragging its feet, the department had finally agreed to provide some clarity on its use of street stops. As councilmembers and reporters pored over the numbers, a stunning picture came into focus: The number of documented stops had risen from 97,296 in Bloomberg's first year in office to 508,540 in 2006. The revelations lit a long fuse on what would become perhaps the central controversy of Bloomberg's mayoralty.[39]

The numbers paint a rough aggregate picture of who was stopped, where, for what, and with what consequences. The number of recorded stops nearly doubled from 2003 to 2004, as the number of officers recovered and the NYPD launched Operation Impact, from 160,851 recorded stops to 313,523, before climbing to a peak of 685,724 in 2011. The most commonly offered justifications were that the person stopped had engaged in "furtive movements" or appeared to be "casing a victim/location"; less than one time out of five did the person stopped fit a relevant criminal description. About half of stops proceeded to a frisk, and around a quarter resulted in the use of physical force by the officer. During the height of stop-and-frisk, some 10 to 13 percent of stops resulted in either a criminal charge or the issuance of a summons, split roughly evenly between the two. Police recovered a gun in one or two out of every one thousand stops, a knife or other weapon roughly once in every one hundred.

The burden of stop-and-frisk fell most heavily on Black and Latino boys and young men in impoverished neighborhoods. Roughly 54 percent of those stopped at the height of stop-and-frisk were Black, though only 23 percent of New Yorkers identified as Black in census records. In the aggregate, Latino New Yorkers were stopped at a slightly higher rate than their share of the population, and like Black New Yorkers, they were more likely to see a stop proceed to a frisk. (Despite being frisked at higher rates, neither Black nor Latino New Yorkers were any likelier to be arrested or issued a summons after a stop than a white New Yorker.) During the height of stop-and-frisk, the NYPD registered more stops in some precincts than there were residents: 204,899 total stops out of a population of some 86,455 in the 75th Precinct in Brownsville, Brooklyn; 130,586 out of a population of 73,116 in East Harlem's 23rd Precinct. Overall, they recorded almost four times as many stops of Black men aged 18–24 as there were Black New Yorkers of that age—bearing out the testimony of many law-abiding young Black New Yorkers that they had been stopped dozens of times.[40]

Kelly and Bloomberg's decisions had profound consequences for everyday life for Black and Latino New Yorkers, particularly those in predominantly working-class or poor neighborhoods. Countless people, the vast majority unarmed and not obviously (or even plausibly) committing or about to commit a crime, were stopped—on the way to school or to work, coming home, hanging out with friends, going to and from the store: a thirteen-year-old in the Bronx thrown against a wall and then into a police wagon with no explanation while walking home from an after-school football game; a Hunter College student walking to the subway after a late night studying at a café who had his laptop broken when the police emptied his bag; a high school student stopped some sixty times who started trying to get himself suspended because the police on school grounds set him too much on edge. "They would enter the classroom very agitated, and not really in a place to learn," one Bronx middle-school teacher recalled. "On the days in which my students were stopped and frisked, their whole day was affected." These were but a few of the consequences of millions of stops.[41]

For those who were stopped and frisked, the consequences reached beyond the event itself. Stop-and-frisk produced a surge in what came to be called "manufactured misdemeanors": Personal possession of small amounts of marijuana was not an enforceable offense, but public display was; when officers ordered people to empty their pockets, they inevitably generated misdemeanor offenses where none would otherwise have occurred. Even when these charges were dismissed by the courts, as many were, they could entail real costs, especially given the backlogged court system and the increasingly dire state of the city's jails. Those who ended up with criminal records could lose access to jobs requiring background checks or city licenses and college scholarships, while immigrants could face deportation. Amid public outrage, Kelly cut the number of arrests sharply in 2011 by issuing an order that public display must be an "activity undertaken of the subject's own volition."[42]

Even for those who escaped the direst consequences of stop-and-frisk, the everyday tenor of life changed. "Achievement-oriented" young people were driven indoors by aggressive policing. Residents of the most heavily surveilled neighborhoods bumped fists or elbows rather than clasp hands when greeting each other because the latter was grounds for a drug search. Friends and families split up when going to the bodega to avoid police attention. Subsequent studies found that New Yorkers experiencing stops felt greater distrust in the police and were less likely to report crimes; were less likely to be civically engaged; were more likely to drop out of school; and were more likely to report trauma and anxiety symptoms.[43]

The impact on individuals rippled out to affect neighborhoods and communities. "The public parks, stoops, streets, and corners once emphasized by social scientists as places to congregate and create meaningful associations are no longer available to members of the community," the sociologist Jan Haldipur wrote after months of fieldwork. "Instead of allowing residents in areas like the southwest Bronx to enjoy nearby public areas, an increased police presence has only helped deepen the wedges between local residents, thus hastening neighborhood disintegration." That this was occurring at precisely the moment when the crime drop and the Bloomberg administration's innovative pro-urban design efforts were enriching the city's public spaces added a wretched irony.[44]

Why did it happen? And why didn't Bloomberg or Kelly—who had issued the department ban on racial profiling—stop it sooner? In an interview with the historian Chris McNickle, Kelly claimed that the numbers had exploded in large part because he insisted that officers fill out their paperwork diligently. Given Attorney General Eliot Spitzer's finding that stops and searches had been grossly underdocumented in the late 1990s, the claim has some measure of plausibility. But the fact that Civilian Complaint Review Board complaints were rising year over year in the first half of the 2000s, with those pertaining to stops-and-frisks rising faster than other kinds, suggests that the skyrocketing numbers were not just an artifact of more accurate reporting. Moreover, the stops appeared to be getting more indiscriminate. "Between 2004 and 2009," the historian Clarence Taylor notes, "incidents in which the officer failed to note a specific suspected crime that triggered the stop increased from 1 percent to 36 percent."[45]

At other times, Bloomberg and Kelly argued that stop-and-frisk was the centerpiece of their strategy to combat the very real problem of gun violence—that the NYPD was following the script James Q. Wilson had provided in 1994. Gun violence mattered deeply to Bloomberg, who exercised powerful leadership on the issue at a time when the federal government was providing little support. Describing gun violence as "our most urgent challenge," he called a group of mayors to Gracie Mansion in April 2006 to form a new organization, Mayors Against Illegal Guns. "What do you say" to the family who lost someone to gun violence? he asked. "That we didn't have the courage to stand up and do something about it? Shame on us if we don't do something about it."[46]

Bloomberg seemed convinced that stop-and-frisk contributed substantially to his campaign against gun violence. "We are not walking away from a strategy that we know saves lives," he pledged in an address at the First Baptist Full Gospel Church in Brownsville, Brooklyn. Critics noted that stop-and-frisk had not recovered many illegal guns: 4.4 million stops and 2.3 million frisks yielded 4,400 guns. (Police recovered 66,000 "deadly devices," mostly knives.) But to Bloomberg and Kelly, this was precisely the point: The threat of a search was encouraging New Yorkers to leave their guns at home. "If you don't run the risk of being stopped, you start carrying your gun, and you do things people do with guns," Kelly argued. "By making it 'too hot to carry,'" he claimed, "the NYPD is preventing guns from being carried on our streets." Yet the inefficiency with which stop-and-frisk took illegal guns off the street and its widespread use for other purposes are hard to ignore, giving such justifications a post-facto quality.[47]

In fact, the proliferation of stop-and-frisk implicated everyone from Bloomberg and Kelly to the NYPD's middle managers down to the officers on the beat and everything from the department's managerial practices to its insulation from the communities it served. Facing intense pressure from headquarters to keep their precincts' crime rates down, precinct commanders not only permitted widespread use of stop-and-frisk but sometimes demanded it—the UF-250 forms that officers filled out after making stops could be used in meetings to demonstrate that they were on the ball. Street-level officers, in turn, felt pressure to produce numbers that would demonstrate their productivity, either out of a desire to rise up the ranks or to avoid poor performance assessments. Some later testified that their precinct commanders had obliged them to meet quotas.[48]

Why would Ray Kelly—a commissioner with relatively strong ties to Black and Latino communities who had been critical of Giuliani's NYPD for squandering a "large reservoir of goodwill" with "dubious stop-and-frisk tactics," someone acutely sensitive to how the department was perceived, who had won plaudits by issuing a ban on racial profiling—be unable to see the damage stop-and-frisk was doing in communities of color? Or did he see it and continue to believe that the benefits outweighed the costs? Kelly has always insisted that he did not curtail stop-and-frisk because he believed it was effective at reducing violence and that most of the beneficiaries of the drop in violence were Black and/or Latino; to make the approach work, he argued, NYPD officers had to "go where the crime is." Kelly has maintained that he believed he had the support of the communities most heavily affected by stop-and-frisk and that the opposition was coming from a grandstanding minority. Polling data seemed to support such claims: Kelly's approval rating was an astonishing 81 percent overall as late as May 2011. Even into 2013, by which time stop-and-frisk had become highly controversial, his approval rating among Black New Yorkers was 63 percent (and 75 percent overall).[49]

But figures like these failed to capture the experiences of young

New Yorkers of color, who were included barely, if at all, in polling samples, and whose trauma found no expression in the outlets the NYPD used to take stock of public opinion. The NYPD (and by extension, Kelly) sought out only a relatively narrow range of community voices—"religious institutions and the official precinct community councils," the urban policy expert Andrew White noted, but not "neighborhood associations, tenant groups, youth service organizations," nor young people themselves and others, such as school principals and teachers, who knew the intimate details of their daily lives. Valuable information that might have contradicted the "grandstanding minority" claim simply did not reach them, in large measure because Kelly and his lieutenants did not seek it out.[50]

And Bloomberg? "I can't explain it," one former aide told McNickle. "I think about this a lot," said another. "If I could go back in time . . . I wish with what I know now, I could have given the mayor a memo that said the stop-and-frisk numbers are a disaster and you need to do something about it." Certainly, part of the answer lies in his regard for Kelly, who had amassed a soaring reputation as a crime fighter and manager, driving down crime rates to almost unimaginable levels while building up a counterterrorism apparatus that rivaled the federal government's. By the end of Bloomberg's second term, Kelly's stature could fairly be likened to a latter-day Robert Moses: imperious, untouchable, and unaccountable, the autonomous, quintessential charismatic bureaucrat. But Bloomberg and his aides, too, ultimately failed to hear the voices that might have convinced them that the NYPD's practices were causing real harm. The closest Bloomberg himself has come to a public accounting was when he was contending for the Democratic nomination for president in 2020. "We weren't on top of things," he allowed, "and we didn't understand just how impactful it is, was, on young men of color who got stopped." If Bloomberg's inaction amounted to a failure of management from the manager par excellence, it also reflected the limits of his style of political leadership, and the limits of an ethical vision wherein, as with Moses, the making of the metropolitan omelet excused the cracking of a few eggs.[51]

AS HIS SECOND TERM DREW to a close, Bloomberg began to search for his next act. After Koch's ill-fated third term, New Yorkers had passed two citywide referenda (backed by a council bill) limiting its mayors to eight years in office. When an exploratory effort at a presidential bid came to naught, though, Bloomberg began to sound out his closest advisers about making an end-run around these measures and pursuing another four years in City Hall. As the fall of 2008 arrived, he gained a clear-cut rationale for doing so: Beginning with the collapse of Lehman Brothers, the world banking system reached the precipice of failure, threatening the city with fiscal and economic ruin. New York needed an experienced and firm hand to guide it through these extraordinary times, Bloomberg argued. Much of the city's civic and media elite agreed. The City Council, some of whose members were themselves term-limited, passed the necessary legislation. Bloomberg would seek to become, after La Guardia, Wagner, and Koch, the fourth three-term mayor in the city's modern history.[52]

Bloomberg's political team anticipated a difficult campaign in the wake of the term limits maneuver and amid the rising populist mood brought on by the Great Recession. They worked hard to clear the field of strong potential challengers, particularly the feisty Brooklyn congressman Anthony Weiner, who dropped out of the race after the Bloomberg campaign convinced him it might be personally embarrassing for him to continue. Only William J. Thompson, an establishment Democrat who had served as president of the Board of Education and New York City comptroller, chose to run against him; amicable and low-key, Thompson struggled to mount the kind of fiery campaign that might have roused populist passions against the billionaire incumbent. Bloomberg squeaked out a four-point victory despite a 14-to-1 spending advantage and a close to 70 percent job approval rating—a testament to how thoroughly his term limit repeal and free campaign spending had disgusted many New Yorkers, but also to the discontents simmering in the city. If less starkly than in the Dinkins-versus-Giuliani contests, the electorate split along racial lines: Black voters, who made up about 23 percent of the electorate, went nearly three to one for Thompson; white voters, still about 46 percent of the electorate even though non-Hispanic whites now accounted for only a third of the city's population, went roughly two to one for Bloomberg.[53]

The surprisingly tight election foretold the course of Bloomberg's third term. One after another, movements arose in opposition to the inequalities that had grown in Bloomberg's New York and the democratic deficiencies deemed responsible for them—discrete manifestations of the larger revolt against inequality and concentrated power emblematized by the Occupy Wall Street movement, which erupted downtown in the fall of 2011. To Chancellor Klein's professed befuddlement, not all parents and students in ostensibly failing schools were eager to see them shuttered and replaced. Some parents, students, educators, and community leaders viewed them as valued neighborhood institutions; perhaps they also feared that losing their neighborhood schools, as the historian Eve Ewing writes, meant "conceding a battle in a much larger ideological war over the future of a city and who gets to claim it." Some spoke of the bonds they had built with teachers and guidance counselors—one student at Paul Robeson High School in Crown Heights told a reporter about a counselor who had run a 5K to help raise money to pay her college application fees. Some, including Haitian Creole–speaking students who were having trouble finding an appropriate ESL program upon the phasing out of Samuel J. Tilden High School in the Bronx, simply did not know where to go next.[54]

For all Bloomberg and Klein's talk of choice, many parents and students felt they had not been offered the one choice that had long been at the heart of campaigns for school equity: well-resourced schools in their own communities, meeting their communities' distinctive needs, and offering a sense of community control, involvement, and empowerment. "You are not closing the white schools," one parent exclaimed during a two-and-a-half-hour meeting regarding the closure of Canarsie High School. "My whole thing is: Why are they giving up on us?" a student asked. Students, teachers, and alumni of schools targeted for closure began holding "Fight Back Friday" rallies outside their buildings. Elected officials sometimes joined. Public meetings of the Bloomberg-appointed Panel for Educational Policy, the agency that made closure decisions, became the schools equivalent of the raucous Rent Guidelines Board meetings. One, held at Brooklyn Tech, lasted more than five hours before the first vote was held. "Even though we know the D.O.E. is going to close the schools no matter what," a senior at University Heights High School in the Bronx explained, "we're here to enter their consciences until they can't sleep at night."[55]

The siting of charter schools represented another point of conflict. As Klein's team studied why the charter movement had lagged in New York, they zeroed in on the challenge of finding suitable locations. "The perfect fix for the real estate problem," Klein wrote, "was to make existing classroom space available to charters, and this is exactly what we decided to do." For traditional public schools, this could mean losing nonclassroom spaces and sharing access to cafeterias, libraries, and playgrounds. Some relatively advantaged parents were sometimes able to fend off co-locations in their school buildings: New Explorations in Science, Technology, and Mathematics on the Lower East Side defeated Klein's attempt to put a charter school in its building in 2006. Less-powerful constituencies often had to watch as better-resourced charters ate away at their facilities—teachers at P.S. 15 in Red Hook, Brooklyn, avoided walking their students past rooms being used by a co-located charter school, lest their students catch sight of their "sparkling-clean classrooms and computers."[56]

Charter opponents and skeptics were numerous and strong enough to pose a real challenge to Bloomberg, Klein, and the charter operators, especially in Albany, where Sheldon Silver remained a strong ally of the UFT. Because the 1998 law had established a numerical cap on the number of new charter schools, Silver seemed to have the leverage to slow the growth of the movement, or at least to insist that co-locations be approved by parents of the affected children. But the pro-charter forces quickly learned how to work Albany. When Silver tried to hold the line in 2010, the billionaires Kenneth Langone, Paul Tudor Jones, Stanley Druckenmiller, and Rupert Murdoch formed a tax-exempt organization, a 501(c)(4), that launched a series of TV ads and undertook door-to-door canvassing in key districts. Using federal money from Barack Obama's Race to the Top program as leverage, they succeeded in splitting Silver's caucus and getting the cap raised.[57]

Looking back at the history of school reform in 2011, Deborah Meier was struck by real doubts about the movement she had been an important part of. She remained proud of the schools she had helped create. But she worried about how the small-schools-and-choice approach had been institutionalized—particularly how it had been combined with that program of testing and "high standards" she had objected to so strenuously in the 1980s. "We had unqualified success" in the early 1990s, she recalled. But "even as we enjoyed our triumphs, another train was leaving the station. At first, these new reformers didn't sound unfriendly and even picked up a lot of our language—about school autonomy, empowerment, family-teacher engagement, engaged learning. . . . Never once did I imagine that we'd literally turn schools over to chain-store operators, to do with the poor whatever they chose—as long as they could produce test scores not much worse than their public rivals." She accused the new reform movement of turning schools into "Dickensian drudge mills." And she noted that the way choice had been implemented was contributing to "a step backward in the movement to school integration by class or race."[58]

In the spring of 2006, Meier met over lunch with her old adversary, Diane Ravitch, to prep for a debate on the federal No Child Left Behind law. To their mutual surprise, they discovered that they shared "a similar reaction to many of the things that are happening in education today." Both were "appalled" by "the relentless 'test prep' activities that have displaced good education in far too many urban classrooms." Both believed that small schools had been a good idea that "has too often been subverted by the mass production of large numbers of small schools, without adequate planning or qualified leadership and with insufficient thought given to how they might promote class and racial integration, rather than contribute to further segregation." Both were struck by how students were being assigned to " 'schools of choice' that the students themselves ha[d] not chosen" as the larger schools were closed down. "And all of this," they noted, "is happening in the name of equity and 'closing the achievement gap' and other unimpeachable rhetoric." At the end of the lunch, Ravitch told Meier that she would be glad to see one of her grandchildren attend one of Meier's schools.[59]

Ravitch was, in fact, undergoing a remarkable transformation. Klein believed that Ravitch had "played as big a part as anyone in calling America's school reform movement into existence by prominently articulating the core ideals—accountability, choice, and innovation—that animated it"; she had advised and supported Bloomberg in the 2001 campaign. Yet by the end of the decade she had emerged as a powerful critic of Bloomberg and Klein's reform program. The watershed moment came with the publication in March 2010 of Ravitch's widely read book, *The Death and Life of the Great American School System*, and an accompanying op-ed in the *Wall Street Journal* entitled "Why I Changed My Mind on School Reform." Charter schools, she argued, "tend[ed] to attract the best students in poor neighborhoods," and their test scores and graduation rates may have been inflated by high attrition rates among low-performing students and the disproportionately low numbers of special needs and English-learner students; as more charters opened, she predicted, "the dilemma of educating *all* students will grow sharper." By the end of Bloomberg's mayoralty, when she published another book, *Reign of Error*, she was sharper. "Your efforts to create a dual system of publicly funded schools," she told the reformers, "turns back the clock to the shameful era before the Brown decision."[60]

Nowhere, though, was the backlash against Bloomberg as impassioned as on the issue of stop-and-frisk: In the first half of 2010, the issue exploded into public consciousness. *The New York Times* began running front-page stories on racial bias in police stops. The columnist Bob Herbert, who had once rushed to Kelly's defense, now assailed stop-and-frisk as "Jim Crow policing." This "despicable, racially oriented tool of harassment" was causing "nonstop humiliation of young black and Hispanic New Yorkers, including children," he wrote. "People going about their daily business, bothering no one, are menaced out of the blue by the police, forced to spread themselves face down in the street, or plaster themselves against a wall, or bend over the hood of a car, to be searched. People who object to the harassment are often threatened with arrest for disorderly conduct." The "gruesome, racist practice . . . should offend all New Yorkers," he concluded, "and it should cease."[61]

In 2009, the NYPD acknowledged the existence of a database with the personal information of a vast number of people who had been stopped—the overwhelming percentage of whom, of course, had not been charged with a crime or issued a summons. In 2010, the database became the first flashpoint in a broader political movement to curtail the abuses of stop-and-frisk. State Senator Eric Adams and Assemblyman Hakeem Jeffries introduced legislation requiring that the database keep track only of people who had been convicted of crimes. Governor David Paterson came under intense pressure from

Kelly, who met with him twice to urge a veto. But Paterson knew firsthand what it was like to suffer police surveillance, having himself been stopped three times. "It's a feeling of being degraded," he later remarked. "I think that's what people who it hasn't happened to don't understand." He signed the measure into law.[62]

By this time, stop-and-frisk was losing support even among people who typically backed the NYPD. This group included Senator Adams, who described street stops as a "great crime-fighting tool" but assailed the NYPD's abuse of them. It included a number of retired commanders and other policing experts who viewed the "throw a wide net and see what you can find" approach (as one former NYPD officer put it) as a lazy alternative to the more challenging work of what policing scholars called "focused deterrence." And though New Yorkers did not yet know it, by 2012 it included Michael Bloomberg himself. In a series of meetings, Bloomberg apparently insisted to Kelly that the practice needed to be reformed. The NYPD began to cut back on the number of stops in the spring of 2012, and within a year stops were down by half. By the end of Bloomberg's mayoralty, the journalist Jim Dwyer wrote, stop-and-frisk was "still a court fight, a giant cultural wrestling match. . . . But as part of life in New York, the stop-and-frisk tactic is shrinking fast." Kelly, for his part, quickly pivoted toward a new program called Operation Crew Cut, which trawled social media for evidence of gang membership and subjected the youths in the resulting database to intense surveillance. And by 2013 the NYPD had extended to the entire city its Domain Awareness System, an assemblage of sensors and closed-circuit TVs that collectively amounted to the largest digital surveillance system in the world.[63]

If Bloomberg and Kelly were moving to relegitimize police surveillance behind the scenes, in public they launched a full-voiced defense of stop-and-frisk. When in June 2013 the City Council passed legislation lead-sponsored by Brooklyn councilmen Jumaane Williams and Brad Lander to create an independent inspector general to monitor the NYPD, Bloomberg vetoed it, only to see the council override him. Two months later Judge Shira Scheindlin of the Southern District of New York ruled in a class action suit, *Floyd v. New York*, that the NYPD had violated the Fourth and Fourteenth amendments by consistently failing to meet the constitutional requirement of "reasonable suspicion that criminal activity may be afoot" and engaging in "indirect racial profiling." Bloomberg and Kelly responded defiantly, arguing that their approach had saved the lives of "countless" New Yorkers (as Bloomberg claimed), most of them "Black and Hispanic young men." Bloomberg vowed to appeal Scheindlin's decision, ensuring that stop-and-frisk would be a central issue in the 2013 mayoral campaign.[64]

THOUGH HE WAS NOT ON THE BALLOT, Bloomberg cast a long shadow over the 2013 mayoral election. The leading Republican candidate, former MTA chair and Giuliani-era deputy mayor Joe Lhota, vowed to build on Bloomberg's legacy, starting with retaining Kelly as police commissioner. Candidates for the Democratic nomination had to define themselves in relation to Bloomberg—a task that proved especially difficult for City Council speaker Christine Quinn, who had backed Bloomberg on a number of issues (most notably in his effort to overturn term limits) before leading the council's opposition to him in 2013. When Quinn's support began to fizzle, front-runner status passed to Anthony Weiner, the candidate Bloomberg had most worried about in 2009. Weiner resigned from Congress in 2011 after it was revealed that he had been sending lewd photos to young women via Twitter and other platforms. Having come home to revitalize his career, he was happily calling for a local single-payer health care system when another set of lewd messages, several posted under the alias "Carlos Danger," came to light.[65]

With Quinn tied to Bloomberg and Weiner discredited, the Democratic primary became a race between William Thompson, Jr., running again after his near-miss in 2009, and Public Advocate Bill de Blasio, a longtime veteran of the city's progressive politics. A great admirer of New York's social democratic tradition—at family gatherings, he once said, it "felt like there were two empty chairs for Franklin Roosevelt and Fiorello La Guardia"—de Blasio had been one of the idealistic young people who entered public service in the Dinkins administration, where he worked as a staffer under political strategist Bill Lynch. In the succeeding years, he had built strong connections with the local labor movement and community groups, especially in his home borough of Brooklyn. His political vision, he explained, was one of a "coalition politics tied to labor." His candidacy marked the apparent coming-of-age of a younger generation of post-Dinkins left-liberal politics that was percolating in the city as the Democratic headliners were floundering in the 1990s and early 2000s.[66]

De Blasio found his moment as a vessel for the anti-Bloomberg revolt. He assailed Bloomberg for fostering a "tale of two cities," a line he had borrowed from Dinkins (who had taken it from Mario Cuomo's famous 1984 Democratic National Convention speech). A public school parent, he spoke out against school closures, called for a pause on charter school co-locations, and promised that under his administration, the charter operator Eva Moskowitz of the Success Academy network would not have "the run of the place"—a pledge that in turn inspired Moskowitz to pull students from class and lead them on a protest march across the Brooklyn Bridge. As the father of a Black teenage son, he staked out the left-most position on policing, promising to end the "stop-and-frisk era," rejecting calls for more officers (the only Democratic candidate to do so), and during the general election, vowing to replace Kelly. De Blasio carried the Democratic primary with a broad coalition tilted toward the working and middle classes, then won the general election by the greatest percentage margin of any candidate in the city's modern history save Koch.[67]

FOR PROGRESSIVES, DE BLASIO'S VICTORY represented an opportunity unlike any since the 1960s. De Blasio was taking office under far more auspicious circumstances than Dinkins had. Crime was low, and a mandate for police reform seemed to have been established during the campaign. The white revanchism so central to Giuliani's politics had diminished as a force in city life, a consequence of changing demographics, the long crime drop, and fading memories of the so-called bad old days of the early 1990s. The local economy was prosperous, if hugely unequal. Unlike in the Dinkins years, resources were available for progressive reform. The governmental systems that de Blasio wanted to put toward progressive ends now worked much better thanks to Bloomberg's administrative reforms. And whereas Dinkins had endured a rocky relationship with Mario Cuomo, de Blasio could look forward to a productive working relationship with Andrew Cuomo, who had won his father's old job in 2010 and whom de Blasio had known and supported for years. The long-awaited progressive revival appeared finally to have arrived.

7

A Tale of Two New Yorks

As de Blasio prepared to take office on the first day of 2014, progressives across the nation turned their hopes squarely to New York City for the first time in at least half a century. With Barack Obama's presidency ground down by Republican opposition in Congress, the columnist Michelle Goldberg wrote, "cities are seizing the initiative and becoming laboratories for progressive policy innovation. Amid widespread despair about national politics, cities have become new sources of hope." With de Blasio's rise, those progressive hopes had come to the nation's grandest stage. "The mayor has a remarkable opportunity to make real many progressive policies and prove their merit," California lieutenant governor Gavin Newsom told a reporter. "De Blasio matters. A lot of us are counting on his success." *The Nation* devoted an entire issue to the promise of what it called "the de Blasio moment" and committed a journalist to cover the new administration full time. The attention continued through the administration's early months. MSNBC's Chris Hayes sat down for a prime-time interview with "the man who has conservatives quaking in their boots."[1]

For one bitterly cold morning, the past and future of New York's Democratic Party assembled on the steps of City Hall: the incoming mayor's old boss, David Dinkins, whose tumultuous mayoralty symbolized so many of the party's hopes, frustrations, failures, and underappreciated successes; Charles Schumer, an emerging power in the U.S. Senate Democratic Caucus whose victory over Alfonse D'Amato in 1998 had dealt the first strong blow to the Republican ascendancy in New York politics; and Bill and Hillary Clinton, the former the day's keynote speaker, the latter seated immediately next to the podium—a nod, perhaps, to the fact that she was, on that day, the person most likely to become the next president of the United States. Easy to miss between the ebullient former president and a stoic but visibly unhappy Michael Bloomberg sat de Blasio's old friend and mentor, New York governor Andrew Cuomo. "I don't have a better political friend than Bill de Blasio," Cuomo told reporters afterward. The following years would put that claim to the test—and test the notion of whether the inequalities of the post-fiscal-crisis state could be swept aside as quickly as de Blasio had promised.[2]

THOUGH THE HONEYMOON PERIOD continued into his first months in office, de Blasio had already raised some progressive eyebrows with his appointments, particularly his choice of police commissioner: Bill Bratton, the architect of Broken Windows policing. It was actually a less surprising choice than it might have appeared. Though he had campaigned on the promise to end "stop-and-frisk as we know it," the mayor did not intend to prioritize police reform during his first months in office. De Blasio, who had sought Bratton out for conversations as he was preparing his mayoral bid, trusted the old hand to keep crime rates low and to assuage rank-and-file officers and the city's business community while he pursued his vision of a twenty-first-century New Deal. Bratton recognized as much. "A lot of this [is about] effectively trying to just calm everybody down," he remarked.[3]

Bratton recognized how much had changed in New York since his departure in 1996. "Crime is not, interestingly enough, a big issue at this time," he mused. His primary task, as he saw it, was public relations. "We will all work hard to identify why it is that so many in this city do not feel good about this department that has done so much to make them safe," he remarked in his first policy message to the city. "What has it been about our activities that have made so many feel alienated?"[4]

Because Kelly's NYPD had already cut back sharply on street stops, "ending stop-and-frisk as we know it" was primarily a political task rather than an operational one. At the end of his first month in office, de Blasio, with Bratton by his side, announced that the city would seek a settlement to the *Floyd* decision and would accept the appointment of an independent monitor and a pilot body camera program, among other reforms. Bratton quickly overturned Kelly's practice of channeling rookie officers into Operation Impact; throwing inexperienced officers into high-crime areas, Bratton believed, had contributed to the abuses of stop-and-frisk. Instead, he placed them in traditional precinct assignments, where seasoned officers familiar with their neighborhoods could help them hone the skills and develop the knowledge they needed to be more responsive to community concerns.[5]

Still, Bratton had no intention of stepping away from the enforcement of low-level offenses that had been the hallmark of his first turn as commissioner. Broken Windows "works," he told a meeting of business leaders at the Waldorf Astoria, "and it will remain a cornerstone of the policy." By this time, academic research had begun to cast real doubt on the Broken Windows theory, and many opponents of stop-and-frisk had blamed the theory for encouraging aggressive policing and street harassment. But Bratton, his own image inextricably intertwined with the theory, appeared also to believe that he would be judged by whether disorder reappeared on the city streets—and de Blasio, whose opponents had warned of a return to the "bad old days," seemed to concur. "We will be focusing on ensuring that aggressive begging and the squeegee pests, all of those activities that create fear and destroy neighborhoods . . . don't have the chance to come back," Bratton promised. He brought George Kelling in as a consultant and launched a high-profile campaign against "showtime" subway performers.[6]

Then suddenly the potential consequences of low-level enforcement became all too clear. In March 2014, officials at Police Headquarters briefed commanders in the 120th Precinct about complaints of disorder along a stretch of Bay Street, near Tompkinsville Park on the North Shore of Staten Island, where a small group of mostly middle-aged men sold untaxed cigarettes and drugs. Eric Garner was a forty-three-year-old husband and father of six, a former Parks Department horticulturist who was now providing for his family by importing cigarettes from lower-tax jurisdictions and selling them for a profit in New York. To "park regulars and local shop owners," two reporters noted, "he had been a bright spot, a peacemaker who with his size alone could—and often did—quell disputes." Garner was known for sitting around playing chess and checkers when business was light and for treating neighborhood children when the ice cream truck came around. To the NYPD, he was a "known recidivist" whose presence both symbolized and embodied the kind of disorder that, according to the Broken Windows theory, was supposed to lead to more serious crime.[7]

On July 17, 2014, two officers arrived at the site, including one, Daniel Pantaleo, who possessed a record of excessive use of force. A bystander captured what occurred next on a cell phone camera. As Garner pleaded with the officers not to touch him, Pantaleo sought to subdue him using what Bratton later said appeared to be a chokehold. "Let up, you got him already," a female sergeant urged as

Garner pleaded for breath. Garner went into cardiac arrest and was pronounced dead at the Richmond University Medical Center about an hour after the initial encounter. As video of the chokehold circulated around the world, Garner's searing words—"I can't breathe"—became a rallying cry for what many Black Americans felt dealing with police brutality and surveillance.[8]

Together with the police killing of Michael Brown in Ferguson, Missouri, several weeks later, Garner's death catalyzed a far-reaching movement, at once national and local, for criminal justice and policing reform. In New York, the movement that had developed during the Giuliani years and revived during Bloomberg's third term turned its attention to Broken Windows. "It's the new stop-and-frisk," said the director of the Police Reform Organizing Project. "I think we need to look at whether we still need these arrests," Brooklyn borough president Eric Adams remarked, questioning whether Broken Windows made sense "now that the windows are no longer broken."[9]

Bratton moved quickly to introduce new police training in conflict de-escalation and allowed that, given the crime drop, it might be possible to de-emphasize arrests and summonses. But Broken Windows policing, he insisted, remained "a key part of what we're doing." Most encounters, he argued, came in response to community demands, such as 311 and 911 calls and requests during community meetings; he noted that public opinion polling showed majority support for quality-of-life enforcement across demographics. And if aggressive enforcement seemed to be concentrated in predominantly poor Black and Latino neighborhoods, this was an unfortunate by-product of the fact that those communities needed the most help from police in restoring informal mechanisms of social control. Police simply went where the disorder was, he argued, echoing Raymond Kelly's defense of stop-and-frisk. The issue was not the policy, he claimed, which worked and enjoyed popular support. It was a handful of the people tasked with carrying it out. "The reality is, at this moment, that there are some in the organization who shouldn't be here," he told a meeting of police commanders; this 1 percent of bad officers was "poisoning the well."[10]

De Blasio was deeply shaken by Garner's killing. When a Staten Island grand jury declined to bring charges against Officer Pantaleo, de Blasio spoke freely of his own fears as the parent of a Black teenager and how he recognized and understood the pain of Garner's family. "The tragedy is personal to this family," he said, "but it's become something personal to so many of us. It's put in stark perspective the relationship between police and community. This issue has come to the fore again, and we have to address them [*sic*] with all our might. We can't stop. We have to act, with the assumption that it's all of our jobs to never have a tragedy again—that's what we have to fight for." Patrolmen's Benevolent Association president Patrick Lynch, in response, accused the mayor of throwing the city's police officers "under the bus." Later that month, when an out-of-state man ambushed and killed Rafael Ramos and Wenjian Liu, two on-duty officers sitting in a marked patrol car, Lynch declared de Blasio complicit in the murders, claiming that the "blood on the hands starts at City Hall in the Office of the Mayor" and encouraging officers to show their disgust by refusing to engage in normal policing.[11]

From that moment forward, de Blasio became reluctant to challenge the NYPD directly, relying on Bratton as a kind of buffer between City Hall and the police force. By the spring of 2015, Bratton had enfolded quality-of-life policing into a new—and yet distinctly familiar—strategic approach: neighborhood policing. The approach divided each precinct into four or five sectors, each of which was assigned two carefully chosen and specially trained neighborhood coordinating officers (NCOs) tasked with "get[ting] to know every person within the neighborhood and to understand the problems of the community from the inside out." The program launched in four pilot precincts in Washington Heights and the Rockaways in May 2015 and was up and running in half of all precincts by that fall. De Blasio's criminal justice office augmented the approach the following year with a new project called NeighborhoodStat—the CompStat managerial approach applied to the objectives of community policing, with meetings featuring not only the local police commander and NCOs but also representatives from the Department of Sanitation, NYCHA, "homeless prevention agencies, tenants' associations, building managers, antiviolence organizations, police officers, and residents," all meeting collectively to devise solutions to neighborhood concerns.[12]

Bratton's critics saw his reforms as fundamentally an attempt to shore up the legitimacy of the status quo—an effort to justify, amid yet another round of protest, the preeminent role the police had gained in local governance over the prior thirty years. The manifestations of "disorder" that Broken Windows policing claimed to address, they argued, were symptomatic of broader problems: poverty, homelessness, un- and underemployment, drug abuse, mental health issues, and the underprovision of public services. It was time, the policing scholars Alyssa Aguilera and Alex S. Vitale wrote, to address disorder through approaches other than the enforcement of criminal sanctions. The role of the police, they argued, "should be restricted to responding to truly dangerous conditions [and serving] as gatekeeper to enhanced services"; the resources that went into Broken Windows policing should instead be invested in "nonpunitive mechanisms for addressing community problems": "supportive housing, harm reduction programs, evidence-based drug treatment, and health services that can play a much more positive and sustained role in reducing very real community concerns about disorder and public safety."[13]

For city lawmakers, these critiques raised two key questions. First, where should public resources be directed? Should funds that might previously have flowed to the criminal justice system be diverted instead to organizations and programs addressing social problems in other ways? Or were the police still the city's indispensable institution? During the 2014 budgeting cycle, City Council speaker

Melissa Mark-Viverito of East Harlem called for an additional one thousand officers to help address a modest uptick in violence, a proposal backed by the council's Black, Latino, and Asian Caucus. With Bratton's support, de Blasio rejected the proposal. But the following year Mark-Viverito revived it; critics such as Communities United for Police Reform and the NAACP Legal Defense and Education Fund once again argued that the major investment required would better be devoted to summer employment programs and community-based antiviolence organizations. This time, though, de Blasio acceded, justifying the addition of thirteen hundred new officers as a way of implementing the neighborhood policing plan—clear evidence, some progressives believed, that the seemingly earnest police reformer of 2013 did not intend to pursue the kinds of alternative approaches to governance envisioned by the new generation of activists.[14]

The second question concerned how minor offenses should be governed. Should acts like small-scale marijuana possession, public drinking, and public urination remain criminal offenses, or should they be treated as civil offenses akin to traffic violations? Bratton wanted criminal offenses to remain on the books so that officers could leverage marijuana to target more serious crimes in the Broken Windows fashion—in order to check for outstanding warrants, conduct searches, and collect information. Proponents of decriminalization saw it as a way of reducing the impact of Broken Windows policing, particularly in low-income communities of color where such arrests and criminal summonses were most common.[15]

The first battle over decriminalization involved marijuana possession, a leading contributor to the spike of misdemeanor arrests in the two decades after 1994. In July 2014, Kings County district attorney Kenneth Thompson, elected in the previous fall's progressive wave, announced over Bratton's opposition that his office would stop prosecuting certain low-level marijuana offenses, noting explicitly that contact with the criminal justice system was causing young

New Yorkers of color in particular "problems with jobs, housing, and school." Four months later de Blasio and Bratton announced that the NYPD "would generally" issue summonses rather than make arrests for possession of up to twenty-five grams of marijuana.[16]

The following spring Mark-Viverito proposed expanding decriminalization to encompass a wider range of offenses—public urination, open container violations, littering, and others. The public urination proposal in particular met a swift backlash. The *New York Post*, whose photographers possessed an almost supernatural ability to witness quality-of-life offenses, predicted a coming tsunami, plastering its cover with a shot of a man relieving himself in the middle of Broadway on the Upper West Side. Even progressive Democrats such as Public Advocate Letitia James and Comptroller Scott Stringer thought public urination should remain a criminal offense. "Having grown up in this city in the '70s and '80s," Stringer said, "I am not in favor of people urinating in the street, jumping turnstiles or creating dangerous situations by being drunk." In May 2016, Mark-Viverito was able to win passage of a suite of bills collectively known as the Criminal Justice Reform Act. The measures left criminal penalties on the books but encouraged officers to issue civil rather than criminal summonses. The measure promptly led to a 90 percent reduction in the number of criminal summonses and, consequently, a drop in open warrants and arrests for nonappearance.[17]

While the controversies over Broken Windows policing raged, the NYPD continued to experiment with new modes of surveillance. The ongoing digital revolution offered large organizations of all types new mechanisms to sort and classify New Yorkers. The Department of Education deployed its algorithm to divvy up spots at desirable public schools. Tenant-screening companies started buying Housing Court records and selling the data to landlords who used it to assemble tenant blacklists, a kind of equivalent to the NYPD's stop-and-frisk and gang databases. Now the NYPD moved into the emerging field of "predictive policing," developing algorithms and data-mining capacities that purported to identify when and where future crimes would occur. "The 'Minority Report' of 2002 is the reality of today," Bratton said, describing predictive policing as "the wave of the future." Critics of the approach cited privacy concerns and worried that the data generated by the racialized patterns of enforcement that had characterized Broken Windows policing would become a self-fulfilling prophecy—that unequal policing in the past would lead to bias in predicting the future.[18]

De Blasio and Mark-Viverito took pride in achieving meaningful reform while keeping New York the safest large city in America. Yet the NYPD had not only fended off calls for a fundamental rethinking of the role of policing in the city but also emerged with more officers and an even more extensive imprint in the city's neighborhoods. De Blasio won election in part by communicating his sincere concern about the costs of aggressive policing in communities of color. But to many in the criminal justice reform movement, de Blasio's first term demonstrated just how impervious to reform the NYPD had become.

BILL DE BLASIO CAME AT school politics not only with a different set of ideas and commitments than Michael Bloomberg and Joel Klein but also from a fundamentally different perspective. Bloomberg and Klein had both graduated from public schools; both men subsequently decided that the public school system no longer offered students the same educational possibilities they had enjoyed, and both sent their children to private schools. Both men saw the public schools as a problem to be solved. De Blasio's children, in contrast, attended traditional elementary and middle schools in Park Slope, Brooklyn, where the schools were unusually integrated and typically performed well on assessments. Both went on to selective public high schools: daughter Chiara to Beacon High, one of the schools launched by the alternative schools movement in the 1990s, son Dante to Brooklyn Tech, one of the older schools that admitted students on the basis of a single exam. De Blasio—who had once served on the school board for District 15 in Brooklyn—recognized the shortcomings of the public school system. But as the first mayor with children in the system in at least half a century, he also appreciated the value of the city's traditional public schools. His choice as schools chancellor embodied the system's successes: Carmen Fariña, the daughter of Spanish Civil War refugees, had grown up in the New York City school system as an English-language learner and become the first member of her family to attend college; after a legendary career teaching social studies and literacy at P.S. 29 in Cobble Hill, Brooklyn (her students included the future novelist Jonathan Lethem), she went on to a successful career as a principal, superintendent, and administrator.[19]

De Blasio and Fariña broke from the Bloomberg-Klein program in two primary ways: They replaced Klein's school-closure approach with an initiative that aimed to boost low-performing schools by supplying additional resources; and they sought to slow the expansion of charters and co-locations. Under de Blasio and Fariña's Renewal program, the Department of Education designated ninety-four low-performing schools as "community schools," pairing them with local community organizations, providing them with wraparound services such as mental health clinics, adding nutritional services and training in restorative justice, and providing additional staff that allowed for an extended school day and summer sessions. If the approach hearkened back to an older notion of the public school as a bastion of community life, it also took account of what school closures meant to underserved neighborhoods, as well as the important role the deprivation of goods not usually associated directly with schooling played in educational disparities.

De Blasio formally ended the Renewal program four years and $773 million later, replacing it with an approach called Comprehensive

School Support in which any school could apply for Renewal-type services. The Renewal program's record was mixed. Some schools did improve quickly and exited the program. Others performed so poorly that de Blasio and Fariña reversed course and closed them in spite of their general position against closures. Most fell in between. The experiment was brief and inconclusive enough that analysts drew different conclusions from it. School reform proponents chided de Blasio and Fariña for keeping students in schools they knew were likely to fail and for wasting money that could have been deployed more effectively by charter schools (though it was unclear whether charters could have operated at the scale and devoted the resources necessary to replace so many troubled schools, or would even have wanted to do so). Progressives lauded the approach and pointed to the mixed results as evidence of just how much investment would be necessary to make real progress given the scale of the obstacles facing troubled schools: The Renewal program, despite its eye-catching cost, amounted to only a sliver of the Department of Education's $24 billion annual budget.[20]

As the Renewal program attested, de Blasio was eager to return attention and resources to the traditional public schools and away from the new-schools movement of the Bloomberg-Klein years. He was basically opposed to charters, which he felt had a "destructive impact" (as he had said during the 2013 campaign) on traditional public schools. More than that, he did not believe that charters represented a scalable alternative to traditional public schools and therefore thought that they had received an undue share of resources, attention, and advocacy. Though de Blasio and Fariña's rhetoric toward charters was considerably sterner than their actual decisions—in their second month in office, they approved fourteen out of seventeen co-location requests—given the eagerness of major charter operators to expand and the contests over resources at play, de Blasio and the charter movement were bound to come into conflict.[21]

In March 2014, having already denied several co-location requests, de Blasio moved forward with a campaign pledge to charge charter schools rent for the use of traditional public school buildings—a common practice nationally but not in New York. The mayor had tripped a political wire. The amply resourced and assertive charter movement had already demonstrated its political capability. Now there was a new entrant onto the stage. Since taking office in 2011, Andrew Cuomo had been a supportive but low-key partner in Bloomberg and Klein's school reforms. He had not said much about charter schools, preferring to emphasize testing and accountability—though some of his major campaign donors were committed charter backers.[22]

But to understand fully what Cuomo did that spring, one has to take in the broader political context. As he approached his first bid for reelection, Cuomo was at a critical juncture. A deeply experienced if sometimes unimaginative strategist, he had carved out a position as a post-Clinton fiscal moderate and social liberal—eager to lower taxes on the middle class, relatively solicitous of the wealthy, liberal on issues like gun control and same-sex marriage (the 2011 legalization of which was perhaps his signature achievement), and eager above all else to place himself to the center of his political rivals in the party. In 2012 he encouraged a group of Democrats, who called themselves the Independent Democratic Caucus, to tip control of the State Senate by caucusing with the Republicans, thus allowing Cuomo to define the middle ground. With respect to New York City, Cuomo's strategy involved a delicate balancing act: retain enough support to ensure that he faced no serious challenge from his left and could run up impressive electoral margins in solidly Democratic areas, while using the left as a foil to shore up his own centrist bona fides—and his appeal to suburban voters and big money donors.[23]

Their divergent politics alone would probably have been enough to doom any chance of cooperation between Cuomo and de Blasio, despite their long-running personal friendship. But Cuomo took the perennial, built-in tension between governor and mayor to a new level. An unparalleled political tactician, Cuomo resented mayors under any circumstances—they could only complicate his maneuvers as governor. His dealings with Bloomberg had already made it clear that he thought mayors should attend to local issues and stay out of his way. De Blasio's new New Deal, of course, was premised on exactly the opposite plan of action. At the same time, Cuomo had long been suspicious of potential rivals within the Democratic ranks: To deal with Cuomo, former governor David Paterson once said, was to feel someone sawing the floor out from under your feet.[24]

These tensions came together as Cuomo eyed reelection in 2014. Whether in the service of future ambitions or to secure his political capital in New York (or both), Cuomo wanted to run up an eye-catching margin. Yet his brand of politics was increasingly at odds with the direction of the Democratic Party following a year in which Democratic elites had taken on the lessons of the Occupy Wall Street movement, read Thomas Piketty, and watched Bill de Blasio emerge from the back of the pack and win in a landslide by telling a tale of two cities. Cuomo, in short, wanted to put de Blasio in his place while making an unmissable demonstration of his own political might.

Cuomo fired the opening salvo in January. De Blasio had campaigned for mayor on the promise of a universal prekindergarten program supported by an additional tax on those making over $500,000 a year. Cuomo announced his support for universal pre-K and pledged state support—then launched what one journalist called a "skillfully deployed assault" on de Blasio's funding scheme. De Blasio's camp expressed incredulity that Cuomo would denounce an approach that enjoyed broad public support and was sound in policy terms: The new program would be unquestionably better off with a dedicated funding stream than it would if left to the vagaries of the Albany budget-making project, fittingly nicknamed the Big Ugly. Cuomo and his allies could not believe that de Blasio would not accept Cuomo's offer and declare victory. Cuomo refused to push for the tax, then watched as the city press ran stories about how he had burnished his image as a fiscal moderate at the expense of de Blasio, the political naïf. The episode established a dynamic that would continue until Cuomo resigned from office in August 2021: De Blasio had advanced a proposal that, from the city's perspective, was justified on the merits but threatened a political interest of Cuomo's; Cuomo then used his authority and his mastery of political theater to make de Blasio look amateurish. The city press recognized the appeal of the Cuomo-versus-de Blasio psychodrama, and both politicians' teams, particularly Cuomo's, started to adopt an us-versus-them mentality.[25]

Most of this was still in the future when de Blasio went to Albany in March 2014, to stage a rally in support for his dedicated tax. Unbeknownst to the new mayor, he would not have the scene to himself. Upon hearing about de Blasio's event, Cuomo suggested to Success Academy's Eva Moskowitz that she organize a head-to-head rally to protest de Blasio's proposed charter reforms. Moskowitz let her schools out for the day so that parents and students could bus to Albany, where thousands amassed outside the state capitol and cheered Cuomo as he declared his unyielding support for the charter movement: "We are here today to tell you that we stand with you. You are not alone. We will save charter schools." "De Blasio went into this thinking he and Cuomo were friends," one Democratic politico told reporters, "but Andrew Cuomo doesn't really have friends."[26]

De Blasio proved no match for the charter movement, which spent millions of dollars on rallies, lobbying, and advertising. The mayor's poll numbers began to sag for the first time, and influential business organizations such as the Partnership for New York started to voice concerns. Soon Bill Clinton was calling with advice on how to beat a strategic retreat, and even Sheldon Silver—the UFT's most powerful ally—was ready to sign off on a measure that required the city to provide charters either free space or funds with which to rent comparable facilities. Thereafter Cuomo and the pro-charter forces in the state legislature consistently leveraged the extension of mayoral control of schools—which required state approval—to extract more charter-friendly concessions. The number of charter schools in New York rose from 159 in Bloomberg's last year in office to 216 at the end of de Blasio's first term.[27]

FOR THE FIRST YEAR OR SO of de Blasio's administration, school segregation remained, as it had been since the mid-1970s, a relative afterthought in education discourse. "We cannot change the basic reality of housing in New York City," de Blasio declared. Fariña promised that she had "no intention of touching" the gifted-and-talented admissions test and lauded gifted-and-talented programs for "serving the purpose of communities." Nor would the department aggressively rezone for the purposes of elementary-level integration—"You would find parents who have invested in certain places." The guiding principle, however oft unstated, remained what it had been for decades: Fariña, the *Times* summarized, "intend[ed] no changes that would drive middle- and upper-class families from the system."[28]

But this silence was becoming harder to maintain. The UCLA Civil Rights Project's 2014 report finding New York City's public schools among the most segregated in the nation (and getting worse over the course of the twenty-first century) received significant attention in the local media. Data from the high schools that admitted students on the basis of the Specialized High Schools Admissions Test (SHSAT), particularly Stuyvesant, Brooklyn Tech, and Bronx Science, had gone from an annual embarrassment to an outright scandal: By 2014, only 12 percent of those admitted were Black and/or Latino, compared to 70 percent in the entire system.[29]

In 2015, as the national Black Lives Matter movement pushed structural analysis of racial inequality to the center of national discourse, students, parents, journalists, academics, activists, and politicians in New York seized on the language of segregation to launch perhaps the deepest structural critique of the city school system since the late 1960s. The recovery of desegregation both as a discourse for making sense of the system's inequities and as a policy objective began, in part, at the grassroots. Parents in two districts where the admixture of gentrification and public school choice had produced especially stark disparities, the Upper West Side and the Lower East Side, began to call for district-wide "controlled choice" plans that would consider socioeconomic factors during the matching process. (The city was barred from considering race by the 2007 Supreme Court decision *Parents Involved v. Seattle*.) At roughly the same moment, journalists such as Nikole Hannah-Jones and Errol Louis reintroduced the language of segregation powerfully into discussions of city life. Such writers and advocates were not only pushing for integration; they were also shining a light on the hidden mechanisms of power that allocated resources, opportunity, and decision-making authority in a system where such things were well concealed. They directed attention to the litany of obstacles that parents and children had to negotiate to gain admission to desirable schools, the language of choice and the techno-mystifications of the matching system, and the funding formulas and the shadow budgets of PTA fundraising and philanthropic contributions.[30]

For the moment, these critics found themselves largely frustrated. De Blasio, viewing the SHSAT data, called for better "diversity" but offered no specific steps. Analysts characterized district-level controlled-choice proposals as "small steps," and even these small, highly local reform efforts met strong opposition. De Blasio conspicuously avoided discussing public school segregation for his first five years in office as, by and large, did his Department of Education. De Blasio and Fariña had turned the page on the Bloomberg-Klein era of creative destruction. Yet constrained by the raw power of the charter movement, the structure of de Blasio's political coalition, and the limits of their own vision—and notwithstanding the massive, unequivocal success of universal pre-K—they had yet to realize a clear alternative.[31]

IN FEBRUARY 2015, de Blasio delivered his first State of the City speech. Tensions over policing were at a fever pitch; the movement for school desegregation was gathering force. De Blasio, though, wanted to talk about housing—the linchpin, as he described it, of New York's promise:

> For generations, New York has been a city that unleashed human potential. A place offering opportunity for everyone, no matter how your life's story began; opportunity for innovators and visionaries to write new chapters in our history; and for parents and grandparents to write brighter ones for the next generation.
>
> And here's the hard truth: All of that is at risk today. It's at risk because so many who live in New York struggle to afford to be here. . . . If we do not act—and act boldly—New York risks taking on the qualities of a gated community . . . A place defined by exclusivity, rather than opportunity. And we cannot let that happen.[32]

After his early success with universal pre-K, housing emerged as the issue on which de Blasio's broader progressive ambitions rested. "So far as Bill de Blasio is concerned," the scholar Joseph Viteritti wrote, "all policy roads in his first administration have led to affordable housing."[33]

De Blasio had first laid out his vision the previous spring in a splashy plan entitled Housing New York, meant to outdo the Koch and Bloomberg plans both in scale and in the extent of its redistributive commitments. De Blasio pledged to "build or preserve" 200,000 affordable units over the span of a decade—some 40,000 more than Bloomberg, with a greater share dedicated to New Yorkers with very low incomes. Eighty thousand of those units would be new; 120,000 would be preserved through a variety of strategies aimed at keeping existing units under rent regulation.[34]

De Blasio's efforts at new construction demonstrated not just the challenges of building in New York, but specifically the difficulties of building in a segregated city. With little support from Albany or Washington, the city government instead deployed zoning powers to incentivize the construction of new affordable housing: Through a program called Mandatory Inclusionary Housing (MIH), the city permitted greater densities—and hence bigger profits for developers—in exchange for specified set-asides of affordable units. But where to build? Of the seven areas the de Blasio administration initially targeted for rezoning—East New York, Brooklyn; East Harlem and Inwood in upper Manhattan; Jerome Avenue in the Bronx; Bay Street on Staten Island; and Flushing and Long Island City in Queens—none was particularly affluent; nearly all were predominantly poor or working-class neighborhoods of color with relatively low construction costs and good transportation access. Community groups and longtime residents reasonably feared that new construction would lead developers to target the existing housing stock—and indeed, speculators did try to buy up tenements in neighborhoods selected for upzoning under de Blasio's plan. The plan thus pitted neighborhood-level organizations against citywide forces—the most influential labor unions as well as elements of the business community and the de Blasio administration. Despite considerable opposition from community boards and other local organizations, the City Council approved de Blasio's plan. By the time de Blasio's administration issued its final report on Housing New York in 2021, MIH had yielded more than four thousand permanently affordable units—a tiny share of the 66,000-some units the de Blasio administration was able to build, most of which came through more direct city subsidies.[35]

Though MIH garnered most of the headlines, the larger part of de Blasio's plan focused on preservation—a rearguard action against the destruction of affordable housing that had swept the city during the Bloomberg years. Much of this work was undertaken by the Department of Housing Preservation and Development, which deployed a range of innovative strategies for incentivizing owners to keep their units regulated after they hit the vacancy deregulation threshold or saw their tax abatements expire. The most famous case, again, was Stuyvesant Town and Peter Cooper Village, where the city put together a package of $220 million in tax breaks and loans to keep the roughly five thousand units that had survived the deregulatory bonanza within the system. But smaller-scale examples could be found across the city, particularly in the gentrifying neighborhoods that had been the epicenters of displacement.[36]

But the key, as always, lay in Albany. If the Democrats could regain clear control of the State Senate, de Blasio recognized, the city would have the clout to push Cuomo to the left. The state elections of 2014 thus held the key to his progressive aspirations. De Blasio had long supported New York's Working Families Party, whose vision of a left-labor coalitional politics fit closely with his own, and he brokered a deal whereby the WFP—no admirers of the centrist Cuomo—would grant the governor its nomination in exchange for a pledge to end the Independent Democratic Caucus and thereby secure unified Democratic control in Albany. Cuomo reluctantly agreed, filming a message to the party that journalists likened to a hostage video. De Blasio then took his campaign upstate, stumping for Democratic challengers. It could hardly have gone worse. All five IDC Democrats won, and the Republican Party netted two seats, giving them outright control of the upper chamber.[37]

The stage was thus set for a legislative session that proved absurd even by Albany standards. The 2015 session had barely begun when Sheldon Silver was arrested on federal corruption charges; it was only beginning to wind to a close when Republican Senate majority leader Dean Skelos was indicted for extortion, fraud, and conspiracy. Carl Heastie of the Bronx, who had succeeded Silver as speaker of the Assembly, appeared with de Blasio at a pro-tenant rally in Crown Heights, Brooklyn, a hotbed of harassment and displacement, and announced that enhanced rent laws were going to be the Assembly Democrats' top priority. The *New York Times* editorial board, long a barometer of elite opinion on the issue, departed from nearly a half-century of consistent (and sometimes strident) opposition to regulation, calling on Cuomo to "join Mr. de Blasio in leading a coalition of the honorable, to give some relief to more than two million New Yorkers . . . who live in constant fear of crippling rent increases and displacement from their homes."[38]

The governor appeared ready to do so. On June 6, he announced in an op-ed in the *Daily News* that he believed the state "must eliminate vacancy decontrol or at the very least significantly raise vacancy decontrol thresholds," signaling a notable shift toward the Assembly Democrats. Then to the astonishment of Democrats and tenant activists, Cuomo stood largely aside as the Senate agreed to lift the deregulation threshold only to $2,700 (indexed this time to Rent Guidelines Board increases). Advocates for the city were aghast at Cuomo's unwillingness to expend any real political capital on their behalf. "By any fair reading of the events of the last Albany session the governor has acted disgracefully" toward the city, the *Times* editorialized. Cuomo's team tried to pin the defeat on de Blasio, accusing him, again, of political naviété; de Blasio, who to this point had taken Cuomo's barbs without much reaction, slammed the governor's "lack of leadership," predicting some kind of "revenge or vendetta" in response. He was not to be disappointed; it would be more or less open warfare between the two old allies from that point forward—by 2018 someone had hung a dartboard with de Blasio's face on it in the Governor's Mansion's pool house.[39]

Having lost in Albany, the de Blasio administration took a number of pro-tenant steps locally. In 2015, with de Blasio's support, the

Rent Guidelines Board issued a rent freeze on one-year leases for the first time in its history; it followed up with another freeze the following year. The city also joined forces with state agencies to create a tenant harassment task force so that city data could be more easily put to use by state enforcement agencies. De Blasio and the City Council also sharply increased spending on tenant legal services and enacted a "right to counsel" law, the nation's first, to ensure that tenants in low-income ZIP codes had access to representation during eviction proceedings. By 2019, one in three tenants facing eviction had a lawyer with them, up from one in one hundred in 2013.[40]

Real as these achievements were, progressive policymakers in New York City faced nearly impossible challenges. High costs and obstacles to new construction both within the five boroughs and in the surrounding metropolitan area; the damaging dynamics of gentrification, a product of the long history of racialized city building; inadequate funding from Albany and Washington for rental support and subsidized affordable housing—all constrained New York's ability to produce the number of units necessary to bring down rents in all but the luxury end of the market. At the same time, the city controlled neither its rent laws nor its system of taxation, which under other circumstances might have provided more money for construction and rehabilitation; and the city's largest stock of deeply affordable housing, the NYCHA public housing projects, were falling into severe disrepair due to years of neglect. It all added up to what the journalist Michael Greenberg likened to a humanitarian emergency, a man-made displacement of people from their homes more commonly associated with civil strife than with everyday life in one of the world's richest cities.[41]

BY THE TIME DE BLASIO WAS UP for reelection in 2017, he had managed to alienate wide swaths of the city. Many on the left considered him ineffective at best, a sellout at worst, incapable of achieving, and perhaps unwilling to achieve, the progressive visions of 2013. Much of the city's press corps and commentariat thought him bumbling and self-important. Yet de Blasio had delivered real gains for his core supporters, and the city was doing well by most of the standard indicators—the local economy was strong, and crime was down despite the sharp reduction in street stops. He won the largest reelection victory since Ed Koch in 1985, albeit again with dismally low voter participation.[42]

Already, though, the progressive resurgence that had elevated de Blasio to national notice had passed him by. Bernie Sanders's 2016 bid for the Democratic presidential nomination galvanized a younger generation of progressives and posed a more searching critique of contemporary capitalism and the political processes bound up with it than liberals had offered for decades. The influence of the Sanders movement rippled through the party, especially after Hillary Clinton's defeat in the 2016 presidential election. "Something fascinating is underway," one columnist wrote in 2018: "After decades of incrementalism, Democrats are now proposing a litany of exciting big ideas."[43]

The elections of 2018 marked a watershed for New York's newest left. Rumblings of a grassroots revolt against the IDC Democrats had started soon after Donald Trump's presidential inauguration, when political mobilization in the city was at a fever pitch; by the time Cuomo and his allies brokered an agreement to bring them back into the regular party fold in April 2018, it was too late for the IDC members to fend off primary challenges. Inspired by the Sanders campaign as well as by resistance to Trump, the challengers were also motivated by the deep inequities of the contemporary city. Former city councilman Robert Jackson, a longtime advocate of more equitable state funding for the city's public schools, took on a well-funded charter school proponent, Marisol Alcantara, in a district on the Upper West Side. Jessica Ramos, who had seen Albany thwart de Blasio's agenda firsthand as a press aide to the mayor, challenged the incumbent José Peralta in Queens. Zellnor Myrie, raised by Costa Rican immigrants in a rent-stabilized apartment in Prospect–Lefferts Garden, left a high-paying job at Davis, Polk to take on Jesse Hamilton in central Brooklyn specifically because the rent laws were up for renewal. "My mom's story," he explained, "would not have been possible without rent regulation." Alexandria Ocasio-Cortez's stunning June primary victory over longtime Queens congressman Joseph Crowley not only vaulted the young Bronx native to overnight political superstardom but also provided the state-level progressive challengers with proof of concept. More established left-leaning Democrats—de Blasio, Congressmen Hakeem Jeffries and Jerry Nadler—and key labor unions lent their support, and in the September primaries the anti-IDC forces ousted six out of eight caucus members statewide.[44]

As the rising generation of progressives pulled the Democratic Party to the left, the presidency of Donald Trump pushed New York state toward the Democratic Party. In November 2018, the Democrats flipped eight seats in the State Senate, securing firm control in Albany for the first time in the state's modern political history (with the exception of one brief, tumultuous period in 2009–10). Cuomo, sensing the new mood and hoping to leverage it to his advantage, kicked off 2019 with a major address at the townhouse Franklin and Eleanor Roosevelt had once shared on East 63rd Street. "What would FDR do today?" he asked, unfurling an agenda that included ending vacancy deregulation and making the largest investment in housing in state history. "FDR will look down and smile on all of us," he promised. A rush of progressive legislation followed: more money for public schools, public housing, and the New York City subway system; bail reform; congestion pricing; codified reproductive rights; protections for undocumented immigrants; marijuana decriminalization; stronger gun laws; early voting provisions; ambitious greenhouse gas reduction goals; and more.[45]

But the heart of the new progressive agenda was housing. Democrats vowed not only to get rid of high-rent and vacancy deregulation but also to do away with the vacancy bonus, lock in preferential rents, eliminate pass-alongs for major capital improvements, and ban tenant blacklists assembled from the housing court database—and to make all these changes permanent, thus ending the end-of-session brinksmanship that had given Senate Republicans the leverage to chip away at regulations. Working hand in hand with the new generation of politicians, tenant organizers young and old launched a carefully designed program of protests and rallies in the city and in Albany.

Still, the real estate industry had one card to left to play. Developers and landlords had showered campaign donations on Andrew Cuomo over the years, and as it became clear that the Democratic bills had a real chance of passing, some of the biggest names in the business—Durst, LeFrak, Rudin—got the governor on the phone. Cuomo, to their horror, told them there was nothing he could do for them and suggested they call their legislators instead. "There is no negotiation," he told reporters; "I will sign the best bill they can pass." "I'm in shock," one REBNY board member told reporters. "I think many of us in the industry are in shock." In the months after Cuomo signed the Housing Stability and Tenant Protection Act of 2019, a *Wall Street Journal* study found, new eviction cases dropped by 46 percent.[46]

FIFTY YEARS HAD NOW PASSED since the first signs of the economic turbulence that pushed New York to the brink in the 1970s and facilitated the political interventions that laid the groundwork for the city's reconstruction on frankly inegalitarian terms. As de Blasio, following in John Lindsay's footsteps, launched a quixotic bid for the presidency, New York was, by common measures, doing as well as at any time during that period. Crime remained at historic lows. The local economy was exceptionally strong and much more diverse than it had been during the Wall Street boom years of the 1980s and late '90s. More than five decades after the Immigration Act of 1965, newcomers who had arrived from around the world had helped stabilize its neighborhoods and lend it a new vitality.

But such sunny indicators told only part of the story. The most important—in many ways the fundamental fact of the contemporary city—was mass poverty. Schools, housing, and policing—all were profoundly shaped by the structural fact of racialized concentrated poverty, and by the fact that American cities were left to address the consequences of poverty largely on their own, with a national government that vacillated between gridlock and active opposition to their cosmopolitan aspirations.

As a consequence, inequality remained entrenched throughout city life. The NYPD had cut back on stop-and-frisk, yet young New Yorkers of color remained far more likely than others to experience harassment, surveillance, and punishment at the hands of the police. Working-class New Yorkers enjoyed better housing conditions than at any point since before the 1970s and, thanks to the renascent tenant movement, greater security against eviction and harassment. But more than half of rental households were officially burdened, spending more than 30 percent of their income on rent, and about one in four were severely rent-burdened, spending more than half. This left the people whose labor made the city run the choice of spending what before the 1970s would have been a staggering share of their income on housing, or moving ever farther away from the metropolitan core. Historic rates of homelessness persisted, with nearly one in ten children in the city's public schools lacking permanent housing. The city had taken meaningful steps to provide more low-income New Yorkers the chance at a good, well-resourced education. But segregation had survived, and the proliferation of new schools had created new divisions in place of old ones.[47]

And because of persistent poverty and inequality, the undisputed successes of the post-fiscal-crisis era rested on fragile foundations. The city was far safer than it had been in the 1970s and '80s. Yet if New York and other cities had demonstrated that it was possible to cut back sharply on violence without addressing the "root causes" of crime, it had not planted and nurtured the roots of nonviolence: Absent an economy and social structure that worked for everyone, the sociologist Patrick Sharkey wrote in 2018, the period of historically low crime rates amounted to an "uneasy peace." Public efforts and private investment had brought the housing stock to its best state in years. But the toxic combination of slack construction, stagnant tenant incomes, and insufficient government support meant that millions of New Yorkers remained a few strokes of bad luck away from losing their homes; and while the 2019 law reduced harassment and profiteering, it raised new questions about how the housing stock could be maintained. And if the city's new and improved schools helped boost graduation rates (and, less certainly, test scores), persistent segregation and inequality left the city's schools ill-prepared should New York suffer another major crisis.[48]

In the half-century ending in 1970, New Yorkers had built a city for the working-class. That city fell apart when the economic underpinnings of the old working class disappeared and the fault lines wrought by racialized investment and political marginalization slipped and spread into full-blown crisis. In the half-century that followed, New Yorkers built a city that could function amid deep, intergenerational, concentrated, compounded deprivation. It did not work the same for everyone, and the systems that made it work for some imposed costs and violence on others. The result was not only an unjust status quo, but also a basic instability in the city's foundations should sudden storms once again arise.

STILL, AS THE 2010S DREW TO A CLOSE, many New Yorkers on the left looked forward with hope. The progressive infatuation with de Blasio that marked the beginning of his term had long since faded; in fact, the unrealized promises of his mayoralty drove many younger New Yorkers to question the kind of city-level pragmatic progressivism he represented. In the wake of the 2018 elections, the marriage of city and state power and the resurgence of the left embodied by Ocasio-Cortez and her state-level counterparts posed the most profound challenge yet to the governing arrangements that had emerged in the aftermath of the fiscal crisis.

One warm day in October 2019, America's eyes were indeed fixed on New York. Bernie Sanders, the walking embodiment of the city's social democratic tradition and the godfather of its progressive revival, had recently suffered a heart attack. He chose to return to the presidential campaign trail with a speech in Queensbridge Park, a legacy of Franklin Roosevelt and Fiorello La Guardia's New Deal, perched at the western edge of what had become one of the most diverse places on earth, the Borough of Queens. Introducing him was the paragon of the new generation of progressives, the Bronx native and U.S. congresswoman Alexandria Ocasio-Cortez. In the crowd, conducting his first canvassing event in an upstart campaign to represent the area in the state assembly, was a young idealist who had found his voice in politics through Sanders's example: Zohran Mamdani.[49]

Ocasio-Cortez spoke of growing up in the aftermath of arson and abandonment in the Bronx neighborhood of Parkchester. "Let's listen to our history," she urged, describing how her family spent everything it had to move to a better school district in suburban Westchester County. "That's when I got my first taste of a country who allows their kids' destiny to be determined by the ZIP code that they're born in." Sanders concluded his own speech with a creed for a new politics of solidarity: "I wantcha all to take a look around and find someone you don't know," he said in his mid-century

Brooklynese, tapping the air with his right index finger for emphasis. "Maybe somebody who doesn't look kinda like you; maybe somebody [who] might be of a different religion than you; maybe they come from a different country. My question now to you is, are you willing to fight for that person who you don't even know as much as you're willing to fight for yourself?"[50]

"The future once happened *here*," Mario Cuomo had remarked to the New York state legislature in 1985, gesturing back to the days when New York had served as a laboratory of reform, hoping to inspire a new era of egalitarian politics that never quite arrived. For one bright fall day, at least, it seemed like it might once more.[51]

Postscript

"We *are* interdependent," Bill Clinton told the frozen crowd at Bill de Blasio's first inauguration. "Look around. We can't get away from each other. We have to define the terms of our dependence."[1]

How to define the terms of mutual dependence? The question has been at the heart of New York City's public life ever since the contours of the modern city emerged across the nineteenth century. Drawn from the hinterlands of the growing nation, from the impoverished agricultural regions of Germany, Ireland, and southern Italy, from the shtetls of the Pale of Settlement and the villages of Galicia, from Cuba and Poland and Spain, millions of people had crowded together on the island of Manhattan. The contagions of fire and disease; the crowded, filthy streets and choking air; the dark workshops—the inescapable, tangible symptoms of interdependence had all but forced New Yorkers to consider how to live together. Monumental waterworks, the building of great parks and transit lines, expansion into the soon-to-be-consolidated boroughs, the rise of public health agencies and workplace regulations and labor unions, consumer movements and a New Deal that promised to provide the things that made for a decent life to those who could not afford to buy them—all these represented responses to what contemporaries had dubbed "the social question." So too did the hulking arsenals the city's elites erected as a hedge against the "dangerous classes" in the late nineteenth century and the efforts to close off the flow of immigrants through Ellis Island in the early twentieth.

The social question was never an easy one to answer. In the decades after 1914, millions of new New Yorkers arrived from the southeastern United States and from Puerto Rico and found themselves constrained in segregated neighborhoods in a way earlier arrivals were not. With the creation and recreation of the segregated metropolis, even the old answers to the social question no longer seemed to work in quite the same way. How to live together when the terms that had been established were terms of inequality? New Yorkers' most recent contests over how to answer that question have been the subject of this book.

THE PLAGUE THAT SWEPT across New York in March and April 2020 was a mass trauma unlike any in a century—more sudden in its onset than the AIDS epidemic, greater in scale than the September 11 attacks and the peak gun violence of the 1980s and '90s. For a moment, the collective trauma of the Covid-19 pandemic seemed to prove Clinton's point. Labor became not only visible but venerated, as countless New Yorkers cracked their windows to cheer and bang cans and drums in gratitude to the nurses, doctors, and paramedics on the front lines. The virus, Governor Andrew Cuomo repeatedly declared, was "the great equalizer": For all the tales of two cities, when it came down to it, New Yorkers could not escape their mutual destiny.[2]

But then, of course, they could. Many people left town, bound for suburbs, beach houses, and country homes. The New Yorkers who remained broke down quickly along class lines: Those who could work from home and those who could not; those whose schools pivoted effectively to remote learning and those whose could not; those who lived in neighborhoods prone to the inevitable spasms of violence that accompanied the quarantine orders and the accompanying breakdown of civic infrastructure and those who did not; those vulnerable to being thrown out of their homes after a missed paycheck or two and those who were not. It will likely take decades to tally the pandemic's full consequences. But it is beyond doubt that both the experience of the pandemic and its enduring effects trace the lines of privilege and deprivation that have defined the contemporary city.[3]

The city's political response to the pandemic echoed eerily its response to the crisis of the 1970s. In the 1970s, key parts of city life had ceased to function well because of New York's deep inequalities; in 2020–21, the virus spread rapidly amid overcrowding and in the context of an economy and welfare system that made it difficult for working people to prioritize their health. In the 1970s, the costs of the crisis had fallen primarily on poor and working-class New Yorkers in disinvested neighborhoods who suffered crumbling housing, underperforming schools, and disorderly, sometimes unsafe streets. During the pandemic, the city's preexisting conditions meant that the burdens of housing insecurity, remote learning, and the uptick in violence that accompanied the breakdown of life-as-usual fell predominantly on poorer New Yorkers. And yet, much as the fiscal crisis had pushed aside the labor and community empowerment politics of the 1960s, the egalitarian politics of the 2010s was for the moment swept away; in the pandemic's wake, the imperative of law and order, the need to secure the city's future by encouraging capital investment and appealing to middle-class and well-to-do residents, took priority.

During the crises of the early 1930s and the mid-1970s, New Yorkers had asked: Will the city survive? The pandemic, the journalist Alyssa Katz noted, raised a different question: What is New York for? It was a question without a single answer. Even in the immediate aftermath of the shelter-in-place orders, New York existed, as ever, to make money: While others asked whether the city would ever recover, Facebook and Google were busy hoovering up office space close to the most desirable residential neighborhoods in Manhattan. At the same time, New York was a place for people to live. For a moment, the city seemed freed to find a nearly forgotten version of itself. "Something has torn and, through the rupture, other elements slip," the writer Jeremiah Moss noted. "On a bone-deep level, beyond the restaurants, shops, and crowds, New York feels more like itself than it has in twenty years." Meanwhile the ambulance sirens howled and the refrigerator trucks lined up and thousands of New Yorkers found their final resting place in mass graves in the city's potter's field on Hart Island.[4]

IN A THIN MANILA FOLDER, stuffed into an archive box at Columbia University, sits the manuscript of the speech David Dinkins had hoped to deliver on election night in 1993. "We are joined by the knowledge that this is a global city of good people—people who have lived, and *will* live, side by side, in peace and in progress," the text reads. "I ask you to take my hand—to take your neighbor's hand—to prepare our city for the century to come."[5]

A bit bland, perhaps—and to his political opponents, more than a bit naïve. Idealistic visions have never survived for long in New York unaccompanied by the hardheaded necessity of making the city work. And yet New York's recent history suggests that the reverse is also true: The city cannot be made to work for long if it works for some at the expense of others.

"Our city of ruins," the urbanist Marshall Berman noted, summing up the sweep of the city's history from the blackout to Bloomberg, "turned out to be a place where people coming from a hundred different places started to talk together and work together in ways people have never quite done before." And yet this radically new experiment, a truly global democratic city, ran up against some of the most deeply rooted forces in American life. New York's problems persist, and will continue to persist, in part because it cannot escape its own history.[6]

All great problems are insoluble, another New Yorker once wrote; the good comes from the continuing struggle. A city of 8 million people, drawn from all parts of the world, living in peace, enjoying the benefits of democracy, and building together a city of tomorrow, a city where no one is left out—such a vision has come to seem naïve and foolish, even dangerous, in much of the United States, and even to some within the city itself. New York's own recent history has shown just how difficult such a vision is to sustain, much less to realize. And yet in New York, there exists the opportunity to struggle for it. Perhaps that is what New York is for.[7]

ACKNOWLEDGMENTS

We all needed more than the usual amount of help during the period in which this book was written. I received more than my share. Thank you to everyone who supported me and my scholarship during the years I was working on this project—particularly Bernard and Irene Schwartz for their generosity in establishing the Bernard and Irene Schwartz Postdoctoral Fellowship at the New-York Historical Society and Eugene Lang College, The New School; to Valerie Paley at N-YHS and my former colleagues in Historical Studies at The New School; to everyone at Albright College, especially John Pankratz; and to my colleagues in the Leadership Studies program and the Political Science department at Williams College. This project could never have come to fruition without you.

Historians are utterly indebted to librarians and archivists during the best of times. The fact that much of the research for this book was undertaken during and in the aftermath of the Covid-19 pandemic means I owe much more. Thank you to the archivists and librarians at the Briscoe Center for American History, the Centro Center for Puerto Rican Studies, Columbia University's Rare Books and Manuscripts Library, the LaGuardia-Wagner Archives at LaGuardia Community College, the Library of Congress, the New York City Municipal Archives, the New York Public Library, the

Rockefeller Archive Center, the Schomburg Center for Research in Black Culture, the Tamiment Library at New York University, the University at Albany, the Williams College Library, and the Woodson Research Center at Rice University who helped me get access to the materials that underpin this study, especially Ryan Reft and Douglas DiCarlo for helping me access materials that were not yet catalogued and Mike Koncewicz for helping me access Tamiment material during the pandemic—a real scholarly lifeline. I am also grateful for research support provided by the Rockefeller Archive Center and Williams College and, not least, for the labors of my student research assistants at Williams, Ben Connor, Sasha Landau, Ella Marx, Eli Miller, Benjamin Platt, and Grady Yuthok Short. Thank you also to Janet Biehl for her attentive copyediting of the manuscript.

I wrote most of the first full draft of this manuscript as an Andrew W. Mellon Foundation Fellow at the New York Public Library's Dorothy and Lewis B. Cullman Center for Scholars and Writers. It was perhaps not the best time to be a Cullman Center fellow, but I can't imagine there was a better place to be a scholar-writer in the 2020–21 academic year. I have no idea what would have happened to this project but for the efforts that Salvatore Scribona, Paul Delaverdac, and Lauren Goldenberg at the Cullman Center and everyone else at the New York Public Library made to keep our work on track. Thank you to my fellow fellows—Burk Bilger, Barbara Demick, Hernán Díaz, Steven Hahn, Peter Kuper, Jennifer Mittelstadt, Nina Munk, Togara Muzanenhamo, Gregory Pardlo, Hanna Pylväinen, Sophia Roosth, Namwali Serpell, Christopher Shinn, Caroline Weber—for your support and suggestions.

Thank you to everyone who has offered support or advice of one kind or another on aspects of this project over the years: Brian Balogh, Kathleen Belew, Salonee Bhaman, Brooke Blower, Casey Bohlen, Leslie Brown, Brent Cebul, N. D. B. Connolly, Sam Crane, Justin Crowe, Sara Dubow, Ansley Erickson, Michael Javen Fortner, Ester Fuchs, Lily Geismer, Ruth Wilson Gilmore, Owen Gutfreund,

Elizabeth Hinton, Ben Holtzman, Meg Jacobs, Nick Juravich, Lisa Keller, Shannon King, Jeffrey Kroessler, Julilly Kohler-Hausmann, Matthew Lassiter, Lauren Lefty, James McAllister, Nicole Mellow, Ruth Messinger, John Mollenkopf, Steve Nafziger, Suleiman Osman, Julia Ott, Natalia Mehlman Petrzela, Sarah Phillips, Peter Pihos, Brian Purnell, Mark Reinhardt, Tim Shenk, Steve Sheppard, Aaron Shkuda, Rob Snyder, Thomas Sugrue, Matthew Tokeshi, Alex Vitale, Tim Weaver, and Carmen Whalen. (To the people I'm sure I'm missing—I'm so sorry!) Thank you also to audiences at the Harvard Kennedy School's Policy and History workshop, the Policy History Conference, the Urban History Association's biennial meeting, the 2015 Violence and the City Conference at CUNY, the NYU History of Education Writing Group, the Columbia City Seminar, LaDale Winling's urban history writing workshop, and the American Political History Conference for your generous feedback on aspects of this book. I am also grateful to Brent Cebul, Lily Geismer, David Greenberg, Kathryn Kish Sklar, Karen Tani, and Moshik Temkin, all of whom I had the pleasure of collaborating with on other projects as I was writing this book. I've learned so much from you. More broadly, I am grateful to all the members of three remarkable research communities who shaped this book and changed the way I think about American political history: scholars of housing policy, education, and the carceral state.

While I was plugging away at this book, some remarkable young scholars were at work reshaping our understanding of late twentieth-century New York, and with it late twentieth-century U.S. history more broadly. I've had the privilege of working with many of them, and it has made this process a lot more fun, if also somewhat more intimidating. I am especially grateful to Amanda Boston, Mike Glass, Dylan Gottlieb, and Pedro Regalado for their comments on part or all of the manuscript. All errors, of course, are mine.

Elizabeth Blackmar and Kim Phillips-Fein both supported this project basically from its inception. I could never have formulated it, much less carried it to completion, without their guidance and wisdom—and their meticulous edits, profound questions, and timely encouragement, to say nothing of their own essential scholarship on twentieth-century New York. When I was midway through, Kim introduced me to Johanna Fernández, another great scholar who helped me see this history more clearly. I'm so deeply grateful to all of you, and so fortunate to have had the chance to work with such brilliant, generous scholars and such wonderful people.

This book's editor, Steve Forman, also supported me at every step of the process, steered me out of countless blind allies, and with his passion for New York and knowledge of its history, helped me both to see the largest questions at stake in this narrative and to make sure I got the finer points right (or at least as right as I was able). Whatever this book contributes would not have been possible without him.

Thank you to the friends I shared the city with all those years ago, and to the friends in Williamstown who have lived with this project. To Charlie, James, Brian, Kelsey, and Jessie—you guys remain the best siblings I could imagine. Keith and Dona, thank you again for all your support over the years.

Alexis, you are the person to whom this book owes the most; thank you for all you did for this project, and for so much more. Mom and Dad, thank you again, for everything. Emerson and Johanna, watching you grow has been one of the joys of my life. One day the city will be yours to find, to lose, and to love.

NOTES

Abbreviations

BC	Briscoe Center for American History, University of Texas at Austin
CCOHC	Columbia Center for Oral History Collection
CCPRS	Centro Center for Puerto Rican Studies, Hunter College, CUNY
LL	Lilly Library, Indiana University
LSL	Lloyd Sealy Library Digital Collections, John Jay College of Criminal Justice
LOC	Library of Congress
LWA	LaGuardia and Wagner Archives, LaGuardia Community College, Queens
NYCMA	New York City Municipal Archives
NYPL	Manuscripts and Archives Division, New York Public Library
NYSA	New York State Archives
RAC	Rockefeller Archive Center
RBML	Rare Books and Manuscripts Library, Columbia University
SCRBC	Schomburg Center for Research in Black Culture
TL	Tamiment Library, New York University
UA	M. E. Grenander Department of Special Collections and Archives, University of Albany
WRC	Woodson Research Center, Rice University
ADB	Records of Mayor Abraham Beame
AC	Deputy Mayor Anthony Carbonetti Subject Files
AJF	Arthur J. Finkelstein Papers
ASPIRA	ASPIRA Papers
BA	Bella Abzug Papers
BE	Babette Edwards Papers
BOE	Records of the New York City Board of Education
CCNYC	Council of the City of New York Collection

CLA	City Legislative Affairs (Records of Mayor Rudolph Giuliani)
DC	Diana Caballero Papers
DD	David Dinkins Papers
DK	Deputy Mayor David Klasfeld Files
DM	Deborah Meier Manuscripts
DND	Records of Mayor David N. Dinkins
DPM	Daniel P. Moynihan Papers
EIK	Records of Mayor Edward I. Koch
ES	Erik Sorensen Files
FR	Deputy Mayor Fran Reiter Files
GOHP	NYPD Guardians Oral History Project
HC	Governor Hugh Carey Central Subject and Correspondence Files
JN	Jack Newfield Papers
JNY	Justice in New York: An Oral History
JVL	Records of Mayor John V. Lindsay
KBC	Kenneth Bancroft Clark Papers
KOHP	Edward I. Koch Administration Oral History Project
LPB	Lee P. Brown Professional Papers
MCH	Metropolitan Council on Housing Records
MMC	Governor Mario M. Cuomo Central Subject and Correspondence Files
MO	Senator Manfred Ohrenstein Subject and Bill Files
MW	Governor Malcolm Wilson Central Subject and Correspondence Files
NARG	Nelson A. Rockefeller Gubernatorial Records
NARVP	Nelson A. Rockefeller Vice Presidential Records
NQ	Chancellor Nathan Quiñones Files
NS	First Deputy Mayor Norman Steisel Files (DND Series 2.1)
NYSTNC	New York State Tenants and Neighbors Coalition Records
OC	Office of Correspondence (Records of Mayor Rudolph Giuliani)
PP	Deputy Mayor Peter Powers Project/Issues Files
PW	Preston Wilcox Papers
REBNY	Real Estate Board of New York Collection
RFWJr	Robert F. Wagner, Jr. Papers, Robert F. Wagner Collection
RG	Robert García Congressional Papers
RL	Deputy Mayor Randy Levine Project/Subject Files
RM	Deputy Mayor Randy Mastro Project Files
RP	Richie Pérez Papers
RPM	New York State Education Department Commissioner Richard P. Mills Subject Files
RS	Deputy Mayor Richard Schwartz Subject Files
RW	Deputy Mayor Rudy Washington Project/Issues Files
RWC	Chancellor Rudolph W. Crew Files
RWG	Records of Mayor Rudolph Giuliani
SC	NYPIRG Straphangers Campaign Records
TC	Deputy Mayor Tony Coles Subject Files
UBP	Papers of the United Bronx Parents
UFT	United Federation of Teachers Records
WHW	William H. Whyte Papers

WL	Deputy Mayor William Lynch Files (DND Series 2.5)
WTL	David Rockefeller Papers, Associates, Warren T. Lindquist Papers
CA	*City Almanac*
C&S	*City & State*
CJ	*City Journal*
CL	*City Limits*
ED-LP	*El Diario–La Prensa*
ESR	*Empire State Report*
GG	*Gotham Gazette*
JAH	*Journal of American History*
JUH	*Journal of Urban History*
MAH	*Modern American History*
NY	*New York*
NYer	*New Yorker*
NYAN	*New York Amsterdam News*
NYDN	*New York Daily News*
NYO	*New York Observer*
NYP	*New York Post*
NYT	*New York Times*
REN	*Real Estate News*
SIA	*Staten Island Advance*
TU	*Times Union (Albany)*
VV	*Village Voice*
WSJ	*Wall Street Journal*

Note: In instances where archival folders were not clearly numbered, I have provided the name as written on the folder. Readers should also be aware that archival citations may vary depending on when and how the collection was consulted. In the twenty-first century, newspapers began publishing articles online before they appeared in print; as a consequence, some of the newspaper articles cited toward the end of the book may appear on different days depending on whether one accesses them using a database (such as ProQuest Historical Newspapers) or through the publications' websites.

Preface

1. Carroll, "For That Big Carey Family . . . ," *NYT*, December 29, 1974; Greenhouse, "Bus Moves Careys . . . ," *NYT*, January 1, 1975; Spagnoli, "Carey Is Gov . . . ," *NYDN*, January 1, 1975; Fallon, "It's a Family Road Show," *NYDN*, January 1, 1975; Susan Carey Dempsey to author, January 16, 2025.

   Greenhouse refers to "biographies of Robert Moses and Gov. Herbert H. Lehman." Fallon specifies that one of the books was Allan Nevins's 1963 *Herbert H. Lehman and His Era*. None of the coverage mentions the title of the Moses biography; the author surmises that it was Caro's, which had been published three months before, rather than Cleveland Rodgers's *Robert Moses, Builder for Democracy*, which was then two decades old.
2. Daniel C. Kramer, *The Days of Wine and Roses Are Over: Governor Hugh Carey*

and New York State (Lanham, MD, 1997), 1–34; Seymour P. Lachman and Robert Polner, *The Man Who Saved New York: Hugh Carey and the Great Fiscal Crisis of 1975* (Albany, NY, 2010), 7–74; Richard Ravitch, *So Much to Do: A Life Full of Business, Politics, and Confronting Fiscal Crises* (New York, 2014), quoted at 55–56.

3. Kramer, *Days of Wine and Roses*, 34.
4. Hugh L. Carey, "Annual Message," *Public Papers of Hugh L. Carey, Fifty-first Governor of the State of New York* (Albany, NY, 1982), 1:19. The New York State Archives provides video: https://www.youtube.com/watch?v=ZTWq9vyjVIY.
5. Andrew Hacker, *The New Yorkers: A Profile of an American Metropolis* (New York, 1975), 5, 153–54. See among others Joshua B. Freeman, *Working-Class New York: Life and Labor Since World War II* (New York, 2000), chap. 15; Jonathan Mahler, *Ladies and Gentlemen, the Bronx Is Burning: 1977, Baseball, Politics, and the Battle for the Soul of a City* (New York, 2005); Kim Phillips-Fein, *Fear City: New York's Fiscal Crisis and the Rise of Austerity Politics* (New York, 2017); Brian Tochterman, *The Dying City: Postwar New York and the Ideology of Fear* (Chapel Hill, NC, 2017), chaps. 7–8; Bench Ansfield, "The Broken Windows of the Bronx: Putting the Theory in Its Place," *American Quarterly* 72, no. 1 (March 2020): 103–27. On the city's image in the 1970s, see esp. Miriam Greenberg, *Branding New York: How a City in Crisis Was Sold to the World* (New York, 2008); on the role of film in its production and dissemination, see James Sanders, *Celluloid Skyline: New York and the Movies* (New York, 2001), chap. 13, and Nathan Holmes, *Welcome to Fear City: Crime Film, Crisis, and the Urban Imagination* (Albany, NY, 2018).

   For homicide numbers, see Monkkonen, "Homicides in New York City, 1797–1999 [and Various Historical Comparison Sites]," National Archive of Criminal Justice Data, March 30, 2006, https://doi.org/10.3886/ICPSR03226.v1. For reduction of the teaching force, see Heather Lewis, *New York City Public Schools from Brownsville to Bloomberg: Community Control and Its Legacy* (New York, 2013), 74. For the loss of housing units, see Temporary Commission on City Finances, *The Effects of Rent Control and Rent Stabilization in New York City: Fifteenth Interim Report to the Mayor* (New York, 1977), 15–17. The loss of housing units in Brooklyn, the Bronx, and parts of Manhattan was offset by new construction elsewhere in the city: According to the U.S. Census, the city added 22,026 total units between 1970 and 1980, despite losing some 823,223 residents. The Bronx lost 57,671 and Brooklyn lost 21,255; Manhattan gained 30,331, Queens gained 12,561, and Staten Island gained 20,726. See "Total Housing Units, New York City and Boroughs, 1940 to 2010," https://www.nyc.gov/assets/planning/download/pdf/data-maps/nyc-population/historical-population/nyc_total_hu_1940-2010.pdf. Such numbers, of course, obscure considerable temporal and spatial variation.
6. "Mayor Bloomberg Delivers 2013 State of the City Address," NYC.gov, February 14, 2013.
7. The data in this paragraph are from the invaluable Opportunity Atlas project at OpportunityAtlas.org. The Carnegie Hill census tract is 36061014802; the East Harlem tract is 36061024200.

   For critical treatments of the concept of "racial disparities," see Adolph Reed, Jr., and Merlin Chowkwanyun, "Race, Class, Crisis: The Discourse of Racial Disparity and Its Analytical Discontents," *Socialist Register* (2012): 149–75; and focused particularly on health, Merlin Chowkwanyun, "What Is a 'Racial Health Disparity'? Five Analytic Traditions," *Journal of Health Politics, Policy, and Law* 47, no. 2 (April 2022): 131–58. This book does not seek to uncover the causes of racial disparities per se; rather it seeks to show how "race" has been a central—and always shifting—element in a set of historical processes by which distributive outcomes and the terms of citizenship have been shaped and reshaped in New York.

8. Michael Goodwin, ed., *New York Comes Back: The Mayoralty of Edward I. Koch* (New York, 2005); Fred Siegel with Harry Siegel, *The Prince of the City: Giuliani, New York and the Genius of American Life* (San Francisco, 2005); Chris McNickle, *Bloomberg: A Billionaire's Ambition* (New York, 2017); Jill Jonnes, *South Bronx Rising: The Rise, Fall, and Resurrection of an American City*, 2nd ed. (New York, 2002); Alexander Von Hoffman, *House by House, Block by Block: The Rebirth of America's Urban Neighborhoods* (New York, 2003); Marshall Berman, "Introduction," in Marshall Berman and Brian Berger, eds., *New York Calling: From Blackout to Bloomberg* (London, 2007), 9–38. See also Patrick Sharkey, *Uneasy Peace: The Great Crime Decline, the Renewal of City Life, and the Next War on Violence* (New York, 2018), on the importance of community-level antiviolence efforts to the crime drop of 1990–2020.

9. William K. Tabb, *The Long Default: New York City and the Urban Fiscal Crisis* (New York, 1982); Kim Moody, *From Welfare State to Real Estate: Regime Change in New York City, 1974 to the Present* (New York, 2007); Kevin Baker, *The Fall of a Great American City: New York and the Urban Crisis of Affluence* (Westport, CT, 2019).

10. Phillips-Fein, *Fear City*, 315, 381n17.

11. See among others Steven Fraser, *Labor Will Rule: Sidney Hillman and the Rise of American Labor* (New York, 1991); Thomas Kessner, *Fiorello H. La Guardia and the Making of Modern New York* (New York, 1989); Roy Rosenzweig and Elizabeth Blackmar, *The Park and the People: A History of Central Park* (Ithaca, NY, 1992), chap. 16; Mason B. Williams, *City of Ambition: FDR, La Guardia, and the Making of Modern New York* (New York, 2013); Gail Radford, *Modern Housing for America: Policy Struggles in the New Deal Era* (Chicago, 1996); Nicholas Dagen Bloom, *Public Housing That Worked: New York in the Twentieth Century* (Philadelphia, 2008), chaps. 2–3; Richard Plunz, *A History of Housing in New York City*, rev. ed. (New York, 2016), chap. 7; Ronald Lawson with Mark Naison, *The Tenant Movement in New York City, 1904–1984* (New Brunswick, NJ, 1986); Roberta Gold, *When Tenants Claimed the City: The Struggle for Citizenship in New York City Housing* (Urbana, IL, 2014); Freeman, *Working-Class New York*, esp. chaps. 4, 6–8; Michael Woodsworth, *Battle for Bed-Stuy: The Long War on Poverty in New York City* (Cambridge, MA, 2016). On WNYC, see Andy Lanset, "How Geopolitics Shaped WNYC's Iconic Station Identification," WNYC.org, June 13, 2014. Marshall Berman mentions it at the outset of his introduction on the city from the three decades after 1977; see Berman, "Introduction," 7.

Parts of the historical literature on gentrification place an equivalent emphasis on the relation of rebuilding to the recreation of inequality. See especially Suleiman Osman, *The Invention of Brownstone Brooklyn: Gentrification and the Search for Authenticity in Postwar New York* (New York, 2011); Brian Goldstein, *The Roots of Urban Renaissance: Gentrification and the Struggle over Harlem*, expanded ed. (Princeton, NJ, 2023); Robert W. Snyder, *Crossing Broadway:*

Washington Heights and the Promise of New York City (Ithaca, NY, 2015), chap. 6 and epilogue; Amanda T. Boston, *The "New" New York: Race, Space, and Power in Gentrifying Brooklyn* (in progress).

12. Robert A. Caro, *The Power Broker: Robert Moses and the Fall of New York* (New York, 1974); Samuel Zipp, *Manhattan Projects: The Rise and Fall of Urban Renewal in Cold War New York* (New York, 2010); Pedro A. Regalado, *Nueva York: Making the Modern City* (Princeton, NJ, in progress); Carl Suddler, *Presumed Criminal: Black Youth and the Justice System in Postwar New York* (New York, 2019); Emily Brooks, *Gotham's War Within a War: Policing and the Birth of Law-and-Order Liberalism in World War II–Era New York City* (Chapel Hill, NC, 2023); Shannon King, *The Politics of Safety: The Black Struggle for Police Accountability in La Guardia's New York* (Chapel Hill, NC, 2024).

On the expansion of ghettoization in New York, see among others Craig Steven Wilder, *A Covenant with Color: Race and Social Power in Brooklyn* (New York, 2000); Wendell Pritchett, *Brownsville, Brooklyn: Blacks, Jews, and the Changing Face of the Ghetto* (Chicago, 2002); Martha Biondi, *To Stand and Fight: The Struggle for Civil Rights in Postwar New York* (Cambridge, MA, 2003), esp. chap. 11; Walter Thabit, *How East New York Became a Ghetto* (New York, 2003); Woodsworth, *Battle for Bed-Stuy*; and Christopher Hayes, *The Harlem Uprising: Segregation and Inequality in Postwar New York City* (New York, 2021).

On postwar struggles for racial justice, see among many others (and in addition to many of the works cited above), Clarence Taylor, *Knocking at Our Own Door: Milton A. Galamison and the Struggle to Integrate New York City Schools* (New York, 1997); Clarence Taylor, ed., *Civil Rights in New York City: From World War II to the Giuliani Era* (New York, 2011); Clarence Taylor, *Fight the Power: African Americans and the Long History of Police Brutality in New York City* (New York, 2018); Miguel Melendez, *We Took the Streets: Fighting for Latino Rights with the Young Lords* (New Brunswick, NJ, 2005); Lorrin Thomas, *Puerto Rican Citizen: History and Political Identity in Twentieth-Century New York City* (Chicago, 2010); Brian Purnell, *Fighting Jim Crow in the County of Kings: The Congress of Racial Equality in Brooklyn* (Lexington, KY, 2013); Brian Purnell and Jeanne Theoharis, eds., *The Strange Career of the Jim Crow North: Segregation and Struggle Outside the South* (New York, 2019); Sonia Song-Ha Lee, *Building a Latino Civil Rights Movement: Puerto Ricans, African Americans, and the Pursuit of Racial Justice in New York City* (Chapel Hill, NC, 2014); Darrel Wanzer-Serrano, *The New York Young Lords and the Struggle for Liberation* (Philadelphia, 2015); and Johanna Fernández, *The Young Lords: A Radical History* (Chapel Hill, NC, 2019).

13. See Destin Jenkins's related observation in the context of public debt financing: Jenkins, *The Bonds of Inequality: Debt and the Making of the American City* (Chicago, 2021), 3. A large (and growing) literature examines how regimes of racial difference have facilitated capital accumulation. For an overview, see Destin Jenkins and Justin Leroy, eds., *Histories of Racial Capitalism* (New York, 2021). The tension between housing-as-home and housing-as-investment, particularly in rental housing, are centered in Matthew Desmond, *Evicted: Poverty and Profit in the American City* (New York, 2016); and Peter Marcuse and David Madden, *In Defense of Housing: The Politics of Crisis* (New York, 2016). Karl Polanyi's classic treatment of "the conflict between the market and the

elementary requirements of an organized social life" refers to twentieth-century efforts to reembed markets as man "restoring his habitation." See Karl Polanyi, *The Great Transformation: The Political and Economic Origins of Our Time* (1944; reprint Boston, 1957), 249. N. D. B. Connolly, *A World More Concrete: Real Estate and the Making of Jim Crow South Florida* (Chicago, 2014), centers rental housing in an earlier era of urban history. For an overview of school and housing politics in twentieth-century U.S. urban history, see Matthew D. Lassiter, "Schools and Housing in Metropolitan America: An Introduction," *JUH* 38, no. 2 (March 2012): 195–204; see also Ansley T. Erickson, *Making the Unequal Metropolis: School Desegregation and Its Limits* (Chicago, 2016).

The historical literature on the politics of policing in postwar American cities is vast and growing. Starting points, in addition to works cited in notes 12 and 16, include Christina B. Hanhardt, *Safe Space: Gay Neighborhood History and the Politics of Violence* (Durham, NC, 2013); Christopher Lowen Agee, *The Streets of San Francisco: Policing and the Creation of a Cosmopolitan Liberal Politics, 1950–1972* (Chicago, 2014); Donna Murch, "Crack in Los Angeles: Crisis, Militarization, and Black Response to the Late Twentieth-Century War on Drugs," *JAH* 102, no. 1 (June 2015): 162–73; Peter C. Pihos, "Policing, Race, and Politics in Chicago" (Ph.D. diss., University of Pennsylvania, 2015); Jordan T. Camp and Christina Heatherton, eds., *Policing the Planet: Why the Policing Crisis Led to Black Lives Matter* (New York, 2016); Alex Elkins, "Battle of the Corner: Urban Policing and Rioting in the United States, 1943-1971" (Ph.D. diss., Temple University, 2017); Max Felker-Kantor, *Policing Los Angeles: Race, Resistance, and the Rise of the LAPD* (Chapel Hill, NC, 2018); Simon Balto, *Occupied Territory: Policing Black Chicago from Red Summer to Black Power* (Chapel Hill, NC, 2019); Anne Gray Fischer, "'Land of the White Hunter': Legal Liberalism and the Racial Politics of Morals Enforcement in Midcentury Los Angeles," *JAH* 105, no. 4 (March 2019): 868–84; Stuart Schrader, *Badges without Borders: How Global Counterinsurgency Transformed American Policing* (Berkeley, CA, 2019); Danielle Wiggins, "'Order as Well as Decency': The Development of Order Maintenance Policing in Black Atlanta," *JUH* 46, no. 4 (July 2020): 711–27; and the essays in Christopher Lowen Agee and Themis Chronopoulos, eds., "Special Section: Urban America and the Police Since World War II," *JUH* 46, no. 5 (September 2020): 951–1116.

14. The policy changes examined here—deregulation, marketization, and more intensive policing and surveillance of public spaces—are often associated with the rising power of business and real estate and the triumph of neoconservative and neoliberal politicians and thinkers. The concept of neoliberalism, in particular, has become central to the study of late twentieth-century American politics and governance despite the fact that scholars dispute what precisely the term means and how well it functions to explain key political processes. One of the critiques of the neoliberalism framework as used here—the turn toward deregulation, the privatization and marketization of formerly public functions, the de-socialization of goods and services, municipal austerity, and other related shifts in governance characteristic of American cities in the last quarter of the twentieth century—has been that it bundles together phenomena and people that might best be considered separately and that it groups together dynamics—such as the clout of business and the push toward privatization—that at important

moments have been at odds. Another strong critique of the framework is that it tends to obscure continuities across time. Still other scholars have written "grassroots" accounts of neoliberalism, pushing at the bounds of the concept by investigating the roles community groups and progressive politicians played in the processes of neoliberalization.

I have tried in this book to address these conceptual problems by focusing on the reconstruction of the democratic state itself. Within each of the three story lines, I have focused on dynamics that are typically considered instances of neoliberalization (or in the case of policing, closely associated with neoliberal restructuring). In writing about housing, I have focused on deregulation, through the decline of rent control and rent stabilization. In discussing policing, I have focused on the re-regulation of public space through quality-of-life policing of streets, parks, and subway stations. In examining public schools, I have focused on the rise of new kinds of schools and the importation of market techniques into the public sphere through the rise of school choice. The chapters are at once chronological and thematic; they are meant to give readers a sense of how the dynamics suggested by the concept of neoliberalism changed over time. They also aim to show how the projects of governance that the city took on in the last fifty years shaped the language of politics, introducing new categories that New Yorkers used to talk about the city's problems and possibilities.

This approach, I think, contributes to our understanding of the neoliberal state in several ways. By following three story lines, this book shows more clearly how phenomena grouped together under the rubric of neoliberalism do and do not relate to each other, the distinctive roles played by different kinds of actors in each area, and the relation of neoliberalization to other dynamics of city politics—the ebb and flow of the local economy, federal policy, city-state relations, the city's changing demographics, the rise and fall of political coalitions. This approach also suggests how long-standing political dynamics and social hierarchies became enfolded in and articulated through new institutions and governing practices. Perhaps most important, by putting the state at the center of the story, I hope to move beyond the conflation of neoliberalism and anti-statism, showing how neoliberalism depended on a strong local state, and, in turn, how the imperatives of statecraft shaped neoliberalization.

On the concept of neoliberalism, David Harvey, *A Brief History of Neoliberalism* (New York, 2005), remains an essential starting point. On the concept of a "neoliberal order," see especially Gary Gerstle, "America's Neoliberal Order," in Nelson Lichtenstein, Gary Gerstle, and Alice O'Connor, eds., *Beyond the New Deal Order: U.S. Politics from the Great Depression to the Great Recession* (Philadelphia, 2019), chap. 14; and Gerstle, "The Rise and Fall(?) of America's Neoliberal Order," *Transactions of the Royal Historical Society* 28 (December 2018): 241–64. On "neoliberal cities," see Neil Brenner, *New State Spaces: Urban Governance and the Rescaling of Statehood* (New York, 2004); Jason Hackworth, *The Neoliberal City: Governance, Ideology, and Development in American Urbanism* (Ithaca, NY, 2007); Timothy P. R. Weaver, *Blazing the Neoliberal Trail: Urban Political Development in the United States and the United Kingdom* (Philadelphia, 2016); and Andrew J. Diamond and Thomas J. Sugrue, eds., *Neoliberal Cities: The Remaking of Postwar Urban America* (New York, 2020). On neoliberal urbanism and ideas about race, see Lester K. Spence, "The Neoliberal City and the Racial Idea," in Richardson Dilworth and Timothy P. R. Weaver, eds., *How Ideas Shape Urban Political Development* (Philadelphia, 2020). On neoliberal political economy and the carceral state, see among others Loïc Wacquant, *Punishing the Poor: The Neoliberal Government of Social Insecurity* (Durham, NC, 2009). Though it does not center the concept of neoliberalism, Ruth Gilmore Wilson, *Golden Gulag: Prisons, Surplus, Crisis, and Opposition in Globalizing California* (Berkeley, CA, 2007), is essential for understanding the relation between the prison state and the economic transformations associated with neoliberalization. Lily Geismer, "Agents of Change: Microenterprise, Welfare Reform, the Clintons, and Liberal Forms of Neoliberalism," *JAH* 107, no. 1 (June 2020): 107–31, calls much-needed attention to the "complexity and spectrum of neoliberalism" in the late twentieth-century United States.

Important works on New York include William K. Tabb, *The Long Default: New York City and the Urban Fiscal Crisis* (New York, 1982); William Sites, *Remaking New York: Primitive Globalization and the Politics of Urban Community* (Minneapolis, 2003); Setha Low and Neil Smith, eds., *The Politics of Public Space* (New York, 2006); Kim Moody, *From Welfare State to Real Estate: Regime Change in New York City, 1974 to the Present* (New York, 2007); Miriam Greenberg, *Branding New York: How a City in Crisis Was Sold to the World* (New York, 2008); Alex S. Vitale, *City of Disorder: How the Quality of Life Campaign Transformed New York Politics* (New York, 2008); Julian Brash, *Bloomberg's New York: Class and Governance in the Luxury City* (Athens, GA, 2011); Jonathan Soffer, *Ed Koch and the Rebuilding of New York City* (New York, 2010); Amy Starecheski, *Ours to Lose: When Squatters Became Homeowners in New York City* (Chicago, 2016); and the essays in Themis Chronopoulos and Jonathan Soffer, eds., "Special Section: After the Urban Crisis: New York and the Rise of Inequality," *JUH* 43, no. 6 (November 2017): 855–959.

For accounts of (public-)privatization in late twentieth-century New York that emphasize the role of non-elites, see Suleiman Osman, "'We're Doing It Ourselves': The Unexpected Origins of New York City's Public-Private Parks During the 1970s Fiscal Crisis," *Journal of Planning History* 16, no. 2 (May 2017): 162–74; and Benjamin Holtzman, *The Long Crisis: New York and the Path to Neoliberalism* (New York, 2021).

For an overview of the concept's use in historical writing, see Kim Phillips-Fein, "The History of Neoliberalism," in Brent Cebul, Lily Geismer, and Mason B. Williams, eds., *Shaped by the State: Toward a New Political History of the Twentieth Century* (Chicago, 2019), 347–62. Critiques of the neoliberalization framework include Daniel T. Rodgers, "The Uses and Abuses of 'Neoliberalism,'" *Dissent* (Winter 2018), and N. D. B. Connolly, "A White Story," *Dissent* (Winter 2018). Works that argue for continuity from the mid- to late twentieth century include Andrew J. Diamond, *Chicago on the Make: Power and Inequality in a Modern City* (Oakland, CA, 2017); and Brent Cebul, *Illusions of Progress: Business, Poverty, and Liberalism in the American Century* (Philadelphia, 2023).

This book does not seek to make a general intervention in the political science literature on urban politics and urban political development. It may, however, suggest the limits of the most common unitary theories of urban politics in making sense of developments across multiple policymaking areas—theories of bureaucracy are especially pertinent to the story about policing told here, whereas the rent-regulation story is more comprehensible in terms of path dependency and interest groups. In all, this analysis is most akin to a polity-centered account in the historical-institutionalist tradition of the development of New York City's neoliberal state, with particular attention to the role of the state government.

15. Starting points in the vast literature on the punitive turn in late twentieth-century U.S. history include Heather Ann Thompson, "Why Mass Incarceration Matters: Rethinking Crisis, Decline, and Transformation in Postwar American History," *JAH* 97, no. 3 (December 2010): 703–34; Elizabeth Hinton, *From the War on Poverty to the War on Crime: The Making of Mass Incarceration in America* (Cambridge, MA, 2016); and Julilly Kohler-Hausmann, *Getting Tough: Welfare and Imprisonment in 1970s America* (Princeton, NJ, 2017). On the centrality of discipline to post-1960s Black liberalism, see Danielle Wiggins, *Black Excellence: Atlanta and the Making of Modern Black Liberalism* (Philadelphia, 2025).
16. On points of consensus in late twentieth-century U.S. political history, see Matthew D. Lassiter, "Political History Beyond the Red-Blue Divide," *JAH* 98, no. 3 (December 2011): 760–64; Bruce J. Schulman, "Neo-Consensus History for the Age of Polarization," *Reviews in American History* 47, no. 3 (September 2019): 479–99; and Gerstle, *Rise and Fall of the Neoliberal Order*.
17. Don DeLillo, *White Noise* (1985; reprint New York, 1999), 65.
18. Cf. Timothy P. R. Weaver, *Inequality, Crime, and Resistance in New York City* (Philadelphia, 2025), which interprets New York City's recent political development in terms of the intercurrence of neoconservative, neoliberal, and egalitarian "political orders." The framework suggested here is indebted to Weaver's and shares significant points of overlap, though as I explain earlier in the preface, I believe that ideas were too protean and institutional dynamics too cross-cutting to sustain the concept of coherent orders. (Weaver also uses the term *tendencies*, which is closer to what is posited here.)

    My approach derives from Daniel T. Rodgers, "Living Without Labels," *Law and History Review* 24, no. 1 (Spring 2006): 173–78, which asks what problems politicians focus on, what solutions make sense to them, how they seek to position themselves, and what "languages" they deploy.

    Wilson quoted in Milo Ward, "A Democracy of Authorities: Broken Windows Policing and the Neoconservative Political Theory of Law and Order," *Perspectives on Politics* (published online by Cambridge University Press, February 13, 2025), 8.
19. Starting points in the enormous literature on race and postwar metropolitan development include Kenneth T. Jackson, *Crabgrass Frontier: The Suburbanization of the United States* (New York, 1985), chap. 11; Thomas J. Sugrue, *The Origins of the Urban Crisis: Race and Inequality in Postwar Detroit* (Princeton, NJ, 1996); Robert O. Self, *American Babylon: Race and the Struggle for Postwar Oakland* (Princeton, NJ, 2003); David M. P. Freund, *Colored Property: State Policy and White Racial Politics in Suburban America* (Chicago, 2007); Colin Gordon, *Mapping Decline: St. Louis and the Fate of the American City* (Philadelphia, 2008); Thomas J. Sugrue, *Sweet Land of Liberty: The Forgotten Struggle for Civil Rights in the North* (New York, 2008), chap. 7; Beryl Satter, *Family Properties: Race, Real Estate, and*

the Exploitation of Black Urban America (New York, 2009); N. D. B. Connolly, *A World More Concrete: Real Estate and the Remaking of Jim Crow South Florida* (Chicago, 2014); Richard Rothstein, *The Color of Law: A Forgotten History of How Our Government Segregated America* (New York, 2017); Keeanga-Yamahtta Taylor, *Race for Profit: How Banks and the Real Estate Industry Undermined Black Homeownership* (Chapel Hill, NC, 2019); Paige Glotzer, *How the Suburbs Were Segregated: Developers and the Business of Exclusionary Housing, 1890–1960* (New York, 2020); and Colin Gordon, *Patchwork Apartheid: Private Restrictions, Racial Segregation, and Urban Inequality* (New York, 2023). The effects of segregation at the intersection of race and class are discussed at greater length in Chapters 1–2.

It should be noted that the social formations that resulted from hypersegregation themselves changed considerably in the years examined in this book. See Brian Purnell, "No Place Like Home: Black Communities and Black Cultures in New York City Since the 1970s," in Johanna Fernández, Kim Phillips-Fein, and Mason B. Williams, eds., *Gotham on the Verge* (Chapel Hill, NC, forthcoming).

20. On the challenges Black New Yorkers faced building coalitions given asymmetries of power and interest, see J. Phillip Thompson, "One Step Forward, Two Steps Back: Liberalism, Race, and Local Democracy," in John Mollenkopf and Ken Emerson, eds., *Rethinking the Urban Agenda: Reinvigorating the Liberal Tradition in New York City and Urban America* (New York, 2001), 200–6, building on Kwame Ture and Charles V. Hamilton, *Black Power: The Politics of Liberation* (1967; reprint 1992), chap. 3.

21. Heather K. Gerken, "Dissenting by Deciding," *Stanford Law Review* 57, no. 6 (May 2005): 1745–805; Jessica Bulman-Pozen and Heather K. Gerken, "Uncooperative Federalism," *Yale Law Journal* 118, no. 7 (May 2009): 1256–310; Heather K. Gerken, "A New Progressive Federalism," *Democracy: A Journal of Ideas* (Spring 2012); Benjamin R. Barber, *If Mayors Ruled the World: Dysfunctional Nations, Rising Cities* (New Haven, CT, 2013); Richard C. Schragger, *City Power: Urban Governance in a Global Age* (New York, 2016); Heather K. Gerken and Joshua Revesz, "Progressive Federalism: A User's Guide," *Democracy: A Journal of Ideas* (Spring 2017).

Chapter 1: Power Failure

1. E.g., Edward N. Costikyan, "Who Runs New York?" *NY*, December 23, 1968, 25–30; Costikyan, "The Ten Most Powerful Men in New York," *NY*, January 5, 1970; 24–27. On *New York*, see Miriam Greenberg, *Branding New York: How a City in Crisis Was Sold to the World* (New York, 2008), 71–96.
2. Robert Daley, "The Struggle for Control in the City . . . ," *NY*, January 14, 1974, 34–47 (at 47); Sam Roberts, "Who Runs New York Now?" *NYT*, April 28, 1985.
3. See especially Kim Phillips-Fein, *Fear City: New York's Fiscal Crisis and the Rise of Austerity Politics* (New York, 2017), 7.
4. The 1970s also saw New York City inadvertently take public ownership of thousands of units of housing and, more intentionally, saw New York State establish a right to shelter, developments discussed in Chapter 2.
5. Joshua B. Freeman, *Working-Class New York: Life and Labor Since World War II* (New York, 2000), 274.

6. Among many others, Suleiman Osman, "The Decade of the Neighborhood," in Bruce J. Schulman and Julian E. Zelizer, eds., *Rightward Bound: Making America Conservative in the 1970s* (Cambridge, MA, 2008), chap. 6; Samuel Zipp, *Manhattan Projects: The Rise and Fall of Urban Renewal in Cold War New York* (New York, 2010). On the production of ruin imagery in 1970s New York, see Rose Diaz, "Moral Panics and Community Narratives: The Case of the Bronx" (Ph.D. diss., New School, 2008); Bench Ansfield, "The Broken Windows of the Bronx: Putting the Theory in Its Place," *American Quarterly* 72, no. 1 (March 2020): 103–27; and Peter L'Official, *Urban Legends: The South Bronx in Representation and Ruin* (Cambridge, MA, 2020).
7. Daniel Bell, "The Three Faces of New York," *Dissent* (Summer 1961): 222–32, at 226; Freeman, *Working-Class New York*, esp. chaps. 1–2.
8. Freeman, *Working-Class New York*, chaps. 9–10; Lizabeth Cohen and Brian Goldstein, "Governing at the Tipping Point: Shaping the City's Role in Economic Development," in Joseph P. Viteritti, ed., *Summer in the City: John Lindsay, New York, and the American Dream* (Baltimore, MD, 2014), chap. 7; Andy Battle, "Runaway: A History of Postwar New York in Four Factories" (Ph.D. diss., Graduate Center, City University of New York, 2019); Herbert Bienstock, "Manpower Directions in New York City in the 70's," *CA*, December 1970, 3–5; Greg David, *Modern New York: The Life and Economics of a City* (New York, 2012): 13–14; Stephen Sondheim, "Another Hundred People," in Sondheim and George Furth, *Company* (1970); Department of City Planning, City of New York, *The Newest New Yorkers: Characteristics of the City's Foreign-born Population* (New York, 2013): 16. On the effects of urban renewal on neighborhood businesses, see esp. Samuel Zipp, *Manhattan Projects: The Rise and Fall of Urban Renewal in Cold War New York* (New York, 2010). Daniel Kay Hertz maps New York's neighborhoods by median family income relative to the metropolitan median at https://danielkayhertz.com/2014/07/09/watch-new-york-citys-middle-class-and-poor-get-pushed-around/.
9. See Preface, note 19. On resistance to integration in postwar New York, see Martha Biondi, *To Stand and Fight: The Struggle for Civil Rights in Postwar New York* (Cambridge, MA, 2003), chap. 11.
10. Emile Schempers, *Law and Community Advocacy: A Case Description of the Use of the Law by United Bronx Parents* (April 1978), 321, in UBP, Box 2, Folder 14, CCPRS; Harlem River Drive, "Harlem River Drive," *Harlem River Drive* (Roulette, 1971).
11. Charles R. Morris, *The Cost of Good Intentions: New York City and the Liberal Experiment* (New York, 1980), 139; Bienstock, "Manpower Directions in New York City in the 70's"; David, *Modern New York*, 13–14; Johanna Fernández, *The Young Lords: A Radical History* (Chapel Hill, NC, 2019), 55. On the long-term consequences of youth unemployment, see Thomas J. Sugrue, *The Origins of the Urban Crisis: Race and Inequality in Postwar Detroit* (Princeton, NJ, 1996), 147.
12. William K. Tabb, *The Long Default: New York City and the Urban Fiscal Crisis* (New York, 1982), 94; Freeman, *Working-Class New York*, 274–75. For contemporary studies of redlining by the New York City Commission in Human Rights and the New York Public Interest Research Group, see MCH, Box 54, Folders 2–4, TL.
13. For an overview of rising operating costs drawing on Bureau of Labor Statistics data, see "Guest Editorial," *REN*, June/July 1974, 7. On the recession of 1969–1971

in New York, see David, *Modern New York*, 20–23. George Sternlieb, *The Urban Housing Dilemma: The Dynamics of New York City's Rent Controlled Housing* (New York, 1972), identified rent control as a cause of underinvestment in the housing stock; Women's City Club of New York, Inc., *"With Love and Affection": A Study of Building Abandonment* (New York, 1977), found that individual landlords in the South Bronx, unlike the landlord organizations that represented them, rarely cited rent control as a consideration in abandonment. Peter Marcuse, *Housing Abandonment: Does Rent Control Make a Difference?* (Washington, DC, 1981), a comparative study, found rent regulation to be neither a necessary nor a sufficient explanation of housing abandonment.

14. Center for Community Change, National Urban League, *The National Survey of Housing Abandonment* (1971), 89; Peter D. Salins, *The Ecology of Housing Destruction: Economic Effects of Public Intervention in the Housing Market* (New York, 1980), 27.

15. Citizens Budget Commission, *Abandoned Buildings—A Time for Action* (New York, 1970); Evelyn Gonzalez, *The Bronx* (New York, 2004), 124–26; Ira S. Lowry, ed., *Rental Housing in New York City*, vol. 1: *Confronting the Crisis* (New York, 1970), 9; Center for Community Change, *National Survey of Housing Abandonment*, 1, 5–15, 97; Ansfield, "Broken Windows of the Bronx," quoted at 106; Bench Ansfield, "The Crisis of Insurance and the Insuring of the Crisis: Riot Reinsurance and Redlining in the Aftermath of the 1960s Uprisings," *JAH* 107, no. 4 (March 2021): 899–921; Bench Ansfield, *Born in Flames: The Business of Arson and the Remaking of the American City* (New York, 2025); Maruca, "Looting Old Buildings . . . ," *NYT*, June 26, 1977. As Ansfield notes, arson resulted not only from disinvestment but also from overinvestment and "predatory inclusion" in the form of fire insurance. See also Stacy Horn, *The Killing Fields of East New York* (New York, 2025).

16. Citizens Budget Commission, *Abandoned Buildings—A Time for Action*, 1; Shipler, "Nathan Says Rents . . . ," *NYT*, November 8, 1969; Shipler, "Sense of Crisis Over Housing Grips Officials," *NYT*, November 16, 1969.

17. Office of the Comptroller, *Comptroller's Report for 1970–1971*, 12. State aid and the property tax accounted for 26.6 percent of municipal revenue; federal aid for 16.6 percent; "other taxes," which included the sales tax, the stock transfer and mortgage taxes, the general corporation and financial corporation taxes, and the commercial rent occupancy tax, for 16.2 percent; "other sources" (rental, interest, services, ferry fares, and water services) for 11.4 percent; and the city's local income tax for 2.6 percent. For an overview of city-state relations in this era, see Gerald Benjamin and Charles Brecher, eds., *The Two New Yorks: State-City Relations in a Changing Federal System* (New York, 1988). The classic work on municipal politics and governance in New York c. 1960, of course, is Wallace S. Sayre and Herbert Kaufman, *Governing New York City* (New York, 1960).

18. Joe Merton, "'I Don't Believe in a Fun City; I Believe in a Safe City': Fear of Crime and the Crisis of Expertise in New York City," *Journal of Policy History* 29, no. 1 (January 2017): 121, 127. On Lindsay's progressive Republicanism, see Geoffrey Kabaservice, "On Principle: A Progressive Republican," in Joseph P. Viteritti, ed., *Summer in the City: John Lindsay, New York, and the American Dream* (Baltimore, 2014), chap. 2.

19. Quoted in Joseph E. Persico, *The Imperial Rockefeller: A Biography of Nelson A. Rockefeller* (New York, 1982), 216. On Rockefeller's Republicanism, see Geoffrey Kabaservice, *Rule and Ruin: The Downfall of Moderation and the Destruction of the Republican Party, from Eisenhower to the Tea Party* (New York, 2012); Richard Norton Smith, *On His Own Terms: A Life of Nelson Rockefeller* (New York, 2014); Marsha E. Barrett, *Nelson Rockefeller's Dilemma: The Fight to Save Moderate Republicanism* (Ithaca, NY, 2024); and Kristoffer Smemo, *Making Republicans Liberal: Social Struggle and the Politics of Compromise* (Philadelphia, 2024). Nicholas Dagen Bloom, *How States Shaped Postwar America: State Government and Urban Power* (Chicago, 2019), details Rockefeller's expansion of the state government.
20. *Rent Control and Its Impact on Housing in New York City: Report of the Mayor's Rent Control Committee, December 1969*, 8–17; Ronan, "Rockefeller Urges . . . ," *NYT*, April 28, 1971. For an overview, see New York State Division of Housing and Community Renewal, Office of Rent Administration, *Rent Regulation After Fifty Years: An Overview of New York State's Rent Regulated Housing, 1993* (Albany, NY, 1994).
21. City of New York, Housing Development Administration, *The Rental Housing Situation in New York City, 1975* (January 1976), 62, 72; Norman Oder, "In Rising Market, Vital Mitchell-Lama Program at Crossroads," *CL*, March 25, 2015.
22. See Martha E. Stark and Doug Turetsky, "Homeward Bound: A Twenty-First-Century Affordable Housing Agenda for New York," in John Mollenkopf and Ken Emerson, eds., *Rethinking the Urban Agenda: Reinvigorating the Liberal Tradition in New York City and Urban America* (New York, 2001), 153.
23. For typical landlord statements, see for example "Rent Control Costing City $400 Million Annually," *REN*, April 1969, 121; "As Ye Sow, So Shall Ye Weep," *REN*, June 1970, 6–8; "What Communism Discards, New York City Keeps," *REN*, August 1970, 8. Real estate organizations began hosting tours of deteriorating neighborhoods in the late 1960s: see, e.g., Fried, "Owners Show . . . ," *NYT*, April 20, 1968.
24. Michael B. Teitz and Stephen R. Rosenthal, *Housing Code Enforcement in New York City* (New York, 1971), 48–49; Shipler, "Leading Democrats Oppose . . . ," *NYT*, May 28, 1970; Gottfried, "New Rent Law . . . ," *NYT*, March 21, 1971; Weisman, "Effort to Repeal . . . ," *NYT*, March 20, 1971. Lindsay was more solicitous of the real estate community than is sometimes remembered. See for instance Lindsay to Fred Berman, June 16, 1967, JVL, Subject Files, "Rent and Rehabilitation," NYCMA.
25. For examples of tenant concerns, see David W. Moore, "The ABC's of MBR: How to Spell Trouble in Landlord/Tenant Relations," *Columbia Journal of Law and Social Problems* 10, no. 2 (Winter 1974); Bella Abzug to John Lindsay, January 15, 1973, BA, Box 364, Folder "Rent Control: Correspondence," RBML. On the lack of an enforcement mechanism, see "Statement of Senators Manfred Ohrenstein and John E. Flynn and Assemblyman Seymour Posner at a News Conference—January 4, 1973," MO, Box 23, Folder "Housing (1972–3) [1]," NYSA. On implementation, see *Final Report of the Temporary State Commission to Make a Study of the Governmental Operation of the City of New York* (April 1973), 69–71; Rosenbaum, "City Battling Turmoil . . . ," *NYT*, November 19, 1972; Asbury, "City

Rent Program . . . ," *NYT*, November 22, 1972; Fried, "City's Bewildering Rent-Control Program," *NYT*, March 11, 1974. For another instance of the Lindsay administration's efforts to rationalize services through the use of computer technology, see Joe Flood, *The Fires: How a Computer Formula, Big Ideas, and the Best of Intentions Burned Down New York City—and Determined the Future of Cities* (New York, 2010).

26. Smith, *On His Own Terms*, 228n; "Ho Hum—Another Election Over," *REN*, November 1970, 6; [Rockefeller Statement], *REN*, June 1971, 9; Farrell, "Governor Signs Measure . . . ," *NYT*, June 3, 1971; Carmody, "Group Sees Housing Spurt . . . ," *NYT*, May 7, 1971; Weisman, "Investment Held Key . . . ," *NYT*, April 29, 1971; Ronan, "Rockefeller Urges Eased . . . ," *NYT*, April 28, 1971; "Hole in the Roof . . . ," *NYT*, April 29, 1971. See also materials in NARG, RG 15, Series 21.2 Hugh Morrow Central Files, Box 22, Folder 230, RAC. For more on REBNY's support for the proposals, see Real Estate Board of New York, "Legislative Action Request" (May 3, 1971), MCH, Box 16, Folder "City Rent Control 1971 #14," TL.

27. Weisman, "Lindsay Protests Passage . . . ," *NYT*, May 28, 1971; Richard A. Brown to Lindsay, July 12, 1971, JVL, Confidential Subject Files, "Albany," NYCMA.

28. Metropolitan Council on Housing, "Legislative Memorandum: Repeal of Vacancy Decontrol and Enactment of Mandatory State-Wide Control," February 21, 1974, MCH, Box 49, Folder "Economics of Real Estate #2," TL; "Statement by Nathan Leventhal . . . Before the Democratic Legislative Task Force on Housing, August 29, 1972," MCH, Box 19, Folder "Rent Control Letters, 1971–72," TL; *Report on Housing and Rents of the Temporary State Commission on Living Costs and the Economy of the State of New York to the Governor and the Legislature* (New York, 1974), 21–23; Citizens Budget Commission, *Strategies to Boost Housing Production in the New York City Metropolitan Area* (August 2020), 7. For the Rockefeller administration, see Hugh Morrow to John Jay Iselin, July 22, 1971, in response to "Here and Now, WNET-TV, June 29, 1971" (transcript); Hugh Morrow to Bob Douglass, January 11, 1972; Nelson Rockefeller to Andrew J. Stein, October 1, 1973, reprinted in press release (Governor—Rent), October 2, 1973; all in NARG, RG 15, Series 21.2 Hugh Morrow Central Files, Box 22, Folder 230, RAC. For the tenant organization perspective, see Metropolitan Council on Housing, "Look Out Tenants!" (flyer), November 7, 1973; Temporary State Commission on Living Costs and the Economy, "Commission Proposes Repeal of Vacancy Decontrol" (press release), February 5, 1974; both in MCH, Box 50, Folder "Rent Control–N.Y. State Comm. On Living Costs and The Economy, 1973–1974," TL.

29. Michael Kramer, "The City Politic," *NY*, March 4, 1974, 4; Donald J. Trump to Malcolm Wilson, April 8, 1974; John F. Forner, Jr., to Trump, April 29, 1974, both in MW, Microfilm Reel 26, NYSA. On the 1973 case, see Mahler and Eder, "'No Vacancies' for Blacks . . . ," *NYT*, August 27, 2016.

30. Roberta Gold, *When Tenants Claimed the City: The Struggle for Citizenship in New York City Housing* (Urbana, IL, 2014), 247–48; *Laws of New York 1974*, chap. 576; New York State Tenants Legislative Coalition, "A Legislative Response to Selected Tenant Issues," October 1974, NYSTN, Series 3, Box 1, Folder 2, UA; New York State Tenants Coalition, "Legislative Memorandum," January 14, 1975, NYSTN, Series 3, Box 1, Folder 5, UA. On the role of the Queens assemblymen,

see Manfred Ohrenstein to Alexander Wolfson, May 28, 1974, MO, Box 22, Folder "Vacancy Decontrol," NYSA. See also Greenhouse, "The Legislature Retains . . . ," *NYT*, May 17, 1974.

31. Connolly, "Owners to Skip Taxes . . . ," *NYT*, January 27, 1974; Oser, "Prewar Apartments on the West Side . . . ," *NYT*, November 1, 1974; Stetson, "Energy Rates Endangering . . . ," *NYT*, December 8, 1974; Gonzalez, *Bronx*, quote at 126. One study of northern Manhattan found that fuel costs had risen from 9 percent to 24 percent of gross income: *REN*, June–July 1974, 7. On housing deterioration in the Bronx, see Lizabeth Cohen, *Saving America's Cities: Ed Logue and the Struggle to Renew Urban America in the Suburban Age* (New York, 2019), 353–56.
32. CPC quoted in Frank S. Kristof, "A 'Housing Shortage' It Isn't," *NYT*, November 28, 1971.
33. Marshall Berman, "Introduction," in Berman and Brian Berger, eds., *New York Calling: From Blackout to Bloomberg* (London, 2007), 11–12, 35. On "juvenile delinquency," see Eric C. Schneider, *Vampires, Dragons, and Egyptian Kings: Youth Gangs in Postwar New York* (Princeton, NJ, 1999); Michael Woodsworth, *Battle for Bed-Stuy: The Long War on Poverty in New York City* (Cambridge, MA, 2016), chap. 1; Carl Suddler, *Presumed Criminal: Black Youth and the Justice System in Postwar New York* (New York, 2019); Shannon King, *The Politics of Safety: The Black Struggle for Police Accountability in La Guardia's New York* (Chapel Hill, 2024), chaps. 6–8.
34. Cannato, *Ungovernable City*, 61, 531 (Lindsay at 61); Eric C. Schneider, *Smack: Heroin and the American City* (Philadelphia, 2008), 117. On the CCRB controversy, see Ruth Cowan, "The New York City Civilian Complaint Review Board Referendum of November 1966: A Case Study of Mass Politics" (Ph.D. diss., New York University, 1970); Cannato, *Ungovernable City*, chap. 5; Clarence Taylor, *Fight the Power: African Americans and the Long History of Police Brutality in New York City* (New York, 2019), chap. 6.
35. "Testimony of Governor Nelson A. Rockefeller at Joint Hearing Before Senate and Assembly Codes Committees, . . . January 30, 1973, 11:00 a.m.," Attachment I, NARG, RG 15, Series 21.2 Hugh Morrow Central Files, Box 33, Folder 349, RAC. On heroin markets in New York, see Schneider, *Smack*, chaps. 6–7.
36. Julilly Kohler-Hausmann, *Getting Tough: Welfare and Imprisonment in 1970s America* (Princeton, NJ, 2017), 42, 44; John V. Lindsay to Nelson Rockefeller, May 6, 1971, JVL, Departmental Files, "New York Governor," NYCMA.
37. "Police to Step Up . . . ," *NYT*, September 10, 1969; Kohler-Hausmann, *Getting Tough*, 58; National Institute of Law Enforcement and Criminal Justice, "Enforcement Policies," in National Institute of Law Enforcement and Criminal Justice, Law Enforcement Assistance Administration, United States Department of Justice, *The Nation's Toughest Drug Law: Evaluating the New York Experience, Final Report of the Joint Committee on New York Drug Law Evaluation* (New York, 1977), 5–6; New York Criminal Justice Coordinating Council, Executive Committee, *Annual Report of the Criminal Justice Coordinating Council [for] 1971* (1971), 39; New York Criminal Justice Coordinating Council, Executive Committee, *Annual Report of the Criminal Justice Coordinating Council [for] 1972* (1972), 34.
38. Commission to Investigate Allegations of Police Corruption—Whitman Knapp, Chairman, *Commission Report (With Summary and Principal Recommendations,*

Issued August 3, 1972) (1972), 91–93; Robert Kane and Michael White, *Jammed Up: Bad Cops, Police Misconduct, and the New York City Police Department* (New York, 2013), 46; "Oral History Interview with Louis R. Anemone," 28–29, JNY, LSL. On the Knapp Commission, see Michael F. Armstrong, *They Wished They Were Honest: The Knapp Commission and New York City Police Corruption* (New York, 2012).

39. Hugh Morrow to Nelson Rockefeller, "Your Appearance on 'Today' Show Friday September 7" (memo), September 6, 1973; Morrow to Rockefeller, October 5, 1973; both NARG, RG 15, Series 21.2 Hugh Morrow Central Files, Box 33, Folder 346, RAC. On the Rockefeller Laws' legislative history, see Kohler-Hausmann, *Getting Tough*, 90–104; and Barrett, *Nelson Rockefeller's Dilemma*, 242–49. Some Black politicians in New York gave rhetorical support to tougher drug laws and policing, though practically none ended up voting for the Rockefeller Drug Laws. For an argument emphasizing the importance of Black support, see Michael Javen Fortner, *Black Silent Majority: The Rockefeller Laws and the Politics of Punishment* (Cambridge, MA, 2015); for a critical assessment of Fortner's argument, see Donna Murch, "Who's to Blame for Mass Incarceration?" *Boston Review*, October 16, 2015. The present author tends to place more emphasis on the fact that the great majority of Black legislators from New York voted against the Rockefeller laws. On national drug policy in the early 1970s, see Matthew D. Lassiter, *The Suburban Crisis: White America and the War on Drugs* (Princeton, NJ, 2023), chap. 4.

40. Ohrenstein quoted in *Knickerbocker News*, January 4, 1973. See also Office of Legislative Research, "Governor Wants to Send Hard Drug Pushers to Jail for Life But Critics Call His Approach Too Harsh, Unconstitutional, Unrealistic," January 18, 1973, p. 8, in NARG, RG 15, Series 21.2 Hugh Morrow Central Files, Box 34, Folder 355, RAC; "Analysis of Testimony at Public Hearings Conducted by the Senate and Assembly Joint Codes Committees," MO, Box 19, Folder "Gov. Drug Bill," NYSA; Kohler-Hausmann, *Getting Tough*, 94 (Lindsay quote); Markham, "'Toughest in the Nation' . . . ," *NYT*, May 13, 1973; Malcolm M. Feeley, *Court Reform on Trial: Why Simple Solutions Fail* (New York, 1983), 124; National Institute of Law Enforcement and Criminal Justice, "Enforcement Policies," in *Nation's Toughest Drug Law*, 2. For the city's official statement of opposition, see Richard A. Brown, "Memorandum in Opposition [to S#6204]," MO, Box 19, Folder "Gov. Drug Bill," NYSA.

41. "Operation Drugs—A Report on Harlem Crime," *NYAN*, April 9, 1977 ("All of us"); "Sutton Asked to Lead Crusade . . . ," *NYAN*, December 27, 1975; Anekwe, "Harlemites Are Lining Up . . . ," *NYAN*, January 10, 1976; H. Carl McCall, "A Hard Line on Crime," *NYAN*, January 10, 1976; Raab, "Police Crack Down on Drugs . . . ," *NYT*, December 7, 1976; Charles B. Rangel to Abraham Beame, November 30, 1976, ADB, Roll 6, Box 88, Folder 4, NYCMA. A strong majority of those arrested during the Operation Drugs campaign—65.4 percent—lived outside Harlem.

42. Raab, "Police Crack Down" ("cynical"); Breasted, "Police Drive Stalks . . . ," *NYT*, January 30, 1977 ("crowds"); Raab, "Sales of Illegal Drugs . . . ," *NYT*, September 14, 1979 ("arrests").

43. Quoted in Benjamin Holtzman, "Expanding the Thin Blue Line: Resident Patrols

and Private Security in Late Twentieth-Century New York," *MAH* 3, no. 1 (March 2020): 47, 50.

44. Jamaica Branch NAACP and Queens CORE, "Why the School Boycott?" (poster), https://www.zinnedproject.org/news/tdih/nyc-school-children-boycott-school/. See Clarence Taylor, *Knocking at Our Own Door: Milton A. Galamison and the Struggle to Integrate New York City Schools* (New York, 1997), chap. 5; Matthew F. Delmont, *Why Busing Failed: Race, Media, and the National Resistance to School Desegregation* (Oakland, CA, 2016), 15; Christopher Bonastia, *The Battle Nearer to Home: The Persistence of School Segregation in New York City* (Stanford, CA, 2022), 69–70.
45. Delmont, *Why Busing Failed*, 30, 32.
46. Adina Back, "Up South in New York: The 1950s School Desegregation Struggles" (Ph.D. diss., New York University, 1997); Taylor, *Knocking at Our Own Door*, 74–83; Delmont, *Why Busing Failed*, 34–36, 40, 42; Bonastia, *Battle Nearer to Home*, 23–45, 55–79. On Baker and New York City school integration, see Barbara Ransby, *Ella Baker and the Black Freedom Movement: A Radical Democratic Vision* (Chapel Hill, NC, 2003), 148–56; On white resistance to school integration before 1964, see also Lisa Yvette Waller, "The Pressures of the People: Milton A. Galamison, the Parents' Workshop, and Resistance to School Integration in New York City, 1960–1963," in Manning Marable and Elizabeth Kai Hinton, eds., *The New Black History: Revisiting the Second Reconstruction* (New York, 2011), chap. 2.
47. Delmont, *Why Busing Failed*, 48; Shapiro, "Segregation Has Been the Story . . . ," *NYT*, March 26, 2019. See the NYPD's surveillance films of the PAT protests, available via the New York City Municipal Archives' website: https://nycma.lunaimaging.com/luna/servlet/NYCMA~3~3. On opposition to integration in New York, see also Clarence Taylor, "Conservative and Liberal Opposition to the New York City School-Integration Campaign," in Taylor, ed., *Civil Rights in New York City: From World War II to the Giuliani Era* (New York, 2011), chap. 5.
48. Sam Roberts, *The New Yorkers: 31 Remarkable People, 400 Years, and the Untold Biography of the World's Greatest City* (New York, 2022), 306–7; Preston Wilcox, ed., "Report of the Education Workshop #1: Control of Schools Within the Black Community: Third Annual Black Power Conference . . . 1968," PWP, MG 235, Box 24, Folder 1, SCRBC; "The Thrust Behind the Surge for Community Control of the Schools Located within Black Communities," 1968, PWP, MG 235, Box 16, Folder 1, SCRBC. On the community control movement, see Heather Lewis, *New York City Public Schools from Brownsville to Bloomberg: Community Control and Its Legacy* (New York, 2013), chap. 2; Sonia Song-Ha Lee, *Building a Latino Rights Movement: Puerto Ricans, African Americans, and the Pursuit of Racial Justice in New York* (Chapel Hill, NC, 2014), chap. 5; Russell Rickford, *We Are an African People: Independent Education, Black Power, and the Radical Imagination* (New York, 2016), 41–45; Russell Rickford, "Black Power as Educational Renaissance: The Harlem Landscape," and Brittney Lewer, "Pursuing 'Real Power to Parents': Babette Edwards's Activism from Community Control to Charter Schools," both in Ernest Morrell and Ansley T. Erickson, eds., *Educating Harlem: A Century of Schooling and Resistance in a Black Community* (New York, 2019), chaps. 9 and 12; and Bonastia, *Battle Nearer to Home*, chap. 5.
49. Preston Wilcox, "The Controversy Over I.S. 201: One View and a Proposal"

1966; Wilcox, "The Meaning of Community Control," 1968; both in PWP, MG 235, Box 24, Folder 1, SCRBC. See also Preston Wilcox, "On the Way to School-Community Control: Some Observations," 1970, PWP, MG 235, Box 24, Folder 1, SCRBC; Taylor, *Knocking at Our Own Door*, 182–84; Lewis, *New York City Public Schools from Brownsville to Bloomberg*, 1–3. On independent Black Power schools in the city, see Viola H. Huang, "Between Protest, Compromise, and Education for Radical Change: Black Power Schools in Harlem in the Late 1960s" (Ph.D. diss., Columbia University, 2019).

50. Jerald E. Podair, *The Strike That Changed New York: Blacks, Whites, and the Ocean Hill–Brownsville Crisis* (New Haven, CT, 2002); Wendell E. Pritchett, *Brownsville, Brooklyn: Blacks, Jews, and the Changing Face of the Ghetto* (Chicago, 2003), chap. 8; Daniel H. Perlstein, *Justice, Justice: School Politics and the Eclipse of Liberalism* (New York, 2004); Lewis, *New York City Public Schools from Brownsville to Bloomberg*, 55–60. On the Ford Foundation's role, see Karen Ferguson, *Top Down: The Ford Foundation, Black Power, and the Reinvention of Racial Liberalism* (Philadelphia, 2013), chap. 4. See also Paul Manning, "TIME BOMB! A Study of the New York City Public School Crisis: Special Report to Governor Nelson A. Rockefeller," NARG, RG 15, Series 21.2, Hugh Morrow General Files, Box 29, Folder 310, RAC.

51. UBP quoted in Lewis, *New York City Public Schools from Brownsville to Bloomberg*, 64. On school choice as a technique for integration, see, e.g., Christopher Jencks, "Is the Public School Obsolete?" *Public Interest* (Winter 1966), 23, 25–26; on support for choice programs by liberals concerned with equality, see Daniel T. Rodgers, *Age of Fracture* (Cambridge, MA, 2011), 215. For a genealogy of the small-schools-and-choice approach in New York, see Ansley Erickson, "Who Decides? Governing New York City Schools Since the Late 1960s," in Johanna Fernández, Kim Phillips-Fein, and Mason B. Williams, eds., *Gotham on the Verge* (Chapel Hill, NC, forthcoming).

52. Jeffrey R. Henig and Stephen D. Sugarman "The Nature and Extent of School Choice," in Sugarman and Frank R. Kemerer, eds., *School Choice and Social Controversy: Politics, Policy, and Law* (Washington, DC, 1999), 19; Andrea Gabor, *After the Education Wars: How Smart Schools Upend the Business of Reform* (New York, 2018), 30–33; Federal Bureau of Investigation (File on Deborah Ellen Meier), DM, Series VIII, Box 15, Folder "FBI file on Meier, 1955–1963," LL, https://archives.iu.edu/catalog/InU-Li-VAB8339aspace_VAB8339-01054.

53. Deborah Meier, "Learning Not to Learn," *Dissent* (November–December 1968): 540–48, at 544; Meier, *The Power of Their Ideas: Lessons for America from a Small School in Harlem*, 2nd ed. (Boston, 2002), 21 ("conceptual and *tangible*"). On the early years of public school choice in District 4, see Seymour Fliegel with James MacGuire, *Miracle in East Harlem: The Fight for Choice in Public Education* (New York, 1993), chaps. 1–10; Gabor, *After the Education Wars*, 32–39; and David L. Kirp, "What School Choice Really Means," *Atlantic* (November 1992), 119–28.

54. "Kenneth Clark: 'Regents to Blame for N.Y. School Segregation,'" *Militant*, February 21, 1975, 9; *Journal of Regents Meeting, November 17–19, 1976*, 434, KBC, Box 485, Folder 6, LOC; [Transcript, "Sunday," WNBC-TV, Channel 4, January 26, 1975, 10:00 a.m.], 5–6, KBC, Box 390, Folder 6, LOC.

55. Genevieve Klein to Joseph W. McGovern, October 16, 1974, in KBC, Box 389,

Folder 9, LOC; Mike Gershowitz, "New Regents Member Will Make Waves," *Long Island Press*, April 7, 1974, 22; Buder, "Regents Dismiss Nyquist," *NYT*, November 20, 1976; Irving Anker, "Chancellor's Report on Programs and Problems Affecting Integration of the New York City Public Schools" (February 1974), 19.

56. Phillips-Fein, *Fear City*, 46–52, at 51.
57. Seymour P. Lachman and Robert Polner, *The Man Who Saved New York: Hugh Carey and the Great Fiscal Crisis of 1975* (Albany, NY, 2010), 104.
58. On the fiscal crisis, see Phillips-Fein, *Fear City*; Lachman and Polner, *Man Who Saved New York*; Morris, *Cost of Good Intentions*; William K. Tabb, *The Long Default: New York City and the Urban Fiscal Crisis* (New York, 1982); Robert W. Bailey, *The Crisis Regime: The MAC, the EFCB, and the Political Impact of the New York City Financial Crisis* (Albany, NY, 1984); Martin Shefter, *Political Crisis/Fiscal Crisis: The Collapse and Revival of New York City* (New York, 1985); Freeman, *Working-Class New York*, 256–70; and the relevant sections of Ester R. Fuchs, *Mayors and Money: Fiscal Policy in New York and Chicago* (Chicago, 1992).
59. "New York City" (speech draft), Robert Hartmann Papers, Box 178, Folder "10/29/75–New York City Speech (3)," Gerald R. Ford Presidential Library, https://www.fordlibrarymuseum.gov/library/document/0269/21969351.pdf; Phillips-Fein, *Fear City*, 100; *NYDN*, October 30, 1975.
60. Phillips-Fein, *Fear City*, 197–201, 206; Jensen, "For the City . . . ," *NYT*, December 10, 1975 (Rohatyn). On the social costs of the fiscal crisis, see esp. Freeman, *Working-Class New York*, 270–83; Phillips-Fein, *Fear City*, esp. chaps. 13–15; and Kim Phillips-Fein, "The Politics of Austerity: The Moral Economy of 1970s New York," in Andrew J. Diamond and Thomas J. Sugrue, eds., *Neoliberal Cities: The Remaking of Postwar Urban America* (New York, 2020), chap. 3.
61. Jacob K. Javits, Undated invitation draft; "Memorandum of Conversation," March 23, 1976; both in WTL, CN FA102, Series 2, Box 64, Folder 518, RAC.
62. Freeman, *Working-Class New York*, 278; David Rockefeller and Harry Van Arsdale to William T. Coleman, Jr., December 30, 1976, WTL, CN FA102, Series 2, Box 64, Folder 532, RAC; Charles J. Orlebeke, *New Life at Ground Zero: New York, Home Ownership, and the Future of American Cities* (Albany, NY, 1997), 14; *Summary Report of the Business/Labor Working Group on Jobs and Economic Regeneration in New York City* (New York, 1977?), 20–23 (emphasis in original). See also *The City in Transition: Projects and Policies for New York: The Final Report of the Temporary Commission on City Finances, June 1977* (New York, 1978), 167, which emphasizes the importance of "meet[ing] economic development and quality of life objectives." On Westway, see William W. Buzbee, *Fighting Westway: Environmental Law, Citizen Activism, and the Regulatory War that Transformed New York City* (Ithaca, NY, 2014). For the city's perspective, see Abraham D. Beame to Percy Sutton, November 8, 1976, ADB, Roll 1, Box 29, Folder 1, NYCMA. On the politics of growth in twentieth-century New York generally, see Daniel Wortel-London, *The Menace of Prosperity: New York and the Struggle for Economic Development, 1865–1981* (Chicago, 2025).

With encouragement from Carey and Koch, David Rockefeller went on to establish the New York City Partnership with the objective of providing a unified voice for the city's largest businesses and establishing "a new model for social problem-solving" by institutionalizing and disseminating the idea of public-private partnerships. Rockefeller described the B/LWG as "the predecessor really of the Partnership." See Greenberg, *Branding New York*, 233–36, 302n5 (at 233); Charles J. Orlebeke, *New Life at Ground Zero: New York, Home Ownership, and the Future of American Cities* (Albany, NY, 1997), 43. See David Rockefeller, "Ingredients for Successful Partnerships: The New York City Case," in Perry Davis, ed., *Public-Private Partnerships: Improving Urban Life* (New York, 1986). The partnership also affiliated with the Chamber of Commerce and Industry (with which it officially merged in the early twenty-first century); on the history of the New York Chamber of Commerce, see Elizabeth Blackmar, "Exercising Power: The New York Chamber of Commerce and the Community of Interest," in Karl Kusserow, *Picturing Power: Portraiture and Its Uses in the New York Chamber of Commerce* (New York, 2013), 189–234.

63. Robert F. Wagner, Jr., "The Threat to Free Tuition at CUNY and to Rent Control Equals Disaster," *VV*, October 13, 1975, 16–17.
64. See J. Phillip Thompson, "One Step Forward, Two Steps Back: Liberalism, Race, and Local Democracy," in John Mollenkopf and Ken Emerson, eds., *Rethinking the Urban Agenda: Reinvigorating the Liberal Tradition in New York City and Urban America* (New York, 2001), 192–93.
65. For overviews of the 1977 campaign, see Jonathan Mahler, *Ladies and Gentlemen, the Bronx Is Burning: Baseball, Politics, and the Battle for the Soul of a City* (New York, 2005); and Jonathan Soffer, *Ed Koch and the Rebuilding of New York City* (New York, 2010), 121–29. Abzug's papers are full of correspondence from non-constituents; see, e.g., E. Allen Ostrander to Abzug, December 21, 1971 (from Mt. Vernon), BA, Box 349, Folder "Housing Correspondence, 1970–1971, n.d.," RBML; and Martin Fishman to Abzug, January 26, 1972 (from Bay Ridge: "It seems like you are the only one out to help people"); Dorothy Covino to Abzug, February 10, 1972 (from Norwood in the Bronx); John Carey to Abzug, March 9, 1972 (from Yorkville: "Since it appears to me that you . . . get things done"); Inez Padilla to Abzug, May 2, 1972 (from New Lots, Brooklyn); all in BA, Box 349, Folder "Housing Correspondence, 1972," RBML.
66. On Cuomo's early career, see Robert S. McElvaine, *Mario Cuomo: A Biography* (New York, 1988), chaps. 6–7.
67. See Soffer, *Ed Koch*, chaps. 2–7.
68. Soffer, *Ed Koch*, 61–64, 108–11 ("political Rubicon" at 108); John Hull Mollenkopf, *A Phoenix in the Ashes: The Rise and Fall of the Koch Coalition in New York City Politics*, 2nd ed. (Princeton, NJ, 1994), 165 ("my experience"); Phillips-Fein, *Fear City*, 286 ("The City of New York").
69. Doug Ireland, "Democratic Dogfight: A Hopeless Welter of Nonissues," *NY*, September 5, 1977, 35. See the discussion in Phillips-Fein, *Fear City*, 284–86. On Abzug, see Leandra Ruth Zarnow, *Battling Bella: The Protest Politics of Bella Abzug* (Cambridge, MA, 2019), 277–83. On Sutton's struggles, see Wilbur C. Rich, *David Dinkins and New York City Politics: Race, Images, and the Media* (Albany, NY, 2007), 30–34.
70. For Koch's post-primary maneuverings, see the excellent treatment in Soffer, *Ed Koch*, 133–42. The best analysis of the primary, runoff, and general election votes is Mollenkopf, *Phoenix in the Ashes*, 101–10. On Cuomo's campaign, see

McElvaine, *Mario Cuomo*, 225–59. For Koch's negotiations with Harlem leaders, see Charles B. Rangel with Leon Wynter, *And I Haven't Had a Bad Day Since: From the Streets of Harlem to the Halls of Congress* (New York, 2007), 206–7; see also Jack Newfield's interview notes in JN, Box 2006–274, Folder "Koch Deal, Basil Paterson Notes," BC. "Code words" in Frank Lynn, "Democratic Mayoral Rivals . . . ," *NYT*, September 2, 1977.

71. Mollenkopf, *Phoenix in the Ashes*, 105–8; see also Jack Newfield's annotated copy of "How the Districts Voted," and Andy Soltis, "Ethnic Vote Was Key," *NYP*, September 20, 1977, in JN, Box 2006–274, Folder "How Koch Got Elected," BC. On Farber, see Dylan Gottlieb, "1-800-BE-ANGRY: Reactionary Media and White Ethnic Conservatism in New York," in Fernández, Phillips-Fein, and Williams, eds., *Gotham on the Verge*.

Chapter 2: Austerity

1. "Text of Address Delivered by Koch . . . ," *NYT*, January 2, 1978. On Koch's mayoralty, see especially Jonathan Soffer, *Ed Koch and the Rebuilding of New York City* (New York, 2010); on the Koch coalition, John Hull Mollenkopf, *A Phoenix in the Ashes: The Rise and Fall of the Koch Coalition in New York City Politics*, rev. ed. (Princeton, NJ, 1994).
2. "Text of Address Delivered by Koch." For Koch's thoughts on gentrification, see Koch to Clark Whelton, December 15, 1982, EIK, Departmental Correspondence Series, Box 0000090, Folder 11 "City Hall Staff—Whelton, Clark [Reganomics (*sic*); Gentrification]," LWA.
3. Business/Labor Working Group, Coordinating Group, "Meeting Notes, November 23, 1976, 2:00 p.m.," WTL, Series 2, CN FA102, Box 64, Folder 532, RAC; "New York City Economic Development Task Force: A Suggested Agenda," n.d., WTL, Series 2, CN FA102, Box 64, Folder 518, RAC. On the BLWG's emphasis on "the necessity of dealing with rent control as a fundamental frustration to the city's economic regeneration," see Warren T. Lindquist to David Rockefeller, June 25, 1976, WTL, Series 2, CN FA102, Box 65, Folder 548, RAC.
4. Hugh Carey to Robert C. Weaver et al., October 20, 1975; Dennis Sullivan to William Woodward, "Report of the Task Force on Housing" (memo), April 14, 1975, all in HC, Microfilm Reel 101, Folder "Housing, Task Force On 12/6/74–10/20/ 75," NYSA; Kaiser, "City's Powers on the Line . . . ," *NYT*, March 14, 1976; Fried, "Moynihan Asks Rent-Control Study . . . ," *NYT*, February 12, 1977; Kaiser, "Beame Says Rent Curbs . . . ," *NYT*, February 17, 1977; West Side Tenants Union, "Rent Controls Can Be Saved" (flyer, 1976), NYSTN, Series 4, Box 1, Folder 7, UA.
5. Greenhouse, "New York Legislature Is Returning . . . ," *NYT*, January 2, 1977; T. N. Hurd, "June 30 Report on New York City" (1976), 4, in "Select Working Papers of Vice President Nelson A. Rockefeller, 1974–1977," Vol. 32, NARVP, Series 18, FA 384, Box 32, RAC (which reported "clear indications" that there would be efforts "to modify or even rescind" rent regulation in 1977); Met Council, "One Year Renewal of ETPA Spells Death to Rent Controls" (press release), June 28, 1976, MCH, Box 3, Folder "Emergency Tenant Protection Act #2," TL (which described the 1976 one-year extension as a "thinly-disguised prelude to the elimination of rent controls" that "paved the way for letting [regulations] die in a

non-[state] election year"); Greenhouse, "Rent Control Pact Reached . . . ," *NYT*, April 27, 1977. This was the common conclusion of those who observed the 1977 session. See for instance Betsy Brown, "Nobody Controls Rent Control," *ESR*, May 1977, 186: "Legislators were unwilling to take a stand on an issue which could affect the outcome of the [mayoral] election." On tenant activism in 1977, which had begun to target the city's seven Republican senators with leafleting campaigns when the Senate GOP announced its intention to extend the laws, see Ronald Lawson with Reuben B. Johnson III, "Tenant Responses to the Urban Housing Crisis, 1970–1984," in Lawson with Mark Naison, *The Tenant Movement in New York City, 1904–1984* (New Brunswick, NJ, 1986), 253.

6. Horsley, "Up, Up and Away . . . ," *NYT*, September 18, 1977; Goodwin, "Middle-Income Families . . . ," *NYT*, March 14, 1979.
7. Coalition for the Homeless, "A History of Modern Homelessness in New York City," in MCH, Box 62, Folder "Housing Facts," TL (SRO unit and resident psychiatric patient figures at 3). See esp. Alex S. Vitale, *City of Disorder: How the Quality of Life Campaign Transformed New York Politics* (New York, 2008), 74–77, 93, 96–97, 109–10; Benjamin Holtzman, *The Long Crisis: New York and the Path to Neoliberalism* (New York, 2021), 179–80. See also Thomas J. Main, *Homelessness in New York City: Policymaking from Koch to de Blasio* (New York, 2016). On the "new homeless," see Peter H. Rossi, *Down and Out in America: The Origins of Homelessness* (Chicago, 2013).
8. See Timothy L. Collins, *An Introduction to the Rent Guidelines Board and the Rent Stabilization System* (New York, 2001).
9. Goodwin, "City's Rent Guidelines Board . . . ," *NYT*, June 28, 1979; Barron, "Guidelines Board: Eight Citizens . . . ," *NYT*, October 14, 1979; Oser, "Inequities Expand . . . ," *NYT*, March 6, 1983.
10. Samuel J. LeFrak, "End Rent Control," *NYT*, August 10, 1982; Rent Stabilization Association of New York City, *A Rational Approach to Housing in the 1980s: Preserving New York City's Rental Apartments* (New York, 1980), 30; Real Estate Board of New York, *Trouble at Home: A Program to Preserve and Develop Rental Housing in New York City* (New York, 1983), 15; Real Estate Board of New York, "Public Perception of Development & Property Ownership: A Public Opinion Poll (September 1985)," Questions 48-51, REBNYC, Box 140033, Folder "REBNY Publications—Reports + Studies—January 1985–September 1985, LWA. On Penn and (especially) Schoen, see Timothy Shenk, *Left Adrift: What Happened to Liberal Politics* (New York, 2024).
11. Rosenbaum, "Reagan Aides Urge . . . ," *NYT*, November 21, 1980; Goodwin, "Plan to Prevent Controls . . . ," *NYT*, November 22, 1980; Molotsky, "D'Amato Urges Fund Cuts . . . ," *NYT*, May 5, 1981; Molotsky, "U.S. Senate Unit Votes Bill . . . ," *NYT*, May 6, 1981; Soffer, *Ed Koch*, 225 (Soffer writes that "Reagan . . . blocked [the measure] at Koch's request"); Tolchin, "Conferees Dropping Penalty . . . ," *NYT*, July 22, 1981; "Summary of Meeting on Tues., February 27, 1984"; Arthur J. Finkelstein to Alfonse D'Amato, October 18, 1983, both in AJF, Box 15, Folder "D'Amato, Alph., General, 1983–1984," LOC; Goldstein, "D'Amato: At Home . . . ," *NYT Sunday Magazine*, February 13, 1983.
12. See Lawson with Johnson, "Tenant Responses to the Urban Housing Crisis," 255–60. Tenants and Neighbors argued that "rental housing, unlike many

other consumer commodities, is directly linked to the public interest; that the price, quality and availability of rental housing is intimately associated with the health, security and general well-being of families, neighborhoods and municipalities." See "New York State Tenant and Neighborhood Coalition Proposed Statewide Rent and Eviction Control Bill Outline—November 1980," in NYSTNC, Series 3, Box 1, Folder 29, UA. For Dearie's argument in favor of his bill, see "Press Release: Dearie Urges Legislature Support Flynn/Dearie Bill; Calls It Cornerstone of Tenant Protections," May 15, 1981, NYSTNC, Series 3, Box 1, Folder 28, UA.

A 1985 study commissioned by the Rent Stabilization Association found that 12 percent of landlords controlled 71 percent of rent-stabilized units. See Eric Weinstock, "Dismantling Rent Regulations: Fiscal Benefits or Fiscal Disaster? . . ." (May 1991), 6, in MCH, Box 62, Folder "Housing Facts + Figures," TL.

13. Chira, "Albany Races Deadline . . . ," *NYT*, June 12, 1983; Daniels, "A Debate Over Extending . . . ," *NYT*, June 17, 1983; "Legislative Memorandum in Support [of] A. 6896," April 25, 1983 NYSTNC, Series 3, Box 2, Folder 19, UA; [handwritten notes for meetings, June 1, 1983, May 25, 1983], NYSTNC, Series 3, Box 2, Folder 22, UA; Lawson with Johnson, "Tenant Responses to the Urban Housing Crisis," 260. Many constituents were convinced that Cuomo had pledged specifically to support the Flynn-Dearie bill; see correspondence in MMC, Box 31 (microfilm), Box "Community Development–Housing–Rent Control–Emergency Tenants Protection Act–Legislation, 7/1/83–12/31/83," NYSA.

14. Mario Cuomo to Lillian Kubersky (of the Rockaway Tenants Council), September 1, 1983, MMC, Box 31 (microfilm), Folder "Community Development–Housing–Rent Control–Emergency Tenants Protection Act–Legislation, 7/1/83–12/31/83," NYSA; Wald, "Tenants Notice a Catch . . . ," *NYT*, September 4, 1983; William P. Rowen, "Rent Regulations Should Never End" (letter), *NYT*, July 23, 1983. For a full legislative history, see Matt Tallmer, "Landlords and Tenants," *ESR*, January 1984, 30–34; on Flynn-Dearie in the 1983 session, see John McKean, "How the Senate Took a Walk on Flynn-Dearie," *CL*, October 1983.

15. Holtzman, *The Long Crisis*, 179–82; Emanuel Tobier, *The Changing Face of Poverty: Trends in New York City's Population in Poverty, 1960–1990* (New York, 1984), 61.

16. Buder, "Schools Open Today . . . ," *NYT*, September 13, 1976; David S. Seeley and Adele Spier, "Productivity in New York City's Schools: Fiscal Reality *and* Educational Quality," *CA* 11, no. 3 (October 1976): 1.

17. Heather Lewis, *New York City Public Schools from Brownsville to Bloomberg: Community Control and Its Legacy* (New York, 2013), 74; William K. Tabb, *The Long Default: New York City and the Urban Fiscal Crisis* (New York, 1982), 30; Nick Juravich, *Para Power: How Paraprofessional Labor Changed Education* (Urbana, IL, 2024), chap. 7; *Testimony by Rudolph F. Crew . . . Before the Senate Finance Committee and the Assembly Ways and Means Committee . . . February 2, 1998*, 4–5, RFC, Series 1150, Box 1150.1, Folder "[January 1998]," BOE, NYCMA.

18. Kim Phillips-Fein and Esther Cyna, "Harlem Schools in the Fiscal Crisis," in Ansley T. Erickson and Ernest Morrell, eds., *Educating Harlem: A Century of Schooling and Resistance in a Black Community* (New York, 2019), chap. 11; "Harlem Parents Want Out of School System; Demand State Funds for Private Education" (press release), February 11, 1975, BE, Box 22, Folder 16, SCRBC;

Genevieve Klein to Babette Edwards, June 27, 1977, BE, Box 23, Folder 1, SCRBC; Simon Anekwe, "Black Parents Seek State Funds for Private Schools," *NYAN*, October 8, 1975; Edwards, "Educational Vouchers for Blacks and Hispanics: Statement to the Democratic Party Platform Committee, May 20, 1976," in BE, Box 23, Folder 1, SCRBC. On Edwards, see Brittney Lewer, "Pursuing 'Real Power to Parents': Babette Edwards's Activism from Community Control to Charter Schools," in Morrell and Erickson, eds., *Educating Harlem*, chap. 12. For a glimpse at how elected representatives, school officials, parents, and children responded to the closure of "underutilized" schools in the South Bronx, see RG, Box 44, Folder 22, CCPRS.

19. Deborah Meier, *The Power of Their Ideas: Lessons for America from a Small School in Harlem* (Boston, 1995), 18; Andrea Gabor, *After the Education Wars: How Smart Schools Upend the Business of Reform* (New York, 2018), 34; Maeroff, "Exploring Alternatives . . . ," *NYT*, January 2, 1982; Lewis, *New York City Public Schools from Brownsville to Bloomberg*, 126.
20. Buder, "Upgraded School Is Urged . . . ," *NYT*, July 2, 1974; Curtis J. Berger, "Away from the Court House and Into the Field: The Odyssey of a Special Master," *Columbia Law Review* 78, no. 4 (May 1978): 713. New York created its first magnet school in 1971, a themed high school in South Jamaica focused on aviation. See Buder, "'Magnet' High Schools . . . ," *NYT*, July 3, 1975. The SHSAT schools, discussed in Chapters 3 and 5, predate the magnet school concept and were not explicitly geared toward integration. See also Anka's budget request in Board of Education News Bureau (press release), January 11, 1974, in BE, Box 28, Folder 4, SCRBC.
21. Kenneth B. Clark, "Reactions to the Report of the Special Master (Curtis J. Berger), Part I: The School Plan," July 15, 1974, 6, 8, KBC, Box 494, Folder 6, LOC. On Clark, see Gerald Markowitz and David Rosner, *Children, Race, and Power: Kenneth and Mamie Clark's Northside Center* (Charlottesville, VA, 1996).
22. Clark, "Reactions to the Report of the Special Master," 3–4.
23. Berger, "Away from the Court House," 710, 715–16, 732–33; Peterson, "School-Integration Order . . . ," *NYT*, July 27, 1974; Buder, "New Twain Integration Plan," *NYT*, February 9, 1975; Peterson, "Tight Security Is Planned . . . ," *NYT*, March 28, 1975.
24. Johnston, "Mini-Schools Seek . . . ," *NYT*, Mar 22, 1981; Berger, "Magnet Schools . . . ," *NYT*, November 10, 1988.
25. Oelsner, "New York's Best Public Schools . . . ," *NYT*, January 23, 1978; Kleiman, "2 'Magnet Schools' Strive . . . ," *NYT*, February 22, 1983; Daley, "Special School in Harlem . . . ," *NYT*, February 23, 1988; Berger, "Teachers of the Gifted . . . ," *NYT*, March 16, 1988; Hertling, "Rules for Magnet Schools Set," *EducationWeek*, June 5, 1985; Bender, "Moynihan Bill to Provide Funds . . . ," *Newsday*, June 11, 1984; "Talking Points for Magnet School Desegregation Amendment"; "Statement of Senator Daniel Patrick Moynihan"; "Sen. Moynihan Welcomes President Reagan's Support for Magnet Schools" (press release), January 25, 1988; all in DPM, Box II:1111, Folder 8, LOC.
26. Robert Kane and Michael White, *Jammed Up: Bad Cops, Police Misconduct, and the New York City Police Department* (New York, 2013), 48.
27. Tabb, *Long Default*, 42; Benjamin Holtzman, "Expanding the Thin Blue Line:

Resident Patrols and Private Security in Late Twentieth-Century New York," *MAH* 3, no. 1 (March 2020), 59–60; Buder, "Berkowitz Is Described . . . ," *NYT*, August 12, 1977.

28. Holtzman, "Expanding the Thin Blue Line," 59–61; Randy Young, "Do-It-Yourself Patrols," *NY*, February 8, 1982, 37.
29. Benjamin Holtzman, "Remaking Business Districts," in Johanna Fernández, Kim Phillips-Fein, and Mason B. Williams, eds., *Gotham on the Verge* (Chapel Hill, forthcoming); Vitale, *City of Disorder*, 128–29, at 128; Holtzman, "Expanding the Thin Blue Line," 65. On privatization and public space, see Elizabeth Blackmar, "Appropriating 'the Commons': The Tragedy of Property Rights Discourse," in Setha Low and Neil Smith, eds. *The Politics of Public Space* (New York, 2006). On New York in particular, see Sharon Zukin, *Naked City: The Death and Life of Authentic Urban Spaces* (New York, 2010), esp. chap. 4. On privatization, the state, and power, see Beatrice Hibou, ed., *Privatising the State*, rev. ed. (London, 2004).
30. On the Guardian Angels, see especially Reiko Hillyer, "The Guardian Angels: Law and Order and Citizen Policing in New York City," *JUH* 43, no. 6 (November 2017): 886–914. See also Nicholas Pileggi, "Guardian Angels: Help or Hype?" *NY* (November 24, 1980), 14–19; Susan Pennell, Christine Curtis, and Joel Henderson, *Guardian Angels: An Assessment of Citizen Response to Crime* (Washington, DC, 1986).
31. Hillyer, "Guardian Angels," quoted at 893 ("mercenaries," "lynch mob," Hamptons, "antagonistic"), 887 "doughnut stands," Cuomo); Mario Cuomo to Jean Guiatiniani, September 16, 1983, MMC, Box 155 (microfilm), Folder "Public Safety–Crime–Prevention–Guardian Angels, N.Y.C.–1/1/83–," NYSA.
32. On the subway and the politics of disorder, see Craig Castleman, *Getting Up: Subway Graffiti in New York* (Cambridge, MA, 1982); Joe Austin, *Taking the Train: How Graffiti Art Became an Urban Crisis in New York* (New York, 2001); Themis Chronopoulos, *Spatial Regulation in New York City: From Urban Renewal to Zero Tolerance* (New York, 2011), chap. 5. See also Dan Bouk, *The Subway Job* (New York, forthcoming).
33. Nathan Glazer, "On Subway Graffiti in New York," *Public Interest* (Winter 1979): 2, 5.
34. Soffer, *Ed Koch*, 323; Dembart, "In the Subways . . . ," *NYT*, March 20, 1979, quoted in Themis Chronopoulos, "The Making of the Orderly City: New York Since the 1980s," *JUH* 46, no. 5 (September 2020): 1090.
35. On Whyte, see Richard K. Rein, *American Urbanist: How William H. Whyte's Unconventional Wisdom Reshaped Public Life* (Washington, DC, 2022); on Whyte and New York, see Thomas Dyja, *New York, New York, New York: Four Decades of Excess, Success, and Transformation* (New York, 2021), 29–30, 36, 40–41. Starting points in the literature on Jacobs include Alice Sparberg Alexiou, *Jane Jacobs: Urban Visionary* (New Brunswick, NJ, 2006) and Peter L. Laurence, *Becoming Jane Jacobs* (Philadelphia, 2016).
36. Jane Jacobs, *The Death and Life of Great American Cities* (1961; reprint New York, 1992), 34–54; William H. Whyte, *The Social Life of Small Urban Spaces* (New York, 1980), 64; Whyte to the Rockefeller Brothers Fund, "Revitalization of Bryant Park–Public Library Front," November 26, 1979, WHW, Box 1, Folder 18, RAC.
37. George L. Kelling and James Q. Wilson, "Broken Windows: The Police and Neighborhood Safety," *Atlantic* (March 1982), 29–30. As the historian Elizabeth Hinton notes, Wilson's interest in the capacity of the police to maintain order

dated back to the 1960s. See Hinton, *From the War on Poverty to the War on Crime: The Making of Mass Incarceration in America* (Cambridge, MA, 2016), 186–87. On the Broken Windows theory in the context of Wilson's political thought, see Milo Ward, "A Democracy of Authorities: Broken Windows Policing and the Neoconservative Political Theory of Law and Order," *Perspectives on Politics* (published online by Cambridge University Press, February 13, 2025).

38. Kelling and Wilson, "Broken Windows," 31 (emphasis in original) and 32.
39. Kelling and Wilson, "Broken Windows," 30–31. On community rights as a feature of American illiberalism, see Steven Hahn, *Illiberal America: A History* (New York, 2024).
40. Kelling and Wilson, "Broken Windows," 35.
41. Edward I. Koch to Robert J. McGuire, March 29, 1982; McGuire to Koch, May 12, 1982; both in EIK, Microfilm roll 26, Box 22, Folder 12, NCYMA.
42. Eli Ginzberg, "Foreign Business: New York City's Number One Growth Industry," *Business Week*, October 30, 1978, 85. On financialization in general, see Greta R. Krippner, *Capitalizing on Crisis: The Political Origins of the Rise of Finance* (Cambridge, MA, 2011); as a feature of post-1960s New York, Themis Chronopoulos and Jonathan Soffer, "Introduction: After the Urban Crisis: New York and the Rise of Inequality," *JUH* 43, no. 6 (November 2017): 855–93; on the relation of the economic restructuring to city politics, John Hull Mollenkopf, "The Postindustrial Transformation of the Political Order in New York City," in Mollenkopf, ed., *Power, Culture, and Place: Essays on New York City* (New York, 1988), chap. 9.
43. Peter C. Goldmark, Jr., "Foreign Business in the Economy of the New York–New Jersey Metropolitan Region," *CA* 14, no. 2 (August 1979): 1–10, at 5–6; Matthew Drennan and Georgia Nanopoulos-Stergiou, "The Local Economy and Local Revenues," in Charles Brecher and Raymond D. Horton, eds., *Setting Municipal Priorities, 1981* (Montclair, NJ, 1980), 23.
44. Peter Hellman, "New York's New Left Bank," *NY*, August 30, 1982, 25–26.
45. Department of City Planning, City of New York, *The Newest New Yorkers: Characteristics of the City's Foreign-born Population* (New York, 2013), 10, 16. For a comparison to earlier periods of immigration to New York, see Nancy Foner, *From Ellis Island to JFK: New York's Two Great Waves of Immigration* (New Haven, CT, 2000).
46. Dylan Gottlieb, "1-800-BE-ANGRY: Reactionary Media and White Ethnic Conservatism in New York," in Fernández, Phillips-Fein, and Williams, eds., *Gotham on the Verge*; Chang-Rae Lee, *Native Speaker* (New York, 1995), 175. For the new immigration and urban history, see A. K. Sandoval-Strausz, *Barrio America: How Latino Immigrants Saved the American City* (New York, 2019). On this phase of immigration to New York, see Nancy Foner, ed., *New Immigrants in New York* (New York, 1987); Peter Kwong, *The New Chinatown* (New York, 1987); Roger Sanjek, *The Future of Us All: Race and Neighborhood Politics in New York City* (Ithaca, NY, 2000); Jesse Hoffnung-Garskof, *A Tale of Two Cities: Santo Domingo and New York After 1950* (Princeton, NJ, 2008); Minju Bae, "One Rise, One Fall: Labor Organizing in New York's Asian Communities, 1970s to the Present" (Ph.D. diss., Temple University, 2020); Hongdeng Gao, "From Medical Schools to Free Clinics: Health Activism and Education in New York's Chinatown, 1950–1980" (Ph.D. diss., Columbia University, 2023);

and Pedro A. Regalado, *Nueva York: Making the Modern City* (Princeton, NJ, in progress).

47. Tobier, *Changing Face of Poverty*, vi, 7, 40, 43, 59, 61, 63. On low wages in the service sector, see Andy Battle, "New Economy, New Politics: New York's Postindustrial Transition," in Fernández, Phillips-Fein, and Williams, eds., *Gotham on the Verge*. On the rise of service work in late twentieth-century American cities, see Gabriel Winant, *The Next Shift: The Fall of Industry and the Rise of Health Care in Rust Belt America* (Cambridge, MA, 2021). For an overview of inequality in New York in this era, see John Hull Mollenkopf and Manuel Castells, eds., *Dual City: Restructuring New York* (New York, 1991).
48. Walter W. Stafford, *Closed Labor Markets: Underrepresentation of Blacks, Hispanics and Women in New York City's Core Industries and Jobs* (New York, 1985), ix, xiv, 45, 134–35. The job categories mentioned in the text were all at least 80 percent white.
49. Tobier, *Changing Face of Poverty*, 57.
50. Daniel Patrick Moynihan, *New York State and the Federal Fisc: IV, Fiscal Year 1979* (1980), 5–6.
51. Calculated from Office of the Comptroller, *Comptroller's Report for 1974–1975*, 12, and New York City Independent Budget Office data, https://www.ibo.nyc.ny.us/RevenueSpending/TaxRevenue.xls.
52. Comprehensive Annual Financial Reports of the Comptroller, in Independent Budget Office of the City of New York, "New York City Fiscal History—Tax Revenues," https://ibo.nyc.ny.us/fiscalhistory.html; Mollenkopf, *Phoenix in the Ashes*, 131; Soffer, *Ed Koch*, 225; "Text of Letter from Mayor Koch . . . ," *NYT*, January 17, 1981. For the modern city's fiscal history, see Lynn A. Weikart, *Follow the Money: Who Controls New York City Mayors?* (Albany, NY, 2009).
53. Mollenkopf, *Phoenix in the Ashes*, 131.

Chapter 3: From Survival to Revival

1. *New York Ascendant: The Report of the Commission on the Year 2000* (New York, 1987), 5–6; LeMoyne, "Panel Formed to Study . . . ," *NYT*, February 18, 1984.
2. On Senator Wagner, see J. Joseph Huthmacher, *Senator Robert F. Wagner and the Rise of Urban Liberalism* (New York, 1968). For Mayor Wagner, Richard M. Flanagan, *Robert Wagner and the Rise of New York City's Plebiscitary Mayoralty: The Tamer of the Tammany Tiger* (New York, 2015); and Chris McNickle, *To Be Mayor of New York: Ethnic Politics in the City* (New York, 1993), chaps. 5–7.
3. Franklin D. Roosevelt to Robert F. Wagner, III, RFWJ, Box 060183, Folder 14, LWA; Robert F. Wagner, Jr., "Curriculum Vitae," RFWJ, Box 060117W, Folder 22, LWA; Michael Kramer, "City Politic: The Resurrection of Robert Wagner," *NY*, December 23, 1974, 8.
4. Laird, "New York Loses . . . ," *NYDN*, November 18, 1993; Michael Ryan, "Back to School: Bobby Wagner Is Koch's Man at the Board of Ed," *NY*, November 10, 1986, 57.
5. *New York Ascendant*, 2, 5, 7–8.
6. *New York Ascendant*, 7, 21–22, 76, 116–18, 143–44. Wagner's handwritten edits on the report's drafts may be found in RFWJ, Box 060111W, Folders 7–9, LWA.

7. "'New York Ascendant': Comments of the Manhattan Borough President on the Report of the Commission of the Year 2000" (1987), 1, 2–3. For Wagner's response, which emphasized points of agreement, see Robert F. Wagner, Jr., to David Dinkins, December 22, 1987, RFWJP, Box 060111W, Folder 5, LWA. Wagner later conceded there had been too little emphasis on race and ethnicity in the commission's report. See Rudy García, "Wagner Admite Inadecuada Atención a los Latinos," *Noticias del Mundo*, May 16, 1988.
8. Peter D. Salins, ed., *New York Unbound: The City and the Politics of the Future* (New York, 1988), vii–viii, 1–2. On the Manhattan Institute's early years, see Alice O'Connor, "The Privatized City: The Manhattan Institute, the Urban Crisis, and the Conservative Counterrevolution in New York," *JUH* 34, no. 2 (January 2008): 333–53; Kim Phillips-Fein, *Fear City: New York's Fiscal Crisis and the Rise of Austerity Politics* (New York, 2017), 280–81.
9. Edward I. Koch, *Mayor: An Autobiography* (New York, 1984), quoted in Norman I. Fainstein and Susan S. Fainstein, "Governing Regimes and the Political Economy of Development in New York City, 1946–1984," in John Hull Mollenkopf, ed., *Power, Culture, and Place: Essays on New York City* (New York, 1988), 189 (Koch quote).
10. Lucy Sante, "My Lost City," *New York Review of Books*, November 6, 2003.
11. Jonathan Soffer, *Ed Koch and the Rebuilding of New York City* (New York, 2010), 320; Basler, "Koch Is Asking Why . . . ," *NYT*, October 8, 1980; Robert Kane and Michael White, *Jammed Up: Bad Cops, Police Misconduct, and the New York City Police Department* (New York, 2013), 50–51.
12. Buder, "New Police Unit . . . ," *NYT*, July 31, 1981; Shipp, "City Makes a Big Issue . . . ," *NYT*, August 30, 1981.
13. Mark H. Moore, *Buy and Bust: The Effective Control of an Illicit Market in Heroin* (Lexington, MA, 1977), esp. chap. 6, at 264.
14. "Limpieza policiaca de traficantes de drogas," *ED-LP*, January 20, 1984. On the Lower East Side real estate market in the early 1980s, see Neil Smith, *The New Urban Frontier: Gentrification and the Revanchist City* (New York, 1996), chap. 9; and Christopher Mele, *Selling the Lower East Side: Culture, Real Estate, and Resistance in New York City* (Minneapolis, MN, 2000), chap. 7. On the Lower East Side drug market, see Lynn Zimmer, *Operation Pressure Point: The Disruption of Street-Level Drug Trade on New York's Lower East Side* (New York, 1987), 2–4; and Eric Schneider, *Smack: Heroin and the American City* (Philadelphia, 2008), chap. 10. Though an outgrowth of disinvestment, the drug economy also helped finance new legitimate businesses and the construction of upmarket co-op housing. See Nicholas Pileggi, "There's No Business Like Drug Business," *NY*, December 13, 1982, 39–40.
15. "En dos años aumentará la venta de droga en NY," *ED-LP*, January 19, 1984; "Policía realiza 1.300 arrestos por drogas en Lower East Side," *ED-LP*, February 7, 1984; Andrew Stein to Koch, June 8, 1982 (enclosing report); Koch to Stein, June 30, 1982; both in EIK, Microfilm roll 4, Box 17, Folder 9, NYCMA (EIK hereafter numbered "Roll–Box–Folder"); Rob DeRocker, "Lower East Side Groups Gear Up . . . ," *Villager*, March 10, 1983; Jeanne Jackson, "Lower East Siders Take Back . . . ," *Villager*, March 24, 1983.
16. Dunlap, "Police Moving to Halt . . . ," *NYT*, January 20, 1984; "Limpieza policiaca de traficantes de drogas"; Wolff, "Three Agencies Joining . . . ," *NYT*, February 26, 1984; Koch to Ward, March 5, 1984; Ward to Koch, March 13, 1984; both in EIK,

51–119–1, NYCMA. Patrick J. Carroll, "Operation Pressure Point: An Urban Drug Enforcement Strategy," *FBI Law Enforcement Bulletin* 58, no. 4 (April 1989): 1–7, details how OPP worked in operation. The initial campaign focused on the area from 14th and Delancey streets, Avenue A, and Bowery in the west to Avenue D and Columbia Street to the east, with particular attention on Rivington, Eldridge, and Forsyth streets, Second to Fourth streets, and Avenues B and C. Ward himself emphasized OPP's visibility and publicity when discussing it as a policing strategy. See Benjamin Ward, "Police/Public Consultation: A Perspective from Police Commissioner Benjamin Ward," in *Models of Police/Public Consultation in Europe* (Cranfield-Wolfson Colloquium, 1984), EIK, 108–230–10, NYCMA.

17. "Oral History Interview with Benjamin Ward," 1992, 109–10, 120, KOHP, CCOHC, RBML; Richard Curtis, "The War on Drugs in Brooklyn, New York: Street-Level Drug Markets and the Tactical Narcotics Team" (Ph.D. diss., Columbia University, 1996), 21; Soffer, *Ed Koch*, 349. For Ward's fascinating biography, see Soffer, *Ed Koch*, 335–37. On New York elites' concern with media depictions of their city in the post-crisis years, see Miriam Greenberg, *Branding New York: How a City in Crisis Was Sold to the World* (New York, 2008).

18. Curtis, "War on Drugs in Brooklyn," 20; Kane and White, *Jammed Up*, 50–52; "Oral History Interview with Ward," 112; Jeanne Mulgrav, "Operation Pressure Point: A Community Perspective," quoted in Curtis, "War on Drugs in Brooklyn," 20–21; Brendan Sexton to Stanley Brezenoff, July 17, 1985, EIK, 51–119–2, NYCMA; Chambers, "Going Cold Turkey . . . ," *NYT*, February 19, 1984; Gross, "In the Trenches . . . ," *NYT*, January 8, 1986; Fein, "In Lobby of Lower East Side . . . ," *NYT*, April 14, 1986.

19. Lynn Zimmer, "Proactive Policing Against Street-Level Drug Trafficking," *American Journal of Police* 9, no. 1 (1990): 43–74 at 64; "Giving the ABCs Back to the Neighborhood," *NYDN*, January 20, 1984; Wolff, "Drug Arrests Mounting . . . ," *NYT*, March 5, 1984; Edward Koch, "Stopping the Drug Epidemic" (op-ed draft, March 20, 1984), EIK, 51–119–2, NYCMA; Rangel, "Police Laud . . . ," *NYT*, April 23, 1985; Fein, "Crime Drop Cited . . . ," *NYT*, January 27, 1985.

20. Koch to Rangel, July 18, 1986, EIK, 52–120–7, NYCMA; Mayor's Office press release, July 18, 1986, EIK, 52–120–5, NYCMA; "Critics Say No to Reagan's Drug Policy," *Black Enterprise* 19, no. 1 (1988): 29; Koch, "Stopping the Drug Epidemic."

21. "Bellamy, in Anticrime Paper . . . ," *NYT*, July 24, 1985; Fernando Ferrer to Brezenoff, April 4, 1985; Dimas Planas Belfort et al. to Ward, [date illegible]; both in EIK, 108–230–10, NYCMA; Johnny Ray Youngblood to Koch, July 3, 1985; Youngblood to Koch, July 17, 1985; both in EIK, 108–230–11, NYCMA; Youngblood to Ward, September 5, 1985, EIK, 108–231–1, NYCMA; Zimmer, *Operation Pressure Point*, 16. On community anticrack efforts in the Bronx, see Noël Wolfe, "Battling Crack: A Study of the Northwest Bronx Community and Clergy Coalition's Tactics," *JUH* 43, no. 1 (January 2017): 18–32.

22. Edward Koch, "Needed: Federal Antidrug Aid," *NYT*, April 27, 1984; David W. Dunlap, "Police Moving to Halt . . . ," *NYT*, January 20, 1984.

23. "Oral History Interview with Ward," 116, 63; Carroll, "Operation Pressure Point," 3–4. In this respect, street-level enforcement was of a piece with the concurrent private-public renovations of the city's parks. On the Central Park Conservancy, see Roy Rosenzweig and Elizabeth Blackmar, *The Park and the People: A History of*

Central Park (Ithaca, NY, 1992), 499–530; Benjamin Holtzman, *The Long Crisis: New York and the Path to Neoliberalism* (New York, 2021), chap. 3.

24. Jeanne Jackson, "Lower East Siders Take Back . . . ," *Villager*, March 24, 1983; Francis Goldin, "The Yupping of Avenue A," *NYT*, August 30, 1985; William R. Greer, "The Fortunes of the Lower East Side . . . ," *NYT*, August 4, 1985.

25. "Oral History Interview with Jeremy Travis," 39, 58, JNY, LSL; George James, "Drug Crackdown Is Expanded . . . ," *NYT*, November 16, 1988; Curtis, "War on Drugs in Brooklyn," 28–29. Ward credited Operation Pressure Point with giving the NYPD a head start in policing crack; see Peter Blauner, "Big Ben: Has Police Commissioner Ward Become a Liability to Koch?" *NY*, April 3, 1989.

On the history of crack in American cities, see David Farber, *Crack: Rock Cocaine, Street Capitalism, and the Decade of Greed* (New York, 2019); Donna Murch, "Crack in Los Angeles: Crisis, Militarization, and Black Response to the Late Twentieth-Century War on Drugs," *JAH* 102, no. 1 (June 2015): 162–73; and Donovan X. Ramsey, *When Crack Was King: A People's History of a Misunderstood Era* (New York, 2023). On the NYPD's response to crack, see Ward to Brezenoff, May 26, 1986, EIK, 15–38–9, NYCMA; Ward to Brezenoff, May 23, 1986; Brezenoff to Ward, June 17, 1986; Francis C. Hall, "Crack Briefing for the Mayor," July 23, 1986; all in EIK, 108–231–4, NYCMA. Ward and City Hall were both especially concerned that the rise of crack corresponded with a reversal of four years of declining crime statistics—a development that was, Ward lamented to Deputy Mayor Stan Brezenoff, receiving "considerable media attention."

26. Bernadette Fiore and Martha Schiff, *Operation Pressure Point, 1/19/84-2/18/84: Final Report on Arrest Characteristics and Criminal Court Outcomes* (New York, 1984); Roberta Kaye and Dynda Andrews to Koch and Patrick Mulhearn, July 24, 1986, EIK, 108–231–4, NYCMA; David F. Weiman and Christopher Weiss, "The Origins of Mass Incarceration in New York State: The Rockefeller Drug Laws and the Local War on Drugs," in Steven Raphael and Michael A. Stoll, eds., *Do Prisons Make Us Safer?: The Benefits and Costs of the Prison Boom* (New York, 2009), 97; Jack Norton, "Little Siberia, Star of the North: The Political Economy of Prison Dreams in the Adirondacks," in *Historical Geographies of Prisons: Unlocking the Usable Carceral Past*, Karen Morin and Dominique Moran, eds. (New York, 2015), 180; Saladin Ambar, *American Cicero: Mario Cuomo and the Defense of American Liberalism* (New York, 2018), 49, 84, 183n61; "Crack Possession Law . . . ," *NYT*, June 30, 1988. Koch characterized Cuomo's proposals as "a throwback to the harsh, but largely ineffective Rockefeller drug laws." Kevin Frawley to Koch, EIK, 52–120–8, NYCMA. On the role of prosecutors, see John Pfaff, *Locked In: The True Causes of Mass Incarceration and How to Achieve Real Reform* (New York, 2017).

The lead authors of Cuomo's counterpart to the Commission on the Year 2000, Jeryl L. Mumpower and Warren F. Ilchman, were urging the state's leaders to begin thinking about alternatives to incarceration. See Mumpower and Ilchman, "Conclusion," in Mumpower and Ilchman, eds., *New York State in the Year 2000* (Albany, NY, 1988), 13–14.

27. Weiman and Weiss, "Origins of Mass Incarceration in New York State," 88; Correctional Association of New York and the New York State Coalition for Criminal Justice, "Imprisoned Generation: Young Men Under Criminal Justice Custody in New York State" (September 1990), 2.

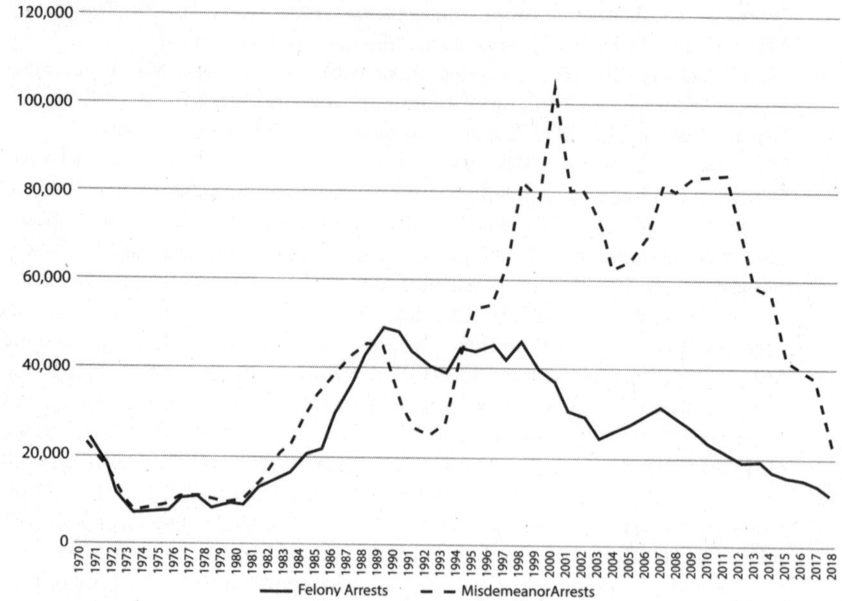

Drug arrests in New York City, 1970–2018, Office of Information Technology Services, "Adult Arrests 18 and Older by County: Beginning 1970," https://data.ny.gov/Public-Safety/Adult-Arrests-by-County-Beginning-1970/rikd-mt35.

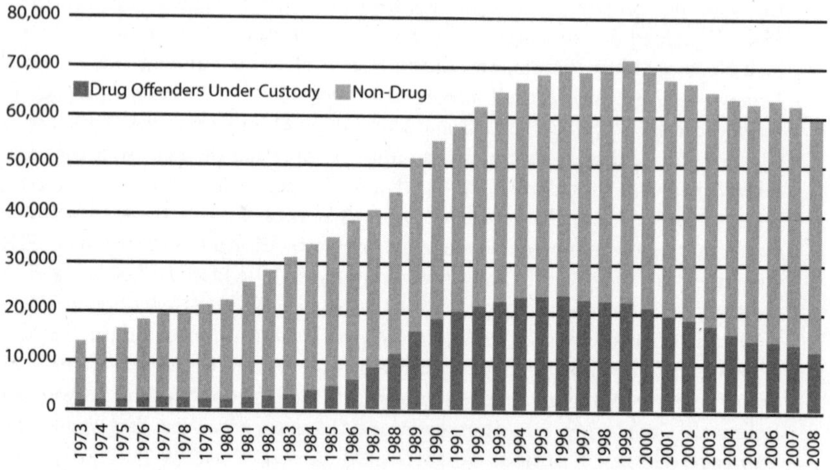

Drug offenders and nondrug offenders under custody by year in New York State, 1973–2008, Division of Criminal Justice Services, Criminal Justice Research Report, *New York State Felony Drug Arrest, Indictment and Commitment Trends, 1973–2008* (February 2010), 6.

28. Dylan Gottlieb, *Yuppies: The Bankers, Lawyers, Joggers and Gourmands Who Conquered New York* (Cambridge, MA, 2026).
29. For the number of new housing units approved by year in New York City, 1961–2019, see Citizens Budget Commission, *Strategies to Boost Housing Production in the New York City Metropolitan Area* (August 2020), 7. Edward Glaeser, Joseph Gyourko, and Raven Saks, "Why Is Manhattan So Expensive? Regulation and the Rise in Housing Prices," *Journal of Law and Economics* 48, no. 2 (October 2005): 331–69, remains the starting point in the large literature on development restrictions. Daniel Garodnick, "When Zoning Goes Too Far," *Vital City*, April 29, 2024, and David Schleicher, "Why Does Everything Cost So Much?" *Vital City*, April 16, 2025, point specifically at the 1961 zoning code. See also Ezra Klein and Derek Thompson, *Abundance* (New York, 2025), which synthesizes the literature on constraints on new housing production in metropolitan areas to make an argument about regulation and the origins of the contemporary housing crisis.

    In 1986, Koch asked a group of leading developers to identify the most important causes of the city's high construction costs. They identified, in order, the following: Higher labor and financing costs due to a code differences and labor differentials; higher land acquisition costs and greater difficulties assembling development sites; delays owing to overlapping departmental jurisdictions; restrictive zoning (particularly the mid-1980s downzonings of some seven hundred residential blocks); and high local fees and taxes. See Koch to Lewis Rudin, December 24, 1985; "Statement by Mayor Edward I. Koch," March 6, 1986; Richard M. Rosan et al. to Koch, March 3, 1986; and "Real Estate Industry Housing Construction Cost Reduction Program," n.d.; all in EIK, Departmental Correspondence Series, Box 0000031, Folder 20 "City Hall Staff, Biderman, Abraham (Middle Income Housing; Family Shelters)," LWA.
30. "Dearie Study Predicts 16,000 Rental Apartments Will Be Converted into Co-operative Ownership in 1980" (press release), January 17, 1980, RG, Box 46, Folder 17, CCPRS; Sternlieb, "Surprising Costs of the Co-op Boom . . . ," *NYT*, June 3, 1984; Adam Brodheim, "Bigger Houses, Fewer Homes: Dwelling Unit Consolidation in New York City" (M.Sc. thesis, Columbia University, 2023). Co-op and condo conversions data may be found in Rent Guidelines Board, *Housing NYC: Rents, Markets and Trends, 1999* (1999), 116; see also Kirk Johnson, "Pace of Co-op Conversions Slacking," *NYT*, December 2, 1984; Kirk Johnson, "From Brooklyn to Jersey . . . ," *NYT*, October 6, 1985. On co-op conversion in 1970s and '80s New York, see especially Holtzman, *Long Crisis*, chap. 2; on co-ops and condos more broadly, see Matthew Gordon Lasner, *High Life: Condo Living in the Suburban Century* (New Haven, CT, 2012).
31. Chavez, "On West Side . . . ," *NYT*, May 24, 1986.
32. Shenon, "22 Indicted . . . ," *NYT*, May 2, 1984; Blair, "6 More Landlords . . . ," *NYT*, November 1, 1984. See Robert M. Morgenthau, *Report of the Special Housing Unit of the Office of the District Attorney, County of New York* (New York, 1985). Another infamous case played out the same year in Manhattan's Chinatown, where investors from Hong Kong and Chinese Burma sought to oust regulated tenants to make way for a thirty-three-story tower on Henry Street. See Peter Kwong, *The New Chinatown* (New York, 1987), 52. See also Holtzman, *Long Crisis*, 186–87.

33. Goodman, "Taxes Hold Primary-Residence Key," *NYT*, June 26, 1983; Wedemeyer, "Enforcing Primary-Residence Rules," *NYT*, September 9, 1984; William Tucker, "Moscow on the Hudson," *American Spectator*, July 1986, 19–21; Tom Wolfe, *The Bonfire of the Vanities* (New York, 1987).
34. Wayne Barrett, *Trump: The Greatest Show on Earth: The Deals, the Downfall, the Reinvention*, rev. ed. (New York, 2016), 79–80; Donald J. Trump with Tony Schwartz, *Trump: The Art of the Deal* (New York, 1987), 253–55; Tucker, "Rent Control: 1,900,000 Lies," *NYDN*, March 5, 1989.
35. Ava Plakins, "The Landlords' Lament," *NY*, January 31, 1983, 39.
36. Wedemeyer, "Q. & A. with Landlords' Advocate," *NYT*, March 24, 1985; Rent Stabilization Association, *A Tale of Two Cities: Rent Regulation in New York City: Does All New York Benefit Equally?* (1986); Dee Wedemeyer, "Q. & A.: Paying the State . . . ," *NYT*, April 28, 1985. REBNY repeated Silverstein's proposal in its letter to Koch, Rosan et al. to Koch, March 3, 1986, cited in note 29.
37. Schmalz, "All in All, It Was a Good Year . . . ," *NYT*, June 30, 1985; Hinds, "Q.&A. with State's Housing Chief," *NYT*, July 14, 1985; "Tenant Unity Coalition Meeting with DHCR Commissioner William Eimicke," April 10, 1986, MCH, Box 53, Folder "Div. Housing Comm. Renewal (DHCR) 1986," TL; Schmalz, "Cuomo Opposes Decontrolling Rents," *NYT*, November 3, 1986; Commission on the Year 2000, *New York Ascendant*, 144; Real Estate Board of New York, *Towards the 21st Century: REBNY Responds to the Report of the Commission on the Year 2000* (November 1987), 2, RFWJ, Box 060111W, Folder 6, LWA.
38. On NYCHA housing in this era, see Nicholas Dagen Bloom, *Public Housing that Worked: New York in the Twentieth Century* (Philadelphia, 2008), chaps. 11–13; on the Koch housing plan, Jonathan Soffer, "The Koch Housing Plan," in Bloom and Matthew Gordon Lasner, eds., *Affordable Housing in New York* (Princeton, NJ, 2016), 273–76, and Soffer, *Ed Koch*, chap. 19; on Cuomo and housing, see Bloom, *How States Shaped Postwar America: State Government and Urban Power* (Chicago, 2019), 228–29. See also City of New York, *Ten Year Housing Plan, Fiscal Years 1989–1998*, in RG, Box 46, Folder 18, CCPRS.
39. Soffer, *Ed Koch*, 295; Andrew White, "Overcrowded Masses," *CL*, October 1992, 20. About half of the new apartments in the Koch housing plan were aimed at middle-class residents; about a quarter were intended for low-income New Yorkers, and another quarter for those with "moderate" incomes. See Martha E. Stark and Doug Turetsky, "Homeward Bound: A Twenty-first-Century Affordable Housing Agenda for New York," in John Mollenkopf and Ken Emerson, eds., *Rethinking the Urban Agenda: Reinvigorating the Liberal Tradition in New York City and Urban America* (New York, 2001), 145–46.
40. White, "Overcrowded Masses," 20; James R. Dumpson and David N. Dinkins, *A Shelter Is Not a Home: Report of the Manhattan Borough President's Task Force on Housing for Homeless Families* (March 1987). On squatters' efforts to defend their homes, see Amy Starecheski, *Ours to Lose: When Squatters Became Homeowners in New York City* (Chicago, 2016).
41. Gerard, "Charles Ludlam . . . ," *NYT*, May 29, 1987; "Rally to Save Everett's Home" (flyer), MCH, Box 51, Folder "Succession Rights," TL; Peg Byron, "Lover of Deceased Director Fights Eviction," UPI Archives, September 8, 1987.
42. Sullivan v. Brevard Associates 66 N.Y.2d 489; Tenant Unity Coalition, "Cuomo

Rapped on Rent Bill: Too Few Tenants Would be Protected" (press release), February 28, 1988, MCH, Box 51, Folder "Succession Rights," TL; "Rally to Save Everett's Home" (flyer). On succession rights amid the AIDS crisis, see Salonee Bhaman, "'For a Few Months of Peace': Housing and Care in the Early AIDS Crisis," *Radical History Review*, no. 140 (May 2021): 78–106.

43. Braschi v. Stahl Associates Co. 74 N.Y. 2d 201 (1989); Gutis, "New York Court Defines . . . ," *NYT*, July 7, 1989; Gary Spencer, "Gay Partner Held Entitled to Lease," *ANHD Weekly Reader*, July 17, 1, 7; William B. Rubenstein to Virginia M. Apuzzo, September 13, 1989; ACLU Lesbian and Gay Rights Project to August 10, 1989, Meeting Participants, Memorandum, August 10, 1989; both in MCH, Box 51, Folder "Succession Rights," TL; David Noh, "Everett Quinton . . . ," *AMNY*, September 10, 2015.
44. Diane Ravitch, "A Good School," *American Scholar* (Autumn 1984), 488. A summary version appeared in the *Wall Street Journal*; see Diane Ravitch, "A School Works in Brooklyn," *WSJ*, June 13, 1984. Thank you to Sasha Horvath, who first called this article to my attention.
45. National Commission on Excellence in Education, *A Nation at Risk: The Imperative for Education Reform: A Report to the Nation and the Secretary of Education*, April 1983; Deborah Meier, "'Getting Tough' in the Schools," *Dissent* (Winter 1984), 61, 70.
46. Diane Ravitch, "A Debate on Education: Diane Ravitch Comments, Deborah Meier Replies," *Dissent* (Spring 1984), 223; Michael B. Katz to Deborah Meier, August 14, 1984, DM, Series: Correspondence, 1927–2009, Subseries: Professional, 1982–2009, Box 5, Folder "General—K," LL, https://archives.iu.edu/catalog/InU-Li-VAB8339aspace_VAB8339-00177.
47. Ravitch, "Good School," 484–85, 490.
48. Perlez, "City to Ease . . . ," *NYT*, September 18, 1986; Perlez, "Opening Up Some Elite . . . ," *NYT*, September 21, 1986; Kriftcher, letter to the editor, "Let the Magnet School Be . . . ," *NYT*, February 9, 1984.
49. Weiss, "Are Neighborhood High Schools . . . ?" *NYT*, February 5, 1984; Weiss, "'Magnet' Schools May . . . ," *NYT*, January 15, 1984; Perlez, "Rethinking 'Career' High School . . . ," *NYT*, August 10, 1986.
50. David N. Dinkins, "New York Must Rid Itself . . . ," *NYT*, July 17, 1986.
51. Advocates for Children of New York, *Public High Schools: Private Admissions: A Report on New York City Practices* (1985); Frank Smith et al., "High School Admissions and the Improvement of Schooling: A Report of the University Consultants," Spring 1986, in NQ, Series 1125, Box 1125.87, Folder 846, BOE, NYCMA; Advocates for Children, "Attention All Educators"; Educational Priorities Panel, "Open Letter to the Chancellor on High School Admissions"; Arthur Auerbach to Nathan Quiñones, Re: "Recommendations of the Committee on Admissions," December 20, 1985; Advocates for Children, "Preliminary Comments on the Consultants' Report on High School Admissions"; Quiñones to Board of Education Committee, Re: "Consultant's Report on High School Admissions," June 3, 1986; Educational Priorities Panel, "Fact Sheet on High School Admissions," July 25, 1986; Robert F. Wagner, Jr., and Nathan Quiñones to Angelo Gonzalez, August 11, 1986; Luis O. Reyes, "Testimony Before the Board of Education . . . Open Hearings on High School Admissions Reforms,"

September 3, 1986; Janet R. Price, "Testimony Before the New York City Board of Education on Proposals to Reform High School Admissions," September 3, 1986; all in ASPIRA, Series VI, Box 30, Folder 2, CCPRS; Perlez, "City to Ease"; Frank Smith to High School Superintendents et al., "High School Memorandum #38: Admissions Policies for the Selection of Students to Screened and Educational Option Schools and Programs," October 6, 1986, NQ, Series 1125, Box 1125.159, Folder 1544, BOE, NYCMA.

52. Ravitch, "Making Good Schools Worse," *NYT*, October 3, 1986; Perlez, "Opening Up Some Elite."
53. Gottlieb, "$500 Million Deal . . . ," *NYT*, January 24, 1985; Fiske, "Lessons: Letting Parents Choose . . . ," *NYT*, January 11, 1989; Diane Ravitch, *The Death and Life of the Great American School System: How Testing and Choice Are Undermining Education*, rev. ed. (New York, 2011), 8. On Bush's move from public school choice to vouchers, see Julie A. Miller, "Bush Stand on School Choice Is Seen Bolder," *EducationWeek*, September 9, 1992.
54. Chris McNickle, *The Power of the Mayor: David Dinkins, 1990–1993* (New Brunswick, NJ, 2013), 29. On the Koch-era scandals, see Soffer, *Ed Koch*, chap. 23. New York City AIDS Memorial's website contains a timeline of cases and deaths in the city; see https://www.nycaidsmemorial.org/timeline.
55. John Mollenkopf, "New York: The Great Anomaly," in Rufus P. Browning, Dale Rogers Marshall, and David H. Tabb, eds., *Racial Politics in American Cities*, 2nd ed. (New York, 1997), 106–9; John Hull Mollenkopf, *A Phoenix in the Ashes: The Rise and Fall of the Koch Coalition in New York City Politics*, 2nd ed. (Princeton, NJ, 1994), 172–73; Soffer, *Ed Koch*, 378–81.
56. See David N. Dinkins with Peter Knobler, *A Mayor's Life: Governing New York's Gorgeous Mosaic* (New York, 2013), 41–50, 56–66, 74–98.
57. Joe Klein, "Can Dinkins Do It?" *NY*, July 31, 1989, 33; Murray Kempton, "The Blame Trade Hits Another Low," *Newsday*, October 10, 1993.
58. Sandra Feldman, [handwritten notes, p. 3], UFT, Series VIII:B, Box 290, Folder 27, TL; David N. Dinkins, "Police Deployment Proposals," July 19, 1989; "Schools for Tomorrow: David Dinkins on Education," June 23, 1989; "Housing New Yorkers: David Dinkins's Agenda for Affordable Housing," n.d.; all in DD, Box 16, Folder 3, RBML.
59. Joshua B. Freeman, *Working-Class New York: Life and Labor Since World War II* (New York, 2000), 318–19; Joseph P. Viteritti, *The Pragmatist: Bill de Blasio's Quest to Save the Soul of New York* (New York, 2017), 108–9; Dinkins with Knobler, *Mayor's Life*, 134; David Duhalde, "What David Dinkins Taught Us," *Jacobin*, November 25, 2020. On pushback from UFT members, see the correspondence in UFT, Series VIII, Box 290, Folder 28, TL. I am grateful to Ruth Messinger for sharing her knowledge of and perspective on Dinkins's candidacy and mayoralty.
60. On Giuliani's early life and career, see Wayne Barrett, *Rudy! An Investigative Biography of Rudy Giuliani* (New York, 2001), 13–200. On his early political commitments, see also Jarrett Murphy, "Government: Do Mayors Matter? Race, Justice, and the Men in City Hall, 1965–2017," in Benjamin P. Bowser and Chelli Devadutt, eds., *Racial Inequality in New York City Since 1965* (Albany, NY, 2019), 92.

61. Helen Giuliani quoted in Barrett, *Rudy!*, 103; Jack Newfield, *The Full Rudy: The Man, the Myth, the Mania* (New York, 2007), 122; Clines, "Albany's Kingmaker . . . ," *NYT*, November 9, 1994; "Oral History Interview with Louis R. Anemone," 61, JNY, LSL; Elizabeth Kolbert, *The Prophet of Love: And Other Tales of Power and Deceit* (New York, 2004), 39, 44. See Jerald Podair, "'One City, One Standard': The Struggle for Equality in Rudolph Giuliani's New York," in Clarence Taylor, ed., *Civil Rights in New York City: From World War II to the Giuliani Era* (New York, 2011), esp. 217; Jonathan Rieder, *Canarsie: The Jews and Italians of Brooklyn Against Liberalism* (Cambridge, MA, 1985).
62. David Friedlander, "'They Saw the World in This Dog-Eat-Dog, Manichean Way,'" *Vanity Fair*, November 10, 2019. See also Andrew Kirtzman, *Giuliani: The Rise and Tragic Fall of America's Mayor* (New York, 2022), 89.
63. Carroll, "Trial Brightens Giuliani's Future," *Newsday*, November 26, 1986; Auletta, "Off to the Races with Rudy," *NYDN*, April 5, 1987; Adams, "Cindy Adams's Page Six," *NYP*, October 20, 1987; Smilon, "Rudy Holds onto Trump Card," *NYP*, November 21, 1987; Emery, "Wealthy NY Developer to Support Giuliani," *Watertown Daily Times*, November 22, 1987; Lombardi, "'Rudy Who?' . . . ," *NYDN*, December 21, 1987; Tomasky, "Moynihan Preferred to Giuliani . . . ," *NYO*, December 28, 1987; Kivlan, "Molinari Glum . . . ," *SIA*, February 9, 1988; Lynn, "Giuliani Is Said . . . ," *NYT*, December 7, 1988; Sleeper, "The Fall," *New Republic*, June 16, 2022 (1989 campaign). Moynihan's office started keeping a clipping file on Giuliani in April 1986: See DPM, Box II:67, Folders 14–17, Box II:68, Folders 1–2.
64. Barrett, *Rudy!*, 186, 189–93; McNickle, *Power of the Mayor*, 39, 43.
65. McNickle, *Power of the Mayor*, 44; Mollenkopf, *Phoenix in the Ashes*, 180–85; John Mollenkopf, "How 9/11 Reshaped the Political Environment in New York," in Mollenkopf, ed., *Contentious City: The Politics of Recovery in New York City* (New York, 2005), 217.
66. "The Dinkins Administration and the Puerto Rican Community: Lessons from the Puerto Rican Experience with African-American Mayors in Chicago and Philadelphia" (proceedings from a forum held December 13, 1989), DC, Series VII, Box 29, Folder 10, CCPRS.
67. Greg David, *Modern New York: The Life and Economics of a City* (New York, 2012), 51; Robert Fitch, *The Assassination of New York* (New York, 1993), 3–4; Freeman, *Working-Class New York*, 324.
68. Lorch, "Record Year for Killings . . . ," *NYT*, December 31, 1990. For the Dinkins administration's sense of the randomness of crime, see, e.g., "New York City Council Criminal Justice Program," n.d., DND, WL, Box 35, Folder 346, NYCMA.
69. "Bring Back the Death Penalty, Bring Back Our Police!" (advertisement), *NYDN*, May 1, 1989. The ad ran in the *Daily News*, *Newsday*, the *Post*, and the *Times*. See Foderaro, "Angered by Attack . . . ," *NYT*, May 1, 1989. For a sense of just how exploited, depressed, and brutalized disinvested neighborhoods had become by the mid-1990s, see Johanna Fernández, "The Fire This Time: Harlem and Its Discontents at the Turn of the Century," in Manning Marable, ed., *Dispatches from the Ebony Tower: Intellectuals Confront the African American Experience* (New York, 2000), chap. 5. The text alludes to Wu-Tang Clan, "C.R.E.A.M.," from *Enter the Wu-Tang (36 Chambers)* (1993).

70. "Welcome to NY," *NY: The City Journal* (Autumn 1990); Barrett, *Rudy!*, 259, 270; Newfield, *Full Rudy*, 65.

Chapter 4: Gorgeous Mosaic

1. As of this writing, Dinkins's inaugural address can be viewed at https://www.ny1.com/nyc/all-boroughs/politics/2020/11/24/watch--david-dinkins--inaugural-address.
2. Finder, "After Decades of Rises . . . ," *NYT*, November 28, 1990; "A Relic Called Rent Control," *NYT*, August 13, 1991.
3. Malcolm Gladwell, "Why We Must End Rent Control Now," *NY*, May 8, 1995, 38, 40–41.
4. "Remarks of Manhattan Borough President Ruth W. Messinger, Empire State Report Conference on Housing," February 28, 1992, in NYSTNC, Series 1, Box 4, Folder 27, UA. Demographic characteristics calculated by the author from 1993 HVS data in Rent Guidelines Board, *Housing NYC: Rents, Markets and Trends '96* (1996), 102–3, 108–10. *Rent regulated* in this paragraph refers specifically to rent-controlled and rent-stabilized tenants; i.e., it does not include the relatively small number of New Yorkers whose rents were regulated under the Mitchell-Lama program, through regulations on in-rem units, under certain HUD programs, by the city Loft Board, etc.
5. Passell, "Economic Scene: Perestroika for Renters," *NYT*, January 2, 1991; Peter D. Salins and Gerard Mildner, "Does Rent Control Help the Poor?" *CJ* (Winter 1991).
6. Citizens Budget Commission, *Reforming Residential Rent Regulations* (New York, 1991); "Tap the Treasure in Rent Control," *NYT*, April 9, 1991; Peterson, "Leading the Sacred Cow . . . ?" *NYT*, May 19, 1991. For a pro-regulation critique of the CBC's report, see Eric Weinstock, "Dismantling Rent Regulations: Fiscal Benefits or Fiscal Disaster? . . . ," (May 1991), MCH, Box 62, Folder "Housing Facts + Figures," TL.
7. Pérez-Peña, "Landlords Quietly . . . ," *NYT*, May 5, 1997; Sack, "A Test of Wills," *NYT*, June 17, 1993; Steinberg, "Questions About Wealthy . . . ," *NYT*, June 20, 1993; Dao, "Compromise Is Reached . . . ," *NYT*, July 4, 1993. See also the RSA's and CHIP's antiregulation ads in NYSTNC, Series 2, Box 1, Folders 13–16, UA. Marcelo Rochabrun and Cezary Podkul, "The Fateful Vote that Made New York City Rents So High," *ProPublica*, December 15, 2016, describes the RSA's insistence on significant reform: "The association told Guy Velella, a Republican senator from New York City, 'that if you renew the rent laws again without weakening amendments, we're not going to give you any money,' according to tenant lobbyist Mike McKee. McKee said that Vellela, who died in 2011, told him about the threat."
8. Perlez, "Year of Honor . . . ," *NYT*, June 27, 1987; U.S. Department of Education, *Schools That Work: Educating Disadvantaged Children* (Washington, DC, 1987); Seymour Fliegel with James MacGuire, *Miracle in East Harlem: The Fight for Choice in Public Education* (New York, 1993), 169; David Osborne and Ted Gaebler, *Reinventing Government: How the Entrepreneurial Spirit Is Transforming the Public Sector* (New York, 1992). British education policy in turn became an inspiration for neoconservative reformers within the United States. See, e.g., John Chubb

and Terry Moe, *A Lesson in School Reform from Great Britain* (Washington, DC, 1992); David Brooks, "Choosing Schools London Style," *CJ* (Winter 1991).

9. On the distinction between choice for equal opportunity and choice for competition, see Joseph P. Viteritti, *Choosing Equality: School Choice, the Constitution, and Civil Society* (New York, 1999). On the language of choice, see Jeffery R. Henig, *Rethinking School Choice: Limits of the Market Metaphor* (Princeton, NJ, 1995); Ansley Erickson, "The Rhetoric of Choice: Segregation, Desegregation, and Charter Schools," *Dissent* (Fall 2011); and Mary Pattillo, "Everyday Politics of School Choice in the Black Community," *Du Bois Review* 12, no. 1 (2015): 41–71.
10. Jim Sleeper to Deborah Meier, February 10, 1997, DM, Series: Correspondence, 1927–2009, Subseries: Professional, 1982–2009, Box 5, Folder "General—S," LL (emphasis in original), https://archives.iu.edu/catalog/InU-Li-VAB8339aspace_VAB8339-00185.
11. Deborah Meier, "Choice Can *Save* Public Education," *Nation*, March 4, 1991, 266, 268, 270.
12. Andrea Gabor, *After the Education Wars: How Smart Schools Upend the Business of Reform* (New York, 2018), 20, 43, 43.
13. Daniel T. Rodgers, *Age of Fracture* (Cambridge, MA, 2011), 214–19; Raymond Domanico, *Model for Choice: A Report on Manhattan's District 4: Education Policy Paper Number 1* (New York, 1989); Domanico, *Restructuring New York City's Public Schools: The Case for Public School Choice: Education Policy Paper Number 3* (New York, 1990); Domanico, *Putting the Carnegie Report on School Choice in Perspective* (New York, 1992); Domanico, *State of the New York City Public Schools, 2002* (New York, 2002); Public Education Association, "IAF Public School Parents and Community Leaders Demand Improvement from the Board of Education" (press release), March 19, 1997; Raymond Domanico to IAF Metro Organizers, March 23, 1998; Public Education Association, "Metro IAF Parents Charge Chancellor Crew with Delinquency in Educational Dead Zones" (press release), October 29, 1997; in "Raymond Domanico—Industrial Areas Foundation, 1996–1998," BOE, Series 901, Box 23, Series 6.7, Folder 2, NYCMA. For Milton Friedman's famous early call for a system of educational vouchers, see Milton Friedman, "The Role of Government in Education," in Robert Solo, ed., *Economics and the Public Interest* (New Brunswick, NJ, 1955). On the CEI's share of the Manhattan Institute budget, see *NYT*, May 12, 1997.
14. See John Chubb and Terry Moe, *Politics, Markets, and America's Schools* (Washington, DC, 1990). This paragraph quotes from the adapted version that ran in Terry Moe and John Chubb, "Letting Schools Work," *NY: The City Journal* (Autumn 1990).
15. Diane Ravitch and Joseph Viteritti, "Introduction," in Ravitch and Vitieritti, eds., *New Schools for a New Century: The Redesign of Urban Education* (New Haven, CT, 1999); Diane Ravitch, *The Death and Life of the Great American School System: How Testing and Choice Are Undermining Education*, rev. ed. (New York, 2011), 303n5. On small schools, see, e.g., Linda Darling-Hammond, "Restructuring Schools for Student Success," *Daedelus* 124, no. 4 (Fall 1995): 153–62. For a critical take, see Michael Klonsky and Susan Klonsky, *Small Schools: Public School Reform Meets the Ownership Society* (New York, 2008). For later, but pre-Bloomberg, advocacy for small high schools from left-of-center education reformers in New York, see

Norm Fruchter to Tony Coles, October 27, 1999, RWG, ES, Box 02/10/1/005, Folder 0124, NYCMA. On Clinton and the DLC's advocacy of charters, see Lily Geismer, *Left Behind: The Democrats' Failed Attempt to Solve Inequality* (New York, 2022), chap. 8.

16. Berger, "Fernandez to Let Students . . . ," *NYT*, September 16, 1992; Sengupta, "Public Schools: Choice or Chance?" *NYT*, January 5, 1997; Barbanel, "Board of Education Votes . . . ," *NYT*, January 14, 1993; Mark Walsh, "N.Y.C. Choice Plan Will Open Boundaries of 800 Schools," *EducationWeek*, September 23, 1992; "Questions and Answers on New York City Public School Choice, November 23, 1992," in RP, Series VI, Box 39, Folder 2, CCPRS.

17. Dillon, "Friction Over Experimental Schools," *NYT*, May 25, 1995; Mosle, "A City School Experiment . . . ," *NYT*, May 28, 1995; Steinberg, "Top Educator Is Leaving . . . ," *NYT*, October 5, 1996; Rudolph F. Crew to Members of the Board of Education, "Memorandum: Symposium on New Schools," April 30, 1998, RFC, Series 1150, Box 1150.1, Folder "[April 1998]," BOE, NYCMA; Gabor, *After the Education Wars*, 66; Gootman and Herszenhorn, "Getting Small . . . ," *NYT*, May 3, 2005. For the application process, see materials in UFT, Series VIII:B, Box 294, Folder 29. On the role of philanthropy in education reform, see Sarah Reckhow, *Follow the Money: How Foundation Dollars Change Public School Politics* (New York, 2013). See also Ansley Erickson, "Who Decides? Governing New York City Schools Since the Late 1960s," in Johanna Fernández, Kim Phillips-Fein, and Mason B. Williams, eds., *Gotham on the Verge* (Chapel Hill, forthcoming).

18. New York City Coalition for Excellence in Black Education, "An Open Letter to the Press and the New York City Education Community," March 27, 1995, in DC, Series VII, Box 27, Folder 2, CCPRS; Diana Caballero to Heather Lewis, April 5, 1995, DC, Series VII, Box 27, Folder 2, CCPRS.

19. Allison Roda and Amy Stuart Wells, "School Choice Policies and Racial Segregation: Where White Parents' Good Intentions, Anxiety, and Privilege Collide," *American Journal of Education* 119, no. 2 (February 2013), 273; Stone, "Gifted Children's Programs . . . ," *NYT*, May 6, 1990. See also Allison Roda, *Inequality in Gifted and Talented Programs: Parental Choices About Status, School Opportunity, and Second-Generation Segregation* (New York, 2015).

20. "Remarks by Governor Mario M. Cuomo, Citizens' Crime Commission, New York City, Tuesday, September 11, 1990," in DND, WL, Box 35, Folder 343, NYCMA.

21. Brown recounts his life and career in Lee P. Brown with Joseph Green-Bishop, *Outhouse to the White House* (Bloomington, IN, 2022). For his career in Atlanta, see Danielle Wiggins, "'Order as Well as Decency': The Development of Order Maintenance Policing in Black Atlanta," *JUH* 46, no. 4 (July 2020): 711–27. On the Kennedy School, see Christopher Stone and Jeremy Travis, *Toward a New Professionalism in Policing* (Cambridge, MA, 2011).

22. Ray Kelly, *Vigilance: My Life Serving America and Protecting Its Empire City* (New York, 2015), 9–21, 26–43, 69–72 (quote at 71); Eric Pooley, "Bulldog," *NY*, February 22, 1993, 39.

23. David N. Dinkins to Lee P. Brown, August 6, 1990, DND, NS, Box 22, Folder 171, NYCMA; Brown, *Policing New York City in the 1990s: The Strategy for Community Policing* (January 1991), 5; Raymond W. Kelly, *Crime Control Plan: A Citizen/Police Partnership* (c. 1993), 5.

24. George L. Kelling, "The Contagion of Public Disorder," *CJ* (Spring 1991); Kelly, *Crime Control Plan*, 6.
25. Kelly, *Crime Control Plan*, 9.
26. Jerome E. McElroy, Colleen A. Cosgrove, and Susan Sadd, *CPOP: The Research: An Evaluative Study of the New York City Community Patrol Officer Program* (New York, 1990), chap. 7, at 137, 154. For instance, 80 percent of "community leaders" in Sunset Park were white and the "vast majority" were homeowners (137).
27. Dinkins to Brown, August 6, 1990, DND, NS, Box 22, Folder 171, NYCMA; "Mayor David N. Dinkins Unveils Omnibus 'Safe Streets, Safe City' Anti-Crime Program . . ." (press release), October 2, 1990, DND, WL, Box 35, Folder 343; Blumenthal, "Dinkins on Crime . . . ," *NYT*, October 3, 1990; "Oral History Interview with Jeremy Travis," 57, JNY, LSL; *Safe Streets, Safe City: An Omnibus Criminal Justice Program for the City of New York* (New York, 1990); Chris McNickle, *The Power of the Mayor: David Dinkins, 1990–1993* (New Brunswick, NJ, 2013), 74–75, 215–17; Themis Chronopoulos, "The Making of the Orderly City: New York Since the 1980s," *JUH* 46, no. 5 (September 2020): 1097; Sack, "Dinkins Crime Plan . . . ," *NYT*, February 8, 1991; Office of the State Comptroller, "Action Needed to Make the 'Safe Streets, Safe City' Program More Effective" (June 1994), ES-1. For Dinkins's account of the negotiations, see David N. Dinkins with Peter Knobler, *A Mayor's Life: Governing New York's Gorgeous Mosaic* (New York, 2013), 214–20.

    Though most of the opposition to the proposal came from Republicans, Safe Streets, Safe City did engender some opposition from community organizations which, though supportive of community policing in general, believed that the additional police hires would crowd out spending on youth programs and other nonpolice antiviolence measures. See City Project, press release, October 1, 1990, and Penelope W. Pi-Sunyer to Dinkins, October 18, 1990, both in DND, WL, Box 35, Folder 343, NYCMA; see also City Project, *Crime Prevention and Public Safety: A Plan That Will Work* (New York, 1990); J. Phillip Thompson III, *Double Trouble: Black Mayors, Black Communities, and the Call for a Deep Democracy* (New York, 2006), 201–4.
28. Alex S. Vitale, *City of Disorder: How the Quality of Life Campaign Transformed New York Politics* (New York, 2008), 131, 140, 160.
29. Dinkins to Brown, June 21, 1991, DND, WL, Box 3, Folder 34, NYCMA; McNickle, *Power of the Mayor*, 268–270; Kilborn, "New York Police Force . . . ," *NYT*, July 17, 1994.
30. Aaron K. Rosenthal to Ray Kelly, February 5, 1993; Rosenthal to Kelly, February 17, 1993; Rosenthal to Kelly, July 15, 1993; all in LPB, Box 41, Folder 16, WRC; John Marzulli, "Community Cops Program a Bust," *NYDN*, January 24, 1994; Brown quoted in William J. Bratton with Peter Knobler, *Turnaround: How America's Top Cop Reversed the Crime Epidemic* (New York, 1998), xi.
31. Joseph G. Rappaport and Gene Russianoff to Editorial Page Editor, *NYT*, February 5, 1990, and Russianoff and Rappaport to Robert Kiley and Alan F. Kiepper, March 2, 1990, both in SC, Box 4, Folder 6, NYPL; Thomas Dyja, *New York, New York, New York: Four Decades of Excess, Success, and Transformation* (New York, 2021), 176; George Kelling, "Reclaiming the Subway," *CJ* (Winter 1991). See Kelling's account of his work in George L. Kelling and Catherine M. Coles,

Fixing Broken Windows: Restoring Order and Reducing Crime in Our Communities (New York, 1998), 109–10, 114–37.

32. William J. Bratton, "*City Journal* Interview: Victory in the Subways," *CJ* (Summer 1992); Bratton with Knobler, *Turnaround*, 94–95, 138–39, 142.
33. "Summary Statement of William J. Bratton . . . ," September 13, 1990," SC, Box 31, Folder 11, NYPL; Bratton with Knobler, *Turnaround*, 143, 154–56; Bratton, "*City Journal* Interview."
34. Bratton with Knobler, *Turnaround*, 153.
35. Bratton, "*City Journal* Interview."
36. Jonathan Soffer, *Ed Koch and the Rebuilding of New York City* (New York, 2010), 340–42, 345–47; James "Police and Protesters Clash . . . ," *NYT*, May 2, 1990 ("121 complaints"); "Oral History Interview with Jeremy Travis," 60, JNY, LSL; Milton Mollen, Chair, *Commission to Investigate Allegations of Police Corruption and the Anti-Corruption Procedures of the Police Department: Commission Report* (New York, 1994), in Gabriel J. Chin, ed., *New York City Police Corruption Investigation Commissions, 1894–1994* (Buffalo, NY, 1997), 6:10–33, 152–54.
37. Purdum, "A Dinkins Account . . . ," *NYT*, September 19, 1992; Lynn, "Rivals Clash . . . ," *NYT*, August 2, 1989; Roberts, "Brutal Question . . . ," *NYT*, March 21, 1991; McKinley, "Debate on Police Board . . . ," *NYT*, March 27, 1991; Hevesi, "14 on Council . . . ," *NYT*, January 23, 1992; Gottlieb, "Dinkins Will Seek . . . ," *NYT*, June 25, 1992; McKinley, "Dinkins Names . . . ," *NYT*, June 26, 1992.
38. On the 1992 uprising in Washington Heights, see Pedro A. Regalado, "The Washington Heights Uprising of 1992: Dominican Belonging and Urban Policing in New York City," *JUH* 45, no. 5 (September 2019): 961–86. For an overview of the 1992 riot, see Laura Nahmias, "The Forgotten City Hall Riot," *NY*, October 4, 2021. For contemporary accounts, see James C. McKinley, Jr., "Officers Rally . . . ," *NYT*, September 17, 1992 (sign slogans); Liff and Cottman, "Dinkins Slams Rowdy Police . . . ," *Newsday*, September 18, 1992 (Adams and Dinkins quotes). Adams describes his own experiences with the NYPD in "Oral History Interview with Eric Adams, Pt. 1," 2015, GOHP, CCOHC, RBML.
39. McKinley, "Middle Ground Is Sought . . . ," *NYT*, September 22, 1992; Hicks, "Dinkins Announces Accord . . . ," *NYT*, October 30, 1992.
40. For Dinkins as a challenge to the post-fiscal-crisis order, see John Hull Mollenkopf, *A Phoenix in the Ashes: The Rise and Fall of the Koch Coalition in New York City Politics*, 2nd ed. (Princeton, NJ, 1994), 172–73; Nick Juravich, "Ghosts of Party Past: New York's Last Two Democratic Mayors and the 2013 Election," *Dissent* (May 2013). On Dinkins's continuities with the post-fiscal-crisis order, see Freeman, *Working-Class New York*, 324–25; and Kim Phillips-Fein, "New York's Austerity Man," *Public Books*, December 15, 2013. Clarence Taylor, *Fight the Power: African Americans and the Long History of Police Brutality in New York City* (New York, 2019), 160–62, 164, 168–72, emphasizes Dinkins's police accountability efforts. On Dinkins's role in legitimating and advancing quality-of-life policing, see esp. Vitale, *City of Disorder*, esp. chap. 6. Other important works on Dinkins's mayoralty include Thompson, *Double Trouble*, chaps. 5–7; Wilbur C. Rich, *David Dinkins and New York City Politics: Race, Images, and the Media* (Albany, NY, 2007); and McNickle, *Power of the Mayor*.
41. See the FBI figures cited and discussed in McNickle, *Power of the Mayor*, 354–56.

42. Bob Dole, "Foreword," in Alfonse D'Amato, *Power, Pasta, and Politics: The World According to Senator Al D'Amato* (New York, 1995), xii (and Koch's introduction); Lynn, "Aggressive Tactics . . . ," *NYT*, October 20, 1986; Jennifer Senior, "La Dolce Alfonse," *NY*, August 23, 1999; Oreskes, "Cuomo's Solo Campaign . . . ," *NYT*, November 6, 1986. The most extensive work on D'Amato is Leonard Lurie, *Senator Pothole: The Unauthorized Biography of Al D'Amato* (New York, 1994).
43. Wayne Barrett, *Rudy! An Investigative Biography of Rudy Giuliani* (New York, 2001), 201–13; McNickle, *Power of the Mayor*, 25–28.
44. Barrett, *Rudy!*, 250–56.
45. Redburn, "Conservative Thinkers Are Insiders," *NYT*, December 31, 1993. On Giuliani during the 1989 campaign, see Jennifer Raab's recollections in Fred Siegel with Harry Siegel, *The Prince of the City: Giuliani, New York and the Genius of American Life* (San Francisco, 2005), 28.
46. Redburn, "Conservative Thinkers Are Insiders"; Traub, "Intellectual Stock Picking," *NYer*, February 7, 1994, 36–42; McNickle, *Power of the Mayor*, 305.
47. Traub, "Intellectual Stock Picking," 36; [Roger Starr], "Editor's Journal," *CJ* (Spring 1992); George L. Kelling, "Measuring What Matters: A New Way of Thinking About Crime and Public Order," *CJ* (Spring 1992); Fred Siegel, "Reclaiming Our Public Spaces," *CJ* (Spring 1992); Colman Genn and Ray Domanico, "Putting Schools First: Changing the Board of Ed's Priorities," *CJ* (Spring 1992); Peter D. Salins, "Correcting New York's Housing Mistakes," *CJ* (Spring 1992).
48. Siegel with Siegel, *Prince of the City*, 72; McNickle, *Power of the Mayor*, 305–6; Dyja, *New York, New York, New York*, 214 ("plagiarize mine"); Kevin Baker, "Worse than Bush: Rudolph Giuliani and the Politics of Personality," *Harper's*, August 2007, 35; Christoper M. Lyon and Ronald A. Giller, "Rudolph W. Giuliani Vulnerability Study: Prepared for Giuliani for New York, April 8, 1993), A-79. See Fred Smith and Jarrett Murphy, "Meet the New Rudy, Same as the Old Rudy? 1993 Study Exposed Vulnerabilities Now on View," *City Limits*, January 13, 2020.
49. McNickle, *Power of the Mayor*, 280–81; Michael X. Delli Carpini, "Analysis of Dinkins' 'Loyalists' and 'Switchers,'" September 28, 1993, 12, DD, Box 32, Folder 8, RBML.
50. "Analysis of Johnson Poll Data: The Preelection Mood," n.d., 16–17, DD, Box 32, Folder 9, RBML; McNickle, *Power of the Mayor*, 324–25, 346; Michael Tomasky, "The Tawdry Mosaic: Identity Politics in New York City," *Nation*, June 21, 1993. See J. Phillip Thompson's analysis of Dinkins's 1993 campaign in Thompson, *Double Trouble*, 234–39 (and chaps. 7–8 more broadly).
51. McNickle, *Power of the Mayor*, 307–8; Daniel Patrick Moynihan, *Miles to Go: A Personal History of Social Policy* (Cambridge, MA, 1996), 165; Liff, "Pat's All Square with the Mayor," *Newsday*, April 10, 1993; "Statement of Sen. Daniel Patrick Moynihan (D.–N.Y.)" (press release), September 26, 1993, DPM, Box IV:42, Folder 6, LOC: *City Journal* reprinted Moynihan's remarks; see Daniel Patrick Moynihan, "No Surrender: Toward Intolerance of Crime," *CJ* (Summer 1993). See also Moynihan, "Defining Deviancy Down," *American Scholar* 62, no. 1 (Winter 1993): 17–30.

After the election, one future Giuliani administration figure wrote to another that Moynihan was "very supportive of Rudy. He told me that he had to endorse Dinkins, but would really like to work with us." Moynihan responded that he had "very much wanted David Dinkins to win the election." Seifman and Dicker, "Dyson Memo . . . ," *NYP*, February 11, 1994. See also "Statement of Sen. Daniel Patrick Moynihan (D.-N.Y.)" (press release), February 10, 1994, DPM, Box IV:42, Folder 6, LOC.

52. See Mario Cuomo to Ralph Marino, March 19, 1990; Cuomo, untitled press release, June 27, 1990; in MMC, Microfilm Roll 28, Folder "Elections–Initiative & Referendum–1/1/90–12/31/90," NYSA; McNickle, *Power of the Mayor*, 302–3, 311–13, 330; Barrett, *Rudy!*, 275–77. On Staten Island's politics in relation to the city as a whole, see Daniel C. Kramer and Richard M. Flanagan, *Staten Island: Conservative Bastion in a Liberal City* (Lanham, MD, 2012).
53. Ross, "Koch Endorses Giuliani," *NYDN*, October 15, 1993; Manegold, "Assailing Dinkins . . . ," *NYT*, October 15, 1993.
54. Manegold, "Assailing Dinkins"; Purdum, "Giuliani Campaign Theme . . . ," *NYT*, October 24, 1993; Ross, "Koch Endorses Giuliani"; Roberts, "After Wagner's Death . . . ," *NYT*, November 22, 1993.
55. Mollenkopf, *Phoenix in the Ashes*, 210–12; Yang, "Giuliani Admits Using 'Dirty Trick' . . . ," *Guardian*, April 29, 2023.
56. E.g., Julius C. C. Edelstein to Robert F. Wagner, Jr., November 11, 1993; Richard F. Ropiak to Wagner, November 5, 1993; both in RFWJ, Box 060117W, Folder 21, LWA; Roberts, "Robert F. Wagner, Jr. . . . ," *NYT*, November 22, 1993; Treaster, "Autopsy Is Inconclusive . . . ," *NYT*, November 19, 1993; Roberts, "After Wagner's Death"; Laird, "New York Loses . . . ," *NYDN*, November 18, 1993; "A Son of New York," *NYDN*, November 17, 1993.
57. Perry, "Look! Could that Be the Spin Doctor . . . ?" *WSJ*, September 28, 1994; Lombardi, "Pataki & Cuomo Gurus . . . ," *NYDN*, June 10, 1994; Nagourney, "New York's Stealth Governor . . . ," *NYT Magazine*, March 16, 1997; Roberts, "Arthur Finkelstein . . . ," *NYT*, August 19, 2017; Hannes Grassegger, "The Finkelstein Formula," *Das Magazin*, January 12, 2019; Charles Francis, "Secretive Arthur Finkelstein . . . ," *Washington Blade*, September 27, 2022. Finkelstein described his approach on a panel at the eighteenth annual CPAC conference: https://www.youtube.com/watch?v=YGCojpON5Bo.
58. Bruce N. Gyory to Armand D'Amato, November 20, 1987; Armand D'Amato to Arthur J. Finkelstein, November 24, 1987; Finkelstein to Armand D'Amato, December 4, 1987; all in AJF, Box 15, Folder "D'Amato, Alfonse—General—1987–1989," LOC; Nagourney, "New York's Stealth Governor"; Maxfield and Schlesinger, "As the World Spins," *Mother Jones*, March–April 1997, 15; Joseph Bruno, *Keep Swinging: A Memoir of Politics and Justice* (New York, 2016), 66.
59. "Giuliani Talks . . . ," *NYT*, October 25, 1994; Barrett, *Rudy!*, 301, 303; Purdum, "As State Split . . . ," *NYT*, November 10, 1994.
60. Nagourney, "New York's Stealth Governor"; Bruno, *Keep Swinging*, 66–79.
61. Barrett, *Rudy!*, 310–11.

Chapter 5: The Republican Moment

1. Marcelo Rochabrun and Cezary Podkul, "The Fateful Vote that Made New York City Rents So High," *ProPublica*, December 15, 2016, offers an excellent history of the 1994 law; Malavé Dilan quote is from this article. Spigner, Ognibene, and

Eldridge quotes are from "Public Hearing on the Local Laws, Re: Introductory Number 220 (Rent Bill)," March 30, 1994, 7, 17, 27–28, RWG, CLA, Box 13/001, Folder 0005, NYCMA. (Stanley Michels emphasized joint living in the same hearing, p. 9.) For the tenant movement's sense that Vallone had become unreliable, see "Tenant Meeting with Council Speaker Peter Vallone, Friday, December 13, 1991—9:00 AM" (handwritten notes on reverse), NYSTNC, Series I, Box 4, Folder 15, UA; Local Laws of the City of New York for the Year 1994, no. 4. On the role of Vallone's former chief of staff, see Robbins, "Ex-Council Aide . . . ," *NYDN*, March 15, 1994. The breakdown of the council vote may be found in RWG, CLA, Box 13/001, Folder 0005, NYCMA. For additional council testimony on the measure, see CCNYC, Series: Committee Files, Box 050135, Folder 29; and CCNYC, Series: Committee Files, Box 050136, Folders 1–3, LWA.

For Cuomo's statement opposing the 1994 council bill, see Office of the Governor of the State of New York, press release, March 10, 1994, MCH, Box 47, Folder "City Council Campaign '94," TL. See also the more substantive statement from state housing director Donald M. Halperin in Halperin to Peter F. Vallone, March 15, 1994, MCH, Box 47, Folder "City Council Campaign '94," TL, as well as Halperin's testimony to the City Council on Cuomo's behalf. On the tenant movement's attitudes toward Cuomo, see for instance Jenny Laurie to Brian Lawler, June 3, 1994, MCH, Box 47, Folder "Albany 1994," TL.

Though deregulation proponents did not draw the connection explicitly, the reference to "signals" echoed an argument that economists had begun to make that rent regulation impeded new construction (even if the resulting units would be unregulated) because sharp movements in rents sent signals to investors about which housing markets merited new investment. See Anthony Downs, *Residential Rent Controls: An Evaluation* (1988). Note that after MBR, and especially as more units moved from rent control to rent stabilization, New York moved from a "strict" regime to a "temperate" one in Downs's typology.

2. Rochabrun and Podkul, "Fateful Vote"; "Mayor Announces Intent to Sign Rent Stabilization Bill" (press release), March 23, 1994, in MCH, Box 47, Folder "City Council Campaign '94," TL; "Public Hearing on the Local Laws, Re: Introductory Number 220 (Rent Bill)," March 30, 1994, 3–4, 50, RWG, CLA, Box 13/001, Folder 0005, NYCMA. See also Martha K. Hirst to Jack T. Linn, n.d., in the same folder, relaying Commissioner Deborah Wright's preference for a straight extender ("this is not the fight to have"). On the Giuliani administration's deliberations about how to proceed, see Jack Linn to Rudolph W. Giuliani, March 11, 1994, RWG, PP, Box 02/01/014, Folder 0513, NYCMA.
3. Hevesi, "As Battle Looms . . . ," *NYT*, June 16, 1996; Joseph Bruno, *Keep Swinging: A Memoir of Politics and Justice* (New York, 2016), 114; Pérez-Peña, "G.O.P. Leader Urges . . . ," *NYT*, December 6, 1996; "Landlord Offerings to Senate Republicans," NYSTNC, Series 3, Box 9, Folder 21, UA. Assemblyman Pete Grannis of Manhattan, the long-serving chairman of the Assembly Housing Committee, leaked the transition team's report calling for immediate deregulation of buildings with twenty or fewer units and vacancy deregulation for the rest. See "Grannis Blats Secret Pataki Housing Report" (press release), January 27, 1995, in MCH, Box 47, Folder "Pataki 94-95," TL.
4. Geoffrey Gray, "The Obstructionist," *NY*, May 30, 2008; Gerald Benjamin, "The

New York State Legislature—On Balance," in Daniel L. Feldman and Gerald Benjamin, *Tales from the Sausage Factory: Making Laws in New York State* (Albany, NY, 2010), 309.

5. See Gerald Benjamin and Robert C. Lawton, "New York's Governorship: Back to the Future?" in Jeffrey M. Stonecash, ed., *Governing New York State* (Albany, NY, 2001), 137. On Silver's opposition to the construction of new affordable housing on the Lower East Side, see Buettner, "They Kept a Lower East Side Lot . . . ," *NYT*, March 21, 2014.
6. Karen Ceraso, "Mike McKee on Winning the Rent Control Battle," *Shelterforce*, July/August 1997, 25–26; Pérez-Peña, "G.O.P. Leader Urges . . . ," *NYT*, December 6, 1996. The best overview of the 1997 rent war is Craig Gurian, "Let Them Rent Cake: George Pataki, Market Ideology, and the Attempt to Dismantle Rent Regulation in New York," *Fordham Urban Law Journal* 31, no. 2 (2004): 339–411.
7. "Pataki Urges Gradual End . . . ," *NYT*, December 12, 1996.
8. R. Eric Petersen and Jeffrey M. Stonecash, "The Legislature, Parties, and Resolving Conflict," in Stonecash, ed., *Governing New York State*, 156–59; Ceraso, "Mike McKee on Winning the Rent Control Battle," *Shelterforce*, July 1, 1997; Hernandez, "In Battle over Rent Law. . . ," *NYT*, April 7, 1997; Pérez-Peña, "Albany Rally . . . ," *NYT*, May 21, 1997; Nagourney, "Ads Seek to . . . ," *NYT*, April 28, 1997; "The Ad Campaign: Tenant Groups . . . ," *NYT*, May 16, 1997; John Cardinal O'Connor, "Regulating/Deregulating Rent and the Right to Affordable Housing: A Moral Reflection," May 11, 1997, NYSTNC, Series 3, Box 10, Folder 8, UA.
9. "Governor Pataki Offers Responsible Plan to Protect Tenants" (press release), May 12, 1997, in MCH, Box 57, Folder "RRRA '97," TL; Dao, "Pataki Urges . . . ," *NYT*, May 13, 1997; Kolbert, "Great Divide Is Widening . . . ," *NYT*, May 22, 1997.
10. See for instance the tenant campaign's efforts to persuade Roy Goodman, the Republican senator from the Upper East Side and a supporter of the rent laws, to expend more political capital in the effort to get them extended. "There is no way to threaten Goodman in an election," one tenant strategist wrote. "He eats up his opponents. . . . It seems that you have to play to his pride. He can be this year's knight in shining armor. Bruno can't touch him." "Bobby" to "Scott," n.d., MCH, Box 57, Folder "Roy Goodman," NYMA.
11. Ceraso, "Mike McKee on Winning the Rent Control Battle," 27; Stanley W. Hill to "Dear Brothers and Sisters," April 10, 1997; New York State Tenants and Neighbors Coalition, "Tap Into Tenant Power! Sign Up for Tenants and Neighbors Phonebank" (flyer), n.d.; both in MCH, Box 57, "1997 Tenant Lobby Days," TL.
12. See the materials on the 1997 lobbying campaign in MCH, Box 57, Folder "1997 Tenant Lobby Days," TL.
13. Pérez-Peña, "If Legislators Allow . . . ," *NYT*, June 9, 1997; Bouzas, "Realizan marcha en favor de control de alquileres," *ED-LP*, June 13, 1997; Kennedy, "Act Honorably . . . ," *NYT*, June 11, 1997; Kennedy, "Rent-Law Plan Is Criticized . . . ," *NYT*, June 6, 1997; Firestone, "Rent Regulations . . . ," *NYT*, June 11, 1997; Newfield, "Once Again, David Has Beaten Goliath," *NYP*, June 17, 8.
14. *New York State Laws of 1997, Chapter 116*; Michael McKee, "How the Landlords Weakened Our Rent Laws: How Tenants Lost—And How We Can Win Back What We Have Lost," pp. 15–19, in MCH, Box 62, Folder "R 3 (Current)," TL;

Martha E. Stark and Doug Turetsky, "Homeward Bound: A Twenty-first-Century Affordable Housing Agenda for New York," in John Mollenkopf and Ken Emerson, eds., *Rethinking the Urban Agenda: Reinvigorating the Liberal Tradition in New York City and Urban America* (New York, 2001), 147; Bruno, *Keep Swinging*, 115–16; Dao and Pérez-Peña, "Rent War Redux . . . ," *NYT*, June 29, 1997. For Silver's and Pataki's statements on the legislation, see "Silver Declares Victory for Tenants" (press release), June 19, 1997, and "Governor Pataki Announces Final Agreement on Rent Legislation" (press release), June 19, 1997, both in NYSTNC, Series 3, Box 11, Folder 1, UA.

15. Fred Siegel with Harry Siegel, *The Prince of the City: Giuliani, New York and the Genius of American Life* (San Francisco, 2005), 92–94, 190–92 (on Wright and in rem); Stark and Turetsky, "Homeward Bound," 135, 139; Citizens Budget Commission, *Stabilizing the Foundation: Transforming NYCHA to Address Its Capital Needs* (2018); Robert Neuwirth and Rachana Sheth, *New York's Housing Underground: A Refuge and a Resource* (March 2008), cited in Michael R. Glass, "Hidden Apartments: Informal Housing in Metropolitan New York," in Johanna Fernández, Kim Phillips-Fein, and Mason B. Williams, eds., *Gotham on the Verge* (Chapel Hill, NC, forthcoming).
16. Clara Hemphill, *New York City's Best Public High Schools: A Parents' Guide* (New York, 2001).
17. Hemphill, "The Kindergarten Shuffle," *NYT*, April 3, 2005; Richardson, "Desperately Seeking a School," *NYT*, September 25, 1994; Sengupta, "Public Schools: Choice or Chance?" *NYT*, January 5, 1997.
18. Amin, "With Glaring PTA Fundraising Inequities . . . ," Chalkbeat.org, November 27, 2019; Amin and Zimmer, "Find Out How Much . . . ," Chalkbeat .org, December 2, 2019; Kershaw, "An Influx of Queens Students," *NYT*, October 8, 1995; Sengupta, "Parents Say . . . ," *NYT*, December 22, 1996.
19. Sengupta, "In Queens . . . ," *NYT*, February 23, 1999; Lii, "Magnet School Plans . . . ," *NYT*, December 10, 1995.
20. Steinberg, "Parents Fight Plan . . . ," *NYT*, December 1, 1995; Allon, "Gifted Get Marching Orders . . . ," *NYT*, October 13, 1996; Allon, "Parents Win . . . ," *NYT*, January 4, 1998.
21. Hartocollis, "Parents Want . . . ," *NYT*, October 11, 2000.
22. Hartocollis, "New Manhattan High School . . . ," *NYT*, June 12, 2001; Hartocollis, "Board Backs a New School . . . ," *NYT*, November 29, 2001; "Welcome to the Online School Quality Snapshot," New York City Public Schools, https://tools.nycenet.edu/snapshot/2020/02M416/HS/; "Student Data," Student and Educator Report 2017–18, Eleanor Roosevelt High School, https://data.nysed .gov/studenteducator.php?year=2018&instid=800000056094. See also Disare, "How One Manhattan District Has Preserved Its Own Set of Elite High Schools," Chalkbeat.org, June 7, 2018.
23. Zernike, "What New York Schools Get . . . ," *NYT*, February 14, 2001; Norm Fruchter and Christina Mokhtar-Ross, "Historic Steps Toward Funding Equity for NYC's Students," Steinhart.nyu.edu, [n.d.]; Norm Fruchter, "Millennial Prospects: Educating All New Yorkers," in Mollenkopf and Emerson, eds., *Rethinking the Urban Agenda*, 208–10, 217; Hevesi, "Louis Armstrong . . . ," *NYT*, March 26, 1995.

24. See Daniel S. Moak, *From the New Deal to the War on Schools: Race, Inequality, and the Rise of the Punitive Education State* (Chapel Hill, NC, 2022). In 1995, the state Department of Education began pushing the city to take "corrective action" in seventeen low-performing schools, making their continued state registration contingent on meeting certain student performance targets. See Richard P. Mills to Carol Gresser, October 18, 1995, RPM, Box 9, Folder 11, NYSA.
25. Board of Education, City of New York, Executive Session Minutes, May 7, 1997, RFC, Series 1150, Box 1150.2, Folder "[Board Meeting, May 7, 1997]," BOE, NYCMA; Sengupta, "District 26 to Defer . . . ," *NYT*, February 2, 1997.
26. Sengupta, "New York's Chancellor . . . ," *NYT*, February 28, 1997; Belluck, "At Top School . . . ," *NYT*, Mar 12, 1997; Sengupta, "Programs for Gifted Favor Whites . . . ," *NYT*, June 18, 1998; Phoebe V. Redmond to Rudolph F. Crew et al., "Memorandum: Settlement of ACORN OCR Complaint," October 16, 1997, and Linda Colón to Crew, "Re: Case no. 02-96-1118," September 25, 1997, New York City Board of Education Counsel Office, "Access to Information About Schools and Programs," October 21, 1997, all in RFC, Series 1150, Box 1150.3, Folder "[October 22 Executive Session Minutes]," BOE, NYCMA; Belluck, "More Minority Students . . . ," *NYT*, May 8, 1997. See also Margaret R. Harrington to Crew, "Memorandum: Comparison of 1997 and 1998 Specialized Science High School Admissions Data," March 27, 1998, RFC, Series 1150, Box 1150.1, Folder "[April 1998]," BOE, NYCMA.
27. Diane Ravitch, *Slaying Goliath: The Passionate Resistance to Privatization* (New York, 2020), 131–33 (Peterson at 132). On national Democrats' support for charter schools, see Lily Geismer, *Left Behind: The Democrats' Failed Attempt to Solve Inequality* (New York, 2022), chap. 8.
28. "Steering Committee / Sponsors Meeting, September 5, 1995 . . . New York Networks for School Renewal" (meeting notes), 4, UFT, Series VIII:B, Box 288, Folder 10, TL; "New York Networks for School Renewal: An Innovative Model for Systemic School Change," 3, UFT, Series VIII:B, Box 295, Folder 10, TL; Steinberg, "Crew Agrees . . . ," *NYT*, October 24, 1996; "New York City Board of Education 1998 Legislative Agenda," 4, 6, in RFC, Series 1150, Box 1150.1, Folder "April 1," BOE, NYCMA.
29. Sol Stern, "The School Reform that Dares Not Speak Its Name," *CJ* (Winter 1996); Stern, "The Invisible Miracle of Catholic Schools," *CJ* (Winter 1996). On Stern, see Tierney, "Unlikely Voice . . . ," *NYT*, March 8, 1999. Admiration for Catholic schools, building on James Coleman's influential research, also informed Diane Ravitch's interest in school choice. See Diane Ravitch, *The Death and Life of the Great American School System: How Testing and Choice Are Undermining Education*, rev. ed. (New York, 2011), 127. On Coleman's influence on the voucher movement, see Daniel T. Rodgers, *Age of Fracture* (Cambridge, MA, 2011), 218–20.
30. Hernandez, "Charter Schools Gaining Support," *NYT*, February 28, 1998; "Failure of Public Schools in Educational 'Dead Zone,'" *New York Beacon*, April 22, 1998; "Las escuelas Alternativas son una Buena Idea," *ED-LP*, January 17, 1997; "Una Buena alternativa en educación pública," *ED-LP*, March 18, 1998. For the vote on the 1998 charter school law, see "NYS Bill and Veto Jackets: 1998, Chapter 4," NYSA, https://digitalcollections.archives.nysed.gov/index.php/

Detail/objects/32292. As of the 1994–95 school year, students of Hispanic background made up some 37.8 percent of all elementary school students and 21.7 percent of students in gifted-and-talented programs. "Programs Serving Gifted and Talented Students in New York City Public Schools, 1995–1996," Table 1, 6, RFC, Series 1150, Box 1150.2, Folder "Board Meeting, March 5, 1997," BOE, NYCMA. On the community politics of charter schools in Harlem, see Basil Smikle, Jr., "Regimes, Reform, and Race: The Politics of Charter School Growth and Sustainability in Harlem" (Ph.D. diss., Columbia University, 2019).

31. Noliwe Rooks, *Cutting School: The Segrenomics of American Education*, 2nd ed. (New York, 2020), 30–31; Hartocollis, "Test-Tube Babies . . . ," *NYT*, January 3, 1999.

32. Hernandez, "Pataki Proposes . . . ," *NYT*, January 13, 1997; Hernandez, "Legislature Presses . . . ," *NYT*, June 18, 1998; Pérez-Peña, "Albany Passes . . . ," June 19, 1998. On the CEI's role, see Hartocollis, "8 Charter Schools . . . ," *NYT*, June 16, 1999. For the CEI's model charter school legislation, see Center for Educational Innovation, "Model Charter School Legislation," in RPM, Box 36, Folder 4, NYSA.

33. Hernandez, "In Albany, Quiet Clamor . . . ," *NYT*, November 29, 1998; Hartocollis, "Crew Speaks Out . . . ," *NYT*, December 16, 1998; Levy, "Senate Passes Charter . . . ," *NYT*, December 18, 1998; Levy and Hartocollis, "Crew Assails . . . ," *NYT*, December 19, 1998. See Crew's response to the law: "Chancellor Crew and Board of Education Unveil Charter School Plans" (press release), February 1, 1999, RPM, Box 62, Folder 8 (Pt. 1), NYSA. Crew described himself as "a strong proponent of charter schools and the proliferation of new, small schools" but was "critical of the new legislation because it siphons funds from the public school system to entities not accountable to the system or the city" and charged that it "[did] not allow the Chancellor to intervene if they fail."

34. Hartocollis "8 Charter Schools"; Hartocollis, "A Charter School Plan . . . ," *NYT*, November 7, 2001; Brittany Lewer, "Pursuing 'Real Power to Parents': Babette Edwards's Activism from Community Control to Charter Schools," in Ansley T. Erickson and Ernest Morrell, eds., *Educating Harlem: A Century of Schooling and Resistance in a Black Community* (New York, 2019), 288–91. On Sisulu, see Mary C. Bounds, *A Light Shines in Harlem: New York's First Charter School and the Movement It Led* (Chicago, 2014). For a glimpse at the chartering process, see materials in RMP, Box 62, Folder 8 (Pt. 1), NYSA.

The city and state approached several existing alternative schools with the option of converting to charter schools. Some, such as International High School in Queens, did; others, like Beacon High School and El Puente Academy for Peace and Justice in south Williamsburg, Brooklyn, did not. See for instance Chad Vignola to Tony Coles, May 24, 1999, Re: "Parental Involvement in Charter School Conversions," RWG, RL, Box 02/03/002, Folder 0119, NYCMA.

35. On Giuliani's role in the 1997 rent war, see Michael McKee to Randy Mastro, April 21, 1997, RWG, RM, Box 02/04/019, Folder 0456; Pérez-Peña, "Giuliani Says . . . ," *NYT*, June 3, 1997; Kolbert, "A Good Day for the Mayor . . . ," *NYT*, June 5, 1997. For a compilation of Giuliani's public statements on rent regulation, see "Mayor Giuliani's Record on Rent Regulations," RWG, FR, Box 02/09/009, Folder 0358, NYCMA. On Giuliani's Charter School Improvement Fund, see the documents in RWG, ES, Box 02/10/1/001, Folders 0014–0015,

NYCMA; Anthony Coles to Bruce Kovner, November 2, 2000; "Mayor Giuliani Announces Creation of $5 Million Charter School Improvement Fund" (press release), October 31, 2000; "New York City Charter Improvement Fund," n.d.; all in RWG, TC, Box 02/10/002, Folder 046, NYCMA. (Cole's letter to Covner, of the School Choice Foundation, provides the $10 million figure; the press release announcing the $5 million fund later refers to funding "up to $10 million in total grants.") For the voucher plan, Caroline Hendrie, "Giuliani Floats N.Y. Voucher Plan Run by City Hall," *EducationWeek*, April 28, 1999. "Blown up" in Barry, "Raze School System . . . ," *NYT*, April 23, 1999. For Giuliani's 1993 education agenda, see "New York City's Public Schools: Rudy Giuliani's Agenda for Reform"; "Background Paper for the Giuliani Plan for New York's Educational Renaissance"; both in RWG, RS, Box 02/07/003, Folder 0126.

36. Jack Newfield, *The Full Rudy: The Man, the Myth, the Mania* (New York, 2002), 37.

37. William J. Bratton with Peter Knobler, *Turnaround: How America's Top Cop Reversed the Crime Epidemic* (New York, 1998), 343, 345; "Statement of the Real Estate Board of New York in Support of the Mayor's Commitment to Maintain Staffing Levels in the Police Department," April 4, 1994, RWG, PP, Box 02/01/019, Folder 0462, NYCMA; Themis Chronopoulos, "The Making of the Orderly City: New York Since the 1980s," *JUH* 46, no. 5 (September 2020): 1100–1; Jennifer R. Wynn, "Can Zero Tolerance Last? Voices from Inside the Precinct," in Andrea McArdle and Tanya Erzen, eds., *Zero Tolerance: Quality of Life Policing and the New Police Brutality in New York City* (New York, 2001), 111. On the 1994 crime bill, see Naomi Murakawa, *The First Civil Right: How Liberals Built Prison America* (New York, 2014), chap. 4. For the perspective of a Black woman officer on the Giuliani culture shift, see "Oral History Interview with Alicia Parker," 2015, GOHP, CCOHC, RBML.

38. Rudolph W. Giuliani and William J. Bratton, *Police Strategy No. 3: Driving Drug Dealers Out of New York* (1994); Giuliani and Bratton, *Police Strategy No. 5: Reclaiming the Public Spaces of New York City* (1994); Bratton, "Crime Is Down in New York City: Blame the Police," in William Griffiths et al., eds., *Zero Tolerance: Policing a Free Society*, rev. ed. (London, 1998), 34–36. For an account that stresses Bratton's departures from previous practices, see Peter Moskos, *Back from the Brink: Inside the NYPD and New York City's Extraordinary 1990s Crime Drop* (New York, 2025).

39. Bratton with Knobler, *Turnaround*, 197–98; Chronopoulos, "Making of the Orderly City," 1101–2; Rashbaum, "Fat Lips OK by Cop," *NYDN*, October 11, 1995; Heather MacDonald, "America's Best Urban Police Force," *CJ* (Summer 2000) ("problem-solving sessions"). For the perspective of NYPD officers who were part of CompStat's implementation, see Moskos, *Back from the Brink*, chap. 6. For a critical account of CompStat, see John A. Eterno and Eli B. Silverman, *The Crime Numbers Game: Management by Manipulation* (Boca Raton, FL, 2017). See also Franklin E. Zimring, *The City That Became Safe: New York's Lessons for Urban Crime and Its Control* (New York, 2012), 119–21; David Weisburd et al., "Reforming to Preserve: Compstat and Strategic Problem Solving in American Policing," *Criminology and Public Policy* 2, no. 3 (2003): 421–56.

40. Jack Maple with Chris Mitchell, *The Crime Fighter: How You Can Make Your Community Crime-Free* (New York, 1999), 154. Franklin Zimring emphasizes this aspect of Broken Windows; see Zimring, *City That Became Safe*, 125–28, 129–30.

41. Giuliani and Bratton, *Police Strategy No. 5*; Wynn, "Can Zero Tolerance Last?"115. For a later initiative, see "Summer '96 Quality of Life Initiative: Building on Success," RWG, RW, Box 02/08/005, Folder 0136, NYCMA. On the parallel quality-of-life campaign in the subways, see Metropolitan Transit Authority, "New Programs Aimed at Improving Quality-of-Life" (press release), January 10, 1994, SC, Box 28, Folder 4, NYPL. See also Issa Kohler-Hausmann, *Misdemeanorland: Criminal Courts and Social Control in an Age of Broken Windows Policing* (Princeton, NJ, 2018), 67–70; Alex S. Vitale and Brian Jordan Jefferson, "The Emergence of Command and Control Policing in Neoliberal New York," in Jordan T. Camp and Christina Heatherton, eds., *Policing the Planet: Why the Policing Crisis Led to Black Lives Matter* (New York, 2016), chap. 12.
42. "Rudy Giuliani's Strategy to Fight Illicit Drugs in New York City," September 30, 1993, RWG, RS, Box 02/07/003, Folder 0118, NYCMA; Seth Kaye to Peter Powers and Gordon Campbell, January 12, 1994, Re: "Additional Materials from 1/10/94 NYPD Policy Initiatives Meeting with Commissioner Bratton" (and enclosures), RWG, PP, Box 02/01/1/014, Folder 046, NYCMA; Powers to Bratton, August 26, 1994, Re: "Responses to Monthly Reports"; Police Department, City of New York, "Monthly Report—June 1994"; Police Department, "Monthly Report—April 1994"; all in RWG, PP, Box 02/01/020, Folder 0466, NYCMA; Giuliani and Bratton, *Police Strategy No. 3*; Moskos, *Back from the Brink*, 61; Bratton with Knobler, *Turnaround*, 273–78.

    For community perspectives on the campaigns, see CCNYC, Series: Committee Files, Box 050221, Folder 2, LWA. The success of the campaigns varied from one neighborhood to another; in Chelsea, according to community board testimony, the NYPD succeeded in driving much of the drug activity inside; in Washington Heights, more open-air activity persisted.
43. Wilson, "Just Take Away Their Guns," *NYT Sunday Magazine*, March 20, 1994; Giuliani and Bratton, *Police Strategy No. 1*, 16; Cooper, "The Procedure Was Once . . . ," *NYT*, March 29, 1999. For an overview of gun policy under Bratton, see Jeffrey A. Fagan and Garth Davies, "Policing Guns: Order Maintenance and Crime Control in New York," in Bernard Harcourt, ed., *Guns, Crime, and Punishment in America* (New York, 2003), 191–221.
44. Maple with Mitchell, *Crime Fighter*, 155–56; Zimring, *City That Became Safe*, 118–19, 122–24, 210–11; Jeffrey Fagan and Garth Davies, "Street Stops and Broken Windows: Terry, Race, and Disorder in New York City," 48 *Fordham Urban Law Journal* 457 (2000): 457–504. See also the relevant works cited in the following chapter's discussion of stop-and-frisk.
45. For an overview, see Andrew Karmen, *New York Murder Mystery: The True Story Behind the Crime Crash of the 1990s* (New York, 2000); Zimring, *City That Became Safe*, chaps. 3–5; Patrick Sharkey, *Uneasy Peace: The Great Crime Decline, the Renewal of City Life, and the Next War on Violence* (New York, 2018), 55–60.
46. For summaries of press coverage, see Karmen, *New York Murder Mystery*, 8–9; Leonard Levitt, *NYPD Confidential: Power and Corruption in the Country's Greatest Police Force* (New York, 2009), 121–22.
47. Bratton with Knobler, *Turnaround*; Gladwell, "The Tipping Point," *NYer*, June 3, 1996, 32–38; Malcolm Gladwell, *The Tipping Point: How Little Things Can Make a Big Difference* (New York, 2000), 141–46; Maple with Mitchell, *Crime Fighter*.

Gladwell (who appears in this and the following chapter as one particularly articulate representative of a broader tendency in how many influential New Yorkers looked at the city in the 1990s and 2000s) later revisited his assessment of Broken Windows on his podcast, *Revisionist History*. See https://www.pushkin.fm/podcasts/revisionist-history/the-tipping-point-revisited-broken-windows.

48. For Bratton's account, see Bratton with Knobler, *Turnaround*, 276–78, 295–304; and Bratton with Peter Knobler, *The Profession: A Memoir of Community, Race, and the Arc of Policing in America* (New York, 2021), 192. On Safir, see Chronopoulos, "Making of the Orderly City," 1105.
49. Bratton with Knobler, *Profession*, 190.
50. Michael Jacobson, "From the 'Back' to the 'Front': The Changing Character of Punishment in New York City," in Mollenkopf and Emerson, eds., *Rethinking the Urban Agenda*, 172–79.
51. Kocieniewski, "Success of Elite Police . . . ," *NYT*, February 15, 1999. See also Chronopoulos, "Making of the Orderly City," 1106, which emphasizes the role of antinarcotics squads.
52. Eliot Spitzer, *The New York City Police Department's "Stop & Frisk" Practices: A Report to the People of the State of New York from the Office of the Attorney General* (New York, 1999), 72; Chronopoulos, "Making of the Orderly City," 1104; Clarence Taylor, *Fight the Power: African Americans and the Long History of Police Brutality in New York City* (New York, 2019), 162–64.
53. Spitzer, *Police Department's "Stop & Frisk" Practices*, chap. 4 (Bronx pastor at 86–87); Timothy Lynch, "New York's Street Crimes Unit: 'We Own the Night,'" *New York Beacon*, July 26, 2000; Kocieniewski, "Success of Elite Police"; Herbert, "The Police Bullies," *NYT*, March 7, 1997.
54. Lynch, "Street Crimes Unit: 'We Own the Night.'"
55. Thompson and Pierre-Pierre, "Portrait of a Slain Immigrant . . . ," *NYT*, February 12, 1999. Toobin, "The Unasked Question," *NYer*, March 6, 2000, 42–44, reviews the events of that evening based on trial testimony. Footage of the trial is available via CourtTV.com at https://www.courttv.com/title/1-ny-v-boss-et-al-opening-statements/.
56. Cooper, "Officers in Bronx . . . ," *NYT*, February 5, 1999; Toobin, "Unasked Question," 42–44.
57. Goldberg, "The Color of Suspicion," *NYT Sunday Magazine*, June 20, 1999; Yardley, "In 2 Minority Neighborhoods . . . ," *NYT*, March 29, 1999.
58. Thompson, "1,000 Rally . . . ," *NYT*, February 8, 1999; Flynn, "Eight Arrested . . . ," *NYT*, February 23, 1999; Roane, "Sharpton Among . . . ," *NYT*, March 4, 1999; Cooper, "Dinkins Among . . . ," *NYT*, March 16, 1999; Barry, "Daily Protesters . . . ," *NYT*, March 19, 1999; Cooper, "More Tolerance Needed . . . ," *NYT*, March 22, 1999; Cooper, "McCall Is Among . . . ," *NYT*, March 23, 1999; Finkelstein, "Protests in Police Killing . . . ," *NYT*, March 25, 1999; Swarns, "Unlikely Protesters . . . ," *NYT*, March 27, 1999.
59. CityWide Coalition to Stop Giuliani, "Fighting Rudy Giuliani . . . Cop By Cop" (flyer), RP, Series III, Box 14, Folder 8, "Diallo, Amadou," CCPRS; Barry with Connelly, "Poll in New York . . . ," *NYT*, March 16, 1999; Lewis, "Symbolism in Action," *NYT*, March 25, 1999.
60. Cooper, "Street Searches . . . ," *NYT*, March 18, 1999; Pérez-Peña, "Police May

Have . . . ," *NYT*, March 23, 1999; Spitzer, *Police Department's "Stop & Frisk" Practices*, ix; "Police Tactics in Question . . . ," *NYT*, December 4, 1999 ("fit [a criminal] description"); U.S. Commission on Civil Rights, *Police Practices and Civil Rights in New York City* (2000); Weiser, "U.S. Detects Bias . . . ," *NYT*, October 5, 2000.

61. Weiser, "Lawsuit Seeks . . . ," *NYT*, March 9, 1999; *Kelvin Daniels et al. v. The City of New York et al.*, 99 Civ. 1695 (SAS), Stipulation of Settlement; Toobin, "Rights and Wrongs," *NYer*, May 20, 2013, 39; Flynn, "After Criticism . . . ," *NYT*, January 5, 2001.

62. Rashbaum, "Eyeing Crime Rate . . . ," *NYT*, January 21, 2000; Barry, "The Police . . . ," *NYT*, February 27, 2000; Wayne Barrett, *Rudy! An Investigative Biography of Rudy Giuliani* (New York, 2001), 336; Taylor, *Fight the Power*, 199–200. For statistics in Operation Condor, see "Operation C.O.N.D.O.R.: Weekly Activity—Teams & Arrests," RWG, AC, Box 02/06/002, Folder 0067, NYCMA. Because the officers were not working overtime, they were not being paid with Operation Condor money, though they were doing identical work.

The Giuliani administration had created a Police-Community Task Force in the wake of Abner Louima's brutalization; like the CCRB, its members grew frustrated by what they saw as a lack of resources and prioritization. See "Mayor Giuliani Creates a Police/Community Relations Task Force" (press release), August 19, 1997, RWG, AC, Box 02/06/002, Folder 0067, NYCMA; Emira Habiby Browne et al. to Giuliani, December 30, 1997, RWG, RW, Box 02/08/011, Folder 0306, NYCMA

63. Donald J. Trump to Giuliani, August 17, 2000, RWG, OC, Box 01/2000/038, Folder 0725, NYCMA; Wilbert A. Tatum, "It's Giuliani Time Ad Nauseum," *NYAN*, May 13, 1999; David Alejandro Rodriguez to Randy Mastro, RWG, RM, Box 02/04/006, Folder 0174, NYCMA.

64. Heather MacDonald, "New York's Indispensable Institution," *CJ* (Special Issue, 2009).

65. Heather MacDonald, "America's Best Urban Police Force," *CJ* (Summer 2000). The text alludes to Notorious B.I.G., "Everyday Struggle," *Ready to Die* (Arista, 1994). On the growth of the creative industries, see Elizabeth Currid-Halkett, *The Warhol Economy: How Fashion, Art, and Music Drive New York City* (Princeton, NJ, 2008).

66. Commission on the Year 2000, *New York Ascendant* (New York, 1987), 1, 4, 9; Jason Bram, "New York City's Economy Before and After September 11," *Federal Reserve Bank of New York: Current Issues in Economics and Finance* 9, no. 2 (February 2003): 2; Sachs, "City Population Tops 8 Million . . . ," *NYT*, March 16, 2001.

67. Commission on 2000, *New York Ascendant*, 4, 51; Mark K. Levitan and Susan S. Wieler, "Poverty in New York City, 1969–99: The Influence of Demographic Change, Income Growth, and Income Inequality," *FRBNY Economic Policy Review* (July 2008): 15; J. Phillip Thompson, "One Step Forward, Two Steps Back: Liberalism, Race, and Local Democracy," in Mollenkopf and Emerson, eds., *Rethinking the Urban Agenda*, 243n56.

68. For a portrait, see Joseph Berger, *The World in a City: Traveling the Globe Through the Neighborhoods of New York* (New York, 2007), quoted at ix, 93. For median

family incomes in the neighborhoods, see Daniel Kay Hertz's maps at https://danielkayhertz.com/2014/07/09/watch-new-york-citys-middle-class-and-poor-get-pushed-around/. On the African-born population, see Department of City Planning, City of New York, *The Newest New Yorkers: Characteristics of the City's Foreign-born Population* (New York, 2013), 10, 16. On the political behavior of foreign-born Black New Yorkers, see Christina M. Greer, *Black Ethnics: Race, Immigration, and the Pursuit of the American Dream* (New York, 2013).

69. On the 2001 election, see esp. Chris McNickle, *Bloomberg: A Billionaire's Ambition* (New York, 2017), chap. 2.
70. On Bloomberg before the mayoralty, see McNickle, *Bloomberg*, chap. 1; Eleanor Randolph, *The Many Lives of Michael Bloomberg* (New York, 2019), chaps. 1–7.
71. McNickle, *Bloomberg*, chap. 2; Randolph, *Many Lives*, chap. 8, at 91; John Mollenkopf, "How 9/11 Reshaped the Political Environment in New York," in Mollenkopf, ed., *Contentious City: The Politics of Recovery in New York City* (New York, 2005), 208–10.

Chapter 6: City of Choice

1. McCann, "Dessert," *NYer*, September 12, 2001. John Mollenkopf describes the smoke from Ground Zero in "Introduction," Mollenkopf, ed., *The Contentious City: The Politics of Recovery in New York City* (New York, 2005), 5.
2. "Prepared Statement of Cristyne L. Nicholas, President & CEO, NYC & Company," *The State of the U.S. Tourism Industry, Hearing Before the Subcommittee on Commerce, Trade, and Consumer Protection of the Committee on Energy and Commerce, House of Representatives, One Hundred Seventh Congress, First Session, October 17, 2001*, 4:58–63; William C. Thompson, Jr., Comptroller, City of New York, *One Year Later: The Fiscal Impact of 9/11 on New York City* (2002), 26; see also New York City Partnership and Chamber of Commerce, *Working Together to Accelerate New York's Recovery: Economic Impact Analysis of the September 11th Attack on New York City* (2001); Purnick, "Recalling the 70's, Warily," *NYT*, November 11, 2001.
3. "Mayor's Speech . . . ," *NYT*, January 2, 2002; "Mayor Michael Bloomberg's 2003 State of the City Address," *GG*, January 23, 2003.
4. Howard Chernick, ed., *Resilient City: The Economic Impact of 9/11* (New York, 2005).
5. Beth Fertig, *Why cant U teach me 2 read? Three Students and a Mayor Put Our Schools to the Test* (New York, 2009), 13 (Bloomberg quote).
6. Chris McNickle, *Bloomberg: A Billionaire's Ambition* (New York, 2017), 99–100. On mayoral control, see Jeffrey R. Henig and Wilbur C. Rich, eds., *Mayors in the Middle: Politics, Race, and Mayoral Control of Urban Schools* (Princeton, NJ, 2003); Joseph P. Viteritti, ed., *When Mayors Take Charge: School Governance in the City* (New York, 2009). On school funding in the Bloomberg-Klein years, see Leanna Stiefel and Amy Ellen Schwartz, "Financing K-12 Education in the Bloomberg Years, 2002–2008," in Jennifer A. O'Day, Catherine S. Bitter, and Louis M. Gomez, eds., *Education Reform in New York City: Ambitious Change in the Nation's Most Complex School System* (Cambridge, MA, 2011), chap. 3.
7. Eleanor Randolph, *The Many Lives of Michael Bloomberg* (New York, 2019),

175; McNickle, *Bloomberg*, 119, 121; Otterman, "At $145 a Session . . . ," *NYT*, November 21, 2009; Phillips, "After Number of Gifted Soars . . . ," *NYT*, April 14, 2012; Hollander, "Brooklyn Sees Growth . . . ," *WSJ*, May 5, 2014. On school choice under Bloomberg and Klein, see Sean P. Corcoran and Henry M. Levin, "School Choice and Competition in New York City Schools," in O'Day, Bitter, and Gomez, eds., *Education Reform in New York City*, chap. 9.

8. Joel Klein, *Lessons of Hope: How to Fix Our Schools* (New York, 2014), xiii. On equivalent developments in federal education policy, see Daniel S. Moak, *From the New Deal to the War on Schools: Race, Inequality, and the Rise of the Punitive Education State* (Chapel Hill, NC, 2022), esp. chap. 5.

9. Klein, *Lessons of Hope*, 104–8; New York City Independent Budget Office, *Phased Out: As the City Closed Low-Performing Schools How Did Their Students Fare?* (New York, 2016). For a particularly evocative and historically grounded account of one case, see Cobb, "The Life and Death of Jamaica High School," *NYer*, August 24, 2015. For overviews of the Klein-era reforms, see O'Day, Bitter, and Gomez, eds., *Education Reform in New York City*; Joseph P. Viteritti, "Stumbling Through: How Joel Klein Reinvented the New York City Schools," *Journal of School Choice* 6, no. 3 (July 2012): 411–22.

10. Klein, *Lessons of Hope*, 111–12, 114.

11. Raymond Domanico, *State of the New York City Public Schools 2002* (March 2002), 2; Klein, *Lessons of Hope*, 81; Malcolm Gladwell, *Outliers: The Story of Success* (New York, 2008), 266. For a sympathetic account of the charter movement, see Robert Pondiscio, *How the Other Half Learns: Equality, Excellence, and the Battle Over School Choice* (New York, 2019). Moskowitz recounts her efforts in Eva Moskowitz, *The Education of Eva Moskowitz: A Memoir* (New York, 2017).

12. As of 2010, white children made up only 4 percent of charter school students in New York City; students of Asian ancestry were 5 percent. See the DOE data in Medina and Gebeloff, "New York Charter Schools . . . ," *NYT*, June 14, 2010.

13. Taylor, "At Success Academy . . . ," *NYT*, April 7, 2015; González, "Success Academy . . . ," *NYDN*, August 28, 2013.

14. Taylor, "At Success Academy." New York's noncharter public schools of choice, in contrast, eagerly adopted Dual Language instruction, increasingly seen as an added benefit for predominantly English-speaking students in a globalizing economy. See Lauren Lefty, "Bilingual in the Big Apple: Bilingual Education Politics and the Making of New York's Neoliberal Multiculturalism," in Johanna Fernández, Kim Phillips-Fein, and Mason B. Williams, eds., *Gotham on the Verge* (Chapel Hill, NC, forthcoming).

15. Herszenhorn, "Schools to Add . . . ," *NYT*, February 17, 2005; Herszenhorn, "Mixed Signals . . . ," *NYT*, December 10, 2003.

16. Saulny, "Gifted Classes Will Soon . . . ," *NYT*, November 16, 2005; Herszenhorn, "Mixed Signals"; Rutenberg, "Bloomberg Claims Progress . . . ," *NYT*, January 12, 2005; Gootman, "Bloomberg to Give . . . ," *NYT*, January 26, 2005. On the importance assigned to the middle class, see also Eva Moskowitz: "It's the middle class that makes the New York City school system better than Philadelphia or Chicago. If we become a school system of the exclusively poor, we are going to be in big trouble." Saulny, "In Middle Class . . . ," *NYT*, December 27, 2005. And Klein: "I think it is really an asset in New York, unlike many other cities,

to have such a powerful middle class." Purnick, "No Parent Left Unheard . . . ," *NYT*, March 23, 2006.

17. Saulny, "Gifted Classes"; Gootman, "Schools Raise Bar . . . ," *NYT*, October 30, 2007; Otterman, "At $145 a Session." See also Banjo, "Private-School Strivers . . . ," *WSJ*, March 5, 2011; Phillips, "After Number of Gifted Soars."
18. Eduwonkette, "With New Gifted and Talented Rules . . . ?" *EducationWeek*, April 14, 2008; Gootman and Gebeloff, "Gifted Programs Are Less Diverse," *NYT*, June 19, 2008; Eduwonkette, "The Upper West Side Relief Act . . . ," *EducationWeek*, April 17, 2008; Gootman, "City Seeks Looser Rule . . . ," *NYT*, April 10, 2008; Otterman, "City Seeking . . . ," *NYT*, June 22, 2010.
19. Caroline M. Hoxby, Sonali Murarka, and Jenny Kang, *The New York City Charter Schools Evaluation Project: How New York City's Charter Schools Affect Achievement* (September 2009); Center for Research on Educational Outcomes, *Charter School Performance in New York City* (January 2010); Harold S. Bloom, Saskia Levy Thompson, and Rebecca Unterman, *Transforming the High School Experience: How New York City Small Schools Are Boosting Student Achievement and Graduation Rates* (New York, 2010); Taylor, "New York Charters . . . ," *NYT*, December 9, 2016; Marcus A. Winters, *Why the Gap? Special Education and New York City Charter Schools* (September 2013); Winters, *Why the Gap? English Language Learners and New York City Charter Schools* (October 2014); Clara Hemphill and Kim Nauer with Helen Zelon and Thomas Jacobs, *The New Marketplace: How Small-School Reforms and School Choice Have Reshaped New York City's High Schools* (June 2009). See also Norm Fruchter, "New York City's Small Schools," *Voices in Urban Education* 52, no. 1 (November 2023).
20. For an overview, see Rachael A. Woldoff, Lisa M. Morrison, and Michael R. Glass, *Priced Out: Stuyvesant Town and the Loss of Middle-Income Neighborhoods* (New York, 2016). On efforts to desegregate the complexes, see Martha Biondi, *To Stand and Fight: The Struggle for Civil Rights in Postwar New York City* (Cambridge, MA, 2003), 121–36; Roberta Gold, *When Tenants Claimed the City: The Struggle for Citizenship in New York City Housing* (Champaign, IL, 2014), 45–55. On the sale, see Charles Bagli, *Other People's Money: Inside the Housing Crisis and the Demise of the Greatest Real Estate Deal Ever Made* (New York, 2013).
21. Scott, "Mayor Rethinking . . . ," *NYT*, February 24, 2006, quoted in Julian Brash, *Bloomberg's New York: Class and Governance in the Luxury City* (Athens, GA, 2011), 261; Association for Neighborhood and Housing Development, *Real Affordability: An Evaluation of the Bloomberg Housing Program and Recommendations to Strengthen Affordable Housing Policy* (New York, 2013); Martin Filler, "New York: Conspicuous Construction," *New York Review of Books*, April 2, 2015. On redevelopment under Bloomberg, see esp. Brash, *Bloomberg's New York*; and Alessandro Busà, *The Creative Destruction of New York City: Engineering the City for the Elite* (New York, 2017).
22. Lambert, "2 Big Projects . . . ," *NYT*, July 13, 2001; Dewan, "McCall Vows . . . ," *NYT*, October 20, 2002; Pristin and Bagli, "For Sale . . . ," *NYT*, September 13, 2006; Scott, "Complexes' Seller Pushes Profits . . . ," *NYT*, September 23, 2006.
23. Fernandez and Bagli, "Tenants Roiled . . . ," *NYT*, May 27, 2008.
24. Metropolitan Council on Housing, "Preferential Rents: A Fact Sheet for Rent Stabilized Tenants," n.d., MCH, Box 62, Folder "Preferential Rents," TL. Michael

Greenberg, "Tenants Under Siege: Inside New York City's Housing Crisis," *New York Review of Books*, August 17, 2017, emphasizes the importance of large investors; see also Morgenson, "As Investment Firms Buy . . . ," *NYT*, May 9, 2008.

25. Community Service Society, *Making the Rent: Rent Burdens and Hardship Among Low Income New Yorkers* (June 2005), 17, MCH, Box 62, Folder "Housing Facts," TL.
26. Celona, "Judge Denies Bail . . . ," *NYP*, March 11, 2003.
27. Mahoney, "Dems Give in . . . ," *NYDN*, June 21, 2003.
28. Fernandez, "Dueling Bills . . . ," *NYT*, December 24, 2007; Fernandez, "Board Backs Rise . . . ," *NYT*, June 20, 2008; Giuliani's Rent Guidelines Board Chair Edward Hochman to Randy Mastro and David Klasfeld, May 1, 1997, Re: "RGB's Pending Loss of Members," RWG, DK, Box 02/09/1/012, Folder 0378, NYCMA. Hochman also reported receiving thirteen death threats and being pelted with gum and other projectiles during the meeting. Materials in this and the preceding folder provide a useful glimpse into the board's workings in the Giuliani years.
29. Scott, "Despite Protests . . . ," *NYT*, June 28, 2006.
30. *Roberts v. Tishman Speyer Props., L.P.* (2009); Bagli, "Top State Court . . . ," *NYT*, October 23, 2009; Haughney and Bagli, "Ruling Sets Off . . . ," *NYT*, October 23, 2009.
31. New York City Rent Guidelines Board, *2012 Income and Affordability Study* (April 2012), 9.
32. Bellafante, "Rent-Regulation Wars . . . ," *NYT*, March 11, 2012.
33. Levitt, "Kelly Favors the Longshot," *Newsday*, October 22, 2001; Levitt, *NYPD Confidential: Power and Corruption in the Country's Greatest Police Force* (New York, 2009), 40–42, 232–34.
34. "Raymond P. Kelly—Preliminary Analysis (12/21/01)," RP, Series III, Box 16, Folder 5, CCPRS; Michael Myers, *NYP*, December 11, 2001, 33.
35. Baker, "Commissioner Bans Profiling . . . ," *NYT*, March 14, 2002; Rashbaum and Baker, "Police Commissioner Closing . . . ," *NYT*, April 10, 2002; Baker, "Hispanic Officers . . . ," *NYT*, April 18, 2002; Fries, "A Police Group Says . . . ," *NYT*, April 15, 2002; Herbert, "An Odd Accusation," *NYT*, April 18, 2002. For the phrasing of Operations Order 11, see City Council, City of New York, "The Transcript of the Minutes of the Committee on Public Safety," February 23, 2004, CCNYC, Subgroup: Office of the Speaker (Gifford Miller, 2002–2005), "Supporting Documents: Hearing Transcript," https://www.laguardiawagnerarchive.lagcc.cuny.edu/pages/FileBrowser.aspx?LinkToFile=../FILES_DOC/NYCC_DOCS/Attachmants/60421.html, LWA.
36. Ray Kelly, *Vigilance: My Life Serving America and Protecting Its Empire City* (New York, 2015), 183–84.
37. Polgreen, "New Police Crackdown . . . ," *NYT*, January 10, 2003; Rashbaum, "Mayor Extending Focus . . . ," *NYT*, July 2, 2003; Rashbaum and Cooper, "Police Widen Plan . . . ," *NYT*, January 13, 2004; Baker, "City Is Doubling . . . ," *NYT*, December 27, 2007.
38. "Mayor Michael Bloomberg's 2003 State of the City Address"; Dewan, "Safest Big City . . . ," *NYT*, December 16, 2003; Baker and Vasquez, "Police Report Far More . . . ," *NYT*, February 3, 2007; McIntire, "New York's Falling Crime Rate . . . ," *NYT*, October 5, 2005. The "safest big city in America" trope had

appeared sporadically starting in the late 1990s, but Bloomberg was the first mayor to deploy it systematically.

39. Baker and Vasquez, "Police Report."
40. See New York Civil Liberties Union, *Stop & Frisk During the Bloomberg Administration, 2002–2013* (August 2014); Andrew Gelman, Jeffrey Fagan, and Alex Kiss, "An Analysis of the New York City Police Department's 'Stop-and-Frisk' Policy in the Context of Claims of Racial Bias," *Journal of the American Statistical Association* 102, no. 479 (September 2007): 813–23; Delores Jones-Brown, Jaspreet Gill, and Jennifer Trone, "Stop, Question & Frisk Policing Practices in New York City: A Primer" (March 2010).
41. Sultan, "6 People Describe . . . ," Vice.com, February 21, 2020; Dressner and Martinez, "The Scars of Stop-and-Frisk," *NYT*, July 12, 2012; Barnum and Zimmerman, "Stop-and-Frisk Under Michael Bloomberg . . . ," Chalkbeat.org, February 18, 2020.
42. Jan Haldipur, *No Place on the Corner: The Costs of Aggressive Policing* (New York, 2019), xiii, 24; Dwyer, "Out of One Gram . . . ," *NYT*, March 21, 2013; Harris, "Police Memo on Marijuana . . . ," *NYT*, September 23, 2011. See also Amanda Geller and Jeffrey Fagan, "Pot as Pretext: Marijuana, Race, and the New Disorder in New York City Street Policing," *Journal of Empirical Legal Studies* 7, no. 4 (December 2010): 591–633; Bronx Defenders, *The Hidden Tax: Economic Costs of Marijuana Enforcement in the Bronx and New York City* (New York, 2014).
43. Haldipur, *No Place on the Corner*, 33–34; Goldstein, "'Stop-and-Frisk' Ebbs . . . ," *NYT*, September 19, 2014; Jennifer Fratello et al., *Coming of Age with Stop and Frisk: Experiences, Perceptions, and Public Safety Implications* (September 2013); Amy E. Lerman and Vesla Weaver, "Staying Out of Sight?: Concentrated Policing and Local Political Action," *Annals of the American Academy of Political and Social Science* 651 (January 2014): 202–19; Barnum and Zimmerman, "Stop-and-Frisk Under Michael Bloomberg"; Amanda Geller et al., "Aggressive Policing and the Mental Health of Young Urban Men," *American Journal of Public Health* 104, no. 12 (December 2014): 2321–27; Badger, "The Lasting Effects of Stop-and-Frisk . . . ," *NYT*, March 2, 2020.
44. Haldipur, *No Place on the Corner*, xii, 30–31. Nicole Gelinas, *Movement: New York City's Long Battle to Take Back Its Streets* (New York, 2024), pt. 3, details the Bloomberg administration's efforts to reclaim public space from automotive transport. See also Patrick Sharkey, *Uneasy Peace: The Great Crime Decline, the Renewal of City Life, and the Next War on Violence* (New York, 2018), on how the crime drop enhanced the utility of public space in New York.
45. McNickle, *Bloomberg*, 88; Clarence Taylor, *Fight the Power: African Americans and the Long History of Police Brutality in New York City* (New York, 2018), 219.
46. Randolph, *Many Lives*, 203.
47. Taylor, "Stop-and-Frisk Policy . . . ," *NYT*, June 11, 2012; Freeman, "The Political War on the NYPD," *WSJ*, April 5, 2013; McNickle, *Bloomberg*, 92.
48. See the discussion in Floyd v. The City of New York 08 Civ. 1034 (SAS), 64–81, https://ccrjustice.org/files/Floyd-Liability-Opinion-8-12-13.pdf.
49. McNickle, *Bloomberg*, 93 (Kelly quote); Pillifant, "The Gentleman Commissioner . . . ," Politico.com, September 7, 2011; "Poll Gives Ray Kelly . . . ," CBSNews.com, January 17, 2013.

50. White, "Fighting Crime and Gaining Favor," *NYT*, January 20, 2004.
51. McNickle, *Bloomberg*, 94, 306; "Bloomberg Apologizes . . . ," interview by WKRN (Nashville), https://www.youtube.com/watch?v=_FlsyTxbZgo.
52. McNickle, *Bloomberg*, 251–59; Randolph, *Many Lives*, 286–92.
53. Powell and Bosman, "Mayor No Longer . . . ," *NYT*, November 4, 2009; Roberts, "For First Time . . . ," *NYT*, December 25, 2009.
54. Eve L. Ewing, *Ghosts in the Schoolyard: Racism and School Closings on Chicago's South Side* (Chicago, 2020), 159; Yoo, "The Rise & Fall of Paul Robeson High School," *Brooklyn Ink*, February 28, 2011; Willen, "NYC's Strategy for Shutting Schools . . . ," *Hechinger Report*, June 25, 2010.
55. Medina, "At Canarsie High . . . ," *NYT*, December 24, 2007; MacDonald, "Fighting the Closing . . . ," *NYT*, November 19, 2010; Cromidas, "Students, Staff Defend John Dewey . . . ," Chalkbeat.org, January 20, 2012; Otterman and Medina, "Boos and Personal Attacks . . . ," *NYT*, January 27, 2010; Winerip, "In Move to Close . . . ," *NYT*, February 5, 2011. On equivalent dynamics in Chicago, see Mary Pattillo, "Everyday Politics of School Choice in the Black Community," *Du Bois Review* 12, no. 1 (2015): 41–71.
56. Klein, *Lessons of Hope*, 112–13; Herszenhorn, "Charter School Will Not . . . ," *NYT*, June 24, 2006; Medina, "City's Schools Share Space . . . ," *NYT*, November 30, 2009.
57. Steven Brill, *Class Warfare: Inside the Fight to Fix America's Schools* (New York, 2011), 271–73, 324–29.
58. Deborah Meier, "Abandoning the Higher Purposes of Public Schools," *Dissent* (September 2011); Meier, "Can Choice Save Public Education Revised," https://deborahmeier.com/2019/05/09/can-choice-save-public-education-revised/.
59. Deborah Meier and Diane Ravitch, "Bridging Differences," *EducationWeek*, May 23, 2006.
60. Klein, *Lessons of Hope*, 65–66 (at 65); Diane Ravitch, *The Death and Life of the Great American School System: How Testing and Choice Are Undermining Education*, rev. ed. (New York, 2011), 134–47 at 135, 145. For the op-ed, see Ravitch, "Why I Changed My Mind About School Reform," *WSJ*, March 9, 2010; "Dear Reformers: I Didn't Mean to Hurt Your Feelings," *Huffington Post*, October 15, 2013, in Diane Ravitch, *The Wisdom and Wit of Diane Ravitch* (New York, 2019), 123.
61. Herbert, "Jim Crow Policing," *NYT*, February 2, 2010; Herbert, "Watching Certain People," *NYT*, March 2, 2010.
62. Baker, "Council Leaders . . . ," *NYT*, March 11, 2010; Baker, "Paterson Urged to Veto . . . ," *NYT*, July 3, 2010; Eligon, "Taking on Police Tactic . . . ," *NYT*, March 23, 2012; Baker and Rivera, "Paterson to Sign . . . ," *NYT*, July 16, 2010.
63. Baker, "Paterson Urged to Veto"; Baker, "New York Minorities . . . ," *NYT*, May 12, 2010; Dwyer, "In Policing Tactic's Decline . . . ," *NYT*, November 13, 2013; El-Ghobashy, "Street 'Crews' Get New Focus . . . ," *WSJ*, October 2, 2012; McDonough, "How New York City Is Watching You," *C&S*, April 30, 2019; E. S. Levin et al., "The New York City Police Department's Domain Awareness System," https://www.brennancenter.org/sites/default/files/Levine%20-%20Interfaces%20-%20The%20New%20York%20City%20Police%20Department%E2%80%99s%20Domain.pdf. Bloomberg biographer Eleanor Randolph writes: "'After much

internal discussion,' as one aide described a few meetings between the mayor and commissioner without elaboration, Bloomberg told Kelly his people needed to do a better job on the city's roughest streets." Randolph, *Many Lives*, 208.

64. Goodman, "Council Reverses . . . ," *NYT*, August 23, 2013; Floyd v. City of New York, 959 F. Supp. 2d 540 (S.D.N.Y. 2013); "NYC Mayor Bloomberg Plans to Appeal Stop-and-Frisk Decision," PBS *NewsHour*, n.d., https://www.youtube.com/watch?v=iw8BMrF7r8Y. For a comprehensive overview of stop-and-frisk, see Michael D. White and Henry F. Fradella, *Stop and Frisk: The Use and Abuse of a Controversial Policing Tactic* (New York, 2016).
65. On the 2013 campaign, see esp. Joseph P. Viteritti, *The Pragmatist: Bill de Blasio's Quest to Save the Soul of New York* (New York, 2017), 153–58. On Lhota's support for Kelly, see "Where the Mayoral Candidates Stand on Key Issues," *NYT*, October 29, 2013. Weiner's campaign is chronicled in Josh Kriegman and Elyse Steinberg, *Weiner* (Edgeline Films, 2016).
66. Viteritti, *Pragmatist*, 33, 233. The first two chapters of Viteritti's book offer by far the best account of de Blasio's political formation and development.
67. Anand, "De Blasio Takes on . . . ," Chalkbeat.org, April 22, 2013; Diane Ravitch, "New York Schools: The Roar of the Charters," in Ravitch, *Wisdom and Wit of Ravitch*, 181; Barbaro, "De Blasio Positions Himself . . . ," *NYT*, August 20, 2013; "To Make a Safe City Safer," *NYT*, July 22, 2013; Goodman and Goldstein, "For Police Commissioner . . . ," *NYT*, October 18, 2013; Viteritti, *Pragmatist*, 159, 161–63.

Chapter 7: A Tale of Two New Yorks

1. Goldberg, "The Rise of the Progressive City," *Nation*, April 2, 2014; Grynbaum, "De Blasio Draws . . . ," *NYT*, January 1, 2014; *Nation*, January 20, 2014; *All In with Chris Hayes*, February 19, 2014, NBCNews.com. See also two contemporary books making an argument similar to Goldberg's: Bruce Katz and Jennifer Bradley, *The Metropolitan Revolution: How Cities and Metros Are Fixing Our Broken Politics and Fragile Economy* (Washington, DC, 2013), and Benjamin R. Barber, *If Mayors Ruled the World: Dysfunctional Nations, Rising Cities* (New Haven, CT, 2014).
2. Stieb, "The Bill de Blasio–Andrew Cuomo Feud: A Retrospective," *NY*, August 24, 2021.
3. Juan González, *Reclaiming Gotham: Bill de Blasio and the Movement to End America's Tale of Two Cities* (New York, 2017), 178, 180; Joseph P. Viteritti, *The Pragmatist: Bill de Blasio's Quest to Save the Soul of New York* (New York, 2017), 4–5; Goldstein and Goodman, "Bratton Still Sees . . . ," *NYT*, June 17, 2014.
4. Goldstein and Goodman, "Bratton Still Sees"; Goodman and Goldstein, "Bratton Vows . . . ," *NYT*, January 3, 2014.
5. "Mayor de Blasio Announces Agreement in Landmark Stop-and-Frisk Case" (press release), January 30, 2014; "Bratton to Reform Operation Impact," *NYDN*, January 31, 2014; Goodman and Goldstein, "Bratton Vows"; Goodman, "Inexperienced Officers' Role . . . ," *NYT*, February 1, 2014.
6. Goldstein, "Street Stops Still . . . ," *NYT*, March 5, 2014; Coscarelli, "NYPD Vows to Keep . . . ," *NY*, March 5, 2014; Goldstein and Goodman, "Bratton Still Sees."

See esp. Bernard Harcourt, *Illusion of Order: The False Promise of Broken Windows Policing*, rev. ed. (Cambridge, MA, 2005).

7. Goodman and Yee, "Death of a Man . . . ," *NYT*, July 21, 2014; Baker, Goodman, and Mueller, "Beyond the Chokehold . . . ," *NYT*, June 13, 2015.
8. Goldstein, "Safer Era . . . ," *NYT*, July 25, 2014; Baker, Goodman, and Mueller, "Beyond the Chokehold . . . ," *NYT*, June 13, 2015.
9. Goldstein, "Safer Era"; Demby, "What We See in the Eric Garner Video . . . ," NPR .org, July 29, 2014; Chiusano, "Beyond Broken Windows," *Atlantic*, November 12, 2014. On the Black Lives Matter movement, see Keeyanga-Yamahtta Taylor, *From #BlackLivesMatter to Black Liberation* (Chicago, 2016). On the movement against Broken Windows in New York, see Jordan T. Camp and Christina Heatherton, "Ending Broken Windows Policing in New York City: An Interview with Joo-Hyun Kang," in Camp and Heatherton, eds., *Policing the Planet: Why the Policing Crisis Led to Black Lives Matter* (New York, 2016), chap. 4.
10. Goldstein, "Safer Era"; "NYPD Commissioner Bratton on Broken Windows, Community Policing, and More," *Brian Lehrer Show*, WNYC.org, August 12, 2014; Shallwani, "Bratton Tells Police Brass . . . ," *WSJ*, October 2, 2014.
11. "Transcript: Mayor de Blasio Holds Media Availability at Mt. Sinai United Christian Church on Staten Island," NYC.gov, December 3, 2014; Adler, "Meet the Men Who Scared de Blasio . . . ," *C&S*, June 3, 2020.
12. Patrick Sharkey, *Uneasy Peace: The Great Crime Decline, the Renewal of City Life, and the Next War on Violence* (New York, 2018), 150–51; Bratton, "How to Reform the Police . . . ," *NYT*, September 16, 2016. For the outlines of the neighborhood policing plan, see Bratton, *The NYPD Plan of Action and the Neighborhood Policing Plan: A Realistic Framework for Connecting Police and Communities* (2015).
13. Alyssa Aguilera and Alex S. Vitale, "The Limits of Community Policing," *GG*, March 2, 2015; Vitale, "Criminal Justice Reform Act is No Alternative to Broken Windows Policing," *GG*, January 25, 2016.
14. Goldenberg, "De Blasio Adds . . . ," Politico.com, June 23, 2015.
15. Goodman and Flegenheimer, "Mayor and Police Boss . . . ," *NYT*, March 10, 2015.
16. Clifford and Goldstein, "Brooklyn Prosecutor Limits . . . ," *NYT*, July 9, 2014; "Transcript: Mayor de Blasio, Police Commissioner Bratton Announce Change in Marijuana Policy," NYC.gov, November 10, 2014.
17. *NYP*, July 11, 2015; Barkan, "Top New York Democrats . . . ," *NYO*, April 29, 2015; New York City Council, "The Criminal Justice Reform Act: One Year Later" (2017), https://council.nyc.gov/the-criminal-justice-reform-act-one-year-later/; Vitale, "Criminal Justice Reform Act Is No Alternative."
18. Michael Colodner to Judge Pfau, March 22, 2007; Pete Grannis to Jonathan Lippman, October 31, 2006; Grannis et al. to Judith S. Kaye, March 29, 2006; all in MCH, Box 62, Folder "Blacklisting 2006/07," TL; Winston, "Transparency Advocates Win Release . . . ," *Intercept*, January 27, 2018. The Brennan Center's website makes available a number of documents on the NYPD's predictive policing programs at https://www.brennancenter.org/our-work/research-reports/nypd-predictive-policing-documents. See also Andrew Guthrie Ferguson, *The Rise of Big Data Policing: Surveillance, Race, and the Future of Law Enforcement* (New York, 2017).
19. Rubinstein, "Bill de Blasio and a Brief History . . . ," Politico.com, August 23,

2013; Hernández and Baker, "No 'Mary Poppins' . . . ," *NYT*, January 15, 2014; "Teacher's Pet . . . ," *Brooklyn Paper*, January 10, 2013.

20. Shapiro, "$773 Million Later . . . ," *NYT*, February 26, 2019; Zimmerman, "New York City Ends . . . ," Chalkbeat.org, February 26, 2019; Miles Doyle, "CityViews: De Blasio's Renewal Program . . . ," *CL*, December 21, 2017; David E. Kirkland, "The Renewal Schools Program Wasn't a Failure, It Was a Lesson," *NYU Steinhardt Metrocenter Blog*, https://steinhardt.nyu.edu/metrocenter/perspectives/renewal-schools-program-wasnt-failure-it-was-lesson-2019. For reviews of the program, see Marcus A. Winters, *Costly Progress: De Blasio's Renewal Schools Program* (July 2017), and Priscilla Wohlstetter et al., *Strategic Inquiry and New York City's Renewal Schools: Final Evaluation Report* (November 2018). Budget figure from the city's Independent Budget Office, https://ibo.nyc.ny.us/iboreports/new-york-city-school-budgets-2020.html.
21. Turkewitz, "New York City Chancellor Meets . . . ," *NYT*, February 23, 2014; Bellafante, "Hijacking of a Narrative," *NYT*, March 9, 2014.
22. Hernández, "Mayor Says He Will Halt . . . ," *NYT*, February 28, 2014; Decker, "Success Academy Donors . . . ," Chalkbeat.org, January 17, 2017; Waldman, "Andrew Cuomo's Charter Epiphany," Politico.com, March 19, 2014; Bellafante, "Hijacking of a Narrative."
23. On the formation of the IDC, see Zeff, "Another Cuomo Non-Interference Story . . . ," Politico.com, September 2, 2014. For a full-length political biography, see Michael Shnayerson, *The Contender: Andrew Cuomo, a Biography* (New York, 2015).
24. Paumgarten, "Andrew Cuomo, The King of New York," *NYer*, October 12, 2020. On Cuomo's relationship with the Bloomberg administration, see Schnayerson, *Contender*, 304–6, 326–28.
25. Smith, "De Blasio vs. Cuomo: The Next Round," *NY*, January 26, 2014; Kaplan, Craig, and Grynbaum, "Cuomo Burnishes His Brand . . . ," *NYT*, March 6, 2014.
26. Hernández and Craig, "For Cuomo, Pivotal Role . . . ," *NYT*, April 3, 2014; Baker and Hernández, "Mayor and Operator . . . ," *NYT*, March 5, 2014; Bellafante, "Hijacking of a Narrative."
27. Lewis, "Who's Behind the Pro-Charter Schools Group . . . ?" WNYC.org, March 6, 2014; Hernández, "From de Blasio . . . ," *NYT*, March 24, 2014; Hernández and Craig, "For Cuomo, Pivotal Role"; Ash, "N.Y. Budget Deal . . . ," *EducationWeek*, March 31, 2014; Decker, "State Leaders Agree to Deal . . . ," Chalkbeat.org, June 23, 2015; Taylor, "De Blasio Keeps Control . . . ," *NYT*, June 18, 2016; Harris and McKinley, "De Blasio's Concessions . . . ," *NYT*, July 6, 2017; Marcus A. Winters, *New York City's Charter Schools: What the Research Shows* (New York, 2018), 8. For an overview, see Ford, "What's Behind the Bill de Blasio-Eva Moskowitz Feud . . . ?" *CL*, November 5, 2015.
28. "Segregation in New York Schools," *NYT*, May 15, 2017; Hernández, "Schools Chief Vows . . . ," *NYT*, June 18, 2014.
29. John Kucsera with Gary Orfield, *New York State's Extreme School Segregation: Inequality, Inaction and a Damaged Future* (March 2014); Baker, "Status Quo at Elite Schools . . . ," *NYT*, March 12, 2014.
30. E.g., Ford, "Some in Manhattan . . . ," *CL*, November 24, 2015; "'Controlled Choice' for Integrating Schools . . . ," WNYC.org, June 6, 2016; Hannah-Jones,

"Choosing a School for My Daughter in a Segregated City," *NYT Magazine*, June 15, 2016; "Errol Louis on the Segregated City," *Slant Podcast*, June 12, 2017, https://www.cityandstateny.com/articles/opinion/the-slant-podcast/errol-louis-on-the-segregated-city.html; Louis, "Our Pro-Segregation Progressives," *NYDN*, January 15, 2018; "Speaker on School and Housing Segregation," *NY1 Inside City Hall*, May 3, 2018, https://www.ny1.com/nyc/all-boroughs/inside-city-hall/2018/05/04/speaker-on-school-and-housing-segregation. For an overview, see Christopher Bonastia, *The Battle Nearer to Home: The Persistence of School Segregation in New York City* (Stanford, CA, 2022), 210–31. On the value of integration as an educational strategy, see Rucker C. Johnson with Alexander Nazaryan, *Children of the Dream: Why School Integration Works* (New York, 2019); see also Alexandra Freidus, *Unequal Lessons: School Diversity and Educational Integration in New York City* (New York, 2025), on the limits of a constrained vision of integration.

31. Baker, "Status Quo at Elite Schools"; Harris, "Small Steps . . . ," *NYT*, July 5, 2016. See for instance New York City Department of Education, *Equity and Excellence for All: Diversity in New York City Public Schools* (June 2017), which conspicuously avoided using the terms *integration* and *segregation*.
32. "State of the City Remarks by Bill de Blasio, as Prepared for Delivery," NYC.org, February 3, 2015.
33. Viteritti, *Pragmatist*, 224.
34. *Housing New York: A Five-Borough, Ten-Year Plan* (New York, 2014).
35. Savitch-Lew, "Which Neighborhoods . . . ?" *CL*, May 31, 2016; *Housing New York: Final Report* (New York, 2021), 9; "Mayor de Blasio Announces 200,000 Affordable Homes Built or Preserved During This Administration" (press release), NYC.gov, December 22, 2021. For a critical assessment from the right, see Eric Kober, *De Blasio's Mandatory Inclusionary Housing Program: What Is Wrong and How It Can Be Made Right* (New York, 2020); from the left, see the discussion in Sam Stein, *Capital City: Gentrification and the Real Estate State* (New York, 2019), chap. 3. For an example of speculation tied to upzoning, see Haag, "A Hidden Gem . . . ," *NYT*, September 27, 2019.
36. On Stuyvesant Town, see Daniel R. Garodnick, *Saving Stuyvesant Town: How One Community Defeated the Worst Real Estate Deal in History* (Ithaca, NY, 2021); New York City Independent Budget Office, *The Stuyvesant Town–Peter Cooper Village Deal: How Much Affordable Housing Did the City Really Preserve?* (New York, 2018). For other instances, e.g., Kimura "Financing Closes to Preserve 33 Buildings in New York City," *Housing Finance Magazine*, March 16, 2016; Isaacson, "NYC Chalks Up $15M Affordable Housing Preservation Deal," *Multi-Housing News*, April 24, 2019; Michael Greenberg, "Tenants Under Siege: Inside New York City's Housing Crisis," *New York Review of Books*, August 17, 2017. For the administration's perspective, see "De Blasio Administration Launches Neighborhood Pillars Program to Protect Tenants and Preserve Affordability" (press release), December 20, 2018.
37. Jarrett Murphy, "Inside the Working Families Party's Deal with Governor Cuomo," *Nation*, June 2, 2014; Joan Walsh, "'Would Have Been Unconscionable Not To,'" *Salon*, June 9, 2014; Grynbaum, "De Blasio Deflects Blame . . . ," *NYT*, November 5, 2014.
38. Rashbaum and Kaplan, "U.S. Says Assembly Speaker . . . ," *NYT*, January 23,

2015; Craig, "New York Senate Leader . . . ," *NYT*, May 5, 2015; Durkin, "Heastie, de Blasio Promise . . . ," *NYDN*, April 9, 2015; "A Moment to Fix the Housing Laws," *NYT*, May 9, 2015.

39. Andrew Cuomo, "My Affordable Housing Agenda," *NYDN*, June 6, 2015; "Mayor de Blasio Unloads," *NYT*, July 2, 2015; Grynbaum, "'Nothing Left to Lose' . . . ," *NYT*, July 1, 2015; "De Blasio Slams Cuomo for 'Lack of Leadership,'" interview by Errol Louis of NY1, July 6, 2015, https://ny1.com/nyc/all-boroughs/news/2015/06/30/de-blasio-slams-cuomo-for-lack-of-leadership; Fink, "Revenge Is Coming . . . ," *C&S*, January 8, 2017; Farrow, "Cuomo's First Accuser . . . ," *NYer*, March 18, 2021.

40. Navarro, "Panel Freezes . . . ," *NYT*, June 30, 2015; Navarro, "For Second Straight Year . . . ," *NYT*, June 28, 2016; "Mayor de Blasio Signs Three New Laws Protecting Tenants From Harassment" (press release), NYC.gov, September 3, 2015; *New York: Three Years of Progress* (New York, 2017), 21; New York City Human Resources Administration, *Universal Access to Legal Services: A Report on Year Four of Implementation in New York City* (Fall 2021), 5–6.

41. Greenberg, "Tenants Under Siege." On NYCHA, see Regional Plan Association, *NYCHA's Crisis: A Matter for All New Yorkers* (December 2018).

42. For overviews of de Blasio's first-term record, see Viteritti, *Pragmatist*, chaps. 8–10; Juan González, *Reclaiming Gotham: Bill de Blasio and the Movement to End America's Tale of Two Cities* (New York, 2017); and David, "Bill de Blasio Is Cruising . . . ," *Crain's New York Business*, September 24, 2017.

43. Kristof, "A Guide to Democrats' . . . ," *NYT*, March 28, 2019.

44. Bragg, "IDC Could Face . . . ," *TU*, April 12, 2017; Goldmacher, "Democrats in New York . . . ," *NYT*, April 4, 2018; Segers, "Additional Progressive Challengers . . . ," *C&S*, March 6, 2018; Braiker, "A Conversation with State Senator Zellnor Myrie," BKMag.com, August 14, 2023; Colon, "Dems Backing IDC Challengers . . . ," *C&S*, August 15, 2018; Kirby, "The Primary Defeat of New York's 'Independent Democrats,' Explained," *Vox*, September 14, 2018. On Ocasio-Cortez, see Segers, "How Alexandria Ocasio-Cortez . . . ," *C&S*, June 27, 2018; Lynda Lopez, *AOC: The Fearless Rise and Powerful Resonance of Alexandria Ocasio-Cortez* (New York, 2020); Editors of New York Magazine, eds., *Take Up Space: The Unprecedented AOC* (New York, 2022).

45. "Governor Cuomo Unveils 2019 Justice Agenda," https://www.youtube.com/watch?v=aM6lf_ALfHU. See *2019 Justice Agenda: The Time Is Now* (2019 State of the State book), https://www.governor.ny.gov/sites/default/files/atoms/files/2019StateoftheStateBook.pdf; New York State Association of Counties, *2019 New York State Legislative Session Summary: The Impact on New York's Counties: Interim Report on Bills the Legislature Passed* (July 31, 2019).

46. Goodman, Wang, and Ferré-Sadurni, "A Stride for Tenant Protection . . . ," *NYT*, June 13, 2019; "LeFrak, Rudin and Durst Called . . . ," *Real Deal*, June 13, 2019; Barbanel, "New York Evictions Are Plunging . . . ," *WSJ*, November 26, 2019.

47. NYU Furman Center, *State of New York City's Housing and Neighborhoods in 2018*, 24; Amin, "Nearly 10% of New York City Students . . . ," Chalkbeat.org, October 26, 2022.

48. Sharkey, *Uneasy Peace*.

49. Mamdani describes the rally in an October 9, 2020 Facebook post: https://www.facebook.com/photo.php?fbid=341501130609861&id=109392217154088&se

t=a.112956613464315. Thank you to Grady Yuthok Short for calling Mamdani's presence at this event to my attention.

50. "Campaign 2020: Senator Sanders with Representative Ocasio-Cortez," C-SPAN, October 19, 2019, https://www.c-span.org/video/?465364-1/senator-sanders-representative-ocasio-cortez.

51. *Public Papers of Governor Mario M. Cuomo, 1985* (Albany, NY, 1989), 95; "Governor Mario M. Cuomo State of the State Address, 1985," https://www.youtube.com/watch?v=i3s-kVxRM-8. See Saladin Ambar, *American Cicero: Mario Cuomo and the Defense of American Liberalism* (New York, 2017), 85; Fred Siegel, *The Future Once Happened Here: New York, D.C., L.A., and the Fate of America's Big Cities* (New York, 1997), viii.

Postscript

1. "2014 New York City Inauguration," NYC Mayor's Office, https://www.youtube.com/watch?v=cvqfn3RYc9U.
2. "Gov. Cuomo's Coronavirus Update, March 31, 2020," CBS New York, https://www.youtube.com/watch?v=tC1392BFNGw.
3. Robert W. Snyder, *When the City Stopped: Stories from New York's Essential Workers* (Ithaca, NY, 2025), provides a terrific starting point on how New Yorkers experienced the pandemic. Scholars may also wish to consult the following oral history and autoethnography collections: Jeanne Theoharis, Joseph Entin, and Dominick Braswell, "Autoethnographies of a Pandemic from Brooklyn's Epicenter," *Black Perspectives*, October 12, 2020, https://www.aaihs.org/autoethnographies-of-a-pandemic-from-brooklyns-epicenter/; Ellen Noonan and Jacob Remes, "Covid Collections," NYU Digital Humanities, n.d., https://digitalhumanities.nyu.edu/projects/covid-collections/; "New York Responds Online," Museum of the City of New York, https://www.mcny.org/new-york-responds-online; Asif Alam, Queens Memory COVID-19 Project, Queens College, https://www.qc.cuny.edu/library/2020/08/04/queens-memory-covid-19-project/; NYC Covid-19 Oral History, Narrative, and Memory Project, Incite at Columbia University, n.d., https://incite.columbia.edu/projects/nyc-covid-19-oral-history-narrative-and-memory-project; Bronx COVID 19 Oral History Project, https://www.thebronxcovid19oralhistoryproject.com/meet-the-team. This list, of course, only scratches the surface. See also Thomas J. Sugrue, ed., "Preexisting Conditions: What 2020 Reveals About Our Urban Future," *Public Books*, November 19, 2020.
4. Haag, "Manhattan Emptied Out . . . ," *NYT*, October 13, 2020; Jeremiah Moss, *Feral City: On Finding Liberation in Lockdown New York* (New York, 2022), 29. See Katz's podcast series on FAQ NYC Off Cycle.
5. "Remarks by David N. Dinkins Election Night '93," DD, Box 45, Folder 9, RBML, emphasis in original.
6. Marshall Berman, "Introduction," in Berman and Brian Berger, eds., *New York Calling: From Blackout to Bloomberg* (London, 2007), 38.
7. Arthur M. Schlesinger, Jr., *The Vital Center: The Politics of Freedom* (Cambridge, MA, 1949), 254. Schlesinger made this assertion in relation to what he called human nature; I make it in relation to the historical context that shapes and constrains struggles for a decent, humane, and just city.

INDEX

A. Philip Randolph Campus High School (Manhattan), 173
abandonment crisis (1970s), 5, 10, 100, 101; *see also* housing abandonment
Abzug, Bella, 41, 43
Academy of American Studies, 173
active-learning model, 106
Adams, Cindy, 117
Adams, Eric, 146, 229, 242, 243, 251
admissions tests, school, 218–19, 262
Advocates for Children, 110
affluent New Yorkers, 73, 95, 134, 174–75, 177, 178, 202–3, 213–14, 218, 219, 260–61
affordable housing, 221, 226
AFL-CIO, 39
after-school programs, 140, 174
Aguilera, Alyssa, 253
Aid to Families with Dependent Children, 75
AIDS epidemic, 102–4, 112, 122
AIDS project (ACLU), 103–4
air transportation, 70–71
Alcantara, Marisol, 269
Alinsky, Saul, 130
Alliance of Community Organizations for Reform Now (ACORN), 133, 178–79
alternative schools (alternative schools movement), xviii, 58, 59–61, 134, 182, 184
Alvarado, Anthony, 33–34, 58
Amalgamated Clothing Workers, 165
American Civil Liberties Union, 103–4
American Scholar, The, 107
Amsterdam News, 27–28, 200
Anderson, Warren M., 49
Anker, Irving, 35, 57
Annenberg, Walter, 133
Annenberg Foundation, 133–34, 173, 214
antibusing, 34, 42
anticrack laws, 92–93
Anti-Crack Unit (NYPD), 92
anti-police-violence activism, 196–200
armed robbery(-ies), 88, 194
arson (arson-for-hire), xiii, 5, 12, 57, 101
Art of the Deal, The (Trump), 98
Assembly Housing Committee, 54
Association for a Better New York, 153
Association for Neighborhood and Housing Development, 168
Astor Place (Manhattan), 84, 165
Astoria (Queens), 118, 162, 203
Atlanta, Ga., 136
Atlantic, The, 67
Aubry, Jeffrion, 181
Auxiliary Police initiative, 62

Badillo, Herman, 41, 43, 204
Baker, Kevin, 152
Baltimore, Md., 40
Bangladeshi Americans, 203
bankruptcy scares, xii–xiii, xvii, 4; *see also* fiscal crisis (1975)

banks (banking system), 11, 18, 22, 94, 237
Barbaro, Frank, 112
Barrett, Wayne, 159
Barry, Dan, 199
Bay Street (Staten Island), 265
Bayside (Queens), 35, 118
Beacon High School (Manhattan), 133, 173, 256–57
Beame, Abraham, and administration, 36–38, 40, 41, 43, 49
Bedford-Stuyvesant (Brooklyn), 61, 196
Bell, Daniel, 6
Bell, Terrel, 105
Bellamy, Carol, 89
Belle Harbor (Queens), 175
Benedict, Jane, 52
Benjamin Cardozo High School (Queens), 173
Bennett, William, 127
Bensonhurst (Brooklyn), 109, 118, 120
Bensonhurst Tenants Council, 168
Berger, Curtis J., 59–60
Berkowitz, David, 62–63
Berman, Marshall, 23, 280–81
billionaires, 221, 240
Binghamton, N.Y., 49
Bishop Laughlin Memorial High School (Brooklyn), 115
Black and Hispanic Caucus (New York State Assembly), 181
Black Enterprise, 197
Black Lives Matter movement, 262–63
Black nationalism, 115
Black New Yorkers (Black communities)
  and charter schools, 181, 215
  disinvestment from neighborhoods with, 11
  and economic decline, 10
  as educators, 57
  everyday challenges faced by, xxiii, xxvi, 120–21
  Rudy Giuliani and, 117, 152, 225
  in Guardian Angels, 64
  as immigrants, 7, 203
  incarceration of, 93, 193
  and Jewish New Yorkers, 42–43, 121
  Ray Kelly and outreach efforts to, 227, 235
  and Kerner Commission, 14
  and Latino New Yorkers, 112–13, 119
  and liberals, 40–41
  as NYPD officers, 141
  and police abuse, 24, 88, 190, 194, 196–98, 231, 242, 244, 251, 252
  as police officers, 141
  political representation by, 44
  as politicians, 112–15
  poverty among, 73, 74
  in public housing, 96
  in public schools, 30–32, 59–60, 134, 175, 176, 178, 179, 262
  and redlining, 8
  and school vouchers, 57–58, 184
  in Trump Village, 21
  unemployment among, 9, 73–74
  as voters, 238; *see also specific mayoral campaigns and elections*
  and Voting Rights Act, xv
  and war on drugs, 93
  see also specific individuals
Black Power movement, 134
Black Power: The Politics of Liberation (Hamilton and Carmichael), 79
blackout (July 1977), 43
BlackRock, 222
Blanchard, Leslie, 104
block associations, 89, 91, 139, 197
Bloomberg, Michael R., and administration
  campaign spending by, 205
  change of party registration, 204–5
  and Andrew Cuomo, 260
  early career of, 204
  housing under, 220–27, 264–66
  inaugural address of, 210
  and Ray Kelly, 227–36, 242–45
  and Joel Klein, 212–14, 217–19, 238–41, 256–59, 263
  as mayoral leader, xxi, xxiv, 209–12, 246
  NYPD and policing under, 210, 227–37, 242–44, 251
  public schools under, 212–19, 238–42, 256–59, 262, 264
  on recovery of the city, xiii
  2001 mayoral campaign and election, 204–5
  2009 mayoral campaign and election, 237–38
  and 2013 mayoral election, 244–45, 248

boardinghouses, 50, 95
body cameras, 249
bonds, 36–37
Bonfire of the Vanities (Wolfe), 97–98
Boston, Mass., 144, 187, 213
Bowery (Manhattan), 51
Braschi, Miguel, 104
Braschi v. Stahl Associates, 104
Bratton, William J. "Bill," xxii, xxviii, 142–44, 161, 162, 185–92, 192–93, 227, 248–56
Brazil (Brazilian Americans), 192, 203
Brezenoff, Stan, 89, 101
Bright Kids NYC, 213
Brighton Beach (Brooklyn), 118
Brodheim, Adam, 96
"Broken Windows Plus," 229
Broken Windows policing, xx, xxii, 67–69, 85, 138, 139, 142–44, 162, 187–92, 216, 227, 229, 248–51, 253–56
"Broken Windows: The Police and Neighborhood Safety" (Kelling and Wilson), 67–69, 139
Bronx, xv, xvii, 7, 8, 10–11, 14, 22, 54, 58, 89, 112, 117, 164, 174, 189, 194–95, 197, 202–4, 215, 220, 226, 232, 233; *see also specific neighborhoods*
Bronx High School of Science, 108, 173, 174, 262
Bronx River Houses project, 195
Brookings Institute, 131
Brooklyn, xi, xv, xvii, xxiii, 7–8, 10, 21, 30–33, 36, 42, 43, 48, 55–58, 56, 57, 112, 118, 121, 155, 164, 169, 173, 189, 202–3, 226–27, 229, 245, 251; *see also specific neighborhoods*
Brooklyn Bridge, 31, 146, 245
Brooklyn College, 173
Brooklyn College Academy, 173
Brooklyn Heights, 29
Brooklyn Law, 113
Brooklyn Tech, 108, 173, 174, 239, 257, 262
Brooks, David, 150
Brown, Lee P., 136–44, 142, 143–44, 146, 153, 161, 186, 187, 227, 228
Brown, Michael, 251
Brown v. Board of Education, 29, 30, 59, 242
Brownsville (Brooklyn), 8, 10, 32, 40, 89, 231, 234
Bruckner, Saul, 106–7, 109
Bruno, Joseph, 159, 164–66, 168–71, 185, 224–25
Bryant Park, 66–67, 85
Bryant Park Restoration Corporation, 63
budget cuts, xiii, 36, 37, 47, 62, 75–76, 123, 194, 229
Buffalo, N.Y., 40
building codes, 17, 95
building strippers, 12
Bumpurs, Eleanor, 144
Bureau of Labor Statistics (BLS), 9
burglaries, 24, 97, 120, 142, 148
Bush, George H. W., and administration, 111, 120, 130
Bushwick (Brooklyn), 61, 163
business community, 37, 39, 48, 79, 213, 248, 261, 265
business district redevelopment, 6
business improvement districts (BIDs), 63
Business/Labor Working Group (B/LWG), 39, 48, 211
busing, forced, *see* forced busing
Bustelo, Manuel, 79
Butz, Mary, 104–7
buy-and-bust operations, 85–87, 92

Caballero, Diana, 134
California, 75
Callahan consent decree, 51
Campaign for Fiscal Equity, 177
Canarsie (Brooklyn), 118
Canarsie High School, 239
capital flight, 56
capital improvement allowances, 170–71, 222–24
capital markets, 70
Capra, Frank, 158
Carey, Hugh, xi–xiii, xxvii, 37, 38, 41, 42, 44, 48–49, 81
Caribbean Americans, 203
Carmichael, Stokely, 79
Carnegie Hill neighborhood (Manhattan), xiii–xiv
Caro, Robert, xi
Carter, Jimmy, and administration, 5, 44
Caruso, Phil, 146
Casey, William J., 82

Catholic New Yorkers, 44, 118, 155, 167
Catholic schools, 181
celebrities, 98, 99
Center for Collaborative Education (CCE), 130, 133–35, 173, 180
Center for Constitutional Rights, 199
Center for Educational Innovation (CEI), 130–31, 133, 182, 184
Center for New York City Affairs (New School), 219
Central Intelligence Agency, 82
Central Park, 120, 226
Central Park Conservancy, 204
Central Park East Secondary School, 34, 61, 108, 129, 134, 173
Central Park jogger assault (1989), 120
Central Park South (Manhattan), 98
Charlotte Street (Bronx), 5
charter schools, xviii, xxii, 160, 179–85, 212, 214–16, 219, 239–42, 245, 257–59, 261–63, 269
Chase Manhattan Bank, 39
Chelsea (Manhattan), 82, 97
Chicago, Ill., 34, 112, 171, 213
child poverty, 73
Children's Workshop School (Manhattan), 133
China, 71
Chinatown (Manhattan), 102
Chinese Americans, 203
Chisholm, Shirley, 18
Chrysler Building, 222
Chubb, John, 131
Citizens Budget Commission, 12, 126, 186
Citizens Committee for Effective Education, 57–58
citizens' patrols, *see* civilian patrols
City College, 36, 42, 197
City Council, 16, 18, 80, 145, 149, 162, 168, 169, 225, 230, 237, 243, 265, 268
City Hall, 31, 146, 197
City Hall Park, 146
City Journal, 121, 131, 144, 150–51, 181, 186, 201
City Planning Commission, 23, 81–82
City University of New York (CUNY), 40, 49
City-as-School (Brooklyn), 33
civil rights, 29, 42, 110, 118, 197, 198, 217, 220
Civilian Complaint Review Board (CCRB), 42, 147–48, 194, 233
civilian patrols, 62–64, 66, 139
civilian review boards, 146
Clark, Kenneth B., 30, 34–35, 59–60, 219
class inequality, xvi, xxvi
Cleveland, Ohio, 40
Clinton, Bill, and administration, 53, 128, 132, 172, 186, 248, 261, 277, 278
Clinton, Hillary, 248, 269
Coalición de Inquilinos del Norte de Manhattan, 168
Cobble Hill (Brooklyn), 257
cocaine, 86, 191; *see also* crack cocaine
"Cocaine Cowboys" scandal, 189
Codd, Michael, 28, 62–63
Colgate-Palmolive, 130
collaborative R&D labs, 179
College of Staten Island, 174
co-location requests, 258–59
Colombia (Colombian Americans), 71, 203
Columbia Law School, 158
Columbia School of Social Work, 31
Columbia University, 59, 79, 99, 110, 111, 132, 198, 280
Columbine High School shootings, 185
Columbus Avenue (Manhattan), 71
Commission on the Year 2000, 79–81, 100, 201–2, 211
Communications Workers of America, 168
Communities United for Police Reform, 254
community boards, 107–8
community control movement, 33, 57, 181
community empowerment, 31
community leaders, 87–88, 195, 215
community norms, 66
Community Patrol Officer Program (CPOP), 139
Community Planning Boards, 139
community policing, xx, xxvii, 114, 123, 137–41, 144, 147–48, 161, 186–88, 200, 227, 253
community self-regulation, 90
Community Service Society, 177
Company (musical), 7, 9
Comprehensive School Support, 257–58
CompStat, 187, 191, 229, 253

Concerned Citizens for the Education of Gifted and Talented Children, 178
condominiums, 16, 95–96
ConEd, 54, 195, 196
Coney Island (Brooklyn), 59, 108
Congress, xii, 38, 53, 61, 87, 270; *see also* U.S. Senate; *individual congresspeople*
Congress on Racial Equality (CORE), 29
Conservative Party, 44
conservatives, 130, 160, 164
construction, 94–95, 220, 224, 226, 265, 268
construction industry (incl. unions), 9, 48
consultants, 14–15
consumer movements, 277
controlled choice, 263
convention centers, 39
conversions, co-op, 95–96, 111, 222
Co-op City, 10–11
Cooper Union, 225
cooperatives (co-ops), 16, 95–96; *see also* conversions, co-op
cop-on-the-beat approach, 138–39, 143
corporate law sector, 94
corruption, 26, 87, 145, 169, 200, 224
Cortines, Ramón, 178
Costa Rican immigrants, 270
counterterrorism, 236
Covid-19 pandemic, 278–80
CPAC, 157
crack cocaine, 91–93, 120, 191, 199
Crew, Rudy, 178, 180, 183, 214
crime (crime rates), 23–29, 62–70, 72, 120, 122, 148, 161–62, 185–92, 191, 201, 211, 227, 236, 249, 272, 273; *see also specific types of crime*
Criminal Justice Coordinating Council, 25–26
Criminal Justice Reform Act, 255
criminal justice system, 25, 27, 232, 254–55
Cross-Bronx Expressway, 7
Crowley, Joseph, 270
Crown Heights (Brooklyn), 18, 102, 121, 154, 221, 226, 238, 267
Cuban Americans, 33
Cuomo, Andrew, xxi, 246, 248, 259–62, 266, 267, 269–71, 278
Cuomo, Mario, xxi, xxiii, 41–44, 55, 56, 64, 82, 92–93, 100, 101, 103, 112, 118–19, 122–23, 126–27, 135, 137, 140, 149, 154, 155, 158–59, 163–64, 186, 204, 205, 245, 246, 275

Dallas, Tex., 6
D'Amato, Alfonse, xxii, 53–54, 116, 123, 148–49, 153, 155–59, 166–68, 170, 183, 185, 224, 248
data-driven managerialism, 212
Davidoff, Sid, 52
Davis, Polk (law firm), 270
daycare centers, 4
DC 37 (union), 115, 168
de Blasio, Bill, and administration
  and Bill Bratton, 248–56
  children of, 256–57
  and Andrew Cuomo, 248
  and David Dinkins, 245, 246
  and election of 2018, 268–71
  and Carmen Fariña, 257–58, 262
  housing under, 264–68
  as mayoral leader, xxi, xxiv, 246, 247, 268–71, 274
  NYPD and policing under, 248–56
  public schools under, 256–64
  2013 mayoral campaign and election, 245–46, 277
de Blasio, Chiara, 256–57
de Blasio, Dante, 257
de Sapio, Carmine, 42
Dearie, John, 54–56
Death and Life of Great American Cities, The (Jacobs), 66
Death and Life of the Great American School System, The (Ravitch), 241
death penalty, 120
"decentralization," 33
decriminalization, 254–55
"deeply affordable" housing, 101, 268
"deep-rooted social conditions," 138
deinstitutionalization, 50
DeLillo, Don, xxiii
Democratic Leadership Council of New York, 132
Democratic National Convention (1976), 58
Democratic National Convention (1984), 245

democratic socialists, xix–xx, 128
Democratic Socialists of America (DSA), 34, 115
Democrats (Democratic Party)
Americans identifying as, 157
and austerity, 44–45
Abraham Beame and, 36
Michael Bloomberg and, 204–5, 213, 236, 244
Hugh Carey and, xii
and community policing, xx
Andrew Cuomo and, 260, 267
Mario Cuomo and, 41–43, 55, 149, 204, 245
Bill de Blasio and, 245–48
David Dinkins and, 113, 114, 118, 119, 153, 204, 247
erosion of support for, 160–61
and fiscal crisis, 39, 160
Rudy Giuliani and, 115, 154–55, 157–58
Independent Democratic Caucus, 259, 266, 269, 270
Ed Koch and, 42, 43, 55, 89, 112, 149, 204
John Lindsay and, 14, 15, 18, 32
and rent regulation/deregulation, 48–49, 100, 164, 166–68, 171, 271
and school choice, 127
in State Assembly, 13, 154, 213, 225, 266
in State Senate, 19, 266, 270
and tenant rights, 22
Bobby Wagner and, 40, 80, 154–55
see also specific individuals
"demonstration" districts, 32
deportations, 232
deregulation, *see* rent deregulation
desegregation, 30, 31, 35, 57, 59, 60, 263
desk appearance tickets, 193
Detroit, Mich., 6
developers, 95, 147, 271
Dewitt Clinton High School (Bronx), 173
Diallo, Amadou, 195–200, 203, 228–30
Diaz, Rafael, 195
Dickens, Charles, 82
Dilan, Martin Malavé, 163
Dinkins, David, and administration
and Mario Cuomo, 122–23
and Bill de Blasio, 245, 246, 248
and Amadou Diallo murder, 197
early career of, 113
housing under, 124–27, 171
inaugural address of, 122, 135
as Manhattan borough president, 82, 84, 109–10
as mayoral leader, xxi, xxiii, xxiv, 119–23, 280
and *New York Ascendant* report, 82, 84
1989 mayoral campaign and election, 113–15, 118, 204, 238
and 1993 mayoral election, 148, 151–56, 159, 238, 280
NYPD and policing under, 114, 135–48, 153, 154, 161, 185–86, 188, 191, 194, 227, 228
public schools under, 127–35, 178
Dinkins, Joyce, 113
"disorder," concept of, 66–68, 140, 151
Dissent, 105
Do the Right Thing (film), 144
Domain Awareness System, 243
Domanico, Ray, 151
Dominican Republic (Dominican Americans), 71, 146, 203
Donovan, Shaun, 221
Dorismond, Patrick, 199, 203
dot-com bubble, 209–10
Doubleday (publisher), 26
Dowd, Matthew, 145
downzoning, 95
Druckenmiller, Stanley, 240
drugs, illicit, 12, 24–29, 25, 27, 85, 116, 120, 135, 145, 189, 318; *see also* street-level drug markets (open-air drug markets)
Dukakis, Michael, 113
Dwyer, Jim, 243

Earth School (Manhattan), 133
East Brooklyn, 130–31, 220
East Brooklyn Churches coalition, 89
East Flatbush (Brooklyn), 115
East Harlem (Manhattan), xiii–xiv, 8–10, 32, 33, 58, 61, 111, 127, 151, 179, 231, 265
East New York (Brooklyn), 8, 89, 265
East Side antidrug marches (1983), 91
East Side Community High School (Manhattan), 173
Eastern Parkway (Brooklyn), 18

economy, xix, 10, 73, 201–4, 272
Ecuador (Ecuadorian Americans), 71, 203
Education for Economic Security Act (1984), 61
education-option schools (ed-ops), 106–11, 173, 174
Edward R. Murrow High School (Brooklyn), 104–9, 173
Edwards, Babette, xxii, 58, 184
"effort academy," 217
Eimicke, William, 100
El Barrio (Manhattan), 82
El Diario–La Prensa, 79, 86, 181–82
Eldridge, Ronnie, 145, 163
Eleanor Roosevelt High School, 176
elections, presidential
  1972, 115
  1976, 38
  1980, 53, 115–16
  1988, 113, 117
  2016, 269
electricity, 54
1199 health care workers (union), 168
Ellis Island, 36, 278
Elmhurst (Queens), 11, 53, 224
Emergency Financial Control Board (EFCB), 37, 38, 41
Emergency Tenant Protection Act (1974), 22, 51–52, 224–25
energy costs, 10
entrepreneurship, 72
ESL programs, 238
Esposito, Meade, 43
Essence, 197
evictions, 16, 55, 104, 268, 271, 272
Ewing, Eve, 238
exclusion laws, 7

Facebook, 280
"failing" schools, 178
Fair Housing Act (1968), 21
Falcón, Angelo, 119
"family," definition of, 104
Farber, Barry, 44
fare evasion, 143
Fariña, Carmen, 257–58, 262
Farrow, Mia, 98
Federal Bureau of Investigation (FBI), 34
federal mortgage insurance, 8
Federal Reserve, 76, 222
federal taxation, 74–75
Feldman, Sandra, 114, 180
felony arrests and convictions, 92–93, 193
Ferguson, Mo., 251
Fernández, Joseph, 132–33
Ferrer, Fernando, 89, 204
Fields, C. Virginia, 117, 145, 176
Fifth Avenue (Manhattan), 98
57th Street (Manhattan), 220
"Fight Back Friday" rallies, 239
Filler, Martin, 220
finance sector, 48, 75, 94
Financial District (Manhattan), 85; *see also* Wall Street
financialization, xvii, 70, 94, 204
Fink, Stanley, 99
Finkelstein, Arthur J., xxii, 148, 156–58
Finkelstein, Jerry, 21
firehouses, xxvii
fiscal crisis (1975), 4, 36–41, 44, 46, 57, 62, 75, 81, 82, 210, 279
Fisher, Antony, 82
Flatbush (Brooklyn), 203, 226
Fliegel, Seymour, 127, 130, 184
Floyd v. New York, 244, 249
Flushing (Queens), 102, 203, 265
Flynn, John E., 54–56
Flynn-Dearie bill, 54–56, 97
focused deterrence, 243
foot patrols, 68, 68–69, 69–70
forced busing, 34, 42, 59
Ford, Gerald, and administration, xii–xiii, 37–38
Ford Foundation, 32
Fordham neighborhood (Bronx), 226
foreign languages, classes in, 216–17
Forest Hills (Queens), 42, 118
Fort Greene (Brooklyn), 8
Fortune magazine, 66, 176
Fourteenth Amendment, 244
14th Street (Manhattan), 195–96
Fourth Amendment, 190, 244
Frederick Douglass Academy, 173
free markets, *see* market economics
Freedom Summer (1964), 42, 197
Freeman, Joshua, xv–xvi, 5

Freeman, Stanley, 117
Friedman, Milton, 156
fuel costs, 52
Fund for New York City Public Education, 133

Gaebler, Ted, 127–28
Galamison, Milton, 31–32
"Gang of Four," 113
gangs, 227, 243
Garcia, José "Kiko," 146
garment industry, 6, 9, 42
Garner, Eric, 250–52
Garth, David, 43, 155
Gates Foundation, 214
gay rights movement, 102–4
Gelman, Andrew, 198
Genn, Colman, 130, 151
gentrification, 47, 56, 71, 86, 91, 95–97, 125, 171, 203, 220–21, 223, 226, 263, 266, 268
Georgia, 44, 198
ghettoes (ghettoization), xvii, 7, 31
gifted-and-talented programs, xviii, xxvii, 59–61, 107–8, 134–35, 175–76, 178–79, 181, 215–19, 262
Gilder, George, 83
Gilder Lehrman Institute of American History, 173–74
Ginzberg, Eli, 70
Giuliani, Helen, 116
Giuliani, Rudolph "Rudy," and administration
  and Michael Bloomberg, 205, 212
  and Bill Bratton, 161–62
  and Mario Cuomo, 158
  and Alfonse D'Amato, 123, 148, 149
  early career of, 115–18
  fiscal policy, 209
  housing under, 162–72, 225
  as mayoral leader, xxi, xxiii–xxiv, 116–17, 147, 156, 161–62, 204, 213, 246
  and 1989 mayoral election, 118, 121, 146, 148, 149, 238
  1993 mayoral campaign and election, 149–55
  NYPD and policing under, 185–201, 211, 227–29, 235, 251
  and George Pataki, 159
  public schools under, 172–79
  and Donald Trump, 117
Gladwell, Malcolm, 124–25, 192, 215
Glaeser, Edward, 227
Glazer, Nathan, 65, 67, 150
Goldberg, Michelle, 247
Goldin, Harrison, 115
Goldwater, Barry, 156
"Good School, A" (Ravitch), 107
Goodman, Andrew, 197
Goodman, Roy M., 44, 49, 168
Google, 280
"gorgeous mosaic" philosophy, 122, 137, 154
Gottfried, Richard, 103
Gracie Mansion, 234
graffiti, 65, 67, 85, 89, 141, 144, 187–88
Grand Central Partnership, 63
Grand Concourse (Bronx), 18, 221
Grand Street (Manhattan), 165
Grannis, Alexander, 54
Grant, Bob, 72
Great Depression, 76, 119
Great Migration, 7
Great Society, xii, 42, 130
Greek Americans, 203
Green, Mark, 204
Greenberg, Michael, 268
Greenhouse, Linda, 49
Greenpoint (Brooklyn), 221
Greenwich Village (Manhattan), 33, 42, 86, 91, 98, 102–3
Gregorian, Vartan, 79
Griffith, Emlyn I., 35
Guardian Angels, 64
Guinea, 195
Gunn, David, 142
guns and gun violence, 135, 189–90, 231, 234, 259

Hacker, Andrew, xiii
Haiti (Haitian Americans), 71, 199, 238
Haldipur, Jan, 233
Hamilton, Charles V., 79
Hamilton, Jesse, 270
Hannah-Jones, Nikole, 263
Haredi Jews, 121

Harlem (Manhattan), xxii, xxiii, 8–10, 27–28, 34, 43, 44, 57, 61, 64, 82, 87, 88, 101, 113, 114, 127, 130; *see also* East Harlem
Harlem Parents' Union, 58
Harlem River Drive (album), 8–9
Harriman, Averell, xii
Hart Island, 280
Harvard Club, 180
Harvard Kennedy School, 85, 136, 137, 142
Harvard University, 40, 80
Hayes, Chris, 247
Health and Hospitals Corporation, 81
health clinics, xxvii, 4
Heastie, Carl, 267
Hemphill, Clara, 172–74, 219
Hempstead Tenants Council, 168
Henry Street (Manhattan), 165
Herbert, Bob, 195, 229, 242
heroin, 24, 86
High School for Environmental Studies, 173
high schools, 108–9, 213; *see also specific high schools*
Highbridge (Bronx), 226
Hispanic New Yorkers, *see* Latino New Yorkers
historic districts, 95
Hogan, Frank, 27
home rule, 13
homelessness, 51, 56, 73, 93, 94, 101–2, 114, 118, 138, 140, 145, 151, 219, 253, 272
homicides, xiii, 24, 88, 120, 148, 152–53, 189, 191
Honduras, 71
Hoover Institution, 131
hotels, 71
Housing Act (1937), 80
housing, xviii, 11, 82
  under Mayor Bloomberg, 220–27, 264–66
  under Mayor de Blasio, 264–68
  "deeply affordable," 101, 268
  under Mayor Dinkins, 124–27
  during fiscal crisis of 1970s, 51–56
  under Mayor Giuliani, 162–72, 225
  under Mayor Koch, 93–102, 171, 264
housing abandonment, 5, 10–11, 17–20, 22, 50, 57, 101, 274
housing market, 48, 50, 52, 56, 94–95, 99, 101–2, 124, 220–27, 268
Housing New York, 264, 265
Housing Stability and Tenant Protection Act (2019), 271, 273
housing stock, 5–12, 75, 96, 171, 273
Houston, Tex., 136
Howard Beach (Queens), 120
Howard University, 136
Hudson River, 39
Hungary, xxii
Hunter College, 79, 232
Hunter College High School, 173
Hunt's Point (Bronx), 64

identity politics, 153
immigrants and immigration, 7, 9, 71–73, 101–2, 171, 203, 217, 232, 272; *see also specific countries and groups*
Immigration and Nationality Act (1965), 71, 272
incarceration rates, 83, 92–93
  graph, 318
income taxes, 140; *see also* New York City income tax
incrementalism, 269
Independent Democratic Caucus (IDC), 259, 266, 269, 270
Industrial Areas Foundation, 130–31
industrial jobs, loss of, 73
inflation, 7, 10, 15, 36, 55, 73, 76, 170–71, 183
information-based economy, xix
insider trading, 116
Institute for Collaborative Education, 173
Institute for Puerto Rican Policy, 119
institutional investors, 11–12
integration (integration movement), 29, 30, 59; *see also* desegregation
interest rates, 10, 76
intergenerational wealth, 96
international business, 70
investment banking, 95
Inwood (Manhattan), 227, 265
Ipswich, Mass., 157
IS 223 magnet school (Harlem), 61
Israel, xxii
Italian Americans, 7, 9
Italy, 192

J-51 (tax code provision), 50, 56, 226
Jackson, Jesse, 112–13, 115, 118, 119, 156, 197
Jackson, Robert, 269
Jackson Heights (Queens), 203
Jacobs, Jane, 66, 68, 90, 138
jails, 93, 189, 193, 232
Jamaica (country), 71
Jamaica (Queens), 29
James, Letitia, 255
Japan, 192
Javits, Jacob, 39, 53, 75, 158
Jeffries, Hakeem, 242, 270
Jerome Avenue (Bronx), 265
Jewish New Yorkers, 9, 36, 42–44, 118, 121, 155, 165
"Jim Crow policing," 242
John Dewey High School (Brooklyn), 33, 109
Johnson, Lyndon B., and administration, xii, 71
Jones, J. Raymond, 113
Jones, Paul Tudor, 240
juvenile delinquency, 23

Katz, Alyssa, 279–80
Katz, Michael B., 106
Kelling, George, xxii, 67–69, 85, 90, 136, 138, 139, 142, 143, 151, 162, 187, 188, 250
Kelly, Raymond "Ray," xxii, 136–44, 142, 143–44, 146, 161, 186, 227–36, 242–45, 245, 249, 251–52
Kempton, Murray, 113–14
Kennedy, John F., and administration, xii
Kennedy, Robert F. "Bobby," 42, 115
kindergarten tests, 218
King, Peter, 115
Kings County, 254; *see also* Brooklyn
Kingsbridge Heights (Bronx), 226
Klein, Genevieve, 35
Klein, Joel, 212–15, 217–19, 238–41, 256–59, 263
Knapp Commission, 26, 145
knives, 234
Knowledge Is Power Program (KIPP), 215
Koch, Edward "Ed," and administration
  and austerity politics, 53, 83–84
  and Michael Bloomberg, 210, 221
  Commission on the Year 2000 of, 79–81, 100, 201–2, 211
  and Mario Cuomo, 55, 101
  and Alfonse D'Amato, 149
  and David Dinkins, 154
  fiscal policy, 76
  and Rudy Giuliani, 116, 118, 154, 155, 161, 188
  housing under, 93–102, 171, 264
  inaugural address of, 46–47
  as mayoral leader, xvii–xviii, xxi, xxiii, xxiv, 121
  1977 mayoral campaign and election, 42–44
  and 1985 mayoral election, 269
  and 1989 mayoral election, 112–15, 119, 204
  NYPD and policing under, 65–66, 69–70, 75, 84–93, 120, 123, 136, 139, 140, 144–45, 147
  Curtis Sliwa on, 64
  and term-limit law, 237
  and Donald Trump, 98
  and Bobby Wagner, 81
Kolbert, Elizabeth, 116–17, 167
Korean Americans, 121, 203

La Guardia, Fiorello, xiii, xxi, 113, 211, 237, 245, 274
Lab School for Collaborative Studies, 173
labor (labor movement), xvi, xvi–xvii, 6, 55, 115, 119
labor unions, xvii, xxii, 6, 9, 15, 38, 48, 79, 115, 146, 165, 168, 182, 277; *see also specific unions*
LaGuardia High School, 173
Laird, Robert W., 156
Lander, Brad, 222, 225, 243–44
landlords (landlord groups), xviii, xxi, 11–12, 15–18, 20, 22, 51–55, 96–100, 97, 99, 103, 103–4, 126, 160, 165, 166, 169–71, 171, 223–26, 224, 225, 255, 271
Landmark School (Manhattan), 173
land-use restrictions, 17, 95, 147
Langone, Kenneth, 240
Latino New Yorkers, xxvi, 57, 64, 73, 74, 88, 93, 119, 120, 141, 155, 175, 176, 178, 181–82, 190, 193, 194, 197, 198, 215, 219, 225, 227, 231, 235, 242, 251, 262; *see also specific groups and people*

Lauder, Ronald, 149
law and order, 43, 279
Learning Environment Survey, 213
Lee, Chang-Rae, 72
Lee, Spike, 144
LeFrak, Samuel, 53, 271
LeFrak City (Queens), 11, 53
left, the, xvi, xxiv, 106, 259, 268–69, 274
legal industry, 75
Lehman, Herbert, xii
Lehman Brothers, 237
Lehrer, Brian, 174, 198
Leon Goldstein High School for the Sciences (Brooklyn), 173
Lesbian and Gay Rights project (ACLU), 103–4
Lethem, Jonathan, 257
Leventhal, Nathan, 20
Lewis, John, 198
Lhota, Joe, 244
Liberal Party, 15, 43, 89
liberals and liberalism, 33, 39, 40, 42, 119, 123, 128–31, 151–52
Libertarian Party, 58
libertarianism, 129, 156
Life Sciences Secondary School (Manhattan), 176
Lincoln Center, 204
Lindsay, John, and administration, xxi, 3, 14–29, 32–33, 36, 42, 43, 85, 95, 118, 131, 145, 147, 160, 271
Liu, Wenjian, 252
Local 1180 (Communications Workers of America), 168
Long Island City (Queens), 136, 173–74, 265
Los Angeles Police Department (LAPD), 91
Losing Ground (Murray), 83
Louis, Errol, 263
Lower East Side (Manhattan), 7, 8, 10, 32, 69, 82, 86–88, 91, 101, 109, 165, 191–92, 200, 239, 263
Lower East Side Joint Planning Council, 91
Lower East Side Narcotics Task Force, 86
low-rise neighborhoods, 96
Ludlam, Charles, 102–4
luxury deregulation, 53, 54, 125, 163–64, 170
Lynch, Bill, 115, 118, 245
Lynch, Patrick, 252
MacArthur "genius" award, 111, 130
MacDonald, Heather, 201
Madison Democratic Club (Brooklyn), 36
magnet schools, xviii, 33, 59–62, 108, 111, 173, 175–77, 180, 181, 215
Malcolm X, 41
Malcolm X Grassroots Movement, 197
Maloney, Carolyn, 176
Mamdani, Zohran, 274
Mandatory Inclusionary Housing (MIH), 265–66
Manhattan, 7, 56, 63, 113, 124, 169, 173, 189; *see also specific neighborhoods*
Manhattan College, 115, 136
Manhattan Institute, 82–83, 121, 123, 128, 130, 131, 133, 134, 149–51, 164, 173–74, 182
manufacturing, xix, 6, 9, 72
Maple, Jack, 116, 187–91
Marcuse, Peter, 50, 99
marijuana, 189, 191, 232, 254–55
Marino, Ralph, 126, 159, 164
Mark Twain Junior High School (Brooklyn), 59–60
Mark Twain School for the Gifted and Talented (Brooklyn), 60–61, 108, 175
market economics, xx, 83, 128, 130, 132, 166, 182
Mark-Viverito, Melissa, 253–56
Marshall Scholarship, 80
Mastro, Randy, 200
Math and Science Institute, 179
Maximum Base Rent (MBR), 18–20
Mayors Against Illegal Guns, 234
McCall, H. Carl, 197, 222
McCann, Colum, 209
McGovern, George, 115
McGuire, Robert, 69–70, 85, 86, 139
McNickle, Chris, 233, 236
Medgar Evers College, 173
median incomes, xiii, 50, 73
Medicaid, 75
Medina, Carlos, 127, 130
Meeks, Gregory, 197
Meier, Deborah, xxii, xxviii, 33–34, 58, 61, 105–6, 108, 111, 127–30, 133, 134, 173, 180, 184, 240–41
mental health clinics, 257

mergers and acquisitions, 94
Messinger, Ruth, 56
MetLife, 220, 222, 223, 226
Metropolitan Council on Housing (MetCo), 54, 168
Metropolitan Museum of Art, 204
Metropolitan Transit Authority (MTA), 3, 13, 143, 244
Mexico, 71
Mfume, Kweise, 197
Miami, Fla., 132
Michael J. Petrides School, 174
middle class, xxiv–xxvi, 6, 7, 10, 16, 18, 39–40, 47, 57, 59, 73, 81–83, 101, 203, 217, 220, 222, 259
Middle College High School (Queens), 173
Middle Eastern Americans, 203
Midwood (Brooklyn), 104–7
Midwood High School (Brooklyn), 173
Minnesota, 179
Mississippi, 197
Mitchell-Lama program, 16
Moe, Terry, 131
Molinari, Guy, 155
Mollen, Milton, 145
Mollen Commission, 145–46
Mollenkopf, John, 118
monetary policy, 52, 75
Moore, Mark H., 85–86, 136
"more-is-more" policing approach, 193
Morgenthau, Robert, 97, 169
Morris Avenue (Bronx), 8
Morris Heights (Bronx), 144
mortgages (mortgage insurance), 8, 10, 18, 22, 52
"Moscow on the Hudson," 97
Moses, Robert, xi, 3, 5, 236, 237
Moshulu (Bronx), 226
Moskowitz, Eva, 215, 216, 245, 261
Moss, Jeremiah, 280
Mothers Against Police Brutality, 197
Moynihan, Daniel Patrick, 49, 61, 74–75, 117–19, 148, 149, 153–54, 205
Mr. Smith Goes to Washington (film), 158
MSNBC, 247
Municipal Assistance Corporation (MAC), 37
municipal charter, 13
Murdoch, Rupert, 240
Murray, Charles, 83
Murry Bergtraum High School for Business Careers (Manhattan), 108, 109
Museum of Modern Art, 222
mutual dependence, 277
Myrie, Zellnor, 270

NAACP, 29, 30, 197
NAACP Legal Defense and Education Fund, 254
Nadler, Jerry, 270
Narcotics Division (NYPD), 28
Nassau County, 14, 53, 157–58
Nation, The, 129, 153, 247
Nation at Risk, A: The Imperative for Educational Reform (report), 105–6
National Advisory Commission on Civil Disorders (Kerner Commission), 14
National Congress for Puerto Rican Rights, 197, 199, 227–28
National Labor Relations Act, 80
National Press Club, 37
National Urban League, 11
National Youth Administration, xi–xii
neighborhood coordinating officers (NCOs), 252–53
neighborhood organizations, 63, 86, 236, 265; *see also* block associations
Neighborhood School, 133
NeighborhoodStat, 253
neoconservatives, xix, xx, 84, 116, 121, 123, 130, 161
neoliberalism, xx–xxi, 5
Neptune Avenue (Brooklyn), 59
Netanyahu, Benjamin, xxii
New Deal, xvi, 36, 39, 40, 55, 80, 119, 120, 154, 248, 260, 274, 277
New Explorations in Science, Technology, and Mathematics, 239
New Housing Marketplace Plan, 221
New Left, 41
new liberalism, 128–29
new reform movement, 240–41
New Right, 83
New School, 219
New Visions, 173
New York Ascendant (report), 81–82, 84, 100

New York Beacon, The, 195
New York City Board of Education, 29–33, 35, 57–59, 81, 105, 106, 108–11, 123, 132, 173, 176–80, 237
New York City Board of Estimate, 36, 76
New York City Central Labor Council, 39
New York City Coalition for Excellence in Black Education, 134, 135
New York City Department of Education, 213, 214, 217, 255, 257, 258, 263
New York City Department of Housing Preservation and Development, 221, 266
New York City Department of Rent and Housing Maintenance, 19
New York City Department of Sanitation, 253
New York City Housing Authority (NYCHA), 16, 100–101, 171, 253, 268
New York City Housing Foundation, 114
New York City income tax, 75, 76, 97, 140, 260
New York City Museum School, 173
New York City Transit Authority, 142
New York City Transit Police, 64, 141–43
New York City's Best Public High Schools: A Parents' Guide (Hemphill), 172–73
New York Civil Liberties Union, 145, 228
New York Daily News, xii–xiii, 38, 88, 141, 154, 156, 267
New York magazine, 3, 64, 71, 124, 191
New York Networks for School Renewal, 133
New York Police Department (NYPD)
  beliefs about role of, xxv, 201
  under Mayor Bloomberg, 210, 227–37, 242–44
  and crime wave of 1970s, 62–65
  under Mayor de Blasio, 248–56
  and Amadou Diallo murder, 195–200, 203, 228–30
  under David Dinkins, 114, 135–41, 144–48, 153, 154
  under Mayor Giuliani, 185–201, 211, 227–29, 235, 251
  as "indispensable institution," 201
  under Mayor Koch, 69–70, 75, 84–93
  under Mayor Lindsay, 24–29
  and stop-and-frisk, xxiii, xxvii, 190–91, 194–95, 198–201, 229–36, 242–45, 248–51, 255, 272
  street-policing strategies of, *see* policing, street-level
  and subway system, 65–66, 141–44
New York Post, 117, 153, 228, 255
New York Public Library, 79, 204
New York State, xxii, 13–15, 37, 51, 61, 73, 93, 99, 103, 120, 123, 153, 177, 205, 248
New York State Assembly, xii, xxii, 13–14, 22, 54, 113, 154, 158, 165, 182, 213, 225, 267, 274; *see also individual assemblypersons*
New York State Department of Housing and Community Renewal, 103, 104
New York State Housing Task Force, 48–49
New York State legislature, xxii, 3, 14, 19, 22, 27, 32–33, 35, 49, 56, 80, 92, 100, 126–27, 146, 162, 165, 171, 183, 186, 213, 223, 262, 275; *see also* New York State Assembly; New York State Senate
New York State Senate, xxvii, 14, 19–20, 49, 55, 100, 103, 126, 140, 158, 159, 164–65, 168–70, 213, 224–25, 259, 266–67, 267, 270, 271; *see also individual senators*
New York State Tenants and Neighbors Coalition, 25, 54, 166–68
New York Stock Exchange, 197
New York Times, The, 3, 12, 27, 50, 64, 88, 91, 109–10, 124, 126, 242, 262, 267
New York Times Sunday Magazine, The, 190
New York Unbound (study), 82–84, 121
New York University (NYU), 42, 91, 115, 131–32, 180
New York Yankees, 222
New Yorker, The, 98, 192
Newark, N.J., 40, 42, 67, 68
Newfield, Jack, 116, 185
Newsom, Gavin, 247
96th Street (Manhattan), xiv
Nixon, Richard, and administration, 26–27
No Child Left Behind Act (2001), 214, 241
"no radio" signs, 120
nonenforcement, policy of, street-level, 84
Norman Thomas High School, 108
North Africans, 203

NY: The City Journal, 121; *see also City Journal*
NYC School Help, 213
Nyquist, Ewald, 35, 57–58

Obama, Barack, and administration, 240, 247
Ocasio-Cortez, Alexandria, 270, 274
Occupy Wall Street movement, 238, 260
Ocean Hill (Brooklyn), 32, 40
O'Connor, John Cardinal, 167
office vacancy rates, 71
Ohrenstein, Manfred, 27, 103
oil shocks of 1970s, 10, 22, 52
Olin Foundation, 132
Omnibus Housing Act (1983), 55, 102
Onassis, Jacqueline Kennedy, 42
"One City, One Standard," 152, 190
125th Street (Harlem), xiii
open-air drug markets, *see* street-level drug markets
open-container violations, 188
Operation Condor, 199
Operation Crew Cut, 243
Operation Drugs, 28
Operation Impact, 229–31, 249
Operation Juggernaut, 189, 192
Operation Pressure Point (OPP), 87–93, 136, 161, 186
Orbán, Viktor, xxii
Organization Man, The (Whyte), 66
organized crime, 12, 97, 116
Osborne, David, 127–28
"outer boroughs," 63, 82, 116
Outliers (Gladwell), 215
Owens, Major, 197

Padavan, Frank, 168
Palmieri, Charlie, 8–9
Palmieri, Eddie, 8–9
Panel for Educational Policy, 239
panhandling, 68, 143, 185–86, 188
Pantaleo, Daniel, 250–52
"Parents and Taxpayers" (activist group), 30
Parents Involved v. Seattle, 263
parent-teacher associations (PTAs), 174–75, 263
Park Slope (Brooklyn), xi, 71, 256
Parkchester (Bronx), 274
Partnership for an Upper East Side High School, 176
Partnership for New York, 130, 261
Pataki, George, xxii, 158–59, 164, 166–72, 178, 179, 182–83, 185, 205, 220, 222, 224
Paterson, Basil, 113, 197
Paterson, David, 242–43, 260
path dependencies, xxvi
Patrolmen's Benevolent Association (PBA), 24, 62–63, 146, 148, 252
Paul Robeson High School (Brooklyn), 238
Penn, Mark, 53
people of color, xiv, xvii, 9, 47, 134, 141, 144, 201, 217, 226, 236, 265, 272; *see also* Black New Yorkers; Latino New Yorkers
People's Board of Education, 31–32
Peralta, José, 270
Pérez, Richie, 227–28
permits and permitting fees, 17, 94–95
Peter Cooper Village (Manhattan), 220, 226, 266
Peterson, Paul, 180
Philadelphia, Pa., 34, 40
philanthropy, 3, 75, 123, 129, 133–35, 182, 185, 204, 212, 214, 216, 263
Philippa Schuyler magnet school (Brooklyn), 61
Philippines, 71
Phillips-Fein, Kim, xv–xvi
Piketty, Thomas, 260
Pittsburgh, Pa., 6
planned shrinkage, 12
police brutality and harassment, xiv, xvii, 24, 28, 87, 121, 144, 145, 146, 162, 195–200, 199–200, 229, 242, 249, 251, 272
Police Executive Research Forum, 136
police reform, xxii–xxiii, 5, 144, 187, 246, 248, 251, 254; *see also specific reform efforts*
Police Reform Organizing Project, 251
policing
  under Mayor Bloomberg, 227–37, 242–44, 251
  Broken Windows, xx, xxii, 67–69, 85, 138, 139, 142–44, 162, 187–92, 216, 227, 229, 248–51, 253–56

community policing, xx, xxvii, 114, 123, 137–41, 144, 147–48, 161, 186–88, 200, 227, 253
under Mayor de Blasio, 248–56
under Mayor Dinkins, 141–44
under Mayor Giuliani, 185–92, 211, 227–29, 235, 251
"Jim Crow," 242
problem-oriented, 123, 161, 186, 192–93
of public spaces, xviii, 85–87, 90, 136, 151, 188
quality-of-life, 85–87, 93, 114, 142–44, 147, 161, 185–88, 190–91, 200, 251, 252, 255
street-level, 28, 85–93, 138, 161–62, 190, 193, 211, 229
see also New York Police Department (NYPD)
Politics, Markets, and America's Schools (Chubb and Moe), 131
Port Authority, 3
poverty, xiii–xiv, xvii, xxv, 9–10, 40, 47, 50, 57, 73, 81, 82, 202, 214, 215, 217, 265, 272–73, 279
Power, Pasta, and Politics (D'Amato), 149
Power Broker, The (Caro), xi
Pratt Institute, 144
precinct commanders, 186–87
Precinct Community Councils, 139, 236
predictive policing, 255–56
Princeton University, 40, 80
prisons, 92, 93
privacy concerns, 256
private investigators, 97
privatization, xv, 129
problem-oriented policing, 123, 161, 186, 192–93
problem-solving approach, xxvi–xxvii
professional class, 47
Progressive Era, 211
progressives and progressivism, xvi, xvii, xxii, 15, 33, 35–36, 105, 112, 118, 119, 121–23, 128, 129, 131, 147, 153, 155–56, 171, 180, 245–48, 254–55, 258, 268–71, 274; *see also* liberals and liberalism
property taxes, 7, 10–13, 17, 48, 49, 72, 126, 140, 162, 176, 210, 221
Prospect Park (Brooklyn), 7, 8, 203
Prospect–Lefferts Garden, 270
prostitution, 68, 97, 188
protest movements of 1960s, xvii
P.S. 3 (Manhattan), 33
P.S. 6 (Manhattan), 133, 176
P.S. 9 (Manhattan), 175–76
P.S. 15 (Brooklyn), 239–40
P.S. 29 (Brooklyn), 257
P.S. 154 (Queens), 175
P.S. 163 (Manhattan), 174
P.S. 166 (Manhattan), 175–76
P.S. 308 (Brooklyn), 61
psychiatric hospitals, 50
Public Interest, The, 65
public schools, xiv, xviii, xxiii, 5, 272
under Mayor Bloomberg, 212–19, 238–42, 256–59, 262, 264
under Mayor de Blasio, 256–64
under Mayor Dinkins, 127–35
District 2, 176
District 3, 61, 130, 175–76, 218–19
District 4, 33–35, 58, 61, 127, 130, 184, 216
District 6, 218–19
District 15, 257
District 21, 59
District 26, 178
and fiscal crisis of 1970s, 56–62
under Mayor Giuliani, 172–79
segregation in, 29–36
see also school choice; *specific schools*
public space(s), xviii, 23, 66–67, 85–87, 90, 136, 151, 188, 233
public universities, 4
public urination, 255
public works projects, xvii
public-investment-driven developmentalism, 211
Puerto Rican New Yorkers, xv, xix, 7, 8, 10, 11, 24, 30–33, 41, 59, 61, 72, 86, 112–15, 136, 203, 278
Puerto Rican/Latino Educational Roundtable, 134
punishment, xx, 253, 272

Qatar, 220
quality of life, 39–40, 83, 121
"Quality of Urban Life, The" (*City Journal* special issue), 150–51

quality-of-life policing, 85–87, 93, 114, 142–44, 147, 161, 185–91, 200, 251, 252, 255
Queens, xxiii, 7, 8, 14, 21, 22, 29, 42, 56, 118, 155, 164, 168, 169, 173–74, 177, 189, 202, 203, 265, 270, 274; *see also specific neighborhoods*
Queens League of United Tenants, 168
Queensbridge Park, 274
Quinn, Christine, 244–45
Quiñones, Nathan, 110
Quinton, Everett, 103, 104
quota laws, 7
quotas, police, 235

Race to the Top program, 240
"racial imbalance," 30
racial steering, 7
racism and racialization, xvi, xvii, xxv–xxviii, 8, 11, 60, 64, 73–74, 88, 117, 152, 191, 228, 233, 244, 272
Ramos, Jessica, 269–70
Ramos, Rafael, 252
Rand, Ayn, 156
Rand Institute, 11–12, 18
Randall's Island (Manhattan), 195
Rangel, Charles, 28, 44, 88, 113, 148, 197
Ravitch, Diane, xxii, 104–7, 111–12, 115, 131–32, 180, 241–42
Ravitch, Richard, 49
Raymond Carver Democratic Club, 113
reading scores, 61, 108, 177
Reagan, Ronald, and administration, 53–54, 56, 82, 83, 88, 101, 105, 111, 115–16, 119, 127, 148, 150, 171
Real Estate Board of New York (REBNY), 20, 22, 53, 56, 99–100, 169, 186, 271
real estate industry, 7, 48, 51, 94–95, 102, 163, 167–68
recessions
 of early 1990s, 119–20, 149–50, 152
 of 2001, 209–10
 Great Recession (2008), 237
Red Hook (Brooklyn), 239–40
redevelopment, 6, 17, 91, 97, 102, 204
redlining, 8, 18
regulation-through-perception, 67
Reign of Error (Ravitch), 242
Reinventing Government: How the Entrepreneurial Spirit Is Transforming the Public Sector (Osborne and Gaebler), 128
rejectionist voting, 157–58
remote learning, 279
Renewal program, 257–58
rent deregulation, 53–54, 83, 99–100, 123–27, 162–72, 185, 211, 220–27, 266, 267; *see also* luxury deregulation; vacancy deregulation
rent freeze, 268
Rent Guidelines Board (RGB), 51, 52, 55, 124, 170, 223, 225, 267–68
rent regulation (rent control and rent stabilization), 5, 11, 15–19, 22, 40, 43, 48–50, 55–56, 83, 96–102, 123–27, 151, 170, 185, 226, 267; *see also* rent deregulation
rent stabilization, 15, 16, 22, 51–55, 103–4, 125, 171, 220, 224, 227, 270
Rent Stabilization Association (RSA), 53, 99, 126, 162, 166
rental vouchers, 17
rents (rent hikes), xviii, 11, 12, 15–16, 20, 50, 51–52, 223–24, 225, 226; *see also* rent deregulation; rent regulation (rent control and rent stabilization)
Republican National Convention (1976), 27
Republicans (Republican Party), xii, xx, xxiii, 14, 15, 19, 21, 22, 26, 27, 34–35, 38, 39, 49, 53, 55, 100, 115–18, 123, 126, 140, 148, 149, 153, 154, 156–61, 164–70, 204, 213, 224, 247, 248, 259, 266–67, 271; *see also specific individuals*
restaurants, 70–71, 209
restrictive covenants, 7
"Rethinking New York: Policies for Renewal" (1992 conference), 150–51
rezoning, 221, 262, 265
Richmond University Medical Center, 251
Ridiculous Theatrical Company, 102
Rikers Island (prison), 193
robbery(-ies), 24, 88, 120, 148, 194, 199
Robert F. Wagner, Jr. Institute for the Arts and Technology, 173
Robles, Victor, 145

Rockaways, the (Queens), 252
Rockefeller, David, 39, 40, 48, 211
Rockefeller, Nelson, xii, xxi, 3, 15, 19–20, 20–21, 25–27, 32, 117, 160, 165, 170
Rockefeller Center, 222
Rockefeller drug laws, 26–27, 84
Rockefeller Fund, 66
Rodgers, Daniel, 130
Rohatyn, Felix, 37, 38, 210
Roosevelt, Eleanor, 270
Roosevelt, Franklin D., and administration, xi–xii, 15, 80, 245, 270, 274
Roth, Alvin, 213
Rubenstein, William B., 104
rule of law, 122

Safe Streets, Safe City, 140, 152–53, 186
Safir, Howard, 161, 192–95, 199
St. John's University, xi, xii, 41–42, 137
Salins, Peter, 11, 151
same-sex marriage, 259
Samuel J. Tilden High School (Bronx), 238
San Antonio, Tex., 156
Sanders, Bernie, 269, 274–75
Sante, Lucy, 84
Scheindlin, Shira, 244
Schlesinger, Arthur, Jr., 42
Schoen, Doug, 53
school choice, xviii–xx, 111–12, 123, 127–35, 132–33, 151, 172–79, 212, 241
School Choice Now, 182
"school choice wars," 174
School of Science and Technology, 130
School of the Future, 173
School of Writing and Publishing, 130
school reform movement, 151, 241
School Select NYC, 213
Schools That Work: Educating Disadvantaged Children (handbook), 127
Schumer, Charles "Chuck," 183, 224, 248
screened schools, 108, 110–11
Section 8 program, 17, 48
segregation, xiv, xv, xxv–xxvii, 7–9, 10, 29, 29–36, 30, 35, 47, 60, 74, 129, 176, 202, 262, 272, 273; *see also* desegregation
SEIU, 115
Senate, *see* New York State Senate; U.S. Senate
September 11, 2001, terrorist attacks, 156, 209–10, 220, 227
Serpico (film), 26
service economy (service sector), xix, 73
"severely crowded" households, 101–2
Seward Park High School (Manhattan), 109
sewer taxes, 10
sexual orientation, 122, 228
Shalala, Donna, 79
Sharkey, Patrick, 273
Sharpton, Al, xxii, 149, 197, 228
Shawn, William, 98
Sheepshead Bay (Brooklyn), 98
Sheridan Square (Manhattan), 102
"shopping," 12
short-term notes, 36–37
Showdown '97 coalition, 169
Sidney Hillman Houses (Manhattan), 165
Siegel, Fred, 151
Silver, Sheldon, xxii, 165–66, 170, 182, 185, 213, 225, 240, 261, 266–67
Silverstein, Larry, 100
Simon, Carly, 98
single-room occupancy (SRO) hotels, 50, 95
Sisulu Children's Academy (Manhattan), 183
Skelos, Dean, 267
skid row districts, 51
Sleeper, Jim, 128
Sliwa, Curtis, 64
small-school movement, xviii, 35, 128, 132, 172, 172–74, 182, 211, 212, 214
Smith, Al, xii
Smith, Frank, 110
Social Security Act, 80
social services, 36, 82, 138–39
Solomon Brothers, 204
Son of Sam murders, 62–63
Sondheim, Stephen, 7, 8–9
Soundview (Bronx), 195
South Asian, immigrants from, 203
South Bronx, 5, 8, 10, 22, 33, 57, 101, 181, 215
South Concourse (Bronx), 226
South Crown Heights (Brooklyn), 226
South Korea, 71
Southern District of New York (district court), 115, 116, 198, 244
Spanish Civil War, 257

Spanish-speaking population, 72; *see also* Latino New Yorkers
special needs, students with, 110, 219, 242
Specialized High Schools Admissions Test (SHSAT), 262–63
Spigner, Archie, 163
Spitzer, Eliot, 165, 198, 233
squatters, 101
"squeegee men," 84, 140, 147, 186, 188
"standards-based" approach (incl. standardized tests), 105, 108, 216–17, 240–41
Starr, Roger, 12, 151
State Board of Regents, 34–35, 58, 183–84
State Commission on Living Costs and the Economy, 20–21
State of the City speeches, xiii, 210
State University of New York (SUNY) system, 13, 183–84
Staten Island, 7, 14, 118, 154, 155, 174, 189, 218, 220, 250–52, 265
Staten Island Tech, 174
Stein, Andrew, 20–21, 80, 86
Stern, Sol, 150, 181
Stewart, Michael, 144
Stonewall Inn riot (1969), 102
stop-and-frisk, xxiii, xxvii, 190–91, 194–95, 198–201, 229–36, 242–45, 248–51, 255, 272
"strangers," 68–69
Straphangers Campaign, 142
Strategic Narcotics and Drug (SNAG) teams, 189
Street Crime Unit (SCU), 190, 193–95, 198, 228, 229
street policing (street-level policing), 28, 85–93, 138, 161–62, 190, 192–93, 211, 229
street-level drug markets (open-air drug markets), 25, 83, 85–93, 89, 161, 186, 188–89, 191–92, 199
Stringer, Scott, 255
Stuyvesant High School (Manhattan), 108, 173, 174, 178, 179, 262
Stuyvesant Town (Manhattan), 222, 223, 226, 266
subemployment, 9
subletting, of rent-regulated apartments, 97, 224
subway system, 4, 64–66, 141–44, 152–53, 250
Success Academy network, 215–17, 245, 261
succession rights, 103, 113
Suffolk County, 145
Sunset Park (Brooklyn), 139
surveillance, 23, 34, 63, 90, 243, 251, 255, 272
Sutton, Percy, 20, 28, 41, 43, 43–44, 113, 197

Tactical Narcotics Teams (TNTs), 92, 161
"Tale of Two Cities," 99, 109–10
Tammany Hall, 42
tax abatements, 16, 50
tax breaks, 56
tax code, 50
taxes and taxation, 10, 13, 17, 39, 51, 74–75, 119, 171, 176, 182, 210, 250, 259–61, 266
Taylor, Clarence, 233–34
teacher turnover, 216
Teachers College (Columbia University), 110, 111
teachers' unions, 179–81; *see also* United Federation of Teachers (UFT)
Teamsters, 115
technocratic approach, xxvi–xxvii, 14, 18–19, 154
telecommunications systems, 70
tenant blacklists, 255, 271
tenants (tenant organizations), xxi, xxiii, 11, 15–19, 50–55, 95–100, 97, 99, 123–24, 123–26, 139, 164, 166–71, 185, 220–26, 253, 267, 267–68, 272, 273
tenant-screening companies, 255
Terry v. Ohio, 190
test-prep services, 218
Thatcher, Margaret, 127
theme schools, 110
Third Worldism, 72
34th Street Partnership, 63
Thompson, Kenneth, 254–55
Thompson, William J., 237–38, 245
Time magazine, 191, 192
Times Square, 85
Times Square Alliance, 63
Tishman Speyer, 222–23, 226
Titone, Vito J., 104

Tomasky, Michael, 153
Tompkins Square (Tompkins Square Riot), 140, 144–45
Tompkinsville Park (Staten Island), 250
tourism, 202, 209, 210
Townsend Harris High School (Queens), 173
Trenton, N.J., 113
Triangle Shirtwaist Factory fire, 80
trickle-down urbanism, xxiv
Trinidad and Tobago, 71
triple damages, 55
Troubled Crusade, The: American Education, 1945–1980 (Ravitch), 106
Troy, N.Y., 159
Trump, Donald, xxii–xxiv, xxviii, 21–22, 48, 98, 99, 117–18, 120, 200, 269, 270
Trump, Fred, 21, 48
Trump Village, 21
Tucker, William C., 98
Tudor City (Manhattan), 96
Twitter, 244

UCLA Civil Rights Project, 262
UF-250 (form), 194, 199, 235
UN Headquarters, 96
"under-utilized" schools, 57
unemployment, 6, 9, 73–74, 119
Union Square Partnership, 63
unions, *see* labor unions
United Auto Workers, 168
United Bronx Parents, 33
United Federation of Teachers (UFT), 32, 114, 115, 153, 180, 182, 183, 213, 214, 218, 240, 261
United States National Commission on Excellence in Education, 105
universal prekindergarten, 260, 264
University Heights (Bronx), 226
University Heights High School, 239
University of Pennsylvania, 106
Upper East Side (Manhattan), 49, 96, 133, 168, 176
upper Manhattan, 57, 168, 215, 227, 265; *see also* Inwood; Washington Heights
Upper West Side, 56, 61, 71, 96, 97, 130, 134–36, 163, 174, 217, 263, 269
upward mobility, xvi, 47, 50, 128, 177
upzoning, 265
Urban Development Corporation, xii, 3, 92
urban liberalism, xvi–xvii, 29, 150; *see also* liberals and liberalism; progressivism
urban renewal, xvii, 5–6
Urstadt, Charles, 20
Urstadt Law, 20
U.S. Census, 16, 202, 231
U.S. Conference of Mayors, 88
U.S. Department of Education, 127, 131
U.S. Department of Housing and Urban Development (HUD), 48, 53
U.S. dollar, 70
U.S. Marine Corps, 66, 113, 136–37, 153
U.S. Office of Civil Rights, 178
U.S. Senate, 53, 55, 80, 117, 148, 149, 248; *see also individual senators*
U.S. Supreme Court, 8, 29, 190, 263

vacancy bonuses, 97, 170, 171, 224, 271
vacancy deregulation, 19–22, 53, 54, 56, 100, 162–64, 166, 167, 169–71, 266, 267, 270–71
vacancy rates, 15, 71
Vallone, Peter, 147, 162–64, 169, 185, 204
Van Arsdale, Harry, 39, 48, 211
Vanity Fair, 117
Vera Institute, 139
Vietnam War, 137
Villager, The, 91
Violent Crime Control and Law Enforcement Act, 186
Vitale, Alex S., 63, 253
Viteritti, Joseph, 131–32, 180, 264
Vladeck Houses (Manhattan), 200
Volcker, Paul, 76
Volcker shock, 76
volunteer patrols, 62–63, 63–64
Voting Rights Act (1965), xv
voucher programs, 57–58, 83, 111, 131, 181, 184, 185

WABC, 72
Wadleigh Alternative Arts Middle School (Manhattan), 130
Wadleigh High School (Manhattan), 130
wages, 6, 9, 38, 73, 84
Wagner, Robert F., 40, 79–80, 114, 237

Wagner, Robert F., Jr. (son of Robert F. Wagner), 80
Wagner, Robert F., Jr., "Bobby" (son of Robert F. Wagner, Jr.), xxii, 40, 79–81, 100, 110, 132, 151, 154–56, 201–2, 211
Waldorf Astoria hotel, 249
Wall Street, 3, 76, 82, 112, 182, 197, 209–10, 238, 272
Wall Street crash (1987), 112, 124
Wall Street Journal, 241, 271
war on crime, 28, 89
war on drugs, 26–27, 88, 93, 200
War on Poverty, 75
Ward, Benjamin, xxii, 64, 86–92, 136, 137, 139, 186, 196
Washington, Harold, 112
Washington Heights (Manhattan), 8, 102, 121, 146, 219, 227, 252
Washington Square Park, 85
water taxes, 10
Watkins, Brian, 153
Wealth and Poverty (Gilder), 83
wealthy New Yorkers, *see* affluent New Yorkers
Weaver, Robert C., 48
Weeksville (Brooklyn), 87
Weiner, Anthony, 237, 244–45
Weingarten, Randi, 183, 218
Weinstein, Jack B., 59, 60
welfare, 11, 73, 124, 279
welfare housing allowance, 50, 56
West Africans, 203
West Bronx, 89
West Side Tenants Union, 49
Westchester County, 14, 158, 274
Westchester Tenants Coalition, 168
Westway, 39
Wheeler Avenue (Bronx), 196
White, Andrew, 236
white flight, xxvi, 35
white New Yorkers, 9, 11, 30, 59, 60–61, 74, 109, 118, 119, 134, 174–75, 216, 217, 238
white rage, 120
Whitestone (Queens), 118
"Who Runs New York?" (*New York* magazine annual feature), 3
"Why I Changed My Mind on School Reform" (Ravitch), 241–42
Whyte, William H., 66–68, 90, 138
Wilcox, Preston, xxii, 31
Williams, Jumaane, 225, 243–44
Williamsburg (Brooklyn), 221
Wilson, James Q., xxii, xxiv, 67–69, 85, 90, 138, 139, 162, 187, 188, 190, 234
Wilson, Malcolm, 21–22, 48
WNYC, xvi, 35, 198
Wolfe, Tom, 97–98
working class, xix, 6, 9, 10, 18, 47, 57, 76, 265, 272, 279
Working Families Party (WFP), 266
Working Group on School Organization and Educational Quality (NYU), 131–32
Works Progress Administration (WPA), xiii, xvi
World War II, xii, 13, 42, 80
Wright, Deborah, 171

Yale University, 14, 158
Yorkville (Manhattan), 80
Young Lords, 227
Young Women's Leadership School, 173
Youngblood, Johnny Ray, 89
Youngstown, Ohio, 31
Yuppies, 94

"zero tolerance," xx, 190
zoning, xix, 13, 58, 95, 221, 262, 265